ORLANDO
& CENTRAL FLORIDA
ACCESS®

Orientation

Whether you are a sun and beach worshiper, theme-park aficionado, or lover of nature, Central Florida most definitely has something to tickle your fancy. From the cobblestone streets of historic **St. Augustine**—the nation's oldest city—on the **Atlantic Ocean** to the new **Animal Kingdom** at **Walt Disney World** to the soft white sands of **St. Petersburg** on the **Gulf of Mexico**, there's an adventure a minute in this 200-mile stretch across Florida's middle.

Orlando is at the heart of it all, home of ever-expanding gargantuan amusement parks that draw more than 37 million people to town every year. **Walt Disney World** is the country's top travel destination, with die-hard devotees returning again and again. Just outside Orlando is the charming residential town of **Winter Park**, known for its shops and restaurants. **International Drive** and **Kissimmee** (and **Highway 192**, which connects it to **Walt Disney World**) offer accommodations to visitors exploring the area's theme parks.

Take a walk through working soundstages and seek excitement on the cutting-edge **Twilight Zone Tower of Terror** ride at **Disney-MGM Studios** theme park one day, then smell King Kong's banana breath or try to escape the grip of **JAWS** at **Universal Studios Escape** the next. And if you want to see real animals, two more world-class amusement parks are enticing—**SeaWorld Orlando** and **Busch Gardens** in **Tampa**.

East of Orlando, the **Kennedy Space Center** beckons astronaut wannabes, and **Daytona Beach** just up the coast attracts race-car drivers, bikers, and college students on spring break. At the **Southern Cassadaga Spiritualist Camp** north of Orlando, a group of about 40 spiritualists welcome visitors into their community (see "A Peek into Your Past and Future" on page 31). A little farther up the road

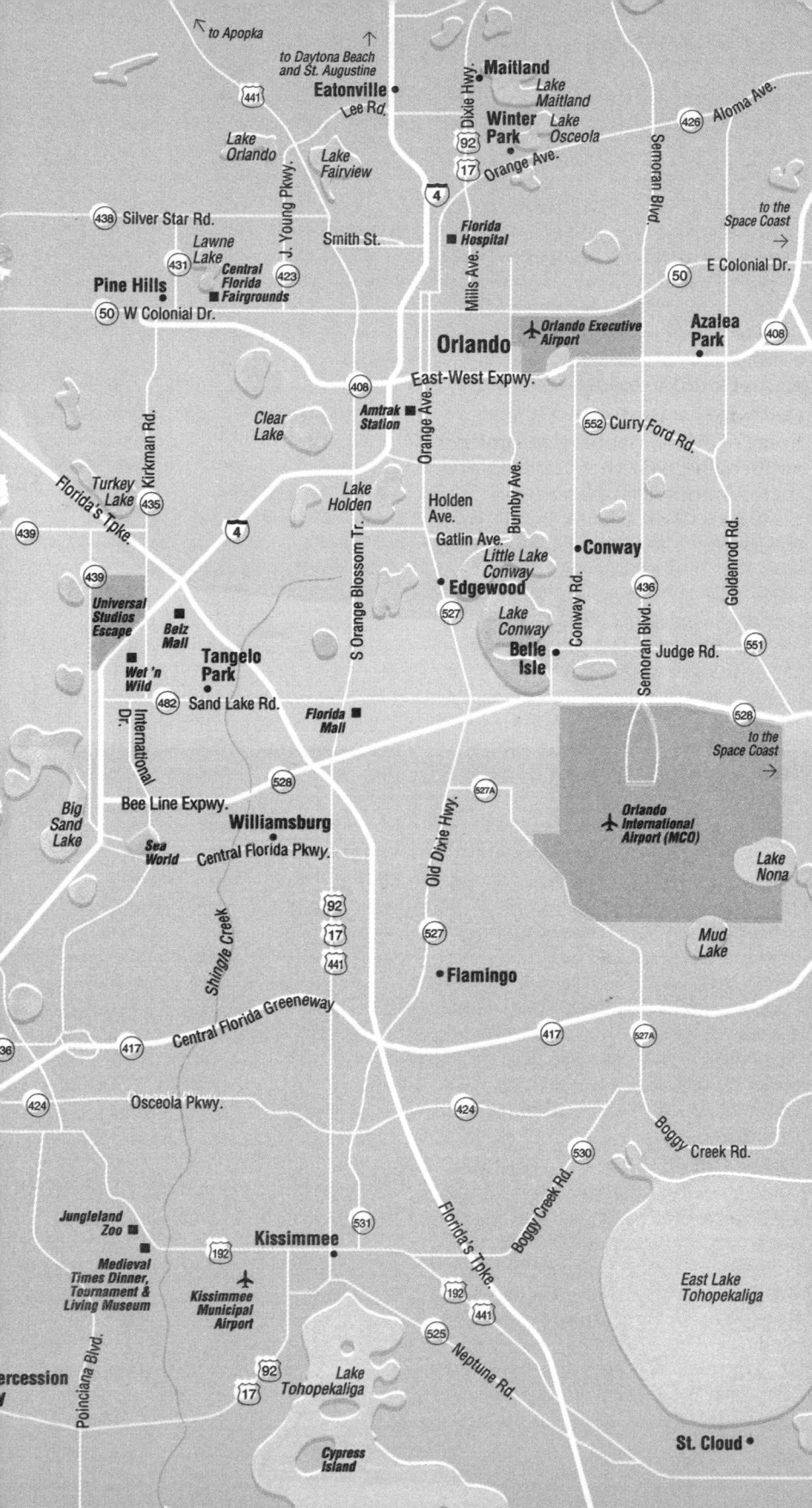

near **Orange City** is **Blue Spring State Park,** a perfect place to spot the endangered manatee, a weed-eating mammal, in its winter refuge. Other natural areas include the scenic **St. Johns River** and **Lake Kissimmee.** And the **Florida Aquarium** in Tampa, one of the largest and most modern in the world, is the place to learn about Florida's underwater habitats.

The earliest known inhabitants of this diverse region were the Timucan Indians, whose aboriginal roots in the area date from 5000 BC. Although the tribe was extinct by 1777, it left many prominent reminders, especially along the coastline in the form of shell mounds. One is **Turtle Mound,** the tallest point of land on Central Florida's east coast, located inside the **Canaveral National Seashore** near **New Smyrna Beach.**

Europeans first came to North America in 1513, when Ponce de León immortalized himself by seeking the Fountain of Youth in St. Augustine. Soon thereafter, the Spanish planted the first orange trees in the New World near St. Augustine. But it wasn't until 1768 that a serious attempt was made to farm the region. Dr. Andrew Turnbull of Scotland received a 60,000-acre land grant that extended from New Smyrna Beach to **Cape Canaveral.** He recruited 1,500 farmers from Turkey and Minorca to work his plantation, but Turnbull's brutal work policies and sporadic Indian raids convinced many farmers to flee to St. Augustine. The colony failed after 10 years.

Later plantations fared far better (Dr. Odet Philippe imported grapefruit from the Bahamas and planted Florida's first citrus groves in the **Pinellas Peninsula** in 1823) until the 1830s, when the US government decided to remove the Seminole Indians to Oklahoma. Many of the Seminole refused to leave their lands, prompting a series of three different wars in the area. During the Second Seminole War of 1835, the Seminole attacked all the plantations that were considered to be on tribal lands and burned and destroyed the major spreads. Even after three wars, the Seminole refused to sign a peace treaty and never surrendered. They are the only Native American tribe today that can make this claim. Most Seminole are currently found in the Everglades, although there is a sizable population around **Ocala.**

In the late 1800s, the coming of the railroad and the improved national transportation system opened up citrus shipping in the urban northeast. Central Florida had already experienced an increase in citrus production 30 years earlier after the end of the Civil War, when the commercialized citrus industry reached a level of about a million boxes. Ten years before the end of the 19th century, that figure jumped fivefold. With the new trains, citrus fruits were shipped throughout the country. Today, more than 12,000 citrus growers cultivate a record 103 million citrus trees on more than 853,000 acres of land in Florida, mostly in the central region of the state. More than 140,000 people work in the citrus or related industries, and the state trails only Brazil in global orange production, and leads the world in grapefruit. The industry generates more than $8 billion in economic activity in the state. Other important sources of income are tomatoes and other vegetables, sugarcane, tobacco, and cattle.

For an area that got such a late start in life, Orlando and Central Florida have more than made up for their years of isolation. Ever since **Walt Disney World** opened in 1971, Central Florida has added one high-tech attraction after another to make it the world's most sophisticated playground. It doesn't hurt that the weather here, as in Southern California, the home of the original Disney theme park, is attractive year-round.

How To Read This Guide

ORLANDO & CENTRAL FLORIDA ACCESS® is arranged by neighborhood so you can see at a glance where you are and what is around you. The numbers next to the entries in the following chapters correspond to the numbers on the maps. The text is color-coded according to the kind of place described.

Restaurants/Clubs: Red   **Hotels:** Blue

Shops/ Outdoors: Green   **Sights/Culture:** Black

& **Wheelchair accessible**

Wheelchair Accessibility

An establishment (except a restaurant) is considered wheelchair accessible when a person in a wheelchair can easily enter a building (i.e., no steps, a ramp, a wide enough door) without assistance. Restaurants are deemed wheelchair accessible only if the above applies and if the rest rooms are on the same floor as the dining area and their entrances and stalls are wide enough to accommodate a wheelchair.

Rating the Restaurants and Hotels

The restaurant ratings take into account the quality, service, atmosphere, and uniqueness of the restaurant. An expensive restaurant doesn't necessarily ensure an enjoyable evening; however, a small, relatively unknown spot could have good food, professional service, and a lovely atmosphere. Therefore, on a purely subjective basis, stars are used to judge the overall dining value (see the star ratings at right). Keep in mind that chefs and owners frequently change, which sometimes drastically affects the quality of a restaurant. The ratings in this guidebook are based on information available at press time.

The price ratings, as categorized at right, apply to restaurants and hotels. These figures describe general price-range relationships between other restaurants and hotels in the area. The restaurant price ratings are based on the average cost of an entrée for one person, excluding tax and tip. Hotel price ratings reflect the base price of a standard room for two people for one night during the peak season.

Restaurants

★	Good
★★	Very Good
★★★	Excellent
★★★★	An Extraordinary Experience
$	The Price Is Right (less than $10)
$$	Reasonable ($10-$15)
$$$	Expensive ($15-$25)
$$$$	Big Bucks ($25 and up)

Hotels

$	The Price Is Right (less than $75)
$$	Reasonable ($75-$150)
$$$	Expensive ($150-$225)
$$$$	Big Bucks ($225 and up)

Map Key

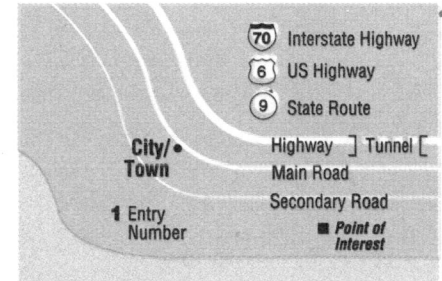

70	Interstate Highway
6	US Highway
9	State Route
City/• **Town**	Highway] Tunnel [
	Main Road
	Secondary Road
1 Entry Number	■ Point of Interest

Area code 407 unless otherwise noted.

Getting to Central Florida

Airports

Orlando International Airport (MCO)

MCO (825.2001) ranks among the top airports in the US for customer service and accommodates more than 27 million passengers annually. It features a three-level main building with parking decks, ticketing, check-in, baggage claim, and ground transportation and car rental; and three terminals that are accessible to the main building by shuttle.

The airport is located 11 miles from downtown Orlando and 20 miles from the gates of **Walt Disney World**.

Airport Services
Airport Emergencies (paramedics) 825.2911
Business Service Center 825.2871

Currency Exchange 825.2147
Customs 825.4300
Immigration...............................826.5870
Information..................825.2352, 825.2355
Lost and Found 825.2111
Parking 825.2070
Police 825.2075
Traveler's Aid.............................825.2352

Airlines
America West 800/235.9292
American 800/433.7300
British Airways 800/247.9297
Continental 295.6000, 800/525.0280
Delta 849.6400, 800/221.1212
Kiwi 800/538.5494
Northwest............................800/225.2525

Southwest	800/435.9792
United	800/241.6522
USAirways	800/428.4322
TWA	800/221.2000
Virgin Atlantic	800/862.8621

Getting to and from Orlando International Airport

By Bus Central Florida's public transportation company is **LYNX** (841.8240). Bus stops are indicated by a round sign with a paw print on it. **LYNX** buses run between the airport and along **International Drive** downtown at half-hour intervals Monday through Saturday from 5:40AM to 11:25PM; hourly on Sunday from 6:15AM to 7:15PM. The trip takes about 55 minutes.

Mears Transportation (422.4561, 423.5566) and **Transtar Shuttle** (856.7777) offer shuttle van service around the clock to and from the airport.

By Car From the airport, take **Route 436 (Semoran Boulevard)** north seven miles to **Route 50 (Colonial Drive).** Make a left turn and go another four miles west to **Orange Avenue** in the heart of downtown Orlando. To make this 11-mile trip to the airport, simply reverse the directions.

The following rental-car companies have 24-hour counters at the airport:

Rental Cars

Avis	825.3700, 800/331.1212
Budget	850.6749, 800/527.0700
Dollar	825.3265, 800/800.4000
Hertz	859.8400, 800/654.3131
National	855.4170, 800/328.4567

By Limousine or Taxi Two companies offer limo and taxi service to and from the airport: **Mears Transportation** (422.4561, 423.5566) and **Transtar Shuttle** (856.7777). Cabs to hotels and attractions are also available at stands at the airport. These taxis are strictly regulated, efficient, and relatively inexpensive.

Other Central Florida Airports

While Orlando is the main hub for airplane travel in Central Florida, the following cities also have airports: **Sanford** (407/324.9681), **Daytona Beach** (904/248.8069), **Gainesville** (352/373.0249), **Melbourne** (407/723.6227), **St. Petersburg** (727/535.7600), and **Tampa** (813/870.8700).

Orlando International Airport, opened in 1981, has grown at twice the rate of any other airport in the US.

There are approximately 455 public and private airports in the state of Florida.

Driving

Getting to this part of Florida by car is a snap. From North Florida, **Interstates 95** and **75** lead to **Interstate 4,** the route through Orlando and **Walt Disney World.** Avoid the **Wildwood** toll gates going to and from Orlando at peak holiday travel times—the traffic can be backed up as much as 20 miles.

Bus Station (Long-Distance)

The long-distance bus station (555 John Young Pkwy, at W Colonial Dr, 292.3422) provides only **Greyhound** (800/231.2222) service throughout the US. It is open 24 hours.

Train Station (Long-Distance)

The **Amtrak** station (1400 Sligh Blvd, between W Miller and W Columbia Sts, 843.7611) is open daily from 7AM to 6PM. Trains arrive from and depart for mostly East Coast destinations.

FYI

Accommodations You'll find every kind of hotel or motel—from glamorous high-rises with huge free-form swimming pools to modest bed-and-breakfast places—in Central Florida. Orlando itself has a staggering 84,000 hotel rooms, more than any other metropolitan area in the country. Still, don't arrive without reservations during national holidays because all the popular inns are likely to be booked.

Climate From December through February the weather can be cold, damp, and rainy. With summer come showers, usually beginning between 2 and 5PM from June through August, the official rainy season. Carry a poncho or umbrella during those months. Or go without to cool off from the blistering heat. Casual attire is the rule here. It's acceptable to wear shorts at lunch into all but the fanciest restaurants. Slacks or a dress are more appropriate evening wear.

Months	Average Temperature (°F)
December-January	51-73
February-May	55-88
June-August	72-92
September-November	65-85

Hours Opening and closing times for shops, attractions, coffeehouses, tearooms, etc., are listed by day(s) only if normal hours apply (opening between 8 and 11AM and closing between 4 and 7PM). In all other cases, specific hours will be given (e.g., 6AM-2PM, daily 24 hours, noon-5PM).

Drinking Florida's legal drinking age is 21. Most bars open around 2PM and close at 1 or 2AM.

Money Banks in Central Florida are generally open Monday through Friday from 9AM to 3PM, but some downtown branches remain open on Fridays until

5PM. There are ATMs throughout the area, and traveler's checks are accepted virtually everywhere. **SunTrust Bank** and **NationsBank** buy and sell banknotes in most major foreign currencies at competitive rates. **SunTrust Bank** is a good place to exchange money, with a branch at **Lake Buena Vista,** across from **Downtown Disney Marketplace** (828.6112). Major branches outside the theme parks include **NationsBank** in the **Williamsburg** area (10900 Orangewood Blvd, at Central Florida Pkwy, 646.3000); and **SunTrust Bank** in Orlando (200 S Orange Ave, at W Church St, 657.4786) and in Tampa (315 Madison St, between N Florida Ave and N Franklin St, 813/224.2121).

Orlando Magicard Save 20 to 50 percent at nearly 100 Central Florida hotels, attractions, restaurants, and other businesses with the **Orlando Magicard,** free through the **Orlando/Orange County Convention & Visitors Bureau.** The card is valid for up to six people, and cardholders just present the card to receive a discount. Call 800/551.0181 (in the US and Canada) or E-mail info@orlandocvb.com for a free card. If you're already in town, stop by the **Official Visitor Center** at 8723 International Drive, open 8AM-7PM 365 days a year.

Personal Safety As in any large metropolitan area, there is crime in Orlando. *Always* lock your car and your hotel room, and *never* open your room door unless you are certain who's on the other side. Most tourist places are safe for walking at night, but use common sense, especially if you're alone. One street to avoid is **South Orange Blossom Trail.**

Publications Orlando's major newspaper is the morning *Orlando Sentinel. Orlando* magazine is a slick monthly, offering local-interest features. *The Weekly,* a giveaway, runs reviews by Liz Langley, Orlando's wittiest entertainment critic, and other articles of interest. The monthly *Florida Sportsman* magazine covers fishing hot spots.

Radio Stations

AM:

540	WQTM	Sports
580	WDBO	News/Talk
740	WWNZ	News/Talk
790	WLBE	Oldies
1030	WONQ	Spanish
1080	WFIV	Spanish
1140	WRMQ	Spanish
1170	WKFL	Sports
1220	WOTS	Oldies
1240	WKIQ	Country
1270	WRLZ	Spanish
1440	WPRD	Spanish
1480	WUNA	Spanish
1600	WOKB	Spanish

FM:

88.7	WLAZ	Spanish
89.9	WUCF	Jazz
90.7	WMFE	Classical
91.5	WPRK	Classical
92.3	WWKA	Country
93.1	WKRO	Rock
96.5	WHTQ	Rock
97.0	WPCV	Country
98.1	WGNE	Country
98.9	WMMO	Adult Contemporary
99.3	WLRQ	Adult Contemporary
99.9	WFKS	Contemporary Hits
100.3	WSHE	Adult Contemporary
101.1	WJRR	Rock
101.9	WJHM	Black Urban/Contemporary
102.7	WHKR	Country
103.1	WLOQ	Jazz
104.1	WTKS	News/Talk
105.1	WOMX	Adult Contemporary
105.9	WOCL	Oldies
106.7	WXXL	Contemporary Hits
107.1	WAOA	Adult Contemporary
107.7	WMGF	Adult Contemporary

Taxes At press time, hotel taxes varied from 4 to 11 percent; sales taxes on meals and purchased goods were 6 percent.

Telephone The area code for **Pinellas** County (St. Petersburg, Clearwater, Treasure Island) is 727; **Hillsborough** County (Tampa) is 813; **Orange, Seminole,** and **Brevard** Counties (Orlando, **Walt Disney World,** the Space Coast, etc.) are 407; **St. Johns** County (St. Augustine) is 904; and **Hardee, Manatee, Sarasota,** and **Polk** Counties are 941. Dial 1 before toll calls and long-distance numbers. At pay phones, local calls cost 35¢; credit card and collect calls have a dollar surcharge.

Time Zone Central Florida is on eastern standard time (EST).

Tipping Taxi drivers receive a 10 to 15 percent tip; waiters 15 to 20 percent; and porters a $3 gratuity.

Visitors' Information Centers

Florida's Space Coast Office of Tourism
2725 St. Johns St, Bldg C, Melbourne, FL 32940
633.2110, 800/USA.1969; fax 633.2112

Greater Daytona Beach Convention & Visitors Bureau
126 E Orange Ave, Daytona Beach, FL 32114
904/255.0415, 800/854.1234

Kissimmee–St. Cloud Convention & Visitors Bureau
PO Box 422007, Kissimmee, FL 34742-2007
847.5000, 800/327.9159

Orlando/Orange County Convention & Visitors Bureau Official Visitor Center
8723 International Dr, Suite 101, Orlando, FL 32819
363.5872, 800/551.0181

St. Augustine–St. Johns County Chamber of Commerce
1 Riberia St, St. Augustine, FL 32084
904/829.5681

St. Petersburg/Clearwater Area Convention & Visitors Bureau
1 Stadium Dr, Suite A, St. Petersburg, FL 33705
727/464.7200, 800/345.6710; fax 727/582.7949

Tampa/Hillsborough Convention & Visitors Association
111 Madison St, Suite 1010, Tampa, FL 33602
813/223.2752, 800/44TAMPA; fax 813/229.6616

Winter Park Chamber of Commerce
150 N New York Ave, Winter Park, FL 32790
644.8281

Phone Book

Emergencies
Ambulance/Fire/Police 911
AAA Emergency Road Service 800/222.4357
Dental Emergency 660.8080

Hospitals
Daytona: Halifax Hospital 904/254.4000
Orlando: Florida Hospital 830.4321
Orlando: Regional Medical Center 841.5111
St. Augustine: Flagler Hospital 904/829.5155
St. Petersburg: St. Petersburg
    General Hospital 727/384.1414
Tampa: Tampa General Hospital 813/251.7000

Pharmacies
Daytona: Walgreen Drug Store 904/252.4734
Orlando: Eckerd Drugs (24 hours) 299.8020
St. Augustine: Walgreen Drug Store 904/829.5358
St. Petersburg: Eckerd Drugs 727/896.3166
Tampa: Eckerd Drugs 813/248.5097
Walt Disney World:
    Turner Drugs (Lake Buena Vista) 828.8125
Poison Control Center 841.5222

Visitors' Information
Amtrak...843.7611
Better Business Bureau 621.3300
Greyhound-Trailways Lines
    Fare and Scheduling Information 800/231.2222
    En Español 800/531.5332
LYNX 841.8240
Time and Temperature................................646.3131
US Customs 825.4300
US Passport Office......................................850.6335
Weather...851.7510

Main Events

January
Zora Neale Hurston Festival of Arts & Humanities, Eatonville Theatrical performances and art exhibits highlight Southern rural African-American culture. The festival usually takes place during the last week in January; call 407/647.3307 for more information.

Speedweeks, Daytona Beach World-famous car races, including the **Rolex 24** and the **Daytona 500**, are run at the **Daytona International Speedway,** usually during the last week in January through the second week in February. For details, call 904/255.0415.

Cypress Gardens' Spring Lights, Winter Haven More than four million twinkling lights transform the theme park into a fantasyland of garden and water creatures. This display usually opens in late January and continues through the second week in April. Call 941/324.2111 for information.

February
Bike Week, Daytona Beach From the last few days in February through the first week in March, the world's largest gathering of motorcyclists— more than 500,000 bikes—converge oceanside, with events ranging from swap meets, cycle displays, and demo rides to concerts and even cole slaw wrestling. If you want to know more, call the Daytona Beach Chamber of Commerce at 904/255.0981.

Silver Spurs Rodeo, Kissimmee Legendary bull riders and cowboys compete in this rodeo, the largest in the eastern United States (also in October). Call 407/847.5118 for details.

Festival Concert Series at Rollins College, Winter Park For nearly 65 years, hundreds of singers and musicians have made this three-day festival in late February, featuring the music of J.S. Bach, one of the most anticipated musical events in Central Florida. Call 407/646.2182 to learn more.

Gasparilla Invasion, Tampa In honor of pirate José Gaspar, who took refuge on Florida's west coast, a ship with more than 500 bucaneers sails into **Tampa Bay** to "capture" the city, kicking off this two-day gala the first week in February. They lead a parade into **Ybor City.** For information, call 813/353.8070.

Plant City Strawberry Festival, Plant City This event, which begins during the last week in February and continues through the first week in March, celebrates the harvest with shortcakes, ice cream, and other delicious strawberry-flavored fare. There are also top country-western entertainers and arts and crafts. Plant City is off Interstate 4 between Orlando and Tampa. Call 813/752.9194 for details.

Mardi Gras at Universal Studios Florida A moving, pulsating street party with entertainment, food, and spectacular parades takes place on the theme park's back lot, starting the second week in February and continuing throughout March. Information is available at 407/363.8000.

March

Annual Winter Park Sidewalk Arts Festival One of the most prestigious outdoor fine arts festivals in the Southeast, and the fourth highest rated in the nation, features art, food, music, jazz, and children's activities. The fun lasts for three days during the third week in March; call 407/672.6390.

April

Orlando-UCF Shakespeare Festival, Orlando Shakespearean works are performed from the first days of the month through the first week in May by professional actors at the **Walt Disney World Amphitheater** in downtown's **Lake Eola Park.** Tickets may be obtained by calling 407/245.0985.

Orlando International Fringe Festival, Orlando This 10-day festival of theatrical performances beginning in the middle of the month showcases original works, premiere performances, improvisational comedy, musicals, dramas, mime, and dance in 500 shows by more than 300 performers from around the world. For more information, call 407/648.0077.

Epcot International Flower & Garden Festival Magnificent flower and garden displays are on view in the **World Showcase** from mid-April through the end of May. There are also tours of the gardens, backstage nursery areas, and greenhouses, gardening demonstrations, and lecture series. To learn more, call 407/824.4321.

Isle of Eight Flags Shrimp Festival, Fernandina Beach There's plenty of seafood and entertainment here to celebrate the birthplace of the shrimping industry. The festival begins at the end of April and continues through the first few days of May. Fernandina Beach is one hour north of St. Augustine; take I-95 to Exit 129. Call 904/261.3248 for details.

May

Zellwood Sweet Corn Festival, Zellwood Thousands of ears of fresh corn are consumed at this weekend festival in late May, featuring corn-eating contests, carnival rides, games, arts and crafts, and live country music. Zellwood is on Highway 441 between Apopka and Mount Dora. The number for information is 407/886.0014.

June

Florida Film Festival, Orlando More than 100 films, documentaries, and shorts from around the globe are shown here for 10 days in mid-June, along with seminars, tributes, midnight movies, parties, and a closing weekend awards gala. Information is available at 407/629.1088.

Spanish Night Watch 1740s, St. Augustine Music and pageantry of the Colonial times are relived with a torchlight procession through the **Spanish Quarter** by actors in period dress. Call 800/OLD.CITY to find out more about this three-day event, which usually takes place the third week in the month.

July

Lake Eola Picnic in the Park, Orlando The city celebrates the Fourth with activities, entertainment, and fireworks. For information, call 407/246.2827.

October

Epcot International Food & Wine Festival Authentic flavors of more than 30 ethnic cuisines can be sampled in this monthlong festival, from the third week in October through the third week in November, that celebrates food, beverages, and cultures from around the world. To learn more, call 407/824.4321.

Halloween Horror Nights at Universal Studios Florida The **Universal Studios** back lot is transformed into a maze of mystery and mayhem with haunted houses, special shows, and hundreds of roaming monsters and misfits. The events are held throughout the month on dates announced in advance; call 407/363.8000 for specifics.

Jacksonville Jazz Festival, Jacksonville Top-name entertainers perform throughout the month as part of this festival, billed as the "world's greatest free jazz concert." Call 904/791.4305 for dates and times.

Lake Eola Celebration in the Park, Orlando This weekend party in mid-October, with Disney characters, musicians, food, games, and fireworks, is sponsored by **Walt Disney World.** The number for information is 407/246.2827.

Biketoberfest, Daytona Beach Motorcycle enthusiasts ride into town for a four-day weekend (usually the third weekend in the month) of camaraderie and fun. Call 800/854.1234 for details.

November

Festival of the Masters, Walt Disney World One of the top juried art shows in the southeastern US, this three-day event in mid-November features more than 200 award-winning artists, whose work is displayed on the sidewalks throughout **Downtown Disney.** For details, call 407/824.4321.

December

Holidays Around the World, Epcot Stories, customs, legends, and holiday traditions of the 11 **World Showcase** countries are enacted here, including the **Candlelight Processional,** a retelling of the Christmas story. The festival begins around Thanksgiving and continues through the end of December. Information is available at 407/824.4321.

Spectacle of Lights, Disney-MGM Studios Millions of lights cover the studio's back-lot streets with a blanket of color, including 60 flying angels and two 30-foot carousels. The outrageous display is the creation of Arkansas businessman Jennings Osborne, who gained worldwide attention when the holiday display in his own front yard in Little Rock, Arkansas, drew so many spectators that the Arkansas Supreme Court ruled that he would have to reduce it. Instead, Disney moved the Osborne extravaganza to the **Disney-MGM Studios** in 1995, adding more lights every year. The display goes up around Thanksgiving and remains through the end of December; call 407/824.4321 for details.

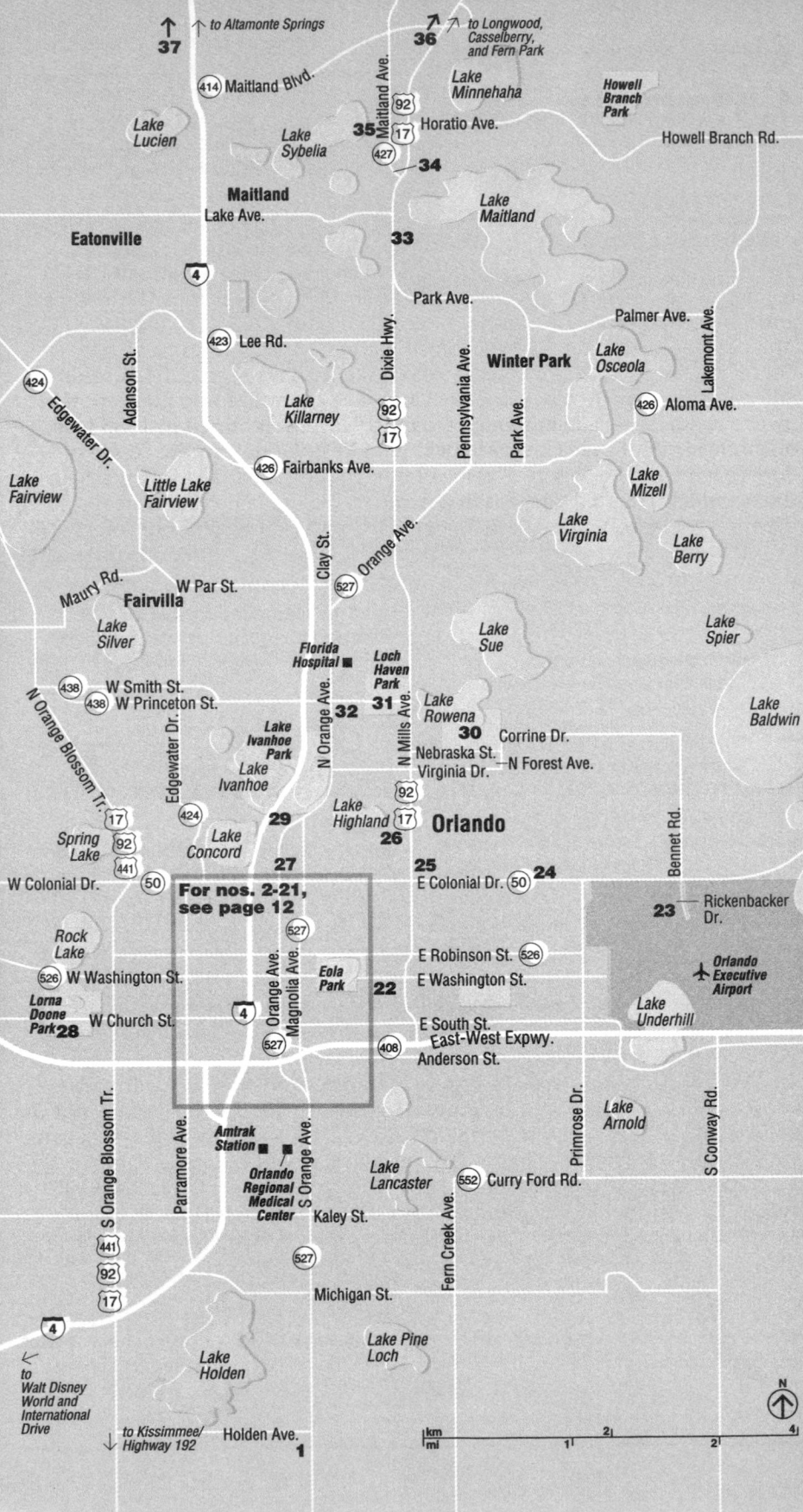

Greater Orlando

Orlando is the heart of **Central Florida**'s vacation wonderland. In fact, Greater Orlando embraces several distinct tourist destinations: **Downtown Orlando, Winter Park, International Drive,** Kissimmee/Highway 192, and, of course, the world's most popular vacation spot, **Walt Disney World**. Orlando has been attracting fun-seeking travelers since the 1920s—decades before Walt Disney set foot in these parts. But little more than a century ago, just after the Civil War, it was just a tiny settlement carved out of a pine tree wilderness.

The origin of the name "Orlando" remains obscure. Unlike many of the region's lyrical place names, such as **Eola, Osceola, Kissimmee** (Kuh-*sim*-ee), and **Ocoee** (Oh-*coe*-ee), it was not bestowed on the area by the Native Americans who first settled here. Most historians trace the name to one Orlando Reeves (or Orlando Rees), who is said to have been either a soldier killed in an Indian attack near **Lake Cherokee** or a well-to-do plantation owner. In any case, a man named Orlando Reeves was buried in 1835 just one mile north of Lake Cherokee next to **Lake Eola**, now in the center of downtown Orlando, where a statue of him stands today. A post office near the burial site adopted Reeves's first name in 1857 to commemorate his death; the town then appropriated the name of the post office—Orlando—in 1876. (Another theory has it that a Shakespeare-loving settler named the town after the protagonist of *As You Like It*.)

The land surrounding Orlando was still open-range cattle country 15 years after the Civil War; on **Main Street** (now **Magnolia Avenue**) the favorite Saturday-afternoon entertainment for cowboys was alligator wrestling. The area began to grow when speculators spread the word about Central Florida's fertile land and salubrious climate. As people arrived, citrus groves became an increasingly important source of revenue and jobs. By the early 1880s Orlando had become a major marketing and supply center for the citrus industry. Soon after, sugarcane, sweet potatoes, and celery also became significant cash crops.

It wasn't long before Orlando became a minor tourist mecca, thanks to its mild climate, pretty lakes, and modest hotel development. As the automobile became affordable, people were eager to drive to new and less developed places. The 1924 completion of **Cheney Highway** (now **Route 50**), which connects Orlando to Florida's east coast and Highway 1, and the opening a year later of **Dixie Highway**, which went through **Apopka**, Orlando, and Kissimmee, made Orlando an even more accessible and popular destination for motorists.

But citrus fruit, not tourism, remained Orlando's primary industry until the 1960s. The nation's space program at **Cape Canaveral**, an hour's drive away, gave a boost to Orlando's growth in the early part of the decade, but the town was still small by most standards when in 1965 a mystery buyer began purchasing large tracts of land in **Orange** and **Osceola Counties**. The buyer was Walt Disney, who in November of 1965 revealed plans to build a $100 million vacationland that would be bigger and better than Disneyland in Anaheim, California. Sadly, Disney died a year later, but his plan nonetheless was carried out. When the **Magic Kingdom**, the first of several major attractions within **Walt Disney World**, threw open its gates in 1971, it forever changed the face of Central Florida. Greater Orlando saw a frenzied building boom in tourist attractions and facilities and in residential areas that has hardly slowed since. In 1990, the region's population surpassed the one million mark (it is now about 1.5 million) and, largely thanks to **Walt Disney World**, Greater Orlando today attracts more than 37 million tourists a year.

Downtown Orlando and Environs

Set apart from the real tourist action, downtown Orlando is nonetheless a popular nighttime spot, thanks to an entertainment complex known as **Church Street Station**, a collection of restaurants, dinner theaters, and bars that lines both sides of **Church Street** between **Garland Avenue** and the railroad tracks. Set in a cluster of renovated Victorian-era buildings, the **Church Street Station** development transformed downtown Orlando, attracting both visitors and local residents to this once-depressed area. The complex also spurred other development downtown. Church Street is now the site of a second shopping-dining-nightclub complex called **Church Street Market** and a popular shopping mall, **Church Street Exchange**. In addition, plans are afoot for a performing arts center and a regional history center, both set to open within the next three years.

Although **Church Street Station** is the most popular tourist attraction in this primarily business district, downtown Orlando has other appealing areas as well. Just a few blocks northeast of Church Street is **Lake Eola**, which is at the heart of a pleasant park with a lakeside walkway, a bandstand, and an open-air theater. **Orange Avenue**, the main shopping area beyond Church Street, is

also a historical district, boasting examples of more than 20 architectural styles from the late 19th and early 20th centuries.

A few miles north of downtown proper at **Loch Haven Park** is the city's main cultural complex, which includes the **Orlando Museum of Art** and the **Orlando Science Center.** Just beyond the city center are the bedroom communities of **Casselberry, Fern Park, Altamonte Springs,** and **Maitland,** home to some of Orlando's best restaurants.

Area code 407 unless otherwise noted.

1 Le Coq au Vin ★★★$$ One of Orlando's finest restaurants, it offers authentic French country cuisine in a warm, homey atmosphere. Set among flowerbeds and shaded by a huge old oak tree, the place has the relaxed yet refined feel of a Brittany country inn. Chef/owner Louis Perrotte offers specialties that include coq au vin, duck *à l'orange,* eggplant Bayou Teche (with crabmeat and shrimp, topped with Cajun hollandaise sauce), and sweetbreads. The service is *parfait.* ♦ French ♦ Tu-F lunch and dinner; Sa-Su dinner. Reservations recommended. 4800 S Orange Ave (between Stratemyer Dr and Holden Ave). 851.6980

2 The Courtyard at Lake Lucerne $$ This hostelry consists of a trio of very attractive buildings, each with its own distinctive personality and decor. **The Norment Parry Inn** (pictured below), built in 1895, is set in Orlando's oldest house. Each of its six rooms was decorated by a different artist or designer. In contrast, Art Deco design carries through all 12 guest rooms at the **Wellborn.** Perhaps the loveliest of the three is the **Dr. Phillips House,** with three rooms (including a honeymoon suite) that reflect the Edwardian style of this restored turn-of-the-century home. Nice touches, including fresh flowers, make this a fine choice for travelers weary of sterile modern hotels. Complimentary continental breakfast is served each morning on the veranda of the **Dr. Phillips House,** and a complimentary carafe of wine greets visitors upon arrival. ♦ 211 N Lucerne Cir E (between Delaney Ave and East-West Expwy). 648.5188, 800/444.5289; www.travelbase.com/destinations/orlando/lake-lucerne/

Norment Parry Inn at The Courtyard at Lake Lucerne

3 City Hall Fast-growing Orlando has a distinctive, high-profile $33-million municipal building, readily visible from Interstate 4 and the East-West Expressway. Designed by **Harwood K. Smith** in 1991, the 267,000-square-foot structure is capped by a 120-foot-high copper dome. ♦ M-F; Sa-Su noon-5PM; guided tours available upon request. 400 S Orange Ave (at W South St). 246.2121

4 SunTrust Center At 35 stories high, this is Orlando's tallest building. Designed by **Skidmore, Owings & Merrill** in 1988, the pink-granite structure is topped with four distinctive teal-green pyramids. The center's plaza is adorned with a fountain, plants, and a modern sculpture. ♦ M-F. 200 S Orange Ave (at W Church St). 237.4882

5 Church Street Station What used to be a city block of run-down hotels, office buildings, and stores is now a lively complex of upscale bars, restaurants, and shops on both sides of Church Street. Often overlooked in all the nighttime revelry that takes place here are the details. Bob Snow, the Orlando businessman who created the complex, searched all over Europe and the United States for the antiques and old architectural elements now found in the many bars and restaurants here. The former **South Florida Railroad** station, built in 1881, serves as the complex's administrative offices. Some people still refer to this street of party places as **Rosie's,** short for Rosie O'Grady's Good Time Emporium, which was the first bar to open here. A varied crowd— families and couples, tourists and locals— fills the complex at night to see the shows at **Rosie O'Grady's,** the **Cheyenne Saloon & Opera House,** and the **Orchid Garden Ballroom.** There's one admission fee in the evening that covers all three shows; for those who just wish to shop, stroll, eat, and drink, there's no admission charge. ♦ Admission after 5PM for shows. Parking fee at all times. Daily 11AM-2AM. 129 W Church St (between S Orange and S Garland Aves). 422.2434; fax 425.4312 &

Within Church Street Station:

Rosie O'Grady's Good Time Emporium

A Dixieland revue led by the "Red Hot Mama" and the "Baron of Bourbon Street," and featuring can-can and Charleston dancers and singing waiters, ensures a fun evening here. But the decor of this hot spot, set in the former **Orlando Hotel** (ca. 1904), is interesting in its own right. The 800-pound chandelier once graced the First National Bank of Boston; guests sit on turn-of-the-century benches from Pensacola's L&N Railroad Depot; the bentwood chairs in the balcony encircling the bar come from the dining room of an English monastery; and when you go up to the bar to order from the light menu of sandwiches and hot dogs, you talk through a bank teller's cage from the 1870s. ♦ Admission. Shows: M-Th, Su 7:15PM, 8:30PM, 10PM; F-Sa 7:15PM, 8:30PM, 10PM, 11:30PM. 422.2434

Apple Annie's Courtyard What was once a meat locker and vacant lot is now a friendly bar full of lush greenery, wicker, and all sorts of intriguing architectural details; it serves tropical cocktails and frozen specialty drinks. The Church Street entrance features the wrought-iron gates of an 18th-century English country estate. The mirrors on the east wall were created in mid–18th-century Vienna. Some booths are actually old church pews, which fit in quite nicely considering the bar itself was a communion rail of an 18th-century French Catholic church. "Tropical Tuesdays" feature drink specials and live bluegrass and folk music. ♦ M-Th, Su 11AM-1AM; F-Sa 11AM-2AM; entertainment Tu 4-7PM. 422.2434

Lili Marlene's ★$$$ A bit pricey, but where else can you eat at Al Capone's very own dining table? It's the one with the green velvet–covered chairs. The two chairs at the head of the table have steel running through the tall chairbacks so that no one could sneak up and shoot the gangster from behind. As at the other **Church Street Station** restaurants, this plush Victorian-style dining spot is chock-full of antiques from around the world, many with an aviation theme, such as the scale models of World War I aircraft suspended from the ceiling. The phone booth between the lavatories was actually an oak confessional from the same French Catholic church that provided the pews used as dining booths. The atmosphere is upscale, but informal; some diners dress up, but casual attire is fine as well. The food is nothing special, but you can't go wrong with a veal chop or a pasta dish. ♦ American ♦ M-Sa lunch and dinner; Su brunch and dinner. Reservations recommended. 422.2434

Church Street Station

Phineas Phogg's Balloon Works When it opened in 1979, this club—where a DJ spins Top 40 hits—was one of the few places where you could dance in downtown Orlando. Although there are now a few more dance spots in town, this place still gets quite crowded, especially around midnight, when an eclectic over-21 crowd stops in after a downtown concert or ball game. Arrive before the crush to check out the memorabilia and photos of famous balloonists, including Colonel Joe Kittinger, the first solo pilot to cross the Atlantic Ocean in a balloon. His 1984 trip from Caribou, Maine, to Cairo Montenotte, Italy, aboard *Rosie O'Grady's Balloon of Peace* lasted 86 hours and covered 3,543 miles. The club features nickel draft beer on Wednesday from 6:30 to 7:30PM. Patrons must be 21 years old to enter. ♦ M-Tu, Th-Su 8PM-2AM; W 6:30PM-2AM. 422.2434

COMMANDER RAGTIME'S

Commander Ragtime's Midway of Fun, Food, and Games The name pretty much says it all. This family-oriented spot offers pool tables, pinball machines, video games, and large-screen TVs that are usually tuned to sporting events. Look up between dangling replicas of World War I planes to find a maze of electric train tracks. Six computer-operated trains are constantly in motion, crisscrossing and sharing tracks. Fast-food stands offer standard fare such as hamburgers, hot dogs, and chicken fingers. ♦ M-Th, Su 11AM-11PM; F-Sa 11AM-midnight. 422.2434

Cheyenne Saloon & Opera House ★$$ Many consider this to be the jewel of the **Church Street Station** complex. It took more than two years to build this showcase from 250,000 feet of golden oak lumber that was once a century-old Ohio barn. Anyone who works here is proud to point out the 11 original Frederic Remington sculptures and the antique guns on the barroom wall; one set was owned by outlaw Jesse James. Climb the stairs to the upper level for a great view of the entire saloon. Check out the 1885 solid rosewood Brunswick pool table and the original tapestries from Buffalo Bill and Annie Oakley's "Wild West Show." Look to the front of the saloon to see an outstanding stained-glass window, a memorial to the Grand Army of the Republic that once hung in a Philadelphia courthouse. Each chandelier has a story, too: Three of them came from beer baron Joseph Schlitz's home in St. Louis, and six are from the Philadelphia mint. The menu features barbecue platters, such as pork spare-ribs, smoked pork tenderloin, and barbecued chicken and ribs; Fridays there's an all-you-can-eat lunch buffet. You'll find rip-roarin' dancing and live country entertainment nightly. ♦ Barbecue ♦ Admission for show. Daily lunch and dinner. Entertainment M-Th, Su 8:45PM, 10:15PM, 11:45PM; F-Sa 8:45PM, 10:15PM, 11:45PM, 1AM. Country dance lessons Su 2-6PM. 422.2434

Orchid Garden Ballroom Live rock 'n' roll from the 1950s to the present is enjoyed by young and old within a Victorian arcade filled with wrought iron, brick floors, and stained-glass windows. The dance floor is a balcony above the bandstand. There's a bar, but no food is served. ♦ Admission. Entertainment M-Th 8PM, 9:30PM, 11PM; F-Sa 8PM, 9:30PM, 11PM, 12:15AM. 422.2434

Crackers Oyster Bar ★★$$$ A Victorian motif prevails at this bar and dining room, which features an open kitchen, a marble-topped bar and tables, and antique furnishings. Patrons savor not only oysters but other seafood dishes—baked or broiled fish, steamed shrimp, clam chowder—as well as Cajun creations like jambalaya and red beans and rice. Or stop in just to sample one of the 26 varieties of beer and catch a sports event on one of the large-screen TVs. ♦ Seafood/Cajun ♦ Daily lunch and dinner (until midnight). 422.2434

Wine Cellar One of Florida's best stocked and most expensive wine stores, with more than 5,000 bottles, is located downstairs next door to **Crackers Oyster Bar**. Wine tastings are held daily, and the staff can always help amateurs make a selection from the bewildering array of choices. ♦ M-Th, Su 4-11PM; F-Sa 4PM-2AM. 422.2434

Bumby Arcade What was once the **Bumby Hardware** store now houses **Bumby Emporium**, a shop filled with **Church Street Station** souvenirs; **Wm. J. Sweet's Ice Cream**; and the **Buffalo Trading Company**, a Western gift shop complete with a stuffed buffalo. ♦ Daily 11AM-11PM. 422.2434

Church Street Exchange Located behind **Rosie O'Grady's** (enter through **Apple**

Annie's Courtyard), this shopping center offers two floors of stores under Victorian tin ceilings. There are more than 50 specialty shops in all, including the nifty **Old Town Magic Shop,** with a magician always on hand, and favorites like **Tokio Electronics, Sam Goody, Victoria's Secret,** and **House of Ireland.** Browsers and buyers can easily spend an entire afternoon here. ♦ Daily 11AM-11PM. 422.2434 &

6 Farmers Market A half-block open-air market offers good prices on produce, baked goods, gourmet coffee, cheese, dried flowers, and houseplants, including a fine selection of orchids. ♦ Sa 7AM-1PM. W Church St (between S Garland and S Hughey Aves). 246.2555

7 Church Street Market Behind the brick facade and beyond the open courtyard with pushcarts, park benches, a clock tower, and turn-of-the-century–style fountains and lamps, this is a modern shopping center. Built in 1988, it includes yuppie favorites such as **The Sharper Image, Brookstone, Compagnie Internationale Express,** and **Häagen Dazs. Behr's Chocolates** lets you see how chocolate and other sweet treats are made. The marketplace is also a popular dining choice, especially for the downtown crowd, featuring **Pizzeria Uno** and the **Olive Garden** for Italian fare, and **Jungle Jim's,** a gourmet burger eatery with a diverse menu and sometimes rather slow service. Not affiliated with **Church Street Station,** it's located about a block east of the complex and the railroad tracks, on the north side of Church Street. ♦ Daily. 55 W Church St (between S Orange and S Garland Aves). 872.3500

Within Church Street Market:

Howl at the Moon Saloon This bar brags that it has the only dueling pianists in town, and the suds and sing-alongs do bring out the crowds. The piano players humorously try to outdo each other beginning at 6PM weeknights and at 8PM on Saturday and Sunday. Don't be shy—sing along. ♦ Cover. M-Th, Su 6PM-1AM; F-Sa 6PM-2AM. 841.4695

Amura Japanese Restaurant ★$$ Sushi is the most requested menu item here, and the 15 seats at the sushi bar are usually filled at lunch and dinner. This restaurant also has two tatami booths, where guests remove their shoes and sit on the floor for dining. If you want to try traditional Japanese food, we suggest the "Love Boat," a sampling of hot dishes from the menu. Or play it safe with either the chicken teriyaki or grilled shrimp, both favorites of regular customers. There's also an impressive selection of Asian beers. ♦ Japanese ♦ Daily 11AM-11PM. 316.8500

Romantic Orlando

The world's top tourist destination isn't often thought of as a romantic spot. However, if you're looking for an idyllic getaway, here are some ideas.

Lake Eola Park in downtown Orlando (bounded by N Osceola and N Rosalind Aves, N Eola Dr, E Central Blvd, and E Washington and E Robinson Sts) was recently voted by readers of *Orlando* magazine "the number one place to propose marriage." There's a pleasant walkway encircling the lake, and fanciful swan paddleboats for rent.

Take a horse-drawn carriage ride under the stars. The nightly excursions start at **Church Street Station** in downtown Orlando (129 W Church St, between S Orange and S Garland Aves, 407/422.2434) with drivers dressed in Victorian garb telling stories about the city's history.

The lovely **Harry P. Leu Gardens** in Orlando (1730 N Forest Ave, north of Nebraska St, 407/246.2620) is the perfect place for a stroll, through 56 acres of natural beauty that includes a southern mansion overlooking a lake, and the largest camellia collection on the East Coast. There's also a formal rose garden where many weddings are held.

Sip Champagne and take a carefree and serene trip through the clouds in a hot-air balloon ride. Several Central Florida companies (see "Flights of Fancy" on page 40) offer trips.

If all this romance leads to marriage, Disney's **Fairytale Weddings** can plan a day to remember, from an intimate ceremony for two to an elegant affair in which the bride arrives in Cinderella's glass coach. Dozens of couples tie the knot every month at **Walt Disney World**—so many, in fact, that Disney built a Victorian **Fairy Tale Wedding Pavilion** that seats 250 and offers a prime view of **Cinderella Castle** in the **Magic Kingdom,** perfectly framed in a window behind the altar. For more information, call 407/828.3400.

7 Sloppy Joe's $$ Key West's most famous bar, where Hemingway was wont to while away the hours, is now a national chain. This Orlando outlet is much noisier and more crassly commercial than the famous original, but a beer and a bowl of conch chowder still taste fine here. The menu is all-American, with such familiar fare as burgers, the eponymous sloppy joes, and several salad choices. And, of course, Hemingway merchandise abounds, with everything from T-shirts to cigarette lighters bearing Papa's round face. ◆ American ◆ Daily lunch and dinner (bar until 2AM). 41 W Church St (between S Orange and S Garland Aves). 843.5825

8 Mulvaney's Irish Pub ★★$ This lively place, frequented by tourists and locals alike, has the feel of a turn-of-the-century Irish pub with its long bar stretching to the back. Known for its selection of imported beers and ales, the pub offers five on tap. Try the shepherd's pie—one of the traditional Irish pub dishes served here—or stick with familiar burgers and sandwiches. There's live entertainment nightly, from Irish music to acoustic folk. ◆ Irish ◆ M-F 11:30AM-2AM; Sa-Su 1PM-2AM. 27 W Church St (between S Orange and S Garland Aves). 872.3296

8 Pebbles ★★★$$ Voted the number one local chain restaurant by readers of *Orlando* magazine, this eatery is known for its consistently outstanding food and prompt and friendly service. Once a five-and-dime store, it's now an intimate tropical restaurant. The fresh fish is superb; so are the pasta and daily specials. An extensive selection of wines and imported ales complements the creative menu, which features such dishes as chicken Vesuvio (chicken breast sautéed with garlic and capers and served on *perciatelli* pasta) and breast of duck with wild mushrooms served on penne pasta with a morel sauce. This is the fourth **Pebbles** restaurant in the area. ◆ American ◆ M-F lunch and dinner; Sa-Su dinner. 17 W Church St (between S Orange and S Garland Aves). 839.0892. Also at: The Crossroads of Lake Buena Vista, Apopka-Vineland Rd (between I-4 and Palm Pkwy), Lake Buena Vista. 827.1111; 2516 Aloma Ave (between Balfour Dr and St. Andrews Blvd). 678.7001; 2110 W Rte 434 (between I-4 and Montgomery Rd), Altamonte Springs. 774.7111

9 Terror on Church Street Ready to encounter a dangerous hunchback? Or a knife-wielding psycho? It's all scary good fun at this theaterlike attraction in which actors spook and shock delighted visitors. The year-round "haunted house" draws late-night crowds, with lines stretching around the corner. Both tourists and residents enjoy the high-tech special effects. Teenagers are especially fond of the mayhem and gore; many return again and again for the 20-minute walk-through. Children under age 10 must be accompanied by an adult. ◆ Admission. M-Th, Su 7PM-midnight; F-Sa 7PM-1AM. 141 S Orange Ave (at E Church St). 649.3327

10 Tanqueray's Bar & Grille ★$$ The centerpiece of this comfortable underground eatery, a few steps down off Orange Avenue, is the bar, which looks like the set of the "Cheers" TV show and is a cozy hangout for locals. At lunchtime you'll find courthouse lawyers on expense accounts who come for the decent steak, chicken quesadillas, or pasta. There's live entertainment on Friday and Saturday nights. ◆ American ◆ Cover charge F-Sa after 9PM. M-F lunch and dinner, until 2AM; Sa dinner, until 2AM; Su club only, 9PM-2AM. 100 S Orange Ave (at E Pine St). 649.8540

11 Le Provence ★$$$ This sophisticated two-level French restaurant fits nicely in the financial section of town. The atmosphere is wonderfully appealing, with a small but attractive upstairs dining room and a larger downstairs room dominated by an impressive 18-foot mahogany-and-brass bar. The ambitious menu changes quarterly, with an emphasis on the freshest ingredients and exquisite dessert pastries. Highlights include oven-roasted scallops with Tuscan ratatouille, osso buco braised in Burgundy with grilled vegetables and gorgonzola risotto, and beef tenderloin grilled with potato cakes and roasted mushrooms. ◆ French ◆ M-Sa lunch and dinner; Su dinner. Reservations recommended. 50 E Pine St (between S Magnolia and S Court Aves). 843.1320

12 Ichiban ★★★$$ Here is one of the few places in Central Florida where fresh sushi is not only available but worth seeking out. Tangy teriyaki and tempura dishes round out the menu. It's casual, with traditional Japanese decor and seating either at tables or at the sushi bar. There's no nonsmoking area. ◆ Japanese ◆ M-F lunch and dinner; Sa dinner. 19 S Orange Ave (between E Pine St and E Central Blvd). 423.2688

Orlando resident Joe Kittinger was the first person to fly solo in a balloon across the Atlantic Ocean. He made his voyage in September of 1984.

Restaurants/Clubs: Red   Hotels: Blue

Shops/🍴 Outdoors: Green   Sights/Culture: Black

Lights, Camera, Reaction:
Central Florida on the Screen

In recent decades, the Orlando region has become a powerhouse of the movie industry, thanks to the working sound stages and production facilities associated with the **Universal Studios** and **Disney-MGM Studios** theme parks. But Central Florida landscapes and lifestyles have played a major supporting role in the movies since as far back as 1915, when Theda Bara gave the world a new word, "vamp," with her performance in *The Devil's Daughter* (also known as *The Vampire*), shot on location in **St. Augustine.**

In that film, the old city was in costume, as the Italian village of the Gabriele d'Annunzio novel *La Gioconda* on which the screenplay was based. Nowadays, Central Florida locations, ranging from retirement colonies to moon-rocket launch sites to alligator swamps to theme parks, are more likely to star as themselves, as in the following films:

Apollo 13 (1995) Tom Hanks, Bill Paxton, and Kevin Bacon play astronauts Jim Lovell, Fred Haise, and Jack Swigert taking off from the **Kennedy Space Center.** This harrowing, only lightly fictionalized version of the disastrous 1970 space flight was directed by Ron Howard.

Armageddon (1998) Bruce Willis is the oil driller who figures out that the way to deflect a killer asteroid is to go into space and blow it up yourself. And how do you get to an asteroid? The plane leaves from **Cape Canaveral.**

China Moon (1994) John Bailey's noir film features Ed Harris as a homicide detective in "Polk County" (**Lakeland** and **Tampa**) who knows more about murder than anybody in Florida but gets fatally confused when he meets up with Madeleine Stowe.

Cocoon (1985) A terrific cast of older folks (Don Ameche, Wilford Brimley, Hume Cronyn, Maureen Stapleton, Jessica Tandy, Gwen Verdon) play the residents of a senior citizens' home in **St. Petersburg** who find that the swimming pool next door has mysterious rejuvenating powers. Aliens have something to do with it, but you don't want to pay too much attention to the plot.

The Creature from the Black Lagoon (1954) This 3-D classic stars Whit Bissell and Jack Carlson as scientists on a fossil-hunting expedition in Amazonia who discover a kind of humanoid—and homicidal—lungfish. Julie Adams shines as the woman the gill-man falls for. Considerable portions of it were filmed underwater in **Marineland.**

Gutterdog Love (1998) Jeremy Hammer's film stars Stephan Eder and Shari Weber as a sitcom producer and his fiancée encountering the sexy but lethal seamy side of life in a corrupt little town in **Pinellas County.**

H.E.A.L.T.H. (1979) Robert Altman's spoof of the health food industry is set at a convention at the fabulous **Don CeSar Beach Resort** in St. Petersburg.

Glenda Jackson, Carol Burnett, James Garner, and Lauren Bacall are the chief intriguers, with Alfre Woodard as the beleaguered hotel manager.

Lethal Weapon 3 (1992) Mel Gibson, Danny Glover, Joe Pesci, and Rene Russo run through their extremely fast paces in **Clearwater** and Orlando this time, with an outrageous chase sequence involving two armored cars and the wrong lane of an expressway.

Marvin's Room (1996) In Broadway director Jerry Zaks's film debut, shot in the middle of **Walt Disney World** at **Lake Buena Vista,** Diane Keaton and Meryl Streep are the respectively self-sacrificing and selfish sisters who come to terms with each other when the former has leukemia and the latter may have the matching bone marrow. Fine acting brings the movie up above the level of the formula tearjerker.

My Girl (1991) Terminally cute Macaulay Culkin is terminally ill, but the point of this movie is the performance of 11-year-old Anna Chlumsky as his plucky and peculiar best friend. **Sanford** is the small town where her father (Dan Aykroyd) runs a funeral home and blunders into romance with Jamie Lee Curtis.

Parenthood (1989) Ron Howard explores the pains and pleasures of having offspring across four generations of a suburban **Gainesville** family with a Robert Altman–sized cast including Steve Martin, Mary Steenburgen, Dianne Wiest, Jason Robards, Tom Hulce, Martha Plimpton, and Keanu Reeves.

Passenger 57 (1992) During the occasional moments when the action of this airplane-hijack thriller, starring Wesley Snipes, is on the ground, it's in Sanford and Orlando.

Senior Week (1987) Where the boys are is in **Daytona Beach** now, and they're as silly as ever, if not even sillier. Michael St. Gerard and Jennifer Gorey star.

Strategic Air Command (1955) General Jimmy Stewart plays an ex–World War II bombing ace *and* baseball star, married, naturally, to June Allyson. He gets into yet another uniform at **MacDill Air Force Base** in **Tampa,** and prepares to drop the Big One on Moscow. Fortunately, it turns out not to be necessary.

The Waterboy (1998) Adam Sandler does his usual stuff, pleasing to some and repellent to others, in Orlando; here, he's the football-team waterboy who turns out to know how to tackle. **De Land** provides the bayou home where the hero and his mother (Kathy Bates) dine on étoufféed swamp snake.

We Shall Return (1963) The story of this Cold War drama of a Cuban exile patriarch, César Romero, whose son, Anthony Ray, secretly supports Fidel Castro and plots to foil the Bay of Pigs invasion, was set in Miami but filmed in Daytona and St. Augustine.

13 Wall Street Cantina ★$ When the weather's cool, the prized seats are on the sidewalk in front of this bright little eatery. It's a downtown business crowd during the day, but the place gets crazy after dark, with live music Tuesday through Thursday and Sunday. Margaritas are the most ordered drink during happy hour, from 4 to 7PM Monday through Friday. The food is typical deli fare with a Tex-Mex flair, including tasty sandwiches and hamburgers—try the "CEO" burger or the "Broker" salad. ◆ American/Tex-Mex ◆ Daily lunch and dinner. Wall St Plaza (between N Court and N Orange Aves). 420.1515

14 Zuma Beach Club The former **Beacham Theatre** has been converted into a high-energy disco that makes you feel as though you're partying on the beach. There are six bars and four levels for dancing. The place attracts a mostly young and enthusiastic crowd, and the hits are spun by a disc jockey. ◆ Cover. M 10PM-3AM; T 7PM-3AM; W-Th 9PM-3AM; F 7PM-3AM; Sa-Su 9PM-3AM. 46 N Orange Ave (between W Central Blvd and W Washington St). 648.8363

14 Sapphire Supper Club ★★$$ Formerly the **Downtown Jazz & Blues Club,** this remodeled place is one of the few beyond Church Street that are lively and open late; it's filled with locals who appreciate live blues and jazz. There are one or more bands on the bill almost every night of the month—the bigger the name, the higher the cover charge. The food is more than your typical bar fare—try the lime pepper chicken or one of several vegetarian selections, such as the popular mozzarella sandwich with plum tomatoes, fresh basil, olive oil, and cracked pepper on French bread. ◆ American ◆ Admission for shows. Tu-Th, Sa-Su dinner; F lunch and dinner. 54 N Orange Ave (between W Central Blvd and W Washington St). 246.1419

15 Barnett Bank Building Neo-Victorian spires top this 28-story office building, constructed in 1987 of silvery reflective-glass walls. A stately entrance leads from the structure's open plaza into an elegant lobby. Two well-known restaurants are located here (see below). ◆ 390 N Orange Ave (at W Livingston St)

Within the Barnett Bank Building:

Harvey's Bistro ★★★$$ There are tables outside on the plaza or inside in the dining room, dominated by an impressive well-stocked bar. On nights the **Orlando Magic** basketball team plays at home, the place overflows with fans. The atmosphere is casual, and the fine fare is served in huge portions; favorites include seared salmon with lobster hash, thin-crust pizza with caramelized onions and spinach, and New England pot roast with roasted-garlic mashed potatoes (the most popular selection). The menu also offers "lite" entrées and soups and salads. There are usually parking spaces on the street in front, or use the center's garage (entrance on Livingston St) and have your ticket validated. ◆ American ◆ M-F lunch and dinner; Sa dinner. Ground floor. 246.6560

Manuel's on the 28th ★★★★$$$ This exclusive restaurant on the top floor has established itself as one of the area's finest. Glass panels run from floor to ceiling, providing every diner with a panorama of downtown Orlando. The spectacular view is matched by a friendly, attentive staff and innovative chefs. The menu, which features "contemporary world cuisine," changes quarterly. Past favorites have included an appetizer of California farm-raised abalone and shrimp in a roasted-garlic sauce, and an entrée of lobster and wood-roasted chicken with coconut lime sauce and fried curry noodles. The beef dishes are usually superb, and the desserts first-rate. Don't be bashful about walking around the dining room to check out the different views; staffers enjoy showing off their restaurant and their city. Parking is available in the building; enter on the Livingston Street side. ◆ Continental ◆ Tu-Sa dinner. Reservations required; jacket required. 28th floor. 246.6580

16 Orlando Downtown Marriott $$ If you would like to enjoy Orlando and its outlying areas but want to remain a bit removed from the crowds at **Walt Disney World** (a 20- to 25-minute drive away), this 300-room hotel is the nicest in the area and a good bet. Formerly an Omni hotel, it's across the street from the **Orlando Arena** and the **Bob Carr Performing Arts Centre,** and right off Interstate 4. The lively sports bar, **Spectators,** is where fans of the **Orlando Magic** basketball team gather before and after the games. There's also a restaurant, but it's nothing special. ◆ 400 W Livingston St (between N Hughey Ave and Pittman St). 843.6664, 800/228.9290; fax 648.5414; www.marriott.com

---

Each week the metropolitan Orlando area hosts an estimated 699,653 visitors.

The tiny enclave of Eatonville is America's oldest incorporated African-American community and was home to Zora Neale Hurston, a famous Harlem Renaissance writer.

17 Bob Carr Performing Arts Centre
This is home to the **Orlando Opera Company** and the **Southern Ballet,** and host to touring Broadway shows and musical groups from rock to classical. With 2,500 seats, it's the largest theater in town, although it does have some drawbacks—less-than-first-rate acoustics, a small stage, and no center aisle. The 32-year-old **Orlando Opera Company** performs four operas each year, one of which is usually a lighter operetta. The opera season customarily runs from November through April. ♦ 401 W Livingston St (at Bob Carr La). Box office 849.2050, event information 849.2001, Orlando Opera Company office 426.1717

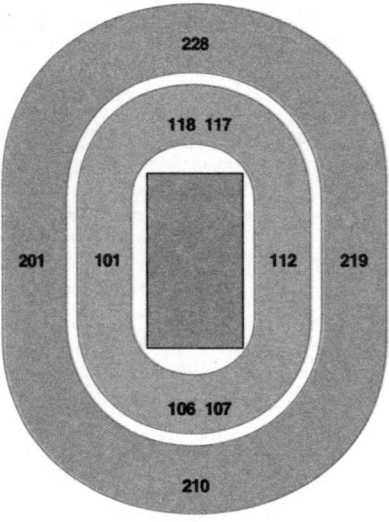

18 Orlando Arena The local tourist tax pays for this well-designed, efficient public building that seats 16,000 (see the seating chart above). Popularly known as the "O-rena," it is home to the **National Basketball Association**'s **Orlando Magic.** The arena, with Art Deco details, hosts a wide range of activities, from hockey games, tractor pulls, and the circus to rodeos, wrestling, and concerts. ♦ 600 W Amelia St (between Revere and N Parramore Aves). Box office 849.2020, event information 849.2001

19 Harley Hotel of Orlando $ This 281-room hotel overlooks beautiful Lake Eola. The rooms have old-fashioned charm, with dust ruffles, pillow shams, and marble-topped bedside tables, and there are nice little touches such as a complimentary newspaper delivered to your door on weekdays. Some of the rooms have views of the lake, and 12 junior suites also have wet bars. Conveniently located, the hotel is only minutes from any destination downtown (complimentary shuttle service is provided) and about 25 minutes from **Walt Disney World.** The restaurant has a good lunch buffet, and there's an outdoor pool. ♦ 151 E Washington St (at N Rosalind Ave). 841.3220, 800/321.2323; fax 849.1839

20 Lake Eola Park Crisscrossed by swan-shaped paddleboats and encircled by a pleasant walkway, Lake Eola forms the heart of this urban park and is a good place to watch the sun set. One of the park's highlights is the **Walt Disney World Amphitheater,** which is the site of occasional free concerts and home of the **Orlando Shakespeare Festival,** a nonprofit professional repertory theater affiliated with the **University of Central Florida;** it produces two of the Bard's plays each spring. ♦ Shakespeare Festival information: 30 S Magnolia Ave, Suite 250, Orlando, FL 32801, 423.6905. Bounded by N Osceola and N Rosalind Aves, N Eola Dr, E Central Blvd, and E Washington and E Robinson Sts

21 Chez Jose $ Sit outdoors or inside at this casual restaurant that serves substantial burritos and other Tex-Mex fare. **Moos Brothers Ice Cream** shares the space, so dessert is just steps away. ♦ Tex-Mex ♦ Daily lunch and dinner. 700 E Washington St (at N Summerlin Ave). 672.8665

22 Dexter's of Thornton Park ★★$$ A local hangout in an up-and-coming downtown neighborhood, it's the second location for this trendy eatery, serving eclectic specialties such as a duck, brie, and caramelized onion sandwich. Wine is offered by the glass. ♦ New American ♦ Daily lunch and dinner. 808 E Washington St (between N Hyer and Hill Aves). 648.2777. Also at: 200 W Fairbanks Ave (between S Park and S New York Aves), Winter Park. 629.1150

23 4th Fighter Group ★$$ Though the food is ordinary, you can sit right next to the window to watch airplanes take off and land at this restaurant located at the **Orlando Executive Airport.** The entrance resembles a fortified bunker, and the inside is like a dim old British country pub, complete with a fireplace and exposed beams. The restaurant is dedicated to the 4th Fighter Group, an elite US fighter pilot unit during World War II. Hanging from the wall are war mementos and pictures of Colonel Donald Blakeslee, whose group escorted the first bombers over Berlin in 1944. Headphones allow patrons to eavesdrop on the control tower and the pilots of landing and departing planes. ♦ American ♦ M-F lunch and dinner, Sa dinner, Su brunch and dinner. 494 Rickenbacker Dr (south of E Colonial Dr). 898.4251

24 La Normandie ★★$$$ Three dining rooms with French country decor provide the setting for such reliable French fare as duck *à l'orange* (a specialty), an outstanding seafood crepe, and a *très magnifique* Grand Marnier soufflé and crème brûlée. Owner Andre Bilheux recommends the *coquille de fruits de mer.* ♦ French ♦ Daily lunch and dinner. 2021 E Colonial Dr (between Garden Plaza and Palm Dr). 896.9976

25 Vinh's ★★$ This modest Vietnamese restaurant is a big hit with downtown lunch crowds and diners in search of something out of the ordinary. Soups are homemade, delicious, and served in huge bowls. One standout: the seafood soup, which brims with shrimp, crab claws, and translucent rice noodles. Other favorites include the sliced egg roll, served on noodles, and *bo seven mon* (beef seven-quart)—thinly sliced beef that guests cook at their tables on ingeniously designed stoves. ♦ Vietnamese ♦ Daily lunch and dinner. 1231 E Colonial Dr (between Shine and N Mills Aves). 894.5007

26 The Forbidden City ★★$$ Forget the pricey Chinese food around the tourist haunts. When chef Steve Chang first worked his magic at **Haifeng Restaurant** near **SeaWorld,** Chinese-food lovers took note. He's now here whipping up good lunches and memorable dinners, including tangy chicken with black bean sauce, orange beef, and an Oriental-style barbecue shrimp dish called *sa chia* shrimp. ♦ Hunan ♦ Daily lunch and dinner. 948 N Mills Ave (between E Marks and Weber Sts). 894.5005

27 One Orlando Center Bright white argon tubes outline this office building's crisp, crystalline contours at night. Pale pink granite walls alternate with glass, creating a stair-step effect that attempts to link the structure architecturally with its less lofty neighbors. Plans call for two more buildings at the site that will make this one—designed by **John Lind** of **Hansen, Lind, Meyer** in 1988—look less like a missing puzzle piece. ♦ 800 N Magnolia Ave (at Park Lake St). 422.7773

The world's largest group of Frank Lloyd Wright–designed buildings is on the campus of Florida Southern College in the small town of Lakeland between Orlando and Tampa.

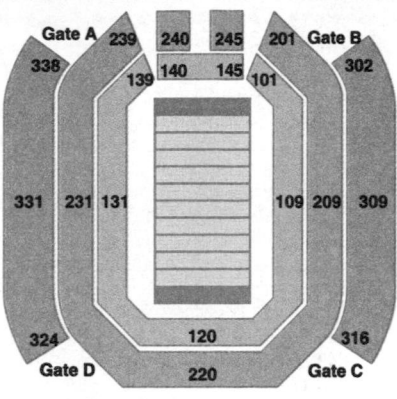

28 Citrus Bowl Previously named **Orlando Stadium,** it holds 70,000 (see the seating chart above) and plans are to eventually expand the stadium to 90,000 seats. But it only fills up completely once a year, for the **Florida Citrus Bowl** football game in January. The **University of Central Florida's** football team, the **Knights,** plays here in front of a steadily increasing number of fans. The stadium is also the site of high-school football games and a few concerts each year. ♦ W Church St (between S Rio Grande and S Tampa Aves). 849.2001

28 Tinker Field This stadium was built in 1921 and named for baseball player Joe Tinker (of Tinker-to-Evers-to-Chance fame), who retired to Orlando after his baseball days were over. It seats more than 5,000 spectators and is home to the **Orlando Cubs,** a Class AA minor-league baseball team affiliated with the **Minnesota Twins.** ♦ 287 S Tampa Ave (between Long and W Church Sts). 872.7593

29 Radisson Plaza Hotel Orlando $$ Some of the 337 rooms at this hotel look out over Lake Ivanhoe, while others face an office building. All have been redecorated in recent years. In addition, a presidential suite has been added, and the club-level rooms are now equipped with such extras as coffeemakers. The lounge has a large-screen TV that's great for sporting events, but the restaurant fare is only so-so—you're probably better off dining outside the hotel. There's an outdoor pool, two tennis courts, a basketball court, and a well-equipped fitness center. Thanks to a high-rise parking garage, you can avoid getting wet during Orlando's rainy summer months. ♦ 60 S Ivanhoe Blvd (between N Orange Ave and Legion Pl). 425.4455, 800/333.3333; fax 425.7440; www.radisson.com

30 Harry P. Leu Gardens
The largest camellia collection on the East Coast is found within these 56 acres of carefully cultivated gardens (the flowers bloom during the winter months). Also

noteworthy are the 50-foot floral clock and the rose garden. Small maps are available to help visitors make their way through the maze of paths. The house, built a century ago, is open to the public, as is the new **Garden House** with rocking chairs on the porch and a splendid view of Lake Rowena. Leu, a successful businessman who grew up in Orlando, purchased the land on the lake in 1936. It was once part of a farm owned by David Mizell, Winter Park's first settler. House tours last about 20 minutes and are conducted every half hour. ♦ Admission. Gardens open daily; house tours 10AM-3PM daily. 1730 N Forest Ave (north of Nebraska St). 246.2620

31 Loch Haven Park North of downtown Orlando, this city park is home to a theater complex and several museums. It's also a favorite spot for staging festivals. Local residents picnic on its grassy meadows and take advantage of its walking/biking trail. ♦ E Princeton and E Rollins Sts (between N Mills Ave and Camden Rd)

Within Loch Haven Park:

Orlando Museum of Art A $7.7-million expansion in 1997 doubled the size of the gallery space, allowing the museum to put more of its collections of pre-Columbian, African, and 19th- and 20th-century American art on display. Now that there's room, look for frequent "blockbuster" exhibitions here. ♦ Admission. Tu-Sa; Su noon-5PM. 2416 N Mills Ave. 896.4231; www.omart.org

Civic Theatre of Central Florida This complex consists of the **Edyth Bush Theatre,** which is the main stage and has seating for 350; the **Ann Giles Densch Theatre for Young People,** which seats 400; and the **Tupperware Theatre,** which seats 140. The theater complex has a six-play MainStage Season. It also stages summer musicals by the **Theatre Arts Group,** a series of plays for children, and a five-play SecondStage Season of adult drama. ♦ Box office M-W; on weekends when there's a performance, also Th-F 9AM-7PM, Sa noon-7PM, and Su noon-4PM. 1001 E Princeton St. 896.7365

Orlando Science Center Exhibits at this new state-of-the-art science center (next door to the old center, which it replaced) include *NatureWorks* (natural sciences), *KidsTown* (early childhood), *Physics Park* (physical science), *Power Station* (energy), *123 Math Avenue* (numbers), *Cosmic Tourist* (earth sciences), *Light Power* (lasers and optics), *Imaginary Landscapes* (computers and simulation), *BodyZone* (health and fitness), and *ShowBiz Science* (entertainment technology).

There's an awesome observatory and a 310-seat **CineDome** featuring large-format films—including *Alaska: Spirit of the Wild,* narrated by Charlton Heston, which was nominated for an Academy Award—and planetarium shows. The center also books international traveling exhibits of all kinds. ♦ Admission. M-Th; F-Sa 9AM-9PM; Su noon-5PM. 810 E Rollins St. 896.7151

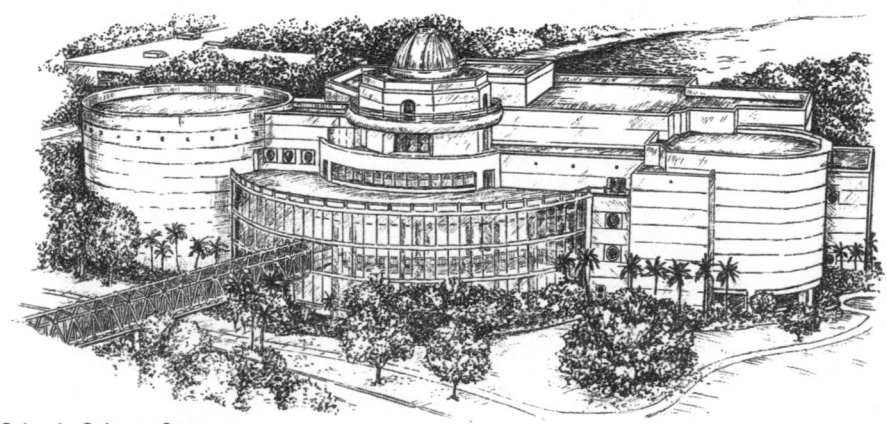

Orlando Science Center

Within the Orlando Science Center:

Orange County Historical Museum
Exhibits chronicle Orange County's past and include a country store and a pioneer kitchen. ♦ Admission. M-Sa; Su noon-5PM. 897.6350

Behind the Orlando Science Center:

COURTESY OF THE ORANGE COUNTY HISTORICAL MUSEUM

Fire Station No. 3 A two-story redbrick building (pictured above) completed in 1926, this is the city's oldest existing firehouse. It now stands less than a mile from its original location. On display are Orlando's old fire trucks, including the horse-drawn American LaFrance Metropolitan steam fire pumper from 1911, and the original leather and metal buckets. ♦ Nominal admission. M-Sa; Su noon-5PM. 897.6350

32 Theatre Downtown This cozy 120-seat theater in a former appliance store specializes in American and contemporary plays that have run successfully on and off Broadway. Works by local playwrights are also performed. ♦ Box office M-F noon-5PM; on performance days, noon-6:30PM and 45 minutes before curtain time. 2113 N Orange Ave (at E Princeton St). 841.0083

33 Enzian Theater Central Florida's first art-film house, this 250-seat theater has comfortable chairs, a reasonably large movie screen, plus food, wine, and beer service during the show. ♦ Admission. 1300 S Orlando Ave (between Magnolia and Manor Rds), Maitland. 629.1088

33 Nicole St. Pierre ★★$$$ This is the new venue for Monique and Georges Vogelbacher, whose venerable Winter Park eatery, the **Cordon Bleu,** burned down in 1995. In a stylish old home, the intimate restaurant (named for their two children, Nicole and Pierre), is adjacent to the **Enzian Theater.** Chef Georges keeps his menu fairly traditional—escargots, *bouillabaisse Provençale,* rack of lamb. But he also includes an ostrich fillet among his "low-fat, low-cholesterol selections." And his crème brûlée is worth the calories. ♦ French ♦ M-F lunch

and dinner; Sa dinner; Su brunch. 1300 S Orlando Ave (between Magnolia and Manor Rds), Maitland. 647.7575

34 Antonio's La Fiamma ★★★$$ For a special lunch or dinner, we recommend the spacious upstairs dining room, with fresh flowers, linen tablecloths, and classical Italian music. The service is pleasant and well timed. Regulars recommend the grilled veal chop or the *zuppa di pesce* with fresh scallops, clams, shrimp, mussels, and calamari, sautéed in white wine and tomato broth and served with garlicky *crostini.* Also try the marinated calamari appetizer or any of the simple pasta offerings. The downstairs deli serves pizzas, sandwiches, and other tasty fare. ♦ Italian ♦ Daily lunch and dinner. 611 S Orlando Ave (between Manor Rd and E Ventris Ave), Maitland. 645.5523

35 Maitland Art Center This quirky museum was created as an artists' retreat in the late 1930s by artist Andre Smith. Today, the stucco and cast-concrete landmark is on the National Register of Historic Places. Featured are changing exhibitions by contemporary American artists. Wall carvings in the garden chapel depict the life of Christ. ♦ Free. M, W-F; Tu 10AM-8PM; Sa-Su noon-4:30PM. 231 W Packwood Ave (between S Maitland Ave and S Lake Sybelia Dr), Maitland. 539.2181

36 Enzo's on the Lake ★★★$$$ Enzo Perlini has been serving the cuisine of his native Rome for more than a decade in this lively setting, a converted ranch-style house on Fairy Lake. The chef, trained in Venice, creates delicate pasta preparations and divine desserts. And you needn't spend big bucks, either, if you order a pasta dish such as *bucatini alla Enzo* (long, tiny pasta tubes in a light sauce of mushrooms, bacon, and peas). For those who prefer to skip the rich and sweet desserts, the restaurant follows the European tradition of offering cheese and fruit after dinner. ♦ Italian ♦ Daily lunch and dinner. 1130 S Hwy 17/92 (between Dog Track Rd and Rte 434), Longwood. 834.9872

37 Maison & Jardin ★★★$$$ A house and garden reminiscent of a Roman villa provide a serene, elegant setting for an exemplary meal. The delicious specialties include macadamia nut–crusted fillet of red snapper with papaya salsa; shrimp and scallops in a saffron beurre blanc; and beef Wellington. Daily specials feature freshly caught fish prepared in a variety of innovative ways. Executive chef Hans Spirig strongly believes in using fresh and, whenever possible, local ingredients; the restaurant even grows its own herbs and vegetables. ♦ Continental ♦ Daily dinner. Reservations recommended. 430 S Wymore Rd (between Spring Valley Rd and Rte 436), Altamonte Springs. 862.4410

Winter Park

With its small-town ambience and tree-lined redbrick roads, Winter Park, a town about four miles northeast of downtown Orlando, feels more like New England than Florida. Spending a day or even an afternoon taking in its shops, galleries, and sights or simply strolling its residential streets provides a pleasant contrast to the theme-park circuit.

Ever since the well-to-do began retreating to cottages and resorts here in the 19th century, Winter Park has been a haven for the rich and famous. Its first white settler, David Mizell, arrived in 1858, when the region was mostly wilderness. Significant development began when, in 1881, two friends from Massachusetts, Loring Chase and Oliver Chapman, bought land for a resort hotel and a community they named Winter Park. Their new town got a boost the very next year when the **South Florida Railroad**, linking Sanford and Tampa, began making regularly scheduled stops here. Residents and winter visitors shopped on **Park Avenue** and lived in family hotels, simple homes, and elegant lakeside cottages.

As did their 19th-century counterparts, most of today's visitors to Winter Park spend a fair amount of time on Park Avenue, with its trendy and distinctive shops, art galleries and museums, and many fine restaurants. One of the avenue's most outstanding attractions is the **Charles Hosmer Morse Museum of American Art**. Its collection of works by Louis Comfort Tiffany represents every period of the artist's life and is considered to be the most comprehensive and interesting Tiffany collection anywhere.

Visitors should also be sure to take the **Scenic Boat Tour**—a relaxing, one-hour narrated cruise that glides through Winter Park's lakes and canals and past impressive mansions. The town also offers many charming parks, small hotels, and the lakeside campus of **Rollins College**.

Winter Park may lack sophistication when measured against New York or San Francisco, but it possesses a graceful character that is lacking in much of neighboring boomtown Orlando.

Area code 407 unless otherwise noted.

1 Rollins College At the south end of posh Park Avenue lies an architectural delight. The campus of this liberal arts college, which has approximately 1,400 students, includes many examples of the Spanish-Mediterranean architectural style. Established in 1885, it is named for Alonzo Rollins, a wealthy Chicago businessman who had moved here for health reasons and contributed $50,000 to the college's founding. Those interested in architecture or in need of a quiet moment will enjoy strolling the tree-shaded pathways that crisscross the 65-acre lakeside campus. ◆ E Fairbanks and S Interlachen Aves. 646.2000

The Walk of Fame at Rollins College in Winter Park has more than 800 inscribed stones that were brought from the homes or birthplaces of famous people.

Rollins College in Winter Park was founded in 1885, the first institute of higher learning in Florida.

On the Rollins College campus:

Walk of Fame In the center of the campus, on the east side of **Carnegie Hall** and across Holt Avenue from the administration building, lies a walkway created by Hamilton Holt, a popular **Rollins College** president who served from 1925 to 1949. The path consists of hundreds of engraved stones, each one in some way connected with a famous person Holt had met. One stone is from the front step of Woodrow Wilson's home in Princeton, another is from the garden of the Paris hotel where Oscar Wilde died, and yet another is from the Atlanta home of Martin Luther King Jr. The walk was inspired by Holt's childhood wanderings through the streets of his New England hometown. Many of the walkways there were made up of stones taken from ancestral homes and engraved with family names. Holt made his mark nationally with several innovative educational ideas. He believed the physical environment should be conducive to learning and that campus buildings at **Rollins** should take advantage of Florida's climate. During his tenure, 32 Spanish-Mediterranean–style buildings were erected here.

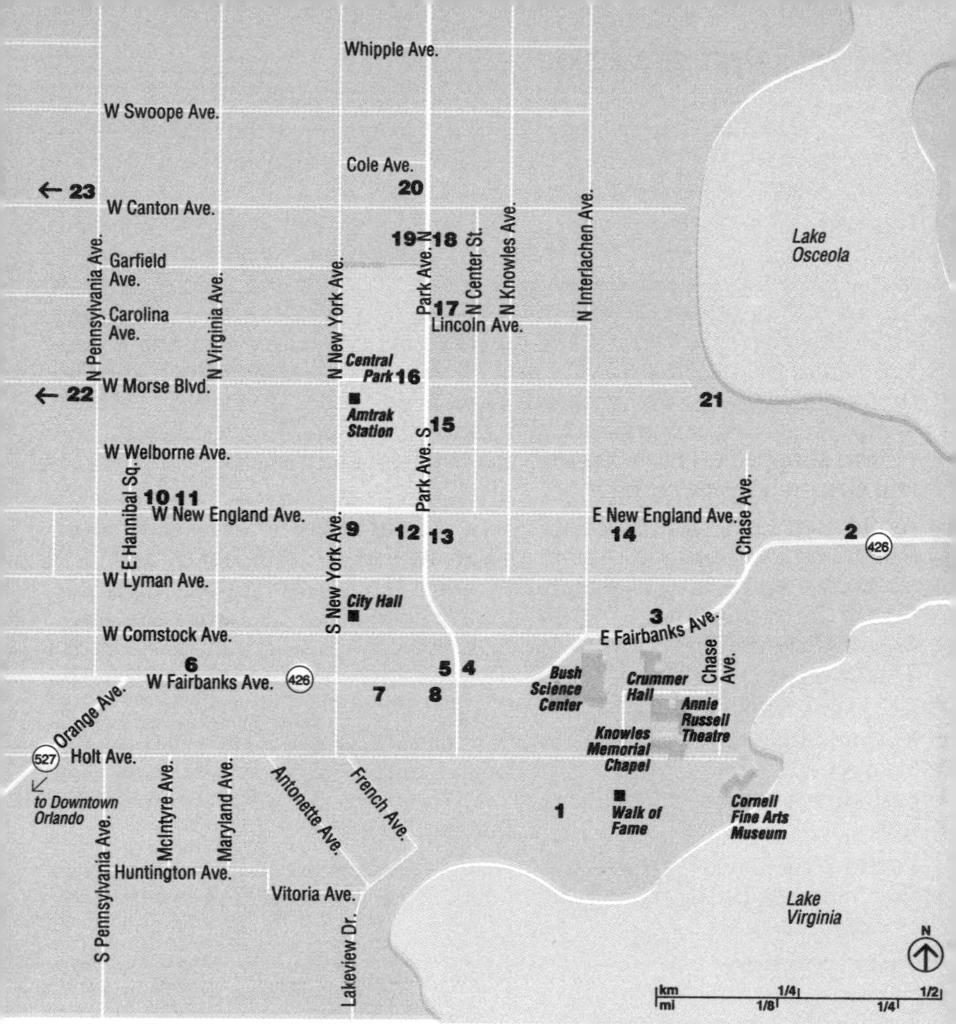

Map

Whipple Ave.

W Swoope Ave.

Cole Ave.

← 23 W Canton Ave.

20

Garfield Ave.

Carolina Ave.

N Pennsylvania Ave.

N Virginia Ave.

N New York Ave.

Park Ave. N

N Center St.

N Knowles Ave.

N Interlachen Ave.

Lake Osceola

19 18

17 Lincoln Ave.

← 22 W Morse Blvd.

Central Park 16

Amtrak Station

Park Ave. S

15

21

W Welborne Ave.

E Hannibal Sq.

10 11
W New England Ave.

S New York Ave.

9

12 13

E New England Ave. **14**

Chase Ave.

2 (426)

W Lyman Ave.

City Hall ■

W Comstock Ave.

3 E Fairbanks Ave.

6 W Fairbanks Ave. (426)

5 4

7 8

Bush Science Center

Crummer Hall

Chase Ave.

Annie Russell Theatre

Orange Ave.

(527) Holt Ave.

Knowles Memorial Chapel

S Pennsylvania Ave.

McIntyre Ave.

Maryland Ave.

Antonette Ave.

French Ave.

1

■ Walk of Fame

Cornell Fine Arts Museum

to Downtown Orlando

Huntington Ave.

Vitoria Ave.

Lakeview Dr.

Lake Virginia

N ↑

| km | 1/4 | 1/2 |
| mi | 1/8 | 1/4 |

Knowles Memorial Chapel The most impressive building on the **Rollins** campus is this place of worship (pictured above), completed in 1932 by **Dr. Ralph Adams Cram** of Boston, the preeminent Gothic architect of the time. Above the chapel's main door is a carved stone bas-relief that depicts a Franciscan friar planting a cross between Seminole Indians on one side and Spanish conquistadores on the other. The linen on the altar is from the 14th century. Take some time to study the stained-glass windows—all but two the work of Wilbur Herbert Burnham of Boston—especially if you plan to compare them with Louis Comfort Tiffany's creations at the **Charles Hosmer Morse Museum of American Art** (see page 30). The chapel plays host to the annual Festival Concert Series in spring. A courtyard garden with a tiled fountain connects with **Annie Russell Theatre** (see below). ♦ M-F, Su. 646.2115

Annie Russell Theatre The Spanish-Mediterranean theme is carried through in the design of this 377-seat theater, dedicated in 1932 and now home to the **Rollins Players,** students who present a regular season of dramatic and musical productions. ♦ 646.2501

Crummer Hall This hall, designed by architect **James Gamble Rogers II** in 1966, houses the **Crummer Graduate School of Business.** Two Tiffany medallion window panels depicting scenes from the life of Christ hang in the lobby closest to Fairbanks Avenue. They were originally sections of a Gothic memorial window (15 feet high and 11 feet wide) made in 1929 for the Greeley Presbyterian Church in St. Louis. ◆ 646.2405

Bush Science Center Just north of the administration building is this structure trimmed in Italian travertine marble. Inside, the science center displays two Tiffany window inserts that were originally part of the same Greeley Presbyterian Church window as the panels in **Crummer Hall.** One insert is tucked away at the end of a hallway to the right as you enter the center's auditorium lobby. The other is beyond the doors to the right of the first panel, on the back wall of a conference room. Neither stained-glass window is as impressive as the panels in **Crummer Hall** (see page 25). ◆ 646.2000

Cornell Fine Arts Museum Set by Lake Virginia, this museum is known for its late–19th-century American art and a complete set of tapestries designed by Alexander Calder. It also boasts a fine collection of Baroque and Italian Renaissance paintings, including *Madonna and Child Enthroned* by Cosimo Rosselli. The Rosselli painting was a gift from Samuel H. Kress, whose collection forms a large part of the National Gallery of Art. ◆ Free. Tu-F; Sa-Su 1PM-5PM. Free tours available M-F by arrangement. 646.2526

2 Albin Polásek Galleries Sculptor and painter Albin Polásek (1879-1965) was born in Moravia, in what is now the Czech Republic. An expert wood-carver when he came to the US at age 22, he studied at the Pennsylvania Academy of the Fine Arts and eventually became head of the Sculpture Department at the Art Institute of Chicago, where he remained from 1916 to 1943 and produced much of his acclaimed work. In 1950 Polásek built a Florida home and studio on three acres of land by Lake Osceola. Although he suffered a stroke that left him paralyzed on his left side, he continued to sculpt here, using his one good hand. In 1961 Polásek married Emily Kubat, and with her occasional help he completed 16 works while in his 80s. Polásek's Lake Osceola home, gardens, and studio are now a series of galleries devoted to his work. In the front gardens, look for a statue of Emily playing a harp, with streams of water forming the strings. Another version can be found in Winter Park's **Central Park.** Outside in front of the main gallery is Polásek's favorite piece, *Man Carving His Own Destiny* (1921), a stone statue of a man chiseling himself from a block of marble. Fiberglass replicas of his *14 Stations of the Cross*—the originals were made in bronze for the St. Cecilia Cathedral in Omaha,

Nebraska—are located in a garden courtyard behind the galleries. Look for the artist himself in the crowd scene of the 12th station. In the main gallery, pay particular attention to the painting of Polásek's bedroom. If you look at it standing to the left of the painting and then from the right, the bed will appear to have moved from one corner to another. After touring the galleries, walk through the artist's house and peek into his bedroom. In which corner is his bed really located? ◆ Free. W-Sa 10AM-noon, 1-4PM; Su 1-4PM; closed July through September. 633 Osceola Ave (between Trismen Terr and Chase Ave). 647.6294

3 The Fortnightly Inn $ The five rooms in this beautifully restored 1922-vintage bed-and-breakfast are just about perfect. Each is thoughtfully decorated with antiques and Oriental and period rugs. **Room No. 1** is a two-room suite done in Empire style, with French doors separating the bedroom from a sunny parlor, a circa-1860 sleigh bed, cabbage-rose chintz curtains, oak floors, and a vintage claw-footed bathtub with shower. **Room No. 4** has a romantic, intimate feel. Its matching curtains and bedding are by Laura Ashley (the designer's sister has stayed in this room); there's a hand-carved walnut bed, an antique lady's writing desk of inlaid fruitwood, and an old-fashioned bathtub tastefully set right in the room (with a screen for the modest). All of the rooms are brightened with fresh flowers and come with a complimentary bottle of cream sherry; all have private baths. Breakfast, which includes coffee or tea with fresh fruit and pastries, is served either in the rooms or in the main dining room. ◆ 377 E Fairbanks Ave (between E Lyman and S Interlachen Aves). 645.4440

4 Cafe de France ★★$$$ This small, charming place has the feel of a Parisian bistro, with high ceilings, a long wooden bar shaded by an awning, and tables crisply done up with white linen and fresh flowers. It's one of several places on Park Avenue known for their desserts, such as a delectable crème brûlée and *tarte tatin* (a traditional French apple tart). Lunch and dinner are served; the rack of lamb and the fresh salmon are consistently fine. ◆ French ◆ Tu-Sa lunch and dinner. Reservations recommended. 526 Park Ave S (between E Fairbanks and E Comstock Aves). 647.1869

5 Shiki ★★★$$ This restaurant is at the top of the list for Japanese cuisine in Central Florida. There's fresh sushi as well as tempura, noodle dishes, and teriyaki. The *gyoza* dumplings (filled with beef and panfried) are a tasty appetizer. The dining room is decorated in traditional Japanese style, with a sushi bar and tatami booths (where diners remove their shoes and sit on mats at low tables), in addition to regular seating. ♦ Japanese ♦ Daily dinner. 525 Park Ave S (between W Fairbanks and W Comstock Aves). 740.8018

6 PR's ★$ This is where the locals go for good Tex-Mex. There's nothing fancy about the place (it's right next to the railroad tracks), but it serves a good margarita, and the ample dishes are authentic. Try the beef and chicken combo fajitas or the *chiles rellenos*. ♦ Mexican ♦ M-Sa lunch and dinner; Su dinner. No reservations accepted. 499 W Fairbanks Ave (between S New York and S Pennsylvania Aves). 645.2225

WINTER PARK
THORNTON PARK

7 Dexter's ★★$ The creative international fare complements the wines at this trendy, friendly wine bar/cafe. **Dexter's** boasts a comprehensive list of wines from around the world, including several good sparkling and dessert wine selections. The wines are available by the glass on a roster that changes monthly. There's a cafe menu that changes monthly too; it's geared toward the season and the month's wine list. The main menu features such favorites as chicken tortilla pie (crispy fried flour tortillas layered with chicken, tomatoes, jalapeños, provolone, sour cream, and scallions) and a Cuban-style pressed duck sandwich (roasted duck with grilled onions and brie pressed between pieces of French bread). The interior looks like a diner, complete with its black-and-white tiled floor and counter lined with old-fashioned spinning stools. ♦ International ♦ Daily lunch and dinner. 200 W Fairbanks Ave (between S Park and S New York Aves). 629.1150. Also at: 808 E Washington St (between N Hyer and Hill Aves), Orlando. 648.2777

8 Brazilian Pavilion ★★$$ You can usually get a table at this friendly little family-run restaurant, where gracious hospitality is part of the experience. Owner Tony Duarte and his wife and daughter are always in the dining room, taking care of the 24 tables, explaining the flavorful Brazilian dishes. Try the *Peixe á Brasileira* (fish and shrimp with onions, tomatoes, peppers, garlic, and olives) or a simple grilled steak with garlic-and-parsley sauce. ♦ Brazilian ♦ Daily lunch and dinner. 140 W Fairbanks Ave (between S Park and S New York Aves). 740.7440

8 Panera Bread ★$ This trendy coffee shop is the meeting place for locals for breakfast, lunch, even a casual dinner. There's only counter service, so you must carry your tray to the table. They offer a large selection of bagels, and the place is famous for its sourdough bread. Sandwiches and soups are satisfying, though a bit pricey. ♦ American ♦ Daily lunch and dinner. 118 W Fairbanks Ave (between S Park and S New York Aves). 645.3939

9 Winter Park Farmers Market A panoply of colors welcomes visitors to this blocklong market, overflowing with fresh flowers and a wide variety of vegetables and herbs. Indulge in delectable homemade banana bread, pick up a dozen fresh bagels, or buy a houseplant for the host who's putting you up. Prices are more than reasonable. ♦ Sa dawn-noon. W New England and S New York Aves

10 Schafer's Caffehaus ★★$ The atmosphere is bohemian, the fare is European—croissants, tarts, Swiss spinach-and-ham pie—in this eclectic little eatery with just six mix-and-match tables and a painted concrete floor. Original artwork hangs on the walls, and it's all for sale. Try anything in the dessert case that strikes your fancy: We recommend the pear Aunt Edith, a buttery cake with fresh pears on the bottom, vanilla cream, and a dollop of meringue. ♦ European ♦ Tu-Su breakfast and lunch. 535 W New England Ave (between S Virginia Ave and Hannibal Sq E). 740.7782; fax 740.8231

Florida's most famous sinkhole opened up in 1981 in Winter Park and swallowed nearly an entire city block, including a house and automobiles.

From 1886 to 1902, The Seminole Hotel in Winter Park was the largest hotel in the state, attracting statesmen and celebrities.

Restaurants/Clubs: Red   **Hotels:** Blue
Shops/♥ Outdoors: Green   **Sights/Culture:** Black

27

Head for the Hills

Despite its name, there isn't really a mountain in **Mount Dora.** The endearing Central Florida town is, however, situated 184 feet above sea level, and that's high in these parts. What Mount Dora does have is rolling hills, beautiful public parks, gorgeous lakes, and plenty of charm. The town is about 30 miles northwest of Orlando on the northeastern shore of **Lake Dora,** named in 1883 for one Dora Ann Drawdy, who moved there with her husband in the mid-1800s (government surveyors christened the lake in her honor as a way of thanking Drawdy for allowing them to camp on her property).

Visitors enjoy the turn-of-the-century architecture; the historic **Lakeside Inn** ($$, 100 Alexander St, south of W Third Ave, 352/383.4101; fax 352/735.2642), where President Calvin Coolidge and his wife vacationed in 1930; and browsing for antiques at the **Art & Antique Union,** housing 16 antiques dealers (331 Donnelly St, between W Third

and W Fourth Aves, 352/735.4003). Just outside of town are **Renninger's Twin Markets** (Hwy 441, north of Rte 46, 352/383.8393). These two adjacent outdoor markets, set on 72 acres, are open only on the weekend. Hundreds of dealers offer everything from antique furniture and toys to old coins and glass by Steuben and Lalique. The markets are packed (except in July and December) on the first weekend of each month, when **Renninger's** holds its Antiques Fairs. On the third weekends in November, January, and February, **Renninger's Extravaganzas** bring nearly a thousand dealers from around the country.

Every October, as many as 1,600 bicyclists gather for the Mount Dora Bicycle Festival, a weekend event offering well-organized rides, a fair, and easy-to-follow mapped routes past orange groves, lakefronts lined with cypress trees, and streets shaded with moss-hung oaks. Bikes are available for rent.

10 Chez Vincent ★★★$$ The decor is unremarkable (though there are linen tablecloths and decent wineglasses), and there are just 12 tables and a small bar, but the traditional French cuisine draws quite a crowd for lunch and dinner. You can't go wrong with the sautéed snails in puff pastry, the warm goat cheese salad, the crepe *bourguignon* (sautéed beef tenderloin tips and mushrooms in a Burgundy sauce), or the *merou Provençale* (grouper with sautéed onions, tomatoes, garlic, and fresh basil in a white wine sauce). ♦ French ♦ Tu-Su lunch and dinner. 533 W New England Ave (between S Virginia Ave and Hannibal Sq E). 599.2929

11 West End Grill ★★$ This casual restaurant started with a walk-up window on the sidewalk and a few picnic tables; now there's a tin roof over the dozen or so tables, but the sides of the restaurant are still open to the elements. Ceiling fans keep it cool in the summer, and heaters hum overhead in the winter months. The menu offers grilled food with fresh herbs, including chicken, beef, pork, and a decent portobello mushroom burger. ♦ American ♦ M, Su lunch; Tu-Sa lunch and dinner. 463 W New England Ave (between S Virginia Ave and Hannibal Sq E). 644.2423

12 Park Plaza Gardens ★★★$$$ Long regarded as one of Central Florida's finest for

both ambience and culinary masterpieces, this restaurant is one of those rare places that prepare fresh fish perfectly. The setting is serene—a greenery-filled atrium with sunlight streaming down through the glass ceiling and artwork (changed monthly) that adorns the walls. Specialties include cedar-plank salmon with horseradish mashed potatoes, and filet mignon with morels. It won't be easy, but try to leave room for dessert; the pastry chef can compete with the best. The restaurant is at the **Park Plaza Hotel,** but it has a separate entrance and different management. ♦ American ♦ M-Sa lunch and dinner; Su brunch and dinner. Reservations recommended. 319 Park Ave S (between W Lyman and W New England Aves). 645.2475

12 Be Be's You'll find classic and trendy children's wear from such notable manufacturers as Florence Eiseman here, as well as dresses and tuxes for First Communion. A little play area in the back keeps fussy children happy while Mom and Pop shop. ♦ Daily. 311 Park Ave S (between W Lyman and W New England Aves). 628.1680

12 Park Plaza Hotel $$ Built in 1921, this property feels like a small, refined European hotel (Paul Newman has been known to discreetly check in on occasion). Each of the

27 rooms has its own personality, though all contain ceiling fans, ferns, and flowers, and each opens onto a balcony where complimentary continental breakfast is served. The best accommodations are the suites facing the avenue, while other rooms have balconies with lovely views of **Central Park**. The lobby is quietly elegant, reminiscent of a sophisticated British drawing room. Romantics should try to reserve the honeymoon suite. ♦ 307 Park Ave S (between W Lyman and W New England Aves). 647.1072, 800/228.7220; fax 647.4081; www.parkplazahotel.com

12 Tuni's The women's apparel here runs from costly linens and sarongs suitable for the Florida climate to trendy slip dresses and brass-and-bone jewelry from India and East Africa. ♦ Daily. 301 Park Ave S (between W Lyman and W New England Aves). 628.1609

13 Red Marq Thousands of greeting cards, many handmade and most unlike those you'll find in a mainstream card shop, are on sale here. There's also a small selection of eclectic gifts—some from New York's Museum of Modern Art and the Guggenheim—as well as a full line of pens and stationery. Even the (free) gift wrapping paper is a standout. ♦ Daily. 308 Park Ave S (between E Lyman and E New England Aves). 647.2336

ᵀᴴᴱ Langford

14 Langford Resort Hotel $ Not fancy, but cozy and right off Park Avenue, this 215-room hostelry is a good value in a good location. There's a heated Olympic-size pool, a spa for facials and massages, a restaurant that also serves great burgers poolside, and a lounge with nightly entertainment. The hotel plays host to a mystery dinner-theater presentation on Saturday nights (reservations required). ♦ 300 E New England Ave (between Chase and S Interlachen Aves). 644.3400; fax 628.1952

15 Williams-Sonoma If you enjoy the catalog, you'll love this pretty store. It has everything for the cook, the kitchen, and the gourmet. Whether you need hard-to-find cooking utensils, the latest cookbooks, or out-of-the-ordinary food items—from unusual pastas to basmati rice—you can find them here. ♦ Daily. 150 Park Ave S (between E Welborne and E Morse Blvd). 628.5900

15 La Venezia Cafe ★★$$ This appealing eatery is part of the Barnie's Coffee & Tea Company chain. The best place to sit is at the outside patio, where you can people watch and gaze at the attractive park across the street. Lunch and dinner selections include wok-seared salmon served over black bean hash; roast pork tenderloin with apple-pear chutney; a grilled vegetable herb focaccia sandwich; and angel-hair pasta with tomatoes and fresh basil. There's a large selection of desserts and they're all out of this world. Open for breakfast on weekends, they serve standard morning fare as well as such specialties as eggs La Venezia (eggs Benedict with sautéed spinach) and the Center Street breakfast (a skillet of herbed, diced potatoes topped with two eggs any style and covered with melted cheese). Service overall is rather slow but better at dinner. ♦ American ♦ M-F lunch and dinner; Sa-Su breakfast, lunch, and dinner. Reservations recommended for dinner. 142 Park Ave S (between E Welborne Ave and E Morse Blvd). 647.7557

16 Central Park This pleasant park, dotted with flowerbeds and oak, palm, and pine trees, is truly central in Winter Park's civic life—not only geographically but also as an important year-round gathering spot. Locals like to buy their lunches from one of the many eateries nearby and bring them here for an impromptu picnic. Children are especially delighted by the occasional sight of an **Amtrak** train traveling right through the center of the park. Several festivals and concert series are held here, but the Winter Park Art Festival, which takes place here on the third weekend in March every spring, reigns supreme. Huge crowds turn the festival into more of a social function than a true art display; as many as 200,000 people turn out to browse and buy anything from acrylic paintings to sculpture to jewelry. For festival information, call the **Winter Park Chamber of Commerce** (644.8281). ♦ W Morse Blvd (between Park and New York Aves)

17 Timothy's Gallery Even if you're only browsing, this gallery is worth a stop. Owner Carolyn Luce has put together one of Florida's largest collections of unusual handmade jewelry and wearables, such as sweaters, jackets, and vests, along with award-winning contemporary works in glass, ceramics, wood, and metal. A new addition to the gallery: art-related specialty books, more than 1,000 titles. This is a great place for gifts or for treating yourself. ♦ Daily. 212 Park Ave N (between Lincoln and E Canton Aves). 629.0707

With more than 39 million square feet of retail space—and still counting—Orlando is the fastest growing retail market in the United States.

The first census, in 1850, showed Central Florida's Orange County had a population of 466. Today, it has 1,255,000 residents.

17 Caswell-Massey A store devoted to fine health and beauty products for both men and women, it offers such specialty items as badger-bristle shaving brushes and Anton Hubner's Therapeutic Bath Oils from the Black Forest. Old photos of Caswell-Massey stores in New York and Rhode Island hang high on the wall. ♦ Daily. 234 Park Ave N (between Lincoln and E Canton Aves). 647.2455

18 The Rune Stone Behind the bright-yellow exterior are all kinds of toys from Europe. The array of model trains, from a small executive tabletop set by Marklin to an indoor-outdoor German set from LGB, will satisfy railroad buffs of all ages. You can purchase nesting dolls from Russia, Hummel or Goebel figurines, and collectible plates from Royal Copenhagen or Bing and Grondahl. The store's name refers to a thousand-year-old Viking tradition of consulting rune stones for guidance through life. ♦ Daily. 326 Park Ave N (between Lincoln and E Canton Aves). 644.9671

18 Maison des Crepes ★★$$$ Nestled in an intriguing courtyard, this is a pleasant place for a casual lunch or a fancy dinner. It's also a romantic, secluded spot to cap off an evening with dessert crepes. Lamb dishes are favorites, including a rich lamb stew and a rack of lamb, as are the crepes St. Jacques (with scallops, shrimp, mushrooms, and gruyère cheese in Newburg sauce). ♦ French ♦ M lunch; Tu-Sa lunch and dinner. 348 Park Ave N (between Lincoln and E Canton Aves). 647.4469

19 Jacobson's High-quality women's clothing (Anne Klein, St. John, and the like) and an excellent selection of children's wear are found here. There's also a beauty salon. ♦ Daily. 339 Park Ave N (between Garfield and W Canton Aves). 645.5005

20 Charles Hosmer Morse Museum of American Art Artist Louis Comfort Tiffany's personal collection of stained glass is housed in this museum, which was moved to its present spacious lodgings in 1995 and includes the recently opened chapel that Tiffany created for the 1893 Chicago World's Fair, considered to be the greatest surviving interior designed by Tiffany. The museum focuses on decorative arts (glass, pottery, furniture), painting, and graphic arts from the 19th and early 20th centuries. All the major trends and styles of that period—Art Nouveau, Arts and Crafts, and Edwardian—are represented. The jewel in the crown, however, is the Tiffany collection, much of which was salvaged by museum founders Hugh Ferguson McKean and Jeanette Morse Genius McKean after a fire at Tiffany's Long Island home in 1957. The collection is rare because it includes many pieces the master himself designed as well as work created in his studio under his supervision. On view are such masterful works as Tiffany's *Red Peony Lamp, Rose Window,* and the *Four Seasons Window,* which was made for the 1900 international exposition in Paris, where the artist gained international recognition as a leader in the Art Nouveau movement. Note the striking ways in which Tiffany added extra dimension to his work by folding the glass while it was still soft. Also on display are examples of Tiffany's other artistic endeavors—paintings, pottery, jewelry, enamels, mosaics, watercolors, and furniture. There are also works by Tiffany's contemporaries and other important artists of the late 19th and early 20th centuries—including John La Farge, **Frank Lloyd Wright,** Maxfield Parrish, and George Inness.The museum opened in 1942 on the **Rollins College** campus, where Hugh McKean was a faculty member (he later served as the college's president and chancellor). Originally called the **Morse Gallery of Art,** it was named in honor of Jeanette McKean's industrialist-philanthropist grandfather. In 1977 the museum was moved to Welborne Avenue. Its present home, with close to 8,000 square feet of exhibition space, nearly doubles what it had previously. Nevertheless, only a fraction of the 4,000 holdings can be displayed at any one time. ♦ Nominal admission. Tu-Sa; Su 1-4PM. 445 Park Ave N (between W Canton and Cole Aves). 645.5311

Charles Hosmer Morse Museum of American Art

A Peek into Your Past and Future

For a quaint, quiet, and memorable vacation experience, visit the scenic and unique community of **Cassadaga**, approximately 45 minutes north of Orlando. The small village is home to the **Southern Cassadaga Spiritualist Camp,** a group of about 40 seers, mediums, and clairvoyants. They attract a steady clientele of the faithful and curious, who journey on **Interstate 4** to Exit 54, where a small road leads into town. Cassadaga has been a haven for spiritualists since 1875,

KEELY EDWARDS

when George Colby left Dale, New York, to seek a winter home for his fellow mediums. Colby said spirits led him to the woods of north Central Florida. Today, the hamlet boasts an odd collection of wood-frame New England–style houses.

If you want to make an appointment with a medium—a person who claims to act as a conduit for messages from the dead—stop at the **Southern Cassadaga Spiritualist Camp Bookstore and Information Center** (1112 Stevens St, 904/228.2880), where they'll help you make an appointment. Or you can just walk around the town until the vibrations from the right house beckon you inside.

21 **Scenic Boat Tours** Since 1938, this tour-boat company has been conveying passengers by shallow-draft boats on Lakes Osceola, Virginia, and Maitland, which are connected by old lumbering canals dug during the 19th century. Boats pass **Rollins College,** formal gardens, and magnificent mansions hidden from the road. Many of the residences began as winter cottages: Sometimes the original structures were torn down and replaced; in other cases the owners just kept adding on. The tour also gives passengers a good view of Albin Polásek's backyard sculptures. In short, it's an interesting and pleasant way to spend an hour. ◆ Fee. Daily. 312 Morse Blvd (east of S Interlachen Ave). 644.4056

22 **Houston's** ★★$$ This popular chain has a lovely location on Lake Killarney with lots of expansive windows facing the water. There is usually a wait for a table, as they take no reservations, but you can sit out back in comfortable wooden chairs or on the dock until your table is ready (they give you a pager to carry). The casual dining room has a lively bar with live piano music, and a trendy open kitchen where you can watch the chefs in action, so it can get a little noisy. Seating is in cushioned booths or at tables, and service is pleasant and fast. Salads are a meal, especially the Pine Room salad, spiked with chicken, jack cheese, and croutons. For a lighter entrée, try the fresh tuna salad. The giant veggie burger with shoestring fries is a favorite. ◆ American ◆ Daily lunch and dinner. Reservations not accepted. 215 S Orlando Ave (at Beachview Ave). 740.4005

23 **Bubbalou's Bodacious BBQ** ★$ There aren't many places in Central Florida where you can get real barbecue, but this is one.

Many swear it's the best around. You'll probably have to squeeze in alongside some strangers to munch on the tender beef ribs or sliced pork because there are only a few picnic tables inside and out. Side orders to try: black-eyed peas and fried okra. ◆ American ◆ Daily lunch and dinner. 1471 Lee Rd (west of N Orlando Ave). 628.1212

Bests

Fred Lounsberry
Executive Vice President of Marketing, Universal Studios Escape

Orlando Science Center This is one of the most exciting buildings in Central Florida, and being inside is like taking a trip through an animated science book.

Lake Eola This lake is a centerpiece of downtown Orlando and provides a wonderful pause during a busy day or a great place to take the family on weekends. The feeling of being in a scenic park while still being able to see tall office buildings nearby is exhilarating.

Lake Wekiva A beautiful nature park, complete with lakes to swim in and trails to wander.

Mount Dora Strolling or driving through Mount Dora is an opportunity to view a wonderfully quaint town. It always brings a sense of calm relaxation.

Park Avenue in **Winter Park** A walk down this street offers great shops and restaurants in an area unlike any other in Central Florida. There is character and charm to the area.

The arts Central Florida's arts community is thriving and you should jump at the chance to attend any of the professional ballet, opera, or orchestra performances that you can.

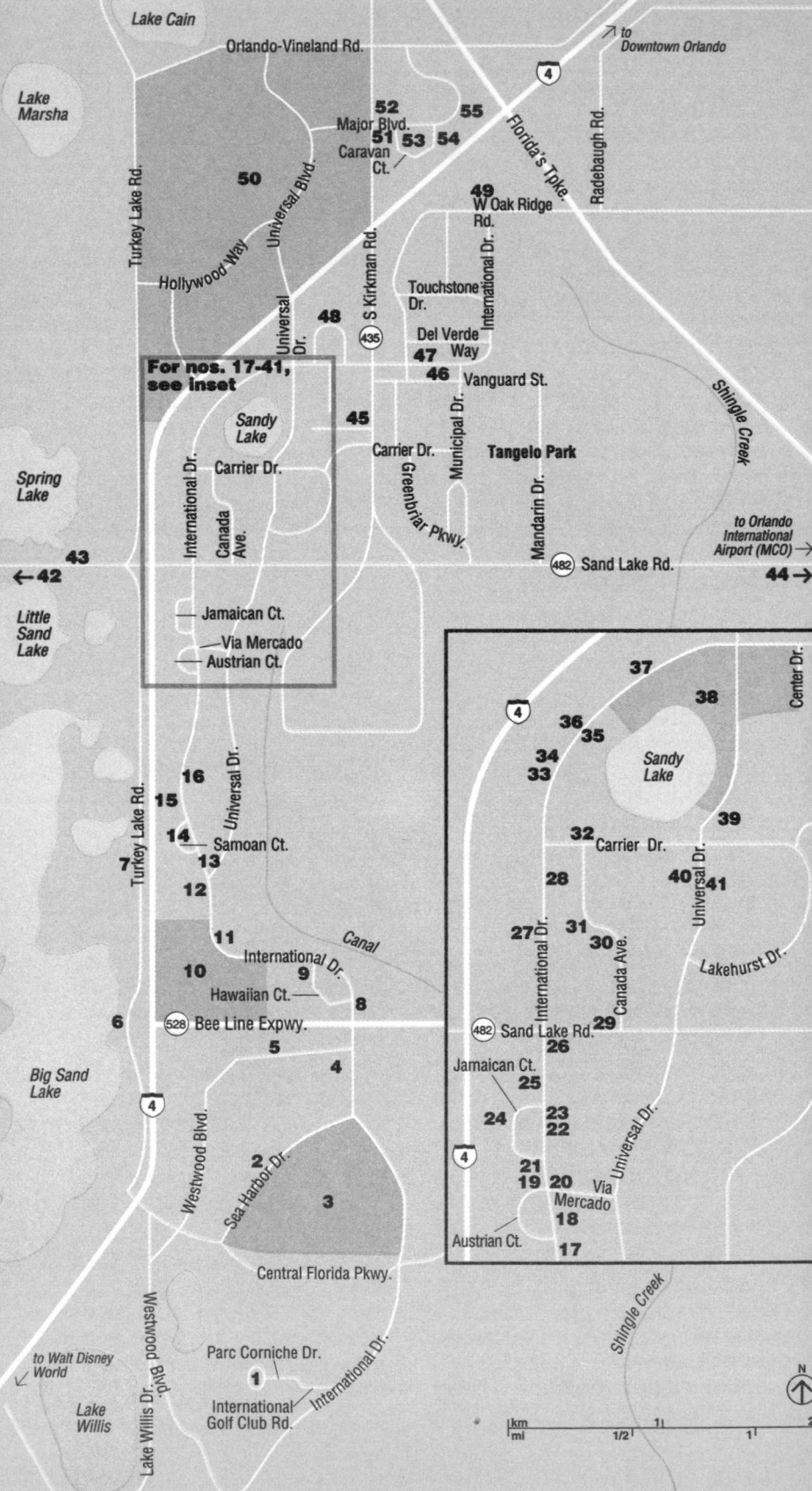

International Drive

At first glance, International Drive seems like nothing more than a collection of T-shirt shops and fast-food joints. It may look that way at second and third glance, too. But if you keep looking you'll see a centrally located tourist strip convenient to some of the area's major tourist attractions and offering a range of hotels to fit all budgets; numerous places to shop, including the nearby **Florida Mall**, Central Florida's largest retail shopping center, and the **Belz Mall**, one of the largest factory outlet complexes in the US; and restaurants galore.

At one end of "I-Drive," as it's known locally, sprawls **SeaWorld Orlando**, a marine-life park that's home to killer whales and gentle manatees. A short drive up the road is **Wet 'n Wild**, one of the most popular water theme parks of Central Florida. A few blocks away from the northern end of International Drive is **Universal Studios Escape**, both a theme park and the largest active motion-picture and television studio outside of Hollywood. In 1997, the three attractions above, plus **Busch Gardens** in Tampa (see "Tampa/St. Petersburg Area"), teamed up to produce the **FlexTicket**, a multi-park package offering all four theme parks for one price. There are actually two options: The first offers five consecutive days of unlimited visits to **Universal Studios**, **SeaWorld**, and **Wet 'n Wild**; the second offers seven consecutive days to the above attractions plus **Busch Gardens**. If you're planning multiple visits to each theme park, the savings are significant. Note that a **FlexTicket** may be purchased at any of the four participating theme parks.

Appropriately, the **Orlando/Orange County Convention Center** is located on International Drive. It's a busy place, as Orlando is considered one of the top five convention destinations in the country, a favorite among business folk and families alike. It is now the sixth-largest center in the US, with four million square feet—more than a million square feet of exhibit space. **Pointe★Orlando**, a major new entertainment complex across from the convention center, features a 21-screen movie theater, interactive museums, nightclubs, theme restaurants, and specialty retailers, including **FAO Schwarz** and **Abercrombie & Fitch**.

Every major hotel chain in the nation, it seems—nearly 60 hotels within the International Drive resort area—has a branch on International Drive, so prices are quite competitive. If you're traveling with children, ask hotels if they have free transportation to the theme parks and complimentary child care programs. Bargain hunters should keep in mind that hotels that do a lot of convention business sometimes offer discounts during their slow periods. Call around, as "unconventional" times vary from hotel to hotel. Most of these properties welcome and are quite suitable for family vacationers.

Although this chapter contains a number of places located a block or two off International Drive, I-Drive is the main drag and the point of reference for visitors. **Interstate 4 (I-4)** has exits at the north end of International Drive (Exit 30B, Kirkman Road), in the middle (Exit 29, Sand Lake Road), and at the south end near **SeaWorld** (Exit 28, Bee Line Expressway). If you are coming up I-4 from the south, you can get off at the **Epcot** exit (Exit 26) and head east on the I-Drive extension.

There is also a convenient public bus service in the International Drive area, **I-Ride** (248.9590), which operates daily from 7AM until midnight, makes 55 stops, including all the major attractions, and charges a nominal fee per ride. Visitors can purchase tickets at 35 locations along International Drive, including three visitors' centers. Also for sale are one-, three-, five-, and seven-day unlimited passes. Children under 12 ride free with an adult.

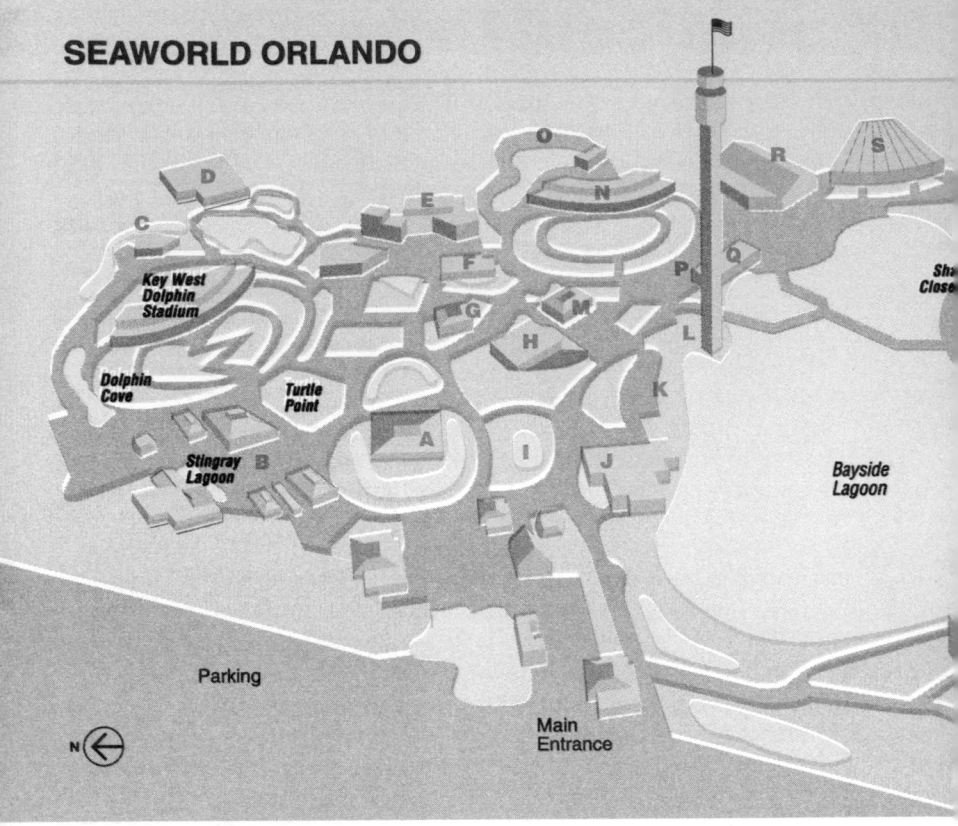

Area code 407 unless otherwise noted.

1 Parc Corniche Condominium Resort Hotel $$ Its location on a lightly developed stretch of International Drive makes this 210-suite hotel a quiet getaway, but you won't be able to walk to any attractions from here. Each suite has a patio or balcony. The three-story building, with its distinctive red-tile roof, sits on the **International Golf Club** grounds. There's also a restaurant and a swimming pool. ♦ 6300 Parc Corniche Dr (west of International Golf Club Rd). 239.7100, 800/446.2721; fax 239.8501; www.parccorniche.com

2 Renaissance Orlando Resort $$$ The atrium lobby, said to be one of the largest in the world, was a pet project of William Jovanovich, the former chairman of the publishing company Harcourt Brace Jovanovich, which once owned a stake in the hotel. The most expensive rooms have balconies that look down on the atrium, where there's a fish pond stocked with huge Japanese carp, an aviary, a two-level lounge and bar, and glass-enclosed elevators. A back elevator allows guests in swimming attire to return to their rooms without walking dripping through the lobby. Facilities include a health club, an Olympic-size pool, an 18-hole golf course, and five restaurants. A much-acclaimed Sunday brunch is served in the atrium; its pastries are particularly delectable.

The 780-room hotel, with 64 suites, is located directly across from **SeaWorld**. ♦ 6677 Sea Harbor Dr (between Central Florida Pkwy and International Dr). 351.5555, 800/HOTELS.1; fax 351.9991; www.renaissancehotels.com &

Within the Renaissance Orlando Resort:

Haifeng ★★★$$ In case you know anyone who still considers the phrase "gourmet Chinese food" to be an inherent contradiction, you may want to take him or her for a special meal at this fine dining spot. The menu reflects all the Chinese regional cooking styles, including Mandarin, Szechuan, Hunan, and Cantonese; specialties include Peking duck and a six-course fixed-price "Imperial Dinner." A sushi bar is a popular new addition. The Asian decor of black lacquer furniture and subdued colors contributes to an intimate and elegant ambience. ♦ Chinese ♦ Tu-Su dinner. Reservations recommended. 351.5555

Atlantis ★★★$$$ Art on the walls, shining crystal, and impeccable service make dinner here a gracious experience. This is one of the best seafood restaurants in Orlando; the fish is fresh and prepared in imaginative ways. Your choices include sautéed red snapper with piña colada butter and grilled tropical fruit, pan-seared sea bass with saffron, fennel, and tomato ragout, and Mediterranean pasta with shrimp, scallops, and mussels in a lemon

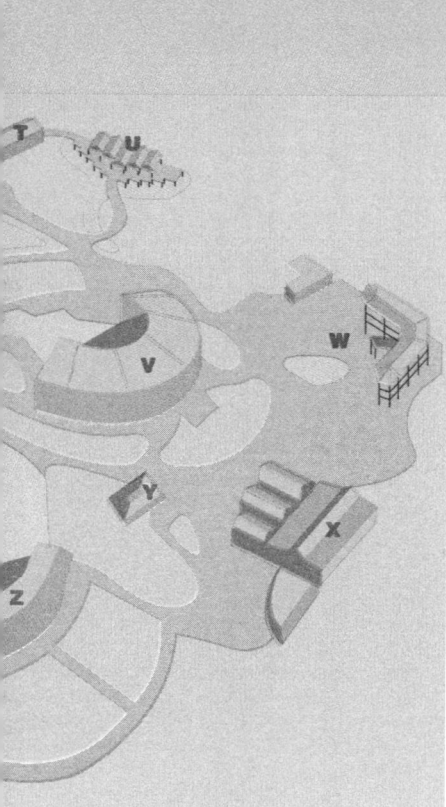

Imposing as it may seem, the entire park can be experienced in a single (long) day. Study the map you receive at the ticket booth. It includes show times, indicates the locations of attractions, shops, and restaurants, and lists the special events for that day. Before you start exploring, stop in at the **Information Center** to make reservations for the two-hour *Aloha Polynesian Luau Dinner and Show,* featuring colorfully costumed dancers and musicians in a South Seas revue. (Or make reservations by calling the appropriate 800 number below; same-day availability is limited.) To enhance the learning aspect of your visit, stop by the **Educational Tour Desk** at the main entrance and ask what tours are available. At the park, you may purchase a **FlexTicket** (see page 33), which admits you to **SeaWorld, Universal Studios, Wet 'n Wild,** and **Busch Gardens** in Tampa.

Most visitors circumnavigate the park clockwise (as described below), but if you arrive at opening time go straight to **Wild Arctic** or **Journey to Atlantis,** where lines are longest later in the day. From there go to see Shamu at **Shamu Stadium,** which puts you near **Shamu's Happy Harbor,** a three-acre playground, just when your troops might want to run off their excitement and cool off in the water-play area. You can save the water-ski show (the least interesting, perhaps because the stars are human) for last. But be sure to consult the park schedule of show times first. Snack bars and food kiosks are found throughout the park. As you would expect, ownership by Anheuser-Busch means beer is readily available. Restaurant and snack bar hours change seasonally; check with the ticket office or the **Food Services Information Center** for hours of operation. Park services include diaper changing and baby nursing areas, first aid, foreign currency exchange, and a 24-hour automated teller machine. Strollers and wheelchairs can be rented. ♦ Admission. Parking and kennel fees. Daily 9AM-7PM (hours vary on holidays and in summer). 7007 SeaWorld Dr (at Sea Harbor Dr). 351.3600, 800/432.1178 in FL, 800/327.2424 ⅃

wine sauce. There are also meat entrées, including rack of lamb and veal chops. ♦ Seafood ♦ M-Sa dinner. Reservations required. 351.5555

Tradewinds Cafe ★$ A casual family eatery, it's a coffeehouse by day and steak house by night. ♦ Coffeehouse/Steak house ♦ Daily 24 hours. 351.5555

SeaWorld.
A D V E N T U R E   P A R K S

3 SeaWorld Orlando Killer whales are the biggest stars at this nearly 200-acre marine animal adventure park, one of Florida's top three tourist destinations. The ever-expanding park regularly introduces new shows and attractions; in 1995 it opened the elaborate "guest experience" (as they call the attractions here) **Wild Arctic,** a simulated helicopter ride to a mock Arctic research station, where visitors observe live Arctic animals (see page 38). In 1996 **Key West at SeaWorld** opened, with such attractions as **Dolphin Cove, Turtle Point,** and **Stingray Lagoon** (see page 36). And the most recent addition is **Journey to Atlantis,** an elaborate water ride that is the park's largest, most expensive addition ever.

Within SeaWorld Orlando (see map above):

A Tropical Reef For a good look at more than a thousand tropical fish, stop at this man-made coral reef, one of the largest in the country. Surrounding the main exhibit are 17 smaller aquariums. Behind the reef is the **Caribbean Tide Pool,** encouraging closer examination of tropical fish and invertebrates such as starfish, sea urchins, and crabs. Inexpensive fast-food stops and shops encircle this attraction.

Restaurants/Clubs: Red   Hotels: Blue
Shops/ ♦ Outdoors: Green   **Sights/Culture:** Black

B Key West at SeaWorld Get within arm's reach of a 300-pound endangered sea turtle, feed squid to a stingray, or listen to dolphins vocalize at this five-acre section of the park. Themed as a "vacation destination" with the quirky ambience of America's southernmost city, this attraction is designed to nurture conservation of the Keys' ecosystems and bring visitors face-to-face with sea creatures they might never encounter in the wild.

Within Key West at SeaWorld:

Dolphin Cove Home to a large community of Atlantic bottlenose dolphins, this 700,000-gallon lagoon features crashing two-foot-high waves, a sandy beach, and easy underwater viewing. Visitors can reach out and touch the dolphins as they surface.

Turtle Point Loggerheads, green, Kemp's ridley, and hawksbill sea turtles are presented in a barrier island–like setting of sand dunes, a contoured beach, rock clusters, and indigenous plant life.

Stingray Lagoon This 40,000-gallon attraction features a mini-cove nursery for newborn rays. Up to 175 Southern, cow-nosed, and blunt-nosed specimens, along with their guitarfish cousins, glide in the lagoon. Visitors can feed and touch the graceful fish (on their backs, so they won't sting), ranging in size from eight-inch babies to five-foot-wide adults.

"Key West Dolphin Fest" Spectacular animal behaviors are showcased in this popular and lighthearted whale and dolphin show at **Key West Dolphin Stadium,** featuring Atlantic bottlenose dolphins and false killer whales (another species of toothed whale that resembles the real thing). ♦ See park schedule for show times

Sunset Square The main thoroughfare pays tribute to the real Key West with novelty banners, lively music, authentic wares, and a wacky street party atmosphere. Nightly "sunset celebrations" feature street performances and live Florida jazz. There are more than two dozen computer games, video displays, and themed interactive graphics throughout the area to create an unusual learning experience.

C Manatees: The Last Generation?
For centuries, seagoing cultures have been intrigued by the manatee, and myths and legends have grown up around this gentle sea mammal. Yet human beings are responsible for placing the manatee on the brink of extinction. Pollution, habitat destruction, and fishing lines have helped to decimate their population—today as few as 1,800 remain. You can get a close-up look at Florida's manatees (also known as sea cows) at this huge, 300,000-gallon habitat. Despite their large size and slow pace, they are often difficult to spot in the wild; here you can observe them at the water's surface as well as underwater. It was as a result of the Marine Mammal Protection Act of 1972 and the Endangered Species Act of 1973 that **SeaWorld** was empowered to organize its Manatee Rescue and Rehabilitation program, which since its inception in 1976 has aided thousands of ill, injured, or orphaned manatees, whales, dolphins, otters, sea turtles, and waterfowl.

D Journey to Atlantis This "immersive" adventure combines a high-thrill water ride with special effects. The ride boasts two of the steepest, wettest, fastest drops in the world. You must be 42 inches tall to ride.

E Penguin Encounter Home to hundreds of these formal-looking fellows and other birds native to the Antarctic and Arctic regions (buffleheads, puffins, murres, and smews), this attraction has a 120-foot people-mover that carries visitors to a viewing area separated from the birds by tempered glass. The habitat is so natural that 6,000 pounds of manufactured snow fall daily. (It's possible to get acceptable pictures through the glass; just don't use a flash.) Beside the viewing area is the **Learning Hall,** with videos on the history of polar exploration. In another room is an exhibit on Arctic birds. The white stucco building sits on a five-acre site that includes a 32,000-square-foot science center, a gift shop, a restaurant, and freshwater ponds.

F Mama Stella's Italian Kitchen $ Kids like the spaghetti and pizza at this counter-service spot; salads are available too. Beer and soft drinks are served. ♦ Italian ♦ Daily lunch and dinner

G Buccaneer Smokehouse This quick-service take-out eatery offers barbecued chicken, beef, and pork.

H SeaWorld Theater Here's a cool, dry refuge when afternoons get too hot or rainy. In the morning and early afternoon, catch *Pets on Stage,* a 25-minute vaudeville show that stars cats, dogs, and a few surprise creatures you won't want to miss. ♦ See park schedule for show times

I Dolphin Nursery Buy some fish here and let the dolphins snatch them out of your hand. If you're lucky, you might be able to reach out and touch the playful sea mammals, but the dolphins seem to take delight in teasing people by staying just out of reach. You'll find it hard to drag yourself away from this attraction, especially if it isn't crowded.

J Bimini Bay Cafe ★$ Set on the edge of the **Bayside Lagoon,** this full-service restaurant specializes in seafood, although it also serves sandwiches, salads, and burgers. The kids' menu features grilled cheese sandwiches, turkey sandwiches, and burgers. Wine and beer are available. ♦ Seafood/American ♦ Daily lunch and dinner

K Luau Terrace Sit on logs and watch the **Hawaiian Rhythms** troupe perform a 25-minute, open-air South Seas revue of Polynesian dances and songs. The stage is on the beach of the **Bayside Lagoon.** At night, the space is known by another name—**Bird Gardens**—and features *Friends of a Feather,* a 25-minute show in which colorful parrots on loan from **Busch Gardens,** Tampa, show off their flying, singing, and acrobatic talents. ♦ See park schedule for show times

L Sky Tower For an overview of the park or a scenic panorama of the area, take this 400-foot ride into the sky. ♦ Nominal admission

M Chicken 'n Biscuit $ Barbecued and fried chicken, desserts, beer, and soft drinks are served at the counter here. The kids' meal features a chicken leg or wing, fries, and a roll. ♦ American ♦ Daily lunch and dinner

N Sea Lion & Otter Stadium The 25-minute *Clyde and Seamore Take Pirate Island* show, featuring the antics of sea lions and otters, takes place in this 3,000-seat stadium. ♦ See park schedule for show times

O Pacific Point Preserve This 450,000-gallon habitat, which duplicates the northern Pacific Coast, is home to sea lions and both harbor and fur seals. It lies directly behind the **Sea Lion & Otter Stadium** (see above), and affords a good view of the speedy, streamlined creatures scientists call pinnipeds (aquatic mammals with flippers) both above and below water.

P Waterfront Sandwich Grill $ Enjoy gourmet sandwiches, burgers, hot dogs, beer, and soft drinks while overlooking the **Bayside Lagoon.** The kids' meal is a hamburger and fries. There's counter service only. ♦ American ♦ Daily lunch and dinner

Q Dockside Chicken & Ribs $ There are barbecue sandwiches or brisket dinners for grown-ups here, and a kid's menu for small fry at this counter-service eatery. ♦ American ♦ Daily lunch and dinner

R Terrors of the Deep One of the world's largest collections of dangerous sea creatures is in residence here in a 630,000-gallon aquarium. Moray eels, lionfish, scorpion fish, blowfish, sturgeon, and barracudas glide around inside the tanks, daring you to take a step closer. A moving sidewalk transports visitors through a tube in the pool; only four inches of clear acrylic separate the humans from the sharks. As you leave the exhibit, enter a viewing room to the right and spend as much time as you like nose-to-nose with these fascinating creatures.

S Nautilus Theatre Adventure awaits you in the form of *Cirque de la Mer,* a nontraditional circus featuring an innovative blend of acrobatics, athletics, comedy, and special effects in a 25-minute show. ♦ See park schedule for show times

T Clydesdale Hamlet Huge Clydesdale horses used in Anheuser-Busch promotions graze in a green paddock here. You can get an even closer view inside the stable, which is open to park guests.

U Anheuser-Busch Hospitality Center Take a break out of the sun and sample the Anheuser-Busch products (i.e., beer), which are free. **The Deli** has indoor and outdoor seating and serves cold-cut platters; there's also a kids' meal (turkey and cheese sandwich, pudding cup). **The Color of Life Theatre,** also on the premises, has a multimedia presentation about the world around us and the need for conservation.

V Shamu Stadium *The Shamu Adventure* features the famed killer whales with more live action and video imagery than ever before. Actor Jack Hanna is the host of the 25-minute large-screen video presentation, which transports the audience to remote locations such as Patagonia and the San Juan Islands to see the whales travel in pods, dive, and pursue prey. The video presentation is interspersed with live-action demonstrations. For instance, footage of killer whales sliding onto a beach in pursuit of sea lion pups is followed by a live beaching demonstration—sans pups. Shamu is one of six killer whales born at **SeaWorld Orlando** since 1985. The stadium holds 5,200 people and 7 million gallons of seawater, some of which sloshes onto the first few rows of seats during the show. (Beware: Saltwater can destroy video or still cameras.) After dark, *Shamu Rocks America* stars killer whales and **SeaWorld** trainers in a 25-minute show with rock 'n' roll music, theatrical effects, and plenty of splashes. ♦ See park schedule for show times

---

Tourism generates 19.2 percent of the total employment in the Orlando metropolitan area, or about 1 out of every 5 jobs.

SeaWorld's animal rescue team is on call 24 hours a day, 365 days a year. In the last five years alone, this team has rescued more than 3,000 injured, orphaned, and stranded marine animals throughout the country.

Next to Shamu Stadium:

Shamu: Close Up!

At this 1.7 million–gallon habitat, guests are able to get closer to killer whales than ever before. Part of the **Shamu Stadium** complex, this facility is used for training and research and as a marine mammal nursery. According to **SeaWorld**, it's the most sophisticated marine-mammal habitat and research facility in the world, with a successful killer whale breeding program. Three eight-foot underwater windows provide views of Shamu and company from every angle. Scientists are constantly monitoring the growth and weight of the whales to learn more about the physiology of these giants.

W **Shamu's Happy Harbor** This three-acre playground directly behind **Shamu Stadium** features both crawlable and climbable structures. Larger kids may want to brave the four-story net climb. Nearby are midway games and an area where kids can play with radio-controlled boats and trucks (for a fee).

X **Wild Arctic** This attraction combines a simulated helicopter ride through the Arctic with real-life encounters with animals that live there. Visitors board cabins that resemble jet helicopters and embark on a "flight" to the Arctic, complete with panoramic (film) views and a fair amount of pitching, surging, and swaying. After the ride, passengers leave the "helicopters" and pass through a chilly passageway to **Base Station Wild Arctic.** Visitors can explore the station, interact with the "scientists," and observe real Arctic animals—polar bears, beluga whales, walruses, harbor seals, and salmon—through floor-to-ceiling windows. Guests can even contribute to actual scientific research, using touch screens to record observed animal behavior. The data become part of the marine park's behavioral studies records.

Y **Mango Joe's Cafe** $ Breakfast is served at this counter-service cafe until 11AM. Otherwise, munch on fajitas, sandwiches, salads, and desserts. The kids' menu offers grilled chicken or beef strips and french fries. ♦ American ♦ Daily breakfast, lunch, and dinner

Z **Atlantis Stadium** Familiar but thrilling stunts are the draws of the 30-minute *Intensity Games,* with world-class athletes competing on water and land in thrilling competitions. This 5,200-seat stadium is also the site of *Red, Bright & Blue Spectacular,* shown in the evening before the park closes and serving as each day's grand finale. The 15-minute extravaganza features patriotic music, lasers, and fireworks. ♦ See park schedule for show times

4 **Sheraton World Resort** $ Located on 25 acres next to **SeaWorld,** this hotel has 800 rooms, a restaurant, and paved paths that wind through tropically landscaped grounds to three pools and five lighted tennis courts. ♦ 10100 International Dr (at Westwood Blvd). 352.1100, 800/341.4292 in FL, 800/325.3535 in Canada, 800/327.0363; fax 352.3679; www.sheratonworld.com &

5 **Wynfield Inn Westwood** $ This 299-room inn has two swimming pools, a pool bar, a restaurant, and a reputation for good management and service. Children age 17 and under stay free in their parents' room. Complimentary coffee, tea, and fruit are always available. ♦ 6263 Westwood Blvd (between International Dr and Central Florida Pkwy). 345.8000, 800/346.1551; fax 345.1508; www.orlando.com/wynfield &

6 **Westgate Lakes Family Resort** $$ Situated on 97 acres beside a lake is one of the most serene all-suite properties in Central Florida. The spacious 391 suites (either on one level or split-level) have fully equipped kitchenettes. A restaurant, cafe, lounge, pool bar and grill, swimming pool, ice-cream parlor, grocery delivery service, and children's activity room make it a full-service resort. ♦ 10000 Turkey Lake Rd (between I-4 and Sand Lake Rd). 345.0000, 800/424.0708; fax 345.5384; www.westgateresorts.com &

7 **Comfort Suites Orlando** $ A solid alternative to the high-priced hotels in the **Walt Disney World** area, this 215-suite hotel provides free continental breakfast, a boon to families who want to grab a bite before setting off to the attractions. In-room microwaves and refrigerators also cut down on meal expenses. Facilities include a restaurant, pool, whirlpool, and cable TV with HBO. ♦ 9350 Turkey Lake Rd (between I-4 and Sand Lake

Rd). 351.5050, 800/27SUITE; fax 363.7953; www.comfortsuitesorlando.com &

8 Country Hearth Inn $ The outside verandas and a rotunda lobby with a patterned tin ceiling and hardwood floors convey Southern hospitality, as do the restaurant, the lounge, and the hotel staff. All 150 rooms have a pleasant, understated decor; there's also a pool on the premises. ♦ 9861 International Dr (between Bee Line Expwy and Universal Dr). 352.0008, 800/447.1890; fax 352.5449; www.countryhearth.com &

9 Omni Rosen $$$ This 1,334-room hotel offers another luxury option near the expanding convention center. Its central location, spacious meeting rooms, and computer hookups in each guest room (200 also have modems) are designed to attract business travelers. Other amenities—including a health club, lighted tennis courts, and a large heated pool—appeal to leisure guests, too. The guest rooms and 80 deluxe suites are light and airy and equipped with the usual hotel amenities; rooms in the bi-level **Omni Club** towers offer special services and other extras. There are three restaurants: **Cafe Gauguin,** which features casual dining; **Red's Deli,** open around the clock; and the **Everglades,** which is the hotel's formal dining room. The intimate bar adjacent to this upscale eatery houses a 12-foot aquarium, which is an attraction in its own right. There's a second bar off the impressive Art Deco lobby. A six-story garage offers covered parking. ♦ 9840 International Dr (at Hawaiian Ct). 354.9840; fax 351.2659; www.omnirosen.com

10 Orlando/Orange County Convention Center Don't ask for a tour; there isn't one. This is a working convention center where trade shows and other events are held. ♦ 9800 International Dr (between Hawaiian and Samoan Cts). 345.9800

11 The Peabody Orlando $$$ Across the street from the **Orlando/Orange County Convention Center,** this elegant 27-story, 891-room luxury hotel caters to both business and leisure guests, but is best known for the ducks that paddle around the lobby fountain. As they do at this hotel's sister location in Memphis, Tennessee, a group of mallards marches into the hotel's marble lobby fountain daily at 11AM and parades out at 5PM with an air of pomp and ceremony that delights onlookers. The tradition began in the 1930s, when general manager Frank Schutt of The Peabody Memphis and his friend Chip Barwick Sr. returned from a weekend hunting trip and came up with the idea of putting a few live ducks in the lobby fountain there.

Beyond its famous feathered residents, this property is noteworthy for its wide range of outstanding restaurants, which makes it unnecessary for guests to venture out onto International Drive in the evening. Guest rooms are large and even have small TVs in the bathrooms. There are four lighted tennis courts, an Olympic-size pool, a children's pool, an outdoor whirlpool, a beauty salon, and the **Peabody Athletic Club,** with 15 Nautilus weight machines. The supervised day-care center is well run, and there is a complete business center. ♦ 9801 International Dr (between Bee Line Expwy and Universal Dr). 352.4000, 800/PEABODY; fax 351.0073; www.peabody-orlando.com

Within The Peabody Orlando:

B-Line Diner ★$$ A sleek 1950s-style diner, it's open around the clock. The to-kill-for desserts are tempting, but those with more willpower may want to order the stacked veggie sandwich. ♦ American ♦ Daily 24 hours. 352.4000 ext 4460

Capriccio ★★★$$$ Dine on carefully prepared Northern Italian dishes in a pretty dining room with a marble floor and tables, soft colors, and a view of the open kitchen. Folks swear by the *petto di pollo Pugliese* (chicken breast grilled with artichokes, capers, roasted garlic, and white wine over angel-hair pasta). The gourmet pizza baked in a wood-burning stove is also wonderful. A lavish brunch takes place on Sundays. ♦ Italian ♦ Tu-Sa dinner; Su brunch. Reservations recommended. 352.4000 ext 4450

Dux ★★★$$$ Rest assured that the hotel with ducks living in it doesn't have duck on the menu (though the butter is shaped like one). Instead, diners enjoy ahi (Hawaiian tuna), seared until it is just rare; Sonoma lamb chops marinated in crushed raspberries, garlic, and marjoram; or skillet-seared sea scallops served over artichoke risotto. The dining room is elegant and formal, with dark wood and crystal chandeliers; the wine list is impressive; and the service is attentive and knowledgeable. ♦ American ♦ M-Sa dinner. Reservations recommended; jacket requested. 345.4550

Orlando/Orange County Convention Center is ranked third in the United States in terms of exhibition space, with more than 1.1 million square feet.

Lobby Bar It's a nice place for a rendezvous, although the drinks are expensive. If you're waiting to see the famous Peabody ducks strut from their home upstairs to the lobby's fountain, be prepared to be caught in the crush (people never seem to tire of this show). Afternoon tea is served weekdays from 3PM to 4:30PM. ◆ Daily 11AM-2AM. 352.4000 ext 4128

Mallards Lounge Sip your drink at the black marble and brass bar or find a seat on one of the overstuffed sofas. Either way, it's an intimate meeting place tucked away from the lobby. ◆ Daily 11AM-2AM. 352.4000 ext 4125

12 Clarion Plaza Hotel $$ This 810-room hotel affords conventioneers a low-cost alternative to the stately **Peabody Orlando** across the street. Each of the large rooms has a safe and most have two double beds. A complete service center for the business traveler includes computer modem hookups. The lobby of this cream-colored 14-story building overlooks a nicely landscaped area with a heated pool and Jacuzzi. ◆ 9700 International Dr (between Hawaiian and Samoan Cts). 352.9700, 800/366.9700; fax 354.5774; www.clarionplaza.com ᕃ

Within the Clarion Plaza Hotel:

Jack's Place ★★$$ This upscale, 99-seat restaurant features seafood, pasta, and steaks. Casually elegant, it is decorated with caricatures of celebrities by Jack Rosen, the owner's father. ◆ American ◆ Daily dinner. 352.9700

Cafe Matisse ★$ A casual place with a buffet as well as à la carte service, this eatery serves basic fare—pasta, meat, and chicken entrées, plus burgers—in a breezy, colorful, and roomy setting. ◆ American ◆ Daily breakfast, lunch, and dinner. 352.9700

Lite Bite This bakery/deli offers take-out service around the clock. Bagels and breakfast items are available in the morning; soups and sandwiches are served the rest of day. ◆ Daily 24 hours. 352.9700

Backstage at the Clarion The 4,000-square-foot nightclub/lounge features Top 40 music (occasionally live) and dancing on a small dance floor. The crowd is mostly over 30 and local, with a smattering of hotel guests. It can get crowded, particularly toward the end of the week. ◆ Cover. Daily 3PM-2AM. 352.9700

Flights of Fancy

Taking to the air is a wonderful way to see Central Florida, and the **International Drive** area offers a number of opportunities for aerial excursions.

Hot-Air Balloons

Many balloon crews take off from fields southwest of Orlando. While prevailing winds govern the flight pattern, there's a fair chance that you'll get a bird's-eye view of the sprawling **Walt Disney World** property. At the very least, you'll fly over lovely, mist-shrouded forests and a surprising number of lakes. As the morning haze burns off, you might glimpse replanted citrus groves. Be sure to take binoculars or a camera.

Should you opt for a ballooning experience, get to bed early the night before—passengers are picked up at their hotels about an hour before dawn. Considerate pilots often soften the early morning blow with coffee and a sweet roll, and then ask participants to lend a hand with flight preparations. Helping to roll out the hot-air balloon will make you appreciate the singularity of the experience. Once the basket and balloon are hitched together, the wind direction determined, and fuel lines and supplies checked, it's inflation time. In about 10 minutes, what looked like an enormous bolt of fabric is transformed into a bulbous, colorful, and whimsical craft.

Riding in a hot-air balloon is a most serene experience, one that always seems to end too soon. Touchdown is usually celebrated with Champagne and flight certificates. Passengers are then driven back to the starting point. Good sports offer to help repack the equipment, so budget four to six hours for the entire adventure.

For hot-air balloon trips, contact:

Air Sport Aviation 438.7773

Orange Blossom Balloons............239.7677

Rise & Float Balloon Tours 352.8191

SkyScapes Balloon Tours..............856.4606

Helicopters

Helicopter rides involve less time than balloon trips, especially since there's a chopper base conveniently located at 8990 International Drive (see below). Zipping about at 120 mph in a roaring machine is a surefire way to get your adrenaline flowing. The most popular helicopter flights last about 15 minutes and carry four passengers. Pilots fly around—not over—the major attractions, including the **Walt Disney World** complex and **SeaWorld,** then head for the **Butler Chain of Lakes** in southwest **Orange County.** Advance booking is recommended. For tours and charter flights, contact **Air Orlando Helicopters Inc.** (354.1400).

Pointe★Orlando

13 Pointe★Orlando This new shopping, dining, and entertainment complex on 17 acres includes five buildings connected by wide promenades, anchored on one end by an **FAO Schwarz** toy store and the other by **WonderWorks,** a hands-on entertainment center. There are more than 40 shops within **Pointe★Orlando,** including **A/X Armani Exchange,** which sells men's and women's designer clothing; **Victoria's Secret** for upscale lingerie; **Banana Republic** for trendy men's and women's clothing; **Abercrombie & Fitch,** purveyors of traditional men's and women's apparel; and **Disney Worldport,** a center for Disney merchandise. Also within the complex is a 21-screen movie theater. There's ample parking in the attached parking garage. Stores here are open daily until 10PM; restaurants serve dinner until 10:30PM, but bars in the restaurants remain open until 2:30AM (they stop serving alcohol at 2AM). ◆ 9101 International Dr (at Universal Dr). 248.2838; www.pointeorlandofl.com

Within Pointe★Orlando:

Adobe Gila's ★$ You'll find more than 100 different tequilas behind the bar at this casual, open-air cantina, as well as decent tacos and quesadillas. ◆ Mexican ◆ Daily lunch and dinner. 903.1477

Monty's Conch Harbor ★★$ Conch fritters, conch salad, stone crab claws, and a delicious fried fish sandwich bring the locals to **Monty's,** the first in this chain to locate outside of South Florida. ◆ Seafood ◆ Daily lunch and dinner. 696.7507

Dan Marino's Town Tavern ★$$ This is the third location (the other two are in Coral Springs and Ft. Lauderdale) for this upscale restaurant owned by Dan Marino, the popular **Miami Dolphins** quarterback. The menu offers a 28-ounce "cowboy" steak, stuffed veal chops, and a variety of pastas. ◆ American ◆ Daily lunch and dinner. 363.1013

LuLu's Bait Shack ★$ This Delta-Cajun, bayou-themed restaurant and bar is designed to look like an old Louisiana shack. Try the crawfish étoufée, jambalaya, baby back ribs, or Buffalo-style shrimp. The outdoor patio features live jazz and rock music on Thursday, Friday, and Saturday nights. ◆ Southern ◆ Daily lunch and dinner. 351.9595

Johnny Rockets ★$ Grilled burgers and old-fashioned milk shakes and ice cream are the draw in this diner inspired by 1950s malt shops. ◆ American ◆ Daily lunch and dinner. 903.0763

The Players Grill, Home of the NFL Players ★★$$ National Football League players have been spotted here, and NFL memorabilia lines the walls. Try the smoked chicken taquitos, wasabi-crusted salmon, or any of the pizzas. ◆ American ◆ Daily lunch and dinner. 425.6826

WonderWorks Experience the trembling of earthquakes, defy gravity, and try the hands-on activities in the **Bermuda Triangle Corridor, Mystery Lab, Bubble Works,** and other interactive areas in this entertainment center designed to look like an upside-down building. ◆ One admission includes all attractions. Daily. 248.2838

Muvico Pointe 21 Theaters This multiplex also features an IMAX theater to showcase 3-D and large-format films. ◆ Call for show times. 352.3573

Graham Central Station This complex includes **Vortex,** a high-energy dance club; **Bell Bottoms,** a 1970s retro disco; **Memphis Lights,** a jazz and blues room; **Alley Cats,** featuring dueling pianos; **Starz Karaoke;** and an outdoor cafe. One cover charge provides admission to all clubs. ◆ Daily. 363.7900

14 Ming Court ★★★$$ Outstanding food is served at this restaurant, which overlooks a floating garden. Among the many fine choices are Hunan *kung pao* chicken with cashews, peanuts, and walnuts, and crispy Shanghai noodles topped with shrimp and shiitake mushrooms. ◆ Chinese ◆ Daily lunch and dinner. Reservations recommended. 9188 International Dr (at Samoan Ct). 351.9988; fax 352.2524 ㊉

15 Race Rock $$ The real draw here is the racing memorabilia. Celebrity owners Richard and Kyle Petty, Jeff Gordon, and Rusty Wallace all have their stock cars on display. In fact, the restaurant is a mini-museum of vehicles, trophies, and racing exhibits, including the largest monster truck in the world, *Smokin' Joe.* The menu is typical: wings, pizza, and "crashed potatoes" (mashed, of course). ◆ American ◆ Daily lunch and dinner. 8986 International Dr (between Samoan and Austrian Cts). 248.9876; fax 248.9887 ㊉

15 King Henry's Feast $$ It's hard not to gawk at this Tudor-style castle, complete with battlements, tower, and moat, plunked down right on busy International Drive. Visitors arriving at this dinner theater are offered mead, a tasty Old English honey wine, before a five-course banquet of standard-issue roast chicken, ribs, soup, salad, vegetables, and pie. The feast purports to be the royal birthday celebration of King Henry VIII, who prowls about in search of bride number seven. Entertainment includes a sword and fire swallower and a court jester. It's silly, but fun.

♦ American ♦ Admission. Daily (show times vary seasonally). 8984 International Dr (between Samoan and Austrian Cts). 351.5151, 800/883.8181; fax 351.3593 &

15 Embassy Suites $$ You really feel like you're getting away from it all when you enter this property's attractive atrium lobby, with its tile pathways, tropical foliage, and fountains. The 244-suite hotel is one of the best-designed properties along Central Florida's tourist strip. Suites are equipped with wet bars, microwave ovens, refrigerators, and two TVs, and there's a restaurant, an indoor pool, a whirlpool, a sauna, and an exercise room on the premises. Breakfast and a two-hour cocktail reception are complimentary. ♦ 8978 International Dr (between Samoan and Austrian Cts). 352.1400, 800/433.7275; fax 363.1120; www.embassysuites.com &

16 Bahama Breeze ★$$ Located in an airy space with open-beam ceilings and festive with Caribbean colors and calypso music, this dinner-only chain eatery (brought to you by the creators of **Red Lobster** and **Olive Garden**) is a step above many cookie-cutter competitors. Among the offerings are creative dishes inspired by the flavors of the Caribbean, including a decent paella, fresh fish, and an interesting piña colada bread pudding. ♦ Caribbean ♦ M-Sa dinner until 2AM; Su dinner until midnight. No reservations accepted. 8849 International Dr (between Universal Dr and Via Mercado). 248.2499 &

17 The Castle-DoubleTree Resort $$ You can't miss this distinctive hotel, painted in pinks and blues, inspired by **Cinderella Castle** in **Walt Disney World**'s **Magic Kingdom**. There are 216 rooms, including 7 suites, all with refrigerators, TVs, and in-room safes. There's a swimming pool, fitness center, gameroom, and shuttle service to area attractions. ♦ 8629 International Dr (between Universal Dr and Via Mercado). 345-1511; fax 248.8181; www.grandthemehotels.com &

18 Pirate's Cove Two imaginative 18-hole miniature golf courses reward luck more than skill. Hazards include waterfalls and damp rock grottoes. ♦ Admission. Daily. 8501 International Dr (between Universal Dr and Via Mercado). 352.7378

19 Summerfield Suites Hotel $ This property offers 146 suites, all with fully equipped kitchens. The two-bedroom suites have two bathrooms, two telephones, a TV in each bedroom, and a TV/VCR in the living room. One-bedroom suites are also available; they have one bathroom, one telephone, two TVs, and one VCR. Cocktail-hour drinks and breakfast are complimentary, but there's no restaurant on-site. ♦ 8480 International Dr (at Austrian Ct). 352.2400, 800/833.4353; fax 238.0778; www.summerfield-orlando.com &

20 Mercado More than 50 specialty shops, restaurants, and bars are arranged around this Mediterranean-style open courtyard. There's even regular entertainment—from mariachi music to clog dancing. In the evening, lights twinkle in the trees. ♦ Daily. 8445 International Dr (at Via Mercado). 345.9337

Within the Mercado:

Official Visitor Center Get all your touristy questions answered here. Discount coupons, maps, and a handy book of menus from area restaurants, along with two walls' worth of brochures, are yours for the taking. The center is operated by the **Orlando/Orange County Convention & Visitors Bureau.** ♦ Daily. 363.5872

House of Ireland If there are O'Malleys or O'Connells in your life, you should be able to find something for them here. How about a mug with the appropriate coat of arms? ♦ Daily. 352.7791

José O'Day's Mexican Restaurant $ Stop here if you need a Tex-Mex fix. This casual eatery offers a full menu of south-of-the-border standards. Order the sizzling apple pie for dessert. ♦ Tex-Mex ♦ Daily lunch and dinner. 363.0613

The Butcher Shop Steakhouse ★★$$ If you're the kind of person who likes to make dinner even when you're on vacation, here's your chance. Choose a slab of steak from a refrigerated case and cook it at one of the large hickory charcoal pits. If that sounds like too much work, kick back and have a brew while one of the chefs does it for you. The building holds about 320 meat lovers in three big, casual dining rooms that combine a steak house–style decor (mahogany walls and tables, a marble entryway) with tropical colors. ♦ American ♦ Daily dinner. 363.9727

Blazing Pianos This 400-seat audience-participation piano bar is rockin' Central Florida. Three fire-engine–red Yamaha concert grands and a cast of talented and outrageous musicians are the stars of the lively show. There's a quieter separate room for conversation. ♦ Admission. Daily 4PM-2AM. 363.5104, 800/883.8282 &

Bergamo's Italian Restaurant ★$$ Step through the doorway into a trattoria straight out of New York's Little Italy. Among the specialties is *zuppa di pesce alla Bergamo* (king crab, clams, shrimp, mussels, and whitefish sautéed in white wine and garlic, served with linguine). Complement your meal with imported Italian wine and top off the evening with scrumptious homemade desserts. ♦ Italian ♦ Daily dinner. 352.3805

La Grille ★★★$$ Locals flock to this *très* French restaurant for its wonderful food and expert service. The decor is simple yet elegant—framed oil paintings line the walls, and there are hardwood floors and linen tablecloths. The restaurant also features a small bar, and patrons enjoy soft classical music while they dine. The mussels on a warm cheese soufflé make a good starter. Fresh fish, a traditional cassoulet, and delicious lamb shanks are also recommended. Save room for the cheese plate or any of the desserts. ♦ French ♦ Daily dinner. 345.0888

Charlie's Lobster House ★★$$ The extensive menu includes crab cakes, steaks, chicken dishes, and fresh seafood specials. The dining room—done up with dark wood, white tablecloths, and brass lamps—has a classy, nautical look. ♦ American/Seafood ♦ Daily lunch and dinner. 352.6929

Damon's—The Place for Ribs ★$$ Your nose knows the way. The mouth-watering smell of ribs being barbecued is apparent as you approach the **Mercado** from I-Drive. You won't be disappointed at this colorful, casual place with no tablecloths or dress code. ♦ Barbecue ♦ Daily lunch and dinner. 352.5984

Mercado Food Pavilion This is a mall-style food court, with a variety of inexpensive fast-food outlets. We like the **Greek Place** for its pita bread generously stuffed with lamb or beef and topped with tomatoes, onions, and special sauce. ♦ Daily

21 **Ran-Getsu** ★★$$$ Don't be fooled by its location in the midst of Central Florida's biggest tourist strip—this restaurant serves excellent and authentic Japanese cuisine. Menu highlights include teriyaki, sukiyaki, and *yosenabe* (a Japanese bouillabaisse with fresh Florida seafood). Enjoy fresh sushi at the long, curving sushi bar or sit at American-style tables overlooking a Japanese garden and reflecting pool. Occasionally a kimono-clad woman performs sedate Japanese dances to traditional music. ♦ Japanese ♦ Daily dinner. Reservations recommended. 8400 International Dr (at Jamaican Ct). 345.0044; fax 351.0481

22 **Crab House** ★$$ Crabs of all kinds—including Alaskan snow crabs, Maryland-style steamed crabs, and soft-shell crabs—can be savored at this very touristy spot. Florida stone crabs are a favorite (ask first if they're in

season to be sure they're fresh). A variety of fish may be ordered from the "fresh catch" menu, and there's pasta for landlubbers. The decor sticks determinedly to the nautical theme, with plenty of lobster traps, fishing poles, and cedar wood. ♦ Seafood ♦ Daily lunch and dinner. 8291 International Dr (between Via Mercado and Sand Lake Rd). 352.6140. Also at: 8496 Palm Pkwy (between Apoka-Vineland Rd and Lake Ave), Lake Buena Vista. 239.1888

Ripley's Believe It or Not!
MUSEUM

23 **Ripley's Believe It or Not! Museum** This attraction is housed in a building that's slanted so severely it looks as if it's about to be swallowed by a Florida sinkhole. The oddities on display include shrunken heads, unusual animals, and model cars made of matchsticks. There are also videos, including one about daredevils who've gone over Niagara Falls in barrels or walked across it on a tightrope. ♦ Admission. Daily 9AM-midnight. 8201 International Dr (between Via Mercado and Sand Lake Rd). 363.4418, 800/998.4418 ⅙

24 **Embassy Suites** $$ The first of the all-suite hotels on I-Drive, it offers 265 units equipped with refrigerators, wet bars, microwave ovens, and two TVs. Facilities include an indoor-outdoor pool, a gameroom, a sauna, a steam room, and an exercise room, but no restaurant. Suites surround an enclosed courtyard where a free full breakfast and evening cocktails are offered daily. ♦ 8250 Jamaican Ct (west of International Dr). 345.8250, 800/362.2779; fax 352.1463; www.embassy-suites.com

25 **Friday's Front Row Sports Grill** $ Name your sport, you can find it here, with 86 TVs to broadcast an astounding variety of competitions. Add 45 video games, five dart boards, shuffleboard, air hockey, pool, and two **NBA** regulation free throws, and you, too, can exercise while you eat. The food is what you'd expect: wings, fajitas, steaks, pizza, pasta, and—the specialty—a half-pound burger. The "Hall of Foam" boasts 100 varieties of bottled beer from around the world, and another 20 on tap. Sports celebrities make regular appearances. ♦ American ♦ Daily lunch and dinner. 8126 International Dr (between Jamaican Ct and Sand Lake Rd). 363.1414 ⅙

26 **Orlando Marriott International Drive** $$ One of Florida's larger hotels, with 1,076 rooms, this property consists of 16 pink-and-teal stucco buildings set on 48 acres. It offers a full complement of on-site facilities,

including three heated outdoor pools, four lighted tennis courts, a health club, three restaurants, two snack bars serving drinks, two small **Pizza Hut** outlets, and a lounge featuring entertainment. For the business traveler, there are meeting rooms and concierge suites. ◆ 8001 International Dr (at Sand Lake Rd). 351.2420, 800/228.9290 in Canada, 800/421.8001; fax 345.5611; www.marriott.com &

27 Quality Inn International $ Owner Harris Rosen boasts that he has the cheapest rates in town—and in fact the prices here are hard to beat. But if you want to stay at this 728-room hotel be sure to book ahead, since the property is a popular choice for tour groups. It has all the usual amenities—a restaurant, two pools, a video arcade, and a bar/lounge. The biggest drawback is the traffic on I-Drive during peak season, which can make getting in and out of the parking lot somewhat tricky. If this place is full, Rosen has two other inexpensive choices on I-Drive: **Quality Inn Plaza** (9000 International Dr, between Samoan and Austrian Cts, 345.8585, 800/999.8585) and **Roadway Inn** (6327 International Dr, between Universal Dr and Sand Lake Rd, 351.4444, 800/999.6327). ◆ 7600 International Dr (between Sand Lake Rd and Universal Dr). 351.1600, 800/825.7600; fax 352.5328; www.tamarinns.com

28 New Punjab Restaurant ★★$$ Here's a fine choice for Indian fare. The Murgh curried chicken and lamb with curry sauce are served with fragrant rice; the garlic-flavored nan, a flat bread baked in a tandoor (clay oven), is heavenly. The pretty pink dining room is accented with paintings of India. ◆ Indian ◆ Tu-Sa lunch and dinner; M, Su dinner. 7451 International Dr (between Sand Lake Rd and Carrier Dr). 352.7887

29 Fun 'n Wheels This family-oriented amusement park draws about a million people a year. The three go-kart tracks are always buzzing; in fact, the 43 go-karts wear out 200 tires each year. There's also a water slide, miniature golf, bumper boats, and video and arcade games. ◆ Nominal fee for each amusement. M-F 6-11PM; Sa-Su 10AM-11PM. 6739 Sand Lake Rd (between Canada Ave and International Dr). 351.5651. Also at: 3711 W Hwy 192 (between Dyer and Armstrong Blvds), Kissimmee. 870.2222

30 Residence Inn by Marriott $ If you have a large family or just need some room to spread out, this 176-suite hotel is a dependable choice. Each suite has a fully equipped kitchen, and there's also a pool. A free buffet breakfast is offered daily and there's a Happy Hour with complimentary drinks Monday through Thursday evenings, but no restaurant. ◆ 7610 Canada Ave (between Sand Lake Rd and Carrier Dr).

345.0117, 800/331.3131; fax 352.2689; www.marriott.com &

31 Dowdy Pavilion Looking for a little rainy-day recreation? Here under one big roof are 32 bowling lanes and an ice-skating rink. On Saturday nights there's moonlight bowling. Snacks are available at both the lanes and the rink. ◆ Admission and rental fees. Bowling M-F, Su 9AM-11PM; Sa 9AM-2AM. Skating Tu-F 7:30-10PM; Sa-Su 1-4PM, 7:30-10PM. 7500 Canada Ave (between Sand Lake Rd and Carrier Dr). Bowling 352.2695, skating 352.9878

32 Enclave Suites at Orlando $ Overlooking a private lake, this 321-suite hotel is far enough off I-Drive to offer a touch of serenity, but close enough to be within walking distance of **Wet 'n Wild** and area restaurants. Suites are spacious, ranging from 660 to 1,200 square feet, with VCRs and fully equipped kitchens. Ask for a unit with a lake view. There's an outdoor and an indoor pool, plus a sauna, a tennis court, and an exercise room. ◆ 6165 Carrier Dr (between Universal and International Drs). 351.1155, 800/457.0077; fax 351.2001 &

33 Dansk Factory Outlet Typically pricey Dansk dinnerware is available here at discounts of 10 to 60 percent. There are limited editions alongside overstocks, seconds, and discontinued patterns. It's the perfect place to pick up wedding gifts. ◆ Daily. 7000 International Dr (between Sand Lake Rd and Universal Dr). 351.2425 &

34 Holiday Inn International Drive Resort $ There are many newer lodging places along the tourist strip, but this 650-room hotel is well managed and always spick-and-span. Other pluses include a huge free-form heated pool, a whirlpool, a pool bar, and a family restaurant. ◆ 6515 International Dr (between Universal Dr and Sand Lake Rd). 351.3500, 800/465.4329; fax 351.5727; www.holiday-inn.com &

Within the Holiday Inn International Drive Resort:

The Comedy Zone Stand-up comics try their luck with the crowds. ◆ Admission. Shows: Tu-Th 8:30PM; F-Sa 8:30PM, 10:30PM. Reservations recommended. 351.3500

35 Congo River Golf & Exploration Co. The two 18-hole miniature golf courses here have a jungle motif. ◆ Admission. Daily 10AM-

11PM. 6312 International Dr (between Universal and Carrier Drs). 352.0042. Also at: 4777 W Hwy 192 (between Seven Dwarfs La and Rte 535). 396.6900

36 Holiday Inn Express International Drive $ The nationwide chain has created an "Express" line of basic, budget hotels, which are a good bet for families. The 217 rooms all have two double beds, and there is a pool. Free continental breakfast is included but there's no restaurant. ♦ 6323 International Dr (between Universal Dr and Sand Lake Rd). 351.4430, 800/365.6935; fax 345.0742; www.enjoyfloridahotels.com &

37 Las Palmas Inn $ Palm trees surround a heated pool out back, away from the commotion of I-Drive. The 262-room hotel is across the street from **Wet 'n Wild** and within walking distance of dining and shopping. ♦ 6233 International Dr (between Universal Dr and Sand Lake Rd). 351.3900, 800/327.2114; fax 352.5597 &

Wet 'n Wild

38 Wet 'n Wild The ever-expanding water park has spawned a host of imitators, but aficionados think this 25-acre original remains the best of the bunch. **Universal Studios Escape** recently purchased the park, so look for even more of an edge against competitors. Teens who find **Walt Disney World**'s **Typhoon Lagoon** or **Blizzard Beach** too tame are satisfied here.

The newest attraction is **Hydra Fighter,** an interactive water ride with riders seated back to back in chairs equipped with water cannons. The rider controls the water pressure that will launch him into the air, sending him twisting and turning. **Fuji Flyer,** a four-passenger toboggan, sends riders flying down a steep, six-story slide through 450 feet of exciting curves. **Bomb Bay,** considered the scariest of the water slides anywhere, is a heart-stopping plunge down a 76-foot-high, nearly vertical slide. Another of the thrill rides, **The Surge,** launches a five-passenger tube from a five-story tower, sending it twisting and turning down 580 feet of banked curves. The wild **Black Hole** journey, in which a two-person raft is propelled by a 1,000-gallon-a-minute blast of water, takes place in near-total darkness highlighted by special lighting and sound effects. Another daredevils' favorite is **Blue Niagara,** which has two intertwined tubes six stories high and 300 feet long.The **Bubba Tub** is much tamer; although the five-passenger inflatable tube starts 60 feet (six stories) up, the slide's wide curves create a fun ride to the bottom. There's also the

relaxing **Lazy River,** where you can float gently in an inner tube and work on your tan. For younger kids, there's a children's water playground that contains miniature versions of some of the big rides as well as a pool for toddlers.

Don't expect more than a hot dog and snack foods from the kiosks, but you can bring your own picnic (no alcohol). At the park you may also purchase a **FlexTicket** (see page 33), which admits you to **Wet 'n Wild, Universal Studios, SeaWorld,** and **Busch Gardens** in Tampa. ♦ Admission. Daily. 6200 International Dr (between Universal and Carrier Drs). 351.1800, 800/992.WILD &

39 The Floridian of Orlando $ A great location—right off I-Drive but away from the heavy traffic and within walking distance of **Wet 'n Wild**—is the drawing card here. The 300 rooms are simply, but nicely, furnished and the food served in the hotel restaurant is basic but good. There's also a pool, a gameroom, and a small gift shop. ♦ 7299 Universal Dr (between Carrier and International Drs). 351.5009, 800/445.7299; fax 363.7807 &

40 Sleuths Mystery Dinner Shows ★$$ There's a mystery afoot, and you're the detective. The fun begins when you enter an English drawing room complete with period furnishings and secret panels. Hot and cold hors d'oeuvres are served as you mingle with other guests and actors playing outrageous characters. The plot unfolds and a murder occurs. During dinner, guests formulate questions for an after-dinner interrogation period. In the end, the murderer is revealed; if you correctly solved the crime you win a prize. One of nine different mystery scenarios is enacted at each dinner; they include an 80th birthday party, a class reunion, a memorial service, and an Italian wedding. An unmemorable four-course dinner and unlimited beer and wine are included in the price of admission. ♦ Admission. ♦ Daily; call for show times. 7508 Universal Dr (between Sand Lake Rd and Carrier Dr). 363.1985, 800/393.1985 &

41 Siam Orchid ★★$$ A nice find in a tourist area, it offers good food in beautiful surroundings. The dining room is adorned with carved wood pieces, statues, and authentic artifacts, and the waiters and waitresses are dressed in colorful native Thai costume. Diners can choose to sit Asian-style at a low table (there's space underneath for your legs) or at standard Western-style tables. The food is very good, but dishes are not as spicy as the menu indicates, so you might consider ordering the next-hottest version. Specialties include roast duck with honey and a whole deep-fried fish in a sauce of chili,

45

garlic, and peppers. ♦ Thai ♦ Daily dinner. 7575 Universal Blvd (between Lakehurst and Carrier Drs). 351.0821

42 Marketplace The stores are fairly standard, but this shopping center does house several good restaurants, as well as a 24-hour **Goodings** grocery. ♦ 7600 Dr. Phillips Blvd (north of Sand Lake Rd)

Within the Marketplace:

Chamberlin's ★★$ The food is fresh and well prepared at this, the only health-food store in Central Florida. Choose a healthful entrée, a hearty salad, a sandwich, or a thick smoothy fruit drink at the cafeteria-style restaurant. ♦ American ♦ M-Sa lunch and dinner; Su lunch until 5PM. 352.2130

Christini's Ristorante Italiano ★★ $$$$ The pasta is homemade (the fettuccine Alfredo is a favorite among regulars) and the fish soup with shrimp, lobster, and clams is good at this attractive, romantic restaurant embellished with Italian paintings, sculpture, and ceramics. Occasionally a strolling musician adds to the ambience. The staff is attentive; the owner charming. The food is good, but the atmosphere is better. ♦ Italian ♦ M-Sa dinner. Reservations recommended. 345.8770

43 Days Inn Orlando Lakeside $ Location and price make this 690-room hotel a good choice. It's on the west side of I-4, a block from the **Marketplace** shopping center. Other pluses include three pools, a playground, a romantic boardwalk that leads to a sandy beach, and free meals for children 12 and under at the hotel restaurant. ♦ 7335 Sand Lake Rd (between Turkey Lake Rd and Dr. Phillips Blvd). 351.1900, 800/777.3297; fax 363.1749; www.thhotels.com ⑤

44 Florida Mall Located five miles east of International Drive, this is Central Florida's largest retail shopping center, with 200 stores. A major expansion is underway, adding another department store and dozens of smaller shops. There's a **Sears** as well as all the usual mall specialty shops, from **Athlete's Foot** to **Zales Jewelers**. ♦ Daily. 8001 S Orange Blossom Tr (at Sand Lake Rd). 851.6255

45 Gateway Inn $ Popular with British tourists, this 355-room hotel is within walking distance of **Wet 'n Wild** and offers a free shuttle to **Walt Disney World** and other area attractions. There are two pools, a playground, and a family restaurant. ♦ 7050 S Kirkman Rd (between Precision and International Drs). 351.2000, 800/432.1179 in FL, 800/327.3808; fax 363.1835 ⑤

45 Hampton Inn $ Part of a value-priced hotel chain, it boasts a quiet location just off International Drive. The 170 comfortable rooms have queen- or king-size beds, refrigerators, and microwave ovens. There's a small fitness center and a pool. Continental breakfast is included in the rate, but there's no restaurant. ♦ 7110 S Kirkman Rd (between Precision and International Drs). 345.1112, 800/763.1100; fax 352.6591 ⑤

46 Passage to India ★★★$$ The best Indian food available in the area is provided by owner Uday Kadam, a native of Bombay who left an 11-year career with Marriott Corporation to open this excellent and warmly hospitable restaurant. Experiment by ordering a selection of appetizers; they're served with a variety of chutneys. ♦ Indian ♦ Daily lunch and dinner. 5532 International Dr (between Municipal and Grand National Drs). 351.3456

47 Great Western Boot & Western Wear Company A good selection of men's western boots by Justin and Dan Post, and a small selection of handmade boots by lesser-known makers such as Stewart of Arizona, are sold here. The women's selection isn't as extensive, but all boots are discounted. ♦ Daily. 5597 International Dr (between Del Verde Way and Grand National Dr). 345.8103

48 Malibu Grand Prix and Castle Batting cages for hardball and softball and formula-style race cars draw teens and twenty-somethings to this amusement center. You must be 18 and have a driver's license, or 16 with a learner's permit and your parents present, to drive the cars. There are also arcade games and miniature golf. ♦ Fee for each activity. Daily. 5863 American Way (north of International Dr). 351.7093 ⑤

49 Belz Factory Outlet World If you're a careful shopper and know your merchandise, you won't have trouble finding good buys here. The complex consists of two unconnected malls and three smaller annexes; brand-name stores include **Calvin Klein, Guess, Oshkosh B'Gosh, Bass**, and **Levi's**. With nine million visitors annually, this bargain-hunter's paradise is reputed to be one of the largest factory outlet complexes in the country, as well as the second-largest tourist attraction in Central Florida. **Annex II** has a carousel for kids to ride. Note that **Belz** has numerous competitors, all side by side along the same road. ♦ Daily. 5401 W Oak Ridge Rd (between Florida's Tpke and Grand National Dr). 352.9611

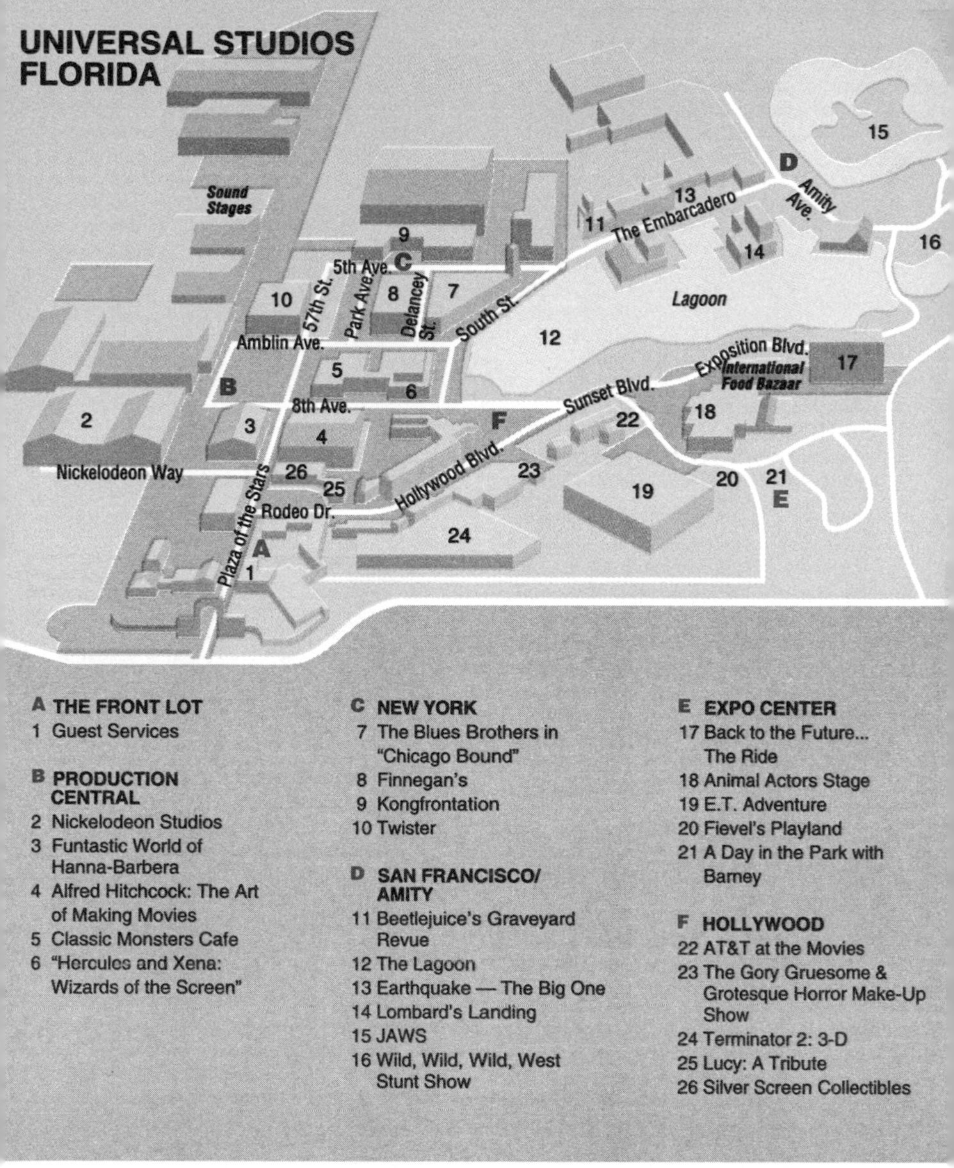

UNIVERSAL STUDIOS FLORIDA

Sound Stages

5th Ave.
57th St.
Park Ave.
Delancey St.
South St.
Amblin Ave.
8th Ave.
Nickelodeon Way
Plaza of the Stars
Rodeo Dr.
Hollywood Blvd.
Sunset Blvd.
The Embarcadero
Amity Ave.
Lagoon
Exposition Blvd.
International Food Bazaar

9 C 7
10
5
6
3 4
2
26 25
1 A
24
23
F
22
19
20 21 E
18
17
11 13
14
15
16
12
D

A THE FRONT LOT
1 Guest Services

B PRODUCTION CENTRAL
2 Nickelodeon Studios
3 Funtastic World of Hanna-Barbera
4 Alfred Hitchcock: The Art of Making Movies
5 Classic Monsters Cafe
6 "Hercules and Xena: Wizards of the Screen"

C NEW YORK
7 The Blues Brothers in "Chicago Bound"
8 Finnegan's
9 Kongfrontation
10 Twister

D SAN FRANCISCO/ AMITY
11 Beetlejuice's Graveyard Revue
12 The Lagoon
13 Earthquake — The Big One
14 Lombard's Landing
15 JAWS
16 Wild, Wild, Wild, West Stunt Show

E EXPO CENTER
17 Back to the Future... The Ride
18 Animal Actors Stage
19 E.T. Adventure
20 Fievel's Playland
21 A Day in the Park with Barney

F HOLLYWOOD
22 AT&T at the Movies
23 The Gory Gruesome & Grotesque Horror Make-Up Show
24 Terminator 2: 3-D
25 Lucy: A Tribute
26 Silver Screen Collectibles

---

50 Universal Studios Escape It may not have the power of The Mouse behind it, but this studio theme park is *the* place to "ride the movies." **Universal Studios** has the edge

UNIVERSAL STUDIOS *Escape*

on authenticity because not only is it a theme park (the fourth most visited in the country), it's also the largest active motion picture and television production studio outside of Hollywood. Some 14 feature films have been shot here, including *Parenthood* and *Psycho IV;* hundreds of TV shows, including "seaQuest DSV" and "America's Funniest People," use the back lot locations and soundstages; and more than 300 commercials and numerous music videos have been shot here. Visitors may see a television show or movie being filmed—and you might even be asked to stand in as an extra. Note, however, that sometimes these sessions are staged (it soon becomes obvious that nothing is really happening). To witness moviemaking in action, check the ever-changing production schedule posted in the **Front Lot,** ask at **Guest Services,** or call ahead (363.8000).**Universal Studios Escape** is the official name of the overall vacation resort being built adjacent to and including the **Universal Studios Florida** theme park. **Universal Studios Escape** includes the existing **Universal Studios Florida,** along with a new theme park named **Universal Studios Islands of Adventure** (see page 54); **Universal Studios CityWalk** (see page 50), a 30-acre entertainment complex featuring themed restaurants, nightclubs, shops, and a 20-screen, 5,000-seat movie megaplex; world-class hotel accommodations; and expanded film and television production facilities.

Opened in 1990, **Universal Studios Florida** is the younger, East Coast cousin of Universal Studios Hollywood, the first movie theme park, which evolved from the Universal Studios' back lot tour. The 444-acre Florida park features more than 30 rides, shows, and attractions; nine state-of-the-art soundstages; and 40 street sets. The park is divided into six areas: **The Front Lot, Production Central, New York, San Francisco/Amity, Expo Center,** and **Hollywood** (see the map on page 47). In the center of the park is an eight-acre **Lagoon**—it serves as a good landmark. To minimize your time in lines, consider the following itinerary: Arrive early and have your ticket in hand when the park opens, then head to **Expo Center** for one of Central Florida's most exciting rides, **Back to the Future . . . The Ride** (lines for this attraction get very long 30 minutes after opening time). From there, head to **JAWS,** get rattled by **Earthquake—The Big One,** go face-to-face with King Kong at **Kongfrontation,** enter the **Funtastic World of Hanna-Barbera,** and fly with **E.T. Adventure** (see pages 49, 51, 52, and 53 for details on the rides). If you don't catch all of the above before 11AM, wait until after 3PM, when the lines dwindle.

Available on Tuesday and Thursday mornings are the all-you-can-eat **Character Breakfasts,** attended by folks dressed up as the Flintstones, Woody Woodpecker, and other cartoon characters. Guests are escorted through the park gates at 7:45AM to the **International Food Bazaar,** where they have breakfast while mingling with the characters. Just as the gates are opened breakfast attendees are given priority entrance to **E.T. Adventure,** one of the rides with the longest lines. Reservations are required for the breakfast; call *at least* 24 hours in advance—two to three days ahead is better (354.6339). Reservations are also recommended for **Lombard's Landing** (see page 52); bookings may be made at **Guest Services,** at the restaurants, or by phone. For a special (and expensive) overview of the park, consider the eight-hour **V.I.P. Tour,** which offers a personalized behind-the-scenes look at the studio. Four-hour tours for small groups also can be arranged for a fee. Both private tours offer priority entrance to attractions (read: You don't have to stand in line), preferred seating, and a guide who recounts fascinating star stories (363.8295 for reservations). Special events take place at **Universal Studios** year-round. For example, during **Halloween Horror Nights** (in October), the park crawls with monsters, maniacs, and mutants from horror films. Note: If you plan to leave **Universal Studios** and return the same day, have your hand stamped; if you plan to return the following day, upgrade your pass on the day of purchase for a substantial saving. Inquire at the **Vacation Planning Center** to the right of the main entrance as you exit. You may also purchase a **FlexTicket** (see page 33), which admits you to **Universal Studios, SeaWorld, Wet 'n Wild,** and **Busch Gardens** in Tampa. ♦ Admission. Parking fee. Daily 9AM-7PM, 9PM, or 10PM, depending on the season. S Kirkman Rd and Major Blvd. 363.8000 ♿

Within Universal Studios Florida (see map on page 47):

A The Front Lot As you pass through the **Universal Studios** turnstiles, you'll find **Guest Services** and the **Lost and Found.** Help is available here for the hearing impaired and for non–English-speaking guests, and you can rent manual or electric wheelchairs, or strollers. You can also check Fido into an air-conditioned kennel for a fee, and behind **Guest Services** are a bank and pay lockers. If you want to catch a glimpse of some real-life moviemaking, check out the chalkboard listing the day's production schedule at the entrance turnstiles (or visit **Guest Services**). You can sign up here to be part of a TV studio audience. On the right side of the path leading into the rest of the park is **On Location,** a shop where you can buy film and camera supplies, and **Beverly Hills Boulangerie,** the first of many food stops, this one serving light snacks. To the left is **Studio Gifts,** the **Fudge Shoppe,** and **Universal Studios Store.**

B Production Central This is the site of such popular attractions as the **Funtastic World of Hanna-Barbera** ride and **Alfred Hitchcock: The Art of Making Movies.** Kids will want to head straight for the **Nickelodeon Studios,** where they may have the opportunity to audition for a show, test games, or be part of a live studio audience.

Within the Production Central area:

Nickelodeon Studios Nickelodeon, reputedly the top children's network in the world, is based in this 90,000-square-foot facility with two 16,500-square-foot soundstages, each seating 250 people, and a three-story main building housing production control rooms and a rehearsal stage. Everything is behind glass walls, so visitors can see what's going on. Of particular interest is the "gak" kitchen, where the famous, gooey

Green Slime beloved of **Nickelodeon** fans is cooked (12,500 gallons annually). Visitors also get to see the **Slime Geyser** and to help "test" new games in the **Game Lab,** where one guest is chosen to be "slimed." A limited number of tickets are available each day for a live taping. Ask a **Nickelodeon Studios** attendant for details. ♦ Tours run from 10:30AM to 5:30PM and last about 45 minutes. 363.8586

The Funtastic World of Hanna-Barbera

The lines are long and slow, and you may wonder why you're wasting time waiting for cartoons . . . but once inside, you'll be glad you did. This is one of the best of the Central Florida simulator-type productions (your seat moves in concert with the action on the screen, but you don't actually go anywhere). The film starts with Bill Hanna and Joe Barbera talking about animation, and before you know it, the audience is part of the show. After a breathtaking movie, you'll have the opportunity to get your hands on some toys—making sound effects, creating voices, and playing the Flintstones' piano with your feet. There's a **Hanna-Barbera Store** on the way out.

Alfred Hitchcock: The Art of Making Movies

Universal produced 10 Alfred Hitchcock movies as well as his TV series. This three-part show begins with clips of Hitchcock movies on a giant screen in the **Tribute Theatre;** brace yourself for the clip from *The Birds.* The second stop is the **Psycho Sound Stage,** where a movie narrated by Tony Perkins reveals how the shower scene in *Psycho* was filmed using 78 camera angles. If you're with children under 13, you might want to skip these first two features, which can be pretty intense, and go straight to the third stop, where audience members are chosen to star in some of Hitchcock's thrillers on re-created sets. Exit via **The Bates Motel Gift Shop.**

Classic Monsters Cafe ★$$ Themed as a horror movie set, this counter-service restaurant features pizza and pasta dishes. They also have devilishly delicious desserts. Stroll around the restaurant and see life-size replicas of the spooky stars themselves, including Frankenstein and Wolf Man. The **Sci-Fi Room** features props from films such as *Abbott and Costello Go to Mars;* the **Crypt Room** displays sets from *Dracula.* ♦ American ♦ Daily lunch and dinner. 363.8769

"Hercules and Xena: Wizards of the Screen"

At this exciting interactive attraction (replacing "Murder, She Wrote" Mystery Theatre), the audience watches a video screen showing how the action-packed TV shows "Hercules: The Legendary Journeys" and "Xena: Warrior Princess" are produced. Then, amid state-of-the-art digital sound effects, actors playing the mythical heroes step onto the stage and select a member of the audience to fight shoulder to shoulder with them.

C New York The big attraction here is **Kongfrontation,** but the street sets are amazing, including **New York**'s **Little Italy** and **Sting Alley,** from Paul Newman's and Robert Redford's film *The Sting.* **Bull's Gym** and other shops are en route as you leave **Production Central** and head over to **Kongfrontation.**

Within the New York area:

The Blues Brothers in "Chicago Bound"

A musical production led by the mischievous duo who belt out the blues is performed on a small stage on the New York street set. Near **The Blues Brothers** is **Doc's Candy,** a sweets shop.

New York

Universal Studios CityWalk

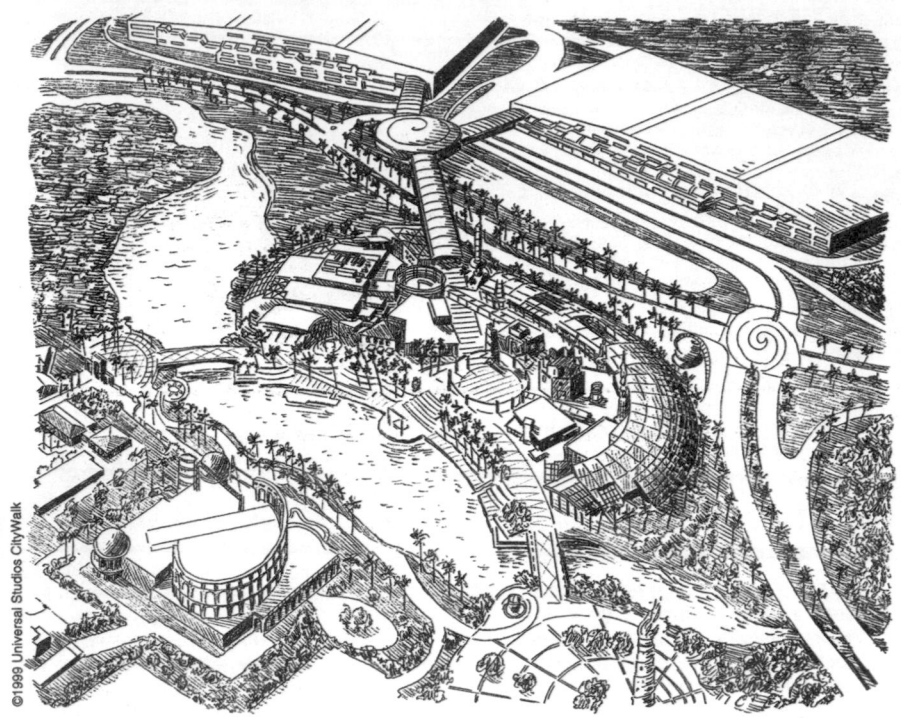

©1999 Universal Studios CityWalk

At the planned 30-acre multibillion-dollar entertainment complex called **Universal Studios CityWalk,** scheduled to open at press time, there will be something for everyone, with a collection of themed restaurants, nightclubs, movie houses, and specialty shops, including:

All New Hard Rock Cafe Orlando The world's largest **Hard Rock Cafe** features music, memorabilia, great food, and the world-famous T-shirts. The new cafe also includes the chain's first-ever dedicated live concert venue **(Hard Rock Live).** Capable of seating up to 2,200 people, with cutting-edge concerts every night, this place looks like the Colosseum in Rome.

Bob Marley—A Tribute to Freedom A one-of-a-kind celebration of music and culture, this tribute to the "King of Reggae Music" will be patterned after Marley's actual home and garden in Kingston, Jamaica, and will commemorate his international musical fame, providing a unique setting for fans to absorb not only his music, but also the Jamaican heritage, lyrical imagery, and essence that inspired it.

Universal Cineplex The 20-screen, 5,000-seat theater complex will offer a full day and evening of entertainment under one roof, with numerous eateries, cafes, and shops.

E! Entertainment Television Production Center The only affiliate studio of **E! Entertainment Television,** this production center will allow **Universal Studios**

CityWalk guests to watch production tapings and live celebrity interviews, as well as to offer their personal opinions on who's hot and who's not.

Emeril's of Orlando Straight from the bayous of Louisiana, this sophisticated, spirited culinary adventure, featuring the restaurant's famed Creole-based "kicky cuisine," is a cousin to the place in New Orleans created by master chef Emeril Lagasse. The new restaurant's focal point will be a bustling, open kitchen where guests can watch chefs design their gourmet creations.

NBA Restaurant The **National Basketball Association** and **Hard Rock Cafe** have teamed up to create this unique dining experience. **NBA** fans can catch a game and enjoy great food. The restaurant will offer exclusive **WNBA** and **NBA** programming and photographs.

NASCAR Cafe The **NASCAR**-themed eatery will feature rows of gleaming **NASCAR** Winston Cup Cars, a surround-sound video wall, electronic and multimedia games, memorabilia, and rare artifacts and collectibles from the world of **NASCAR.** A car racing–theme menu and decor—right down to the eating utensils and pit crew waitstaff—will contribute to the experience, along with a kids' racing arcade.

Pat O'Brien's A replica of New Orleans's favorite watering hole (home of the "Hurricane" drink), it will capture the tavern's Irish charm in the "Main" bar and a "Dueling Pianos" bar next door.

Motown Cafe The restaurant will feature photographs, life-size statues, and memorabilia from some of **Motown**'s most popular artists as well as home-style American and regional cuisines. Visitors will be able to experience the music and culture made famous by such giant hit makers as the **Temptations,** the **Four Tops,** the **Supremes,** the **Jackson Five,** and others who redefined popular music.

City Jazz Universal is teaming up with *Down Beat,* the Jazz Hall of Fame, and the **Thelonious Monk Institute of Jazz** to create this jazz center. It will be designed for live performances, special events, and education.

The Groove Although it may appear to be a dilapidated old theater, this electrifying dance club will really be on the cutting edge. The club will feature state-of-the-art lighting and visual effects,

along with customized audio systems to deliver today's hottest sounds.

Jimmy Buffet's Margaritaville Slip away to this island-style restaurant and enjoy a cheeseburger in paradise. Every corner will bring to life a different Jimmy Buffet classic.

At press time, admission to **Universal Studios CityWalk** had not been determined. There will be no fee to walk around the complex and a nominal fee for each club. Packages will also be available.

Finnegan's ★★$$ Stop in for a pint of Guinness and some surprisingly good Irish pub grub. American favorites, such as burgers and grilled chicken sandwiches, also are served. There's also live entertainment.
◆ Irish/American ◆ Daily lunch, dinner, and snacks

Kongfrontation In the back streets of the New York set is the **Roosevelt Island Tramway Station,** where visitors board the tram for this thrilling ride. Once aboard, passengers are informed that King Kong is menacing New York. You'll first spot him hanging from the Queensboro Bridge; next thing you know, he's grabbed your vehicle and raised it so close to his face that you can smell his banana breath. When he hurls the tram down, passengers experience 1.75 g's of force as they plunge 50 feet at 12 feet per second. The tram (saved by a single cable) then continues to Roosevelt Island, where a videotape of the passengers' reactions to the King's fling plays on an overhead screen. King Kong is said to be the largest computer animated figure ever constructed. Tipping the scale at 12,000 pounds, he stands 32 feet high and has a 54-foot arm span. His fur alone weighs 7,000 pounds. Near **Kongfrontation** is

Safari Outfitters Ltd, a store selling clothes that are more than appropriate for a jungle adventure and a photo opportunity with King Kong.

Twister This walk-through attraction (which replaces Ghostbusters Spooktacular) simulates the sights, sounds, and feel of a tornado. From just 20 feet away, visitors watch driving rains and winds culminating in a five-story cyclone that shatters windows and smashes trucks in its path, finally bursting into a massive funnel of fire. Be prepared to get a little wet. On your way back down Fifth Avenue toward the San Francisco/Amity section, you'll pass **Louie's Italian Restaurant** and **Space Station,** with arcade-type games of skill.

Kongfrontation

©1999 Universal Studios Escape

©1999 Universal Studios Escape

D San Francisco/Amity Two blockbuster rides, **Earthquake—The Big One** and **JAWS,** are in this area; the sets are a sleepy New England village and San Francisco's Fisherman's Wharf.

Within the San Francisco/Amity area:

Beetlejuice's Graveyard Revue The live, 15-minute dance revue with exciting special effects stars all your favorite monsters, including Dracula and Frankenstein, pounding out rock 'n' roll hits. The "ghoul of cool" Beetlejuice, of the **Universal Studios** movie, is master of ceremonies. Across the street from **Beetlejuice's Graveyard Revue** on the waterfront are **Shaiken's Souvenirs; Richter's Burger Co.;** and **Chez Alcatraz,** serving seafood and sourdough rolls.

The Lagoon This lake is used almost daily for shooting, rehearsing, or just trying out new stunts. The *Dynamite Nights Stuntacular* show, featuring stunt artists leaping 60 feet through a three-story wall of fire and performing other death-defying feats, takes place here. It's the best stunt show anywhere, but it's shown only once or twice daily, so check the park entertainment schedule. Particularly good vantage points are the rocks at **Central Park** and the **Battery Park Docks.**

Earthquake—The Big One Charlton Heston, star of the movie *Earthquake,* is the on-screen host of this attraction. Visitors first see how miniaturization, high-speed photography, matte painting, blue-screen technique, and stunts combine to create dazzling disasters. Then everyone is herded into a re-creation of an Oakland subway station and onto a subway car. The car goes under San Francisco Bay and is pulling up to the Embarcadero station in San Francisco when all hell breaks loose. The subway car shakes. Lights blink. Chunks of street fall from above. There's an oncoming subway train and a runaway propane tanker truck heading your way when suddenly a deluge of 60,000 gallons of water rushes down the subway stairs directly at your car! Even more amazing than the mock earthquake (which measures 8.3 on the Richter scale) is how

quickly everything on the set goes back into position before your eyes. Sit on the left side toward the front of the ride for the greatest visual impact. On the waterfront across the street from **Earthquake—The Big One** are **Salty's Sketches,** a portraiture artist, and **Lombard's Landing** (see below).

Lombard's Landing ★★$$ The largest restaurant in the park is set in a re-creation of San Francisco's Fisherman's Wharf on the lagoon. Specialties include Maine lobster, fish-and-chips, and the catch of the day. Steaks, pasta dishes, and sandwiches also are served. The adjacent **Pastry Shop** features cappuccino and a variety of sweet treats. Around the corner are **Quint's Nautical Treasures** and **Boardwalk Snacks,** featuring lemonade, ice cream, yogurt, and hot dogs. ◆ Seafood ◆ Daily lunch and dinner. Reservations recommended. 363.8000

©1999 Universal Studios Escape

JAWS The sharp-toothed shark from the famous movie is out to tear you to shreds. What starts out as a pleasant boat ride turns into a hunt-and-chase situation in which you are the prey of a giant white shark. Naturally, you win, but things get a little dicey for a while. Sit on the left toward the front of the boat if possible. You could get a little wet, but that's part of the fun.

Wild, Wild, Wild West Stunt Show The story line is more than a little corny, but audience members end up with more than a little respect for the acrobatics and stunts the actors perform. Good special effects have been enhancing western movies for years, and this show demonstrates some of the tricks of the trade.

Florida has 7,700 lakes that cover an area of 10 acres or more.

E **Expo Center** More blockbusters are found here: **Back to the Future . . . The Ride** and **E.T. Adventure,** plus **Barney.**

Within the Expo Center area:

Back to the Future . . . The Ride
Here's the attraction all other theme parks wish they had. The four-minute movie portion took two years to make and cost as much as a feature film, and the ride itself employs two specially designed domed theaters with two seven-story Omnimax screens. Christopher Lloyd, the star of *Back to the Future,* sends passengers on a mission to recover high-tech materials stolen by the bully Biff. After climbing into your DeLorean-style car, you blast into the past and zoom through time with the help of the screens, plus flight simulators and special effects. Your bumpy journey takes you through various time periods as the car pitches on hydraulic lifts some 12 feet above the ground. You really do get rocked and rolled (if you have neck problems, avoid this ride). When you get off, you may feel like you've been lifting weights because you've been gripping the restraining bar so tightly. Next to the ride are **Back to the Future . . . The Store** and the **International Food Bazaar,** where numerous monitors play old movies and TV shows. Listen carefully: The stars' voices have been dubbed so they're speaking the language represented by the cuisine—the TV shows are dubbed in Spanish at the Mexican food section, for example.

Animal Actors Stage Benji, Lassie, Mr. Ed, Babe, and the lovable St. Bernard Beethoven join about 50 other animals as they demonstrate what a well-trained animal actor can do. The critters, including skunks, birds, and an orangutan, dodge disasters and save humans in peril. The fast-moving performance is lots of fun. According to Universal, this is the largest assembly of TV animal actors in the world—what makes it especially nice is that most of the dogs and cats are from the pound.

E.T. Adventure Steven Spielberg, the theme park's creative consultant, had John Williams, who won the Academy Award for the *E.T.* score, compose original music for this ride. Spielberg then put together a new story—an *E.T.* sequel for those of you who were disappointed that a movie follow-up never materialized. The ride begins with Spielberg setting the scene: E.T.'s planet is dying, and unless you can get the little space alien back to his planet, it will turn into a wasteland. After walking through a perilous redwood forest, you hop aboard dirt bikes that climb into the sky (with E.T. in the basket on the front). Beneath you is a large city, made up of 250 cars, some 1,000 street lights, and 3,340 miniature city buildings. As you soar ever higher, there are 4,400 illuminated stars. You pedal past the moon through purple perfumed fog. Soon you are on E.T.'s planet, and he begins the work of saving it. Note: Young children love this ride but teens and adults may find it a bit sappy. At **E.T.'s Toy Closet & Photo Spot** you can buy intergalactic phones and E.T. jewelry, and have your photo taken with the adorable little guy.

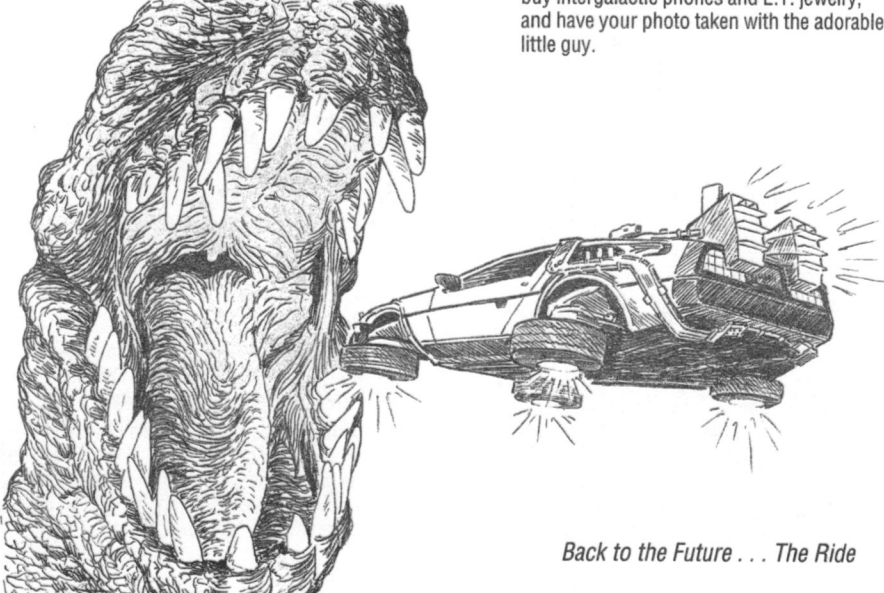

Back to the Future . . . The Ride

Islands of Adventure

©1999 Universal Studios Escape

Scheduled to open at press time, with Academy Award–winning producer and director Steven Spielberg serving as creative consultant, **Universal Studios Islands of Adventure**—the cornerstone of Universal's $2.5-billion expansion—will offer some of the most technologically advanced rides and attractions ever made. **Islands of Adventure** will also cater to the young, with two "lands" designed primarily for children, **Seuss Landing,** featuring characters from Dr. Seuss's world-famous children's books, and **Toon Lagoon,** with comical characters straight from the Sunday funnies. Thrill seekers will flock to the park's other three lands—**Marvel Super Hero Island, The Lost Continent,** and **Jurassic Park** (inspired by the motion picture of the same name).

Seuss Landing

This 10-acre whimsical land brings together characters from some of Dr. Seuss's most memorable books, including *Green Eggs and Ham* and *The Cat in the Hat.* The major draw here will be the **Caro-Seuss-el,** with rider-activated animated characters.

The Cat in the Hat: Ride Inside This ride will take you on a journey through the pages of Dr. Seuss's most famous book. Riding on a six-passenger "couch," you'll encounter whimsical characters such as The Cat in the Hat, Thing 1, Thing 2, and the goldfish who tries unsuccessfully to maintain order in the house.

One Fish, Two Fish, Red Fish, Blue Fish Soaring 15 feet in the air, you'll pilot a giant colored fish through myriad waterspouts and streams. If you listen closely to the instructions given by your fish, you can avoid getting wet. Three 18-foot-tall "squirt posts" will douse unsuspecting riders who don't follow along with the special rhyme.

Caro-Seuss-el This wacky carousel features seven different Seussian characters in what Universal claims will be "the most elaborate carousel ever built." Each of the ride's 54 mounts will be equipped with guest-activated interactive animation.

If I Ran the Zoo This totally interactive playland tells the story of Gerald McGrew and his quest to create a unique zoo filled with strange and unusual animals.

You will be able to wrangle flying water snakes or tickle the toes of a Seussian animal in one of three interactive areas.

Green Eggs and Ham Cafe Sidle up to the giant ham-shaped cafe and order real green eggs and ham. Of course, more traditional meals will be served as well.

Toon Lagoon

Upon entering **Toon Lagoon,** you'll be surrounded by more than 150 lifelike cartoon figures that just a few steps earlier, at the bridge, appeared to be only two-dimensional images. Floating around this animated universe you'll see characters from your favorite Sunday comics, including Popeye, Bullwinkle, Betty Boop, and many more. Attractions here will include **Dudley Do-Right's Ripsaw Falls** and **Popeye & Bluto's Bilge-Rat Barges.**

Dudley Do-Right's Ripsaw Falls You'll join Dudley Do-Right, from the popular 1960s cartoon "Rocky and Bullwinkle," as he sets out on a daring mission to rescue Nell from the evil Snidely Whiplash. You'll embark on a wild and wet adventure around a 400,000-gallon lagoon. Explosive fun awaits as you drop through the rooftop of a dynamite shack and the blast sends you rocketing 15 feet below water level. This will be the first flume ride to ever send guests plummeting below the water surface.

Popeye & Bluto's Bilge-Rat Barges This bumping, twisting, turning white-water raft ride is operated by Popeye's nemesis, Bluto. Before the ride ends, the raft and all 12 occupants will be squirted by water cannons aboard **Popeye's Boat,** spun into an **Octopus Grotto,** and whirled into a fully operational boat wash. Plan on getting completely soaked on this attraction.

Blondie's Deli Home of the Dagwood sandwich, named for the insatiable appetite of the comic-strip hero Dagwood Bumstead, this restaurant (Blondie is Dagwood's wife) will serve an abundance of stacked sandwiches that you purchase by the inch.

Marvel Super Hero Island

This attraction combines unprecedented technology with the familiar faces of popular comic book heroes and villains. You'll experience the gravity-defying inversions of **The Incredible Hulk Coaster,** a plummeting 200-foot drop aboard **Doctor Doom's Fearfall,** and a 3-D ride through the streets of New York with **The Adventures of Spider-Man.**

The Adventures of Spider-Man After a tour of the *Daily Bugle* newspaper, where Peter Parker (a.k.a. Spider-Man) works as a reporter, you realize that the Statue of Liberty has been nabbed by evil villains. You will be enlisted to help Spider-Man retrieve this national treasure and defeat the forces of evil. Hold on tight, because in the midst of the battle Doctor Octopus will zap you with an anti-gravity gun and the ride vehicle will plunge 400 feet into darkness.

The Incredible Hulk Coaster Like the superhero for which the attraction is named, the coaster's track will have a green glow. During the 2-minute adventure, your 32-passenger vehicle will encounter 7 rollovers, 2 subterranean enclosures, and a complete inversion that will leave you feeling weightless. This attraction gets off to a rip-roaring start: The coaster will rocket from zero to 40 mph in two seconds as it begins its initial climb.

Doctor Doom's Fearfall This is a very short experience, but one you will not soon forget. With your feet dangling over the edge of the seat, you'll plunge 200 feet straight down a giant steel tower at an unthinkable speed.

Lost Continent

This "land" seems to have magically appeared from the pages of Greek mythology. If you dare to proceed you'll find yourself in the midst of a medieval forest inhabited by fiery dragons and mythical gods. Climb aboard **Dueling Dragons** for a heart-stopping adventure or catch **The Eighth Voyage of Sinbad,** an entertaining stunt show.

Escape from the Lost City Here, you'll be thrust in the middle of a battle between Poseidon and his archenemy, Zeus. During the clash, more than 350,000 gallons of water and 200 fiery special effects, which explode into 25-foot fireballs, will excite the crowd.

Dueling Dragons One dragon breathes fire, the other ice, but both will thrill you as no other single roller coaster has. This ride features two intertwined tracks that whiz you over, under, and around each other as you travel through the trees of a medieval forest and over **Dragon Lake.** Both dragons will drop from a 125-foot common lift and will be capable of reaching speeds in excess of 55 mph. During one portion of the attraction, the two tracks and their passengers are separated by mere inches. Note: There will be a separate line for those who wish to sit in the very front seat.

The Eighth Voyage of Sinbad Sinbad strikes out once again on his endless search for enormous riches. As he has on previous journeys, he once again encounters life-threatening perils along the way. You'll be on the edge of your seat during this stunt show, which features six water explosions and 50 pyrotechnical effects. The theater seats 1,700 guests, so you'll want to arrive several minutes before show time.

Mythos Restaurant One of the better restaurants at the park, this was designed by world-renowned designer Jordan Mozer and will be nestled in a massive, dormant "volcano." As you feast on gourmet cuisine like pepper-painted salmon or pan-fried crab cakes with lobster sauce and basil, brilliant rainbows will shine over the restaurant's interior.

Jurassic Park

You'll come face-to-face with "living, breathing" dinosaurs as the theme park featured in the motion picture becomes a reality. This "land" will contain some of the most lifelike Audio-Animatronics ever created. Some dinosaurs blink their eyes or actually flinch when touched. Possibly the park's best ride— **Jurassic Park River Adventure**—is located in this "land." Other attractions include the **Discovery Center** and **Pteranodon Flyers.**

Jurassic Park River Adventure It's not a roller coaster, but this attraction will make your heart race. As you travel through the three-dimensional world of **Jurassic Park,** you'll quickly realize something has gone wrong. Suddenly, a five-story Tyrannosaurus rex emerges from the lush jungle. The chase is on. T-rex is an unrelenting hunter and gets within inches of your boat before you plunge 85 feet down one of the world's steepest water descents.

Pteranodon Flyers You'll get a bird's-eye view of **Jurassic Park** as you soar through the air on the backs of these gentle flying dinosaurs. The creatures will coast atop mountainous **Camp Jurassic,** overlooking the tropical landscaping that makes up the island.

Discovery Center Just as it does in the film, this area will house the skeletal remains of a massive T-rex and the laboratories where biochemists work to bring these prehistoric creatures back to life. You'll be able to watch as a seemingly real baby Raptor is hatched.

Dueling Dragons

MATT MORROW/NORTH MARKET STREET GRAPHICS ©1999 Universal Studios Escape

Terminator 2:3-D

MATT MORROW/NORTH MARKET STREET GRAPHICS ©1999 Universal Studios Escape

Fievel's Playland This brightly colored interactive play area is a great place for kids to work off energy. They can talk to Tiger the Cat, who is two stories high; climb a 30-foot spiderweb; or ride the rapids of a water slide.

A Day in the Park with Barney Opened in 1995, this major attraction is geared to preschoolers. TV's purple dinosaur, Barney, and his friends Baby Bop and BJ appear live daily, playing with their little fans and leading them in sing-alongs. There's also a playground that's a replica of the set from the TV show.

F Hollywood This section of the park, which formerly lacked a blockbuster attraction, is now home to Universal's mega magnet, **Terminator 2: 3-D,** an incredibly exciting sound-and-sight extravaganza sure to mesmerize thrill seekers of all ages (see below). Among the street sets in this part of the park is a re-creation of **Hollywood Boulevard.** From here, the state-of-the-art **Radio Broadcast Center** has hosted hundreds of radio stations from around the world; passersby can watch the broadcasts through large windows. Also on the boulevard are **Cafe La Bamba,** an indoor/outdoor cafe serving tacos, Mexican beer, and margaritas; **Mel's Drive-In,** from the movie *American Graffiti,* featuring diner dinners and a 1950s show; **The Dark Room,** a one-hour film developer; **It's a Wrap,** a hip Hollywood boutique; and **Schwab's Pharmacy,** a re-creation of the ice-cream parlor in which Lana Turner was discovered. Around the corner on **Rodeo Drive** is the **Brown Derby Hat Shop,** where *chapeaux* are sold in a reproduction of the landmark restaurant.

Within the Hollywood area:

AT&T at the Movies The technology of the next century is the star of this interactive film about movies past, present, and future.

The Gory Gruesome & Grotesque Horror Make-Up Show Despite the rating "PGGG-13" and the warning that this attraction might be too intense for children under 13, it's not really that gory, gruesome, or grotesque. All the stunts are explained and there are more laughs than gasps. Audience members learn how Michael Keaton became a ghost in the movie *Beetlejuice,* how David Naughton was transformed in *An American Werewolf in London,* and how Linda Blair became a "head-spinner" in *The Exorcist.* Next door is **Cyber Image,** which sells unique merchandise for *Terminator* fans.

Terminator 2: 3-D Featuring superstar Arnold Schwarzenegger and the original *Terminator 2* cast, this "virtual adventure" is the most elaborate and technologically advanced attraction at the theme park. For 12 minutes you're immersed in an action-packed drama with menacing robots and live-action stunt doubles. Be prepared for Schwarzenegger's 1,500-pound Harley to explode off the screen and roar into the theater's stage. It's a $60-million attraction, and worth every penny.

Lucy: A Tribute Review all your favorite "I Love Lucy" episodes and see some of the show's actual costumes and scripts as well as some of Lucille Ball's home movies. At times a dead ringer for the world's favorite comedic redhead appears.

Silver Screen Collectibles A large building is filled with costumes worn by stars, movie posters, scripts, and old letters, all for sale.

51 Holiday Inn Universal Studios $$ Across the street from the entrance to **Universal Studios Escape,** this 256-room hotel offers extra-large rooms with cable TV and a VCR. There's a restaurant and a pool. Other pluses: Kids 18 and under stay free and there's free transportation to **Universal Studios.** ♦ 5905 S Kirkman Rd (between I-4 and Major Blvd). 351.3333, 800/327.1364, 800/327.1364; fax 351.3577; www.holiday-inn.com ♿

52 Radisson Twin Towers Hotel and Convention Center $ Here's one hotel that keeps the light on for you (it's outlined in neon). At the entrance to **Universal Studios Escape,** the 760-room establishment has five restaurants and lounges, a 24-hour deli, 24-hour room service, a health club, a playground, and a small pool with a poolside bar. Guest rooms feature one king or two queen beds; 30 suites are available. There's a shuttle to **Universal Studios,** and a business center with computer hookups. ♦ 5780 Major Blvd (at S Kirkman Rd). 351.1000, 800/327.2110; fax 363.0106; www.go2orlando.com/sponsor/radisson ♿

53 Mystery Fun House/Star Base Omega One of Orlando's oldest attractions, the 15-room **Mystery Fun House** has something for everyone. It features a rolling barrel, a mirror maze, a topsy-turvy room, and a coward's bypass for those too old and blasé or too young and scared. Visitors enter the chambers through a secret door in the fireplace. The complex also has miniature golf and arcade games. The star attraction, however, is Star Base Omega, a laser tag game. ♦ Admission. Daily. 5767 Major Blvd (at Caravan Ct). 351.3355 ♿

54 Days Inn East of Universal Studios $ A good, basic motel, it has 262 rooms with in-room safes and TV sets, and separate pools for adults and children. The **Denny's** restaurant next door is open around the clock. ♦ 5827 Caravan Ct (just south of Major Blvd). 351.3800, 800/327.2111; fax 363.0907; www.daysinneuc.com ♿

55 Delta Orlando Resort $$ A fine choice for families, the sprawling, 800-room hotel at the main entrance to **Universal Studios Escape** occupies 25 acres made attractive with tropical landscaping. Facilities include **Mango's,** a Key West–style restaurant; the **Bistro Boulevard; Studio 70** dance club; two tennis courts; and three heated outdoor pools. **Wally's Kids Club** will look after your little ones if you need a break. There's a free shuttle to **Universal Studios** and nearby shopping spots. ♦ 5715 Major Blvd (between Caravan Ct and Orlando-Vineland Rd). 351.3340, 800/327.8590 in FL, 800/634.4763; fax 345.2872; http://intpro.com/orlando/hotels/delta

Bests

Glenda E. Hood
Mayor, City of Orlando

Lake Eola Park—taking a swan boat ride and attending the Orlando Shakespeare Festival performance.

Orlando Museum of Art—viewing the permanent collection and exhibits.

Church Street Station—taking visitors to downtown's popular historical entertainment destination.

Orlando Arena—watching the **Orlando Magic** play basketball.

Farmers Market—buying fresh produce and plants on Saturday.

City Hall—visiting the art gallery and city store on the ground floor.

Citrus Bowl—watching the **University of Central Florida's** football games.

Dexter's of Thornton Park—enjoying a light bite.

The Courtyard at Lake Lucerne—attending a wedding ceremony at this charming bed-and-breakfast establishment.

Celebration in the Park—enjoying the arts and crafts festival at **Lake Eola** in early November.

Horse-drawn carriage ride—riding through our downtown neighborhood on a beautiful night.

Greg Dawson
Columnist, *Orlando Sentinel*

An airboat ride on the gator-infested **St. Johns River** with a good-ol'-boy guide.

The world's largest collection of Tiffany stained-glass art at the **Charles Hosmer Morse Museum of American Art** in **Winter Park.**

Ron Jon Surf Shop in **Cocoa Beach**—an open-all-night neon Taj Mahal of the hip and the tacky.

A bag of boiled peanuts, available at better roadside stands and convenience stores.

Visiting the **Harry P. Leu Gardens.** A breathtaking variety of plants, flowers, and beautiful landscaping awaits you in this oasis just minutes from downtown Orlando.

The **Scenic Boat Tour** in Winter Park sails past fabulous lakeside mansions and down narrow canals shadowed by monstrous flora.

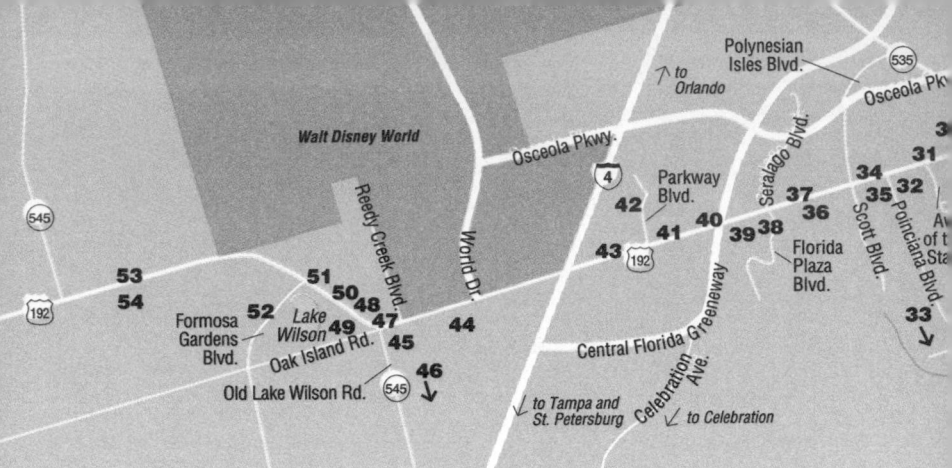

Kissimmee/Highway 192

Three distinct periods characterize the history of Kissimmee (pronounced Kuh-*sim*-ee) and Highway 192, which today form an affordable and busy tourist center convenient to **Walt Disney World**. The region's story begins in the mid-1830s, when a Seminole Indian Chief, Osceola, and his followers arrived in the **Lake Tohopekaliga** area. But by 1837, the chief had already led his people farther south, near **Lake Okeechobee**, where he was reportedly captured by US general Joseph M. Hernandez while standing under a flag of truce. The chief was sent to Fort Moultrie in Charleston, South Carolina, where he died of malaria a year later.

The second phase of the area's known history began in 1881, when Hamilton Disston, a Philadelphia businessman, purchased four million acres from Florida's bankrupt Internal Improvement Fund for 25 cents an acre. Part of the land became **Allendale**, a trading post named after pioneer Major J. H. Allen. It was later called Kissimmee, a Caloosa Indian word meaning "heaven's place," and became a minor transportation hub thanks to **Lake Toho** and a rail line running east to the **St. Johns River**.

Ninety years later, **Walt Disney World** opened and the town started spreading northwest toward US Highway 192. Tourist attractions, affordable lodging, and restaurants soon sprouted along the highway. Today, Kissimmee and neighboring **St. Cloud** are the two largest cities in **Osceola County**, although their combined population is only 42,500. But the new town of **Celebration**, developed by Disney on Highway 192 just east of **Interstate 4**, is projected to add 20,000 residents to the area over the next two decades. The town's charming shopping district already is a new draw for tourists. While the Kissimmee area is best known as a major gateway to **Walt Disney World**, it's also a major cattle producer, with weekly cattle auctions and regularly scheduled rodeos featuring local working cowboys.

Highway 192, also known as **Irlo Bronson Memorial Highway**, **Vine Street**, and **Spacecoast Parkway**, stretches from the heart of downtown Kissimmee past the main **Walt Disney World** entrance. Divided into east and west sections where it intersects with **Highway 92**, it is a hodgepodge of chain hotels, smaller motels, and a variety of minor attractions. New "guide markers" are part of a beautification project, and they help locate hotels, restaurants, or entertainment locations along both sides of Highway 192. The markers are approximately one mile apart, and many businesses refer to the markers when giving directions. Many of the hotels closest to **Walt Disney World** incorporate the term "main gate" into their name to let travelers know

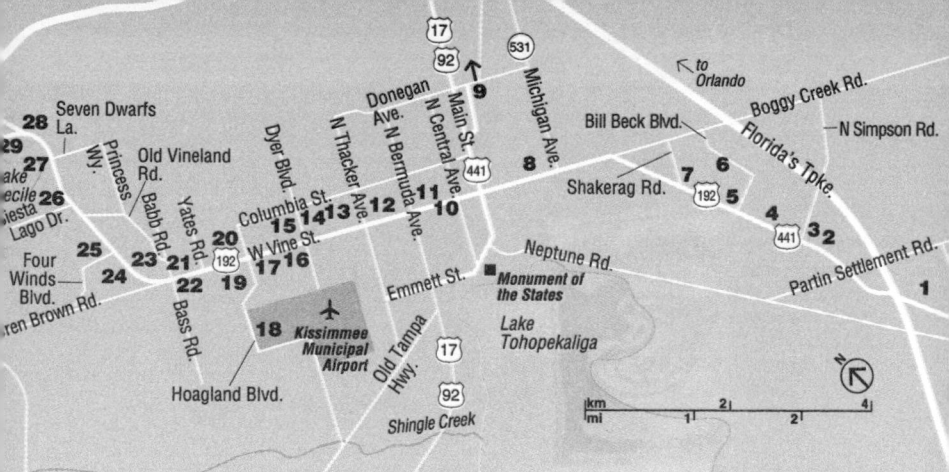

they are about as close as you can get to Mickey Mouse without actually being on Disney property. Hotels often cater to families—some provide free shuttle service to the park (saving parking fees) and free meals for youngsters accompanied by parents.

It's possible to find nice motel rooms along Highway 192 for $40 a night—even less in slow seasons (from the end of April to the beginning of June and from mid-August to the end of September). But to be on the safe side, ask to see a room before you pay for it. If you don't like it, you're sure to find something better, since there are more than 35,000 accommodations in the area. Those seeking a spacious apartmentlike setting as opposed to a no-frills hotel room will find plenty of condominiums and villas available for rent. Call **Guest Services** at the **Kissimmee–St. Cloud Convention & Visitors Bureau** (800/327.9159) for an accommodations directory and the **Central Reservation Line** (800/333.KISS) to book a room.

Although **Walt Disney World** is the main tourist draw, there are other attractions in the Kissimmee/Highway 192 area as well—children's petting farms, tourist reptile exhibits, and amusement areas offering go-karts, bumper boats, paintball, and similar rides and games.

To escape the area's commercial aspects and enjoy some of the great Central Florida outdoors, stay near one of the many lakes in the Kissimmee–St. Cloud area. This is one of the best places in the country for largemouth bass fishing (see "Where the Bass Are" on page 61), and nature lovers can rent a canoe or airboat for some leisurely lake cruising.

Annual events in the area include the Silver Spurs Rodeo in February and October, the Kissimmee Bluegrass Festival in March, the Osceola Art Festival on the shores of Lake Tohopekaliga in September, and the Christmas Boat Parade in December.

Kissimmee is a convenient and economical place to stay while visiting the world's most popular tourist destination. As the local visitors' bureau slogan states, "Location is our biggest attraction."

Area code 407 unless otherwise noted.

1 Osceola Flea & Farmer's Market Open weekends only, this market is a fun place to get a taste of Florida produce (though the vendors also truck in such seasonal produce as Georgia peaches). You'll find local arts and crafts, breads, candies, and even a few tacky souvenirs on display in the 900 booths. ♦ F-Su 8AM-5PM. 2801 E Hwy 192 (at Simmons Rd). 846.2811 &

2 Howard Johnson Kissimmee Lodge $ A quick stop off the Florida's Turnpike, this 200-room hotel has a pool, tennis court, laundry facilities, and, of course, a **HoJo**

restaurant that opens at 7AM for breakfast. The hotel provides a free shuttle to area attractions. ◆ 2323 E Hwy 192 (between Partin Settlement and S Simpson Rds). 846.4900; www.hojo.com ♿

3 Best Western Kissimmee $ This 282-room motel has two swimming pools, a restaurant, a lounge, free in-room movies, and free shuttle service to **Walt Disney World**. ◆ 2261 E Hwy 192 (between Partin Settlement and S Simpson Rds). 846.2221, 800/944.0062; fax 846.1095; bwestern@kissimmee.com; www.orlandolodging.com ♿

4 Days Inn Kissimmee East $ This small, moderately priced 122-room motel has a pool and a laundry room. Some units are efficiencies. There's a restaurant on the premises and a free shuttle service to attractions. ◆ 2095 E Hwy 192 (between S Simpson Rd and Bill Beck Blvd). 846.7136, 800/352.2192; fax 846.7805; www.daysinn.com ♿

4 Stadium Inn $ The 113 rooms here sleep up to four people, and each has a dining area and a fully equipped kitchen. (There's a **Waffle Inn** on the premises if you'd rather not cook.) Some rooms connect to make two-room suites. The pool isn't large, but there is a Jacuzzi. The motel is near **Osceola County Stadium**, where the **Houston Astros** hold spring training. ◆ 2039 E Hwy 192 (between S Simpson Rd and Bill Beck Blvd). 846.7814, 800/221.2222; fax 846.1863

Kissimmee St. Cloud
CONVENTION & VISITORS BUREAU

5 Kissimmee–St. Cloud Convention & Visitors Bureau Stop here for brochures on area amusements, discounts on local attractions, and assistance in finding accommodations. The bureau offers a toll-free central reservations system (800/333.5477), which operates from 7AM to 2AM daily. ◆ Daily. 1925 E Hwy 192 (at Bill Beck Blvd). 847.5000, 800/327.9159; fax 847.0878

6 Osceola County Stadium The **Houston Astros** conduct spring training here. When the major league team moves out in mid-April, the complex is taken over by the **Kissimmee Cobras**, a single-A minor league team. The **Senior Little League World Series** (for 14- and 15-year-olds) is held here in August. ◆ 1000 Bill Beck Blvd (between E Hwy 192 and Boggy Creek Rd). 933.5400

There are more than 125 golf courses and more than 800 tennis courts in greater Orlando.

7 Silver Spurs Arena Kissimmee is cattle country, and this is the place to see real cowboys in action. Professional rodeos take place here several times each year. The first, usually held the last weekend of February, concludes the weeklong Kissimmee Valley Livestock Show and Osceola County Fair at the adjoining **Agricultural Center**. The Silver Spurs Rodeo takes place in February and October. Members of the **Professional Rodeo Cowboys Association** participate in bareback and saddle riding, calf roping, and steer wrestling, and winners walk off with big money. The arena is also the site of the annual Kissimmee Bluegrass Festival in the spring. ◆ Admission. The box office (67.RODEO) opens two months before each rodeo; at other times call the Kissimmee–St. Cloud Convention & Visitors Bureau (847.5000, 800/327.9159; fax 847.0878). 1875 E Hwy 192 (at Shakerag Rd)

8 Flamingo Inn $ This two-story, 40-room pink stucco motel is clean, well-appointed, and has some efficiency units but no restaurant. There's a pool and the rooms are equipped with HBO, refrigerators, and microwave ovens. ◆ 801 E Hwy 192 (between Damon and Kelley Aves). 846.1935, 800/780.7617; fax 846.7225 ♿

9 Tupperware International Headquarters Visitors may no longer tour the home of the famous Tupperware plastic food containers, but the 2,000-seat theater still draws well-known pop artists, rock and country bands, and other performing groups. There's also a convention center. For convention center information call 847.1800, in Orlando 826.4475. For theater box-office information call 847.1802, 826.4450 in Orlando. ◆ Hwy 441 (between Osceola Pkwy and Central Florida Greeneway)

9 Gatorland A Florida BD (Before Disney) attraction, it's a little hokey, but the exhibits are interesting and educational—and the price is right. Visitors enter through a 20-foot-high set of gaping gator jaws, a landmark in Central Florida since 1962 (though the park has been around since 1949). The jaws lead to a boardwalk bridge spanning a seven-acre lake filled with an enormous number of reptiles of all sizes. You can buy fish to feed the alligators, but they often ignore the offerings because they're so well fed. Gators of all ages can be observed at the park. This is an active alligator farm and research center that works closely with the **University of Florida**. Besides the famous gator jaws, the park is best known for its three entertaining

and educational shows, running about 15 minutes each and performed several times daily. *Gator Wrestlin' Cracker-Style* is a demonstration of how Florida cowboys used to go one-on-one with the beasts. The *Snakes of Florida* show features poisonous and nonpoisonous snakes native to Florida. For the *Gator Jumparoo,* raw chicken halves are suspended from a cable to entice alligators to jump out of the water and snatch them. A recently opened exhibit, "Jungle Crocs of the World," enables visitors to walk through a jungle setting and come face-to-face with, among others, the Australian saltwater crocodile, one of the world's largest and most deadly; American crocodiles; Nile crocodiles; and Cuban crocodiles, the rarest in the world.Visitors board the **Gatorland Express** train (which runs continuously) for a narrated tour of the 50-acre park. On the other side of the lake are covered walkways that lead past monkeys, pygmy goats, Barbados sheep, deer, bears, and wild birds. At the far end of the park is a 2,000-footlong walkway through a cypress swamp that gives visitors an idea of what the area must have been like before civilization arrived. Also on the premises are an 800-seat, open-air gator-wrestling stadium and a 10-acre alligator breeding marsh with a boardwalk and three-level observation tower. From the tower you can see as many as 130 gators guarding their nests and thousands of bird's nests and seven varieties of Florida wading birds. Alligator accessories (belts, handbags, boots) are sold at the gift shop and the snack bar offers deep-fried gator nuggets and smoked gator ribs. ♦ Admission. Daily. 14501 S Orange Blossom Tr (between Osceola Pkwy and Central Florida Greeneway). 855.5496, 800/393.JAWS ♿

10 Lambert Inn $ If you're looking for a clean bed, cable TV, and a cool pool, this two-story, 44-room motel will fill the bill. There's no restaurant. ♦ 410 W Hwy 192 (between N Central and N Orlando Aves). 846.2015; fax 846.8876

11 Walgreen Drug Store When you have an upset stomach, it's nice to know this huge drugstore never closes. ♦ Daily 24 hours. 1003 W Hwy 192 (between N Central and N Bermuda Aves). 847.4222, prescription service 847.5252

12 Super 8 $ This comfortable 83-room motel also offers a few two-bedroom apartments with full kitchens, two swimming pools, a laundry facility, and a guest services desk to answer questions about area attractions. There's free coffee and doughnuts every morning. ♦ 1815 W Vine St (at Magnolia Dr). 847.6121, 800/325.4348

13 Holiday Inn Kissimmee Downtown $ Local owners keep loyal fans coming back to this sprawling, 200-room motel, complete with two big swimming pools, a gameroom, a Jacuzzi, and a tennis court. Children under 18 stay free with their parents. ♦ 2009 W Vine St (at N Thacker Ave). 846.2713, 800/624.5905; fax 846.8695; www.holiday-inn.com ♿

Within the Holiday Inn Kissimmee Downtown:

Black Angus Restaurant $$ The specialties here are steaks and seafood, but it's also a good place to start the day before beginning your assault on nearby theme parks. An all-you-can-eat breakfast buffet is available from 8AM to noon. There's a children's menu too. ♦ American ♦ Daily breakfast, lunch, and dinner. 846.7117

13 LaSuite Kissimmee Downtown $ A real steal for the price, this 131-room motel is clean, efficiently run, and well located. It also has all the facilities and services of the larger, higher-priced motels, including a lounge, pool, guest services, and a free shuttle to **Walt Disney World**. There's a **Denny's** restaurant next door. ♦ 2407 W Hwy 192 (between N Thacker Ave and Orange Blvd). 933.2400, 800/722.7462; fax 933.1474 ♿

Where the Bass Are

Central Florida lakes and the **St. Johns River** offer some of the finest trophy largemouth bass fishing in the country. Plan your fishing trip for early or late in the day; on long, hot summer days, early mornings almost always see more action. The best time to take a big lunker (eight pounds and over) is in spring, when the females are spawning. If you aren't familiar with Florida bass fishing techniques, you might want to hire a guide in the Kissimmee area to show you the ropes. Florida lakes tend to be shallow, so deep-water techniques simply do not work here. To locate a guide, contact the **Kissimmee–St. Cloud Convention & Visitors Bureau** (800/327.9159).

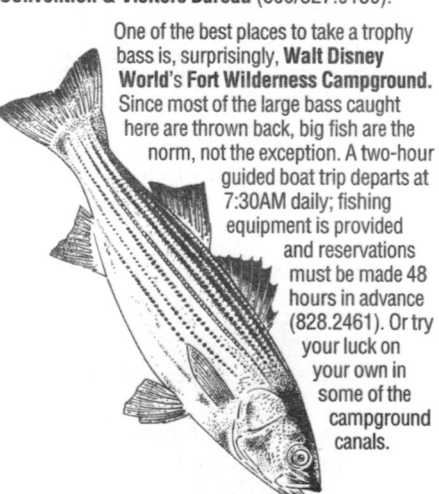

One of the best places to take a trophy bass is, surprisingly, **Walt Disney World**'s **Fort Wilderness Campground**. Since most of the large bass caught here are thrown back, big fish are the norm, not the exception. A two-hour guided boat trip departs at 7:30AM daily; fishing equipment is provided and reservations must be made 48 hours in advance (828.2461). Or try your luck on your own in some of the campground canals.

A Step Back in Time

Century-old **Silver Springs** may have been upstaged by **Walt Disney World**, but for natural beauty it hasn't been outclassed. The park's most famous attraction is the **Silver River**, home to 14 fast-flowing springs. Some Tarzan movies were filmed here, as was Lloyd Bridges's "Sea Hunt" TV series. The water is so clear that you can often see more than 80 feet down. The **Jungle Cruise** water safari takes you through an area stocked with exotic animals, including giraffes, zebras, and antelopes. The **Lost River Voyage** is a 30-minute tour aboard a glass-bottomed boat. For close-up looks at deer, wild boar, alligators, and monkeys in the park's interior, take the

Jeep Safari. The park also has the world's largest exhibit of bears, a car museum, a children's play area, a petting zoo, and gift shops. **Silver Springs** is located on Route 40 one mile east of Ocala, on the edge of Ocala National Forest (352/236.2121, 800/274.7458).

THE NEW SILVER SPRINGS It's Alive!

14 Outback Steakhouse ★★$$ The Australian-theme restaurant chain is winning many fans for its wonderful steaks (rib-eye, porterhouse, New York strip, or tenderloin) and its savory side dishes. House specialties include "bloomin' onions" (onions fried just right) and Aussie cheese (homemade fries topped with monterey jack cheese and bacon bits). Pasta dishes are also available. The wait can get long on weekends, but patrons pass the time in a comfortable lounge with a full bar. Meals also are served in the lounge, which is much more lively than the dining room. ♦ American ♦ Daily dinner. 3109 W Hwy 192 (between Orange and Dyer Blvds). 931.0033

15 Tony Roma's $$ If you're looking for a big slab of baby back ribs, this is the place. One of a nationwide chain, it offers standard barbecue dishes in a comfortable, publike setting. ♦ American ♦ Daily lunch and dinner. 3415 W Hwy 192 (between Dyer and Armstrong Blvds). 870.9299

15 Fun 'n Wheels A small family attraction, it has go-karts, bumper boats, a water slide, and video and arcade games. ♦ Nominal fee for each ride. M-F 6-11PM; Sa-Su 10AM-11PM (extended hours in the summer). 3711 W Hwy 192 (between Dyer and Armstrong Blvds). 870.2222. Also at: 6739 Sand Lake Rd (between Canada Ave and International Dr), Orlando. 351.5651

FOX AND HOUNDS

16 Fox and Hounds Pub ★$ Ready for a black-and-tan? If you're a fan of imported beer, you know that's a pale ale, such as Bass,

topped with Guinness stout. It's just the ticket for mellowing out after a hard day of waiting in line at theme parks. Traditional pub grub, such as a ploughman's plate (cheese, bread, pickle, and salad) or steak-and-kidney pie, is served. Look for the red British phone booth out front. ♦ Pub ♦ Daily lunch and dinner. 3514 W Hwy 192 (between Dyer and Armstrong Blvds). 847.9927

17 Four Points Sheraton $$ One of the nicer places on this tourist strip, this 225-suite lodging offers a pool with a nicely landscaped deck and a Jacuzzi, free continental breakfast, a lounge, and a gameroom. Children under 12 stay free. There's no restaurant, but there is a small deli. ♦ 4018 W Hwy 192 (between Armstrong Blvd and Airport Rd). 870.2000, 800/228.5150; fax 870.2010 ♿

18 Flying Tigers Warbird Restoration Museum A World War II aircraft restoration facility has been turned into a terrific museum filled with decals, models, and other World War II memorabilia, most of which is for sale. You can tour a huge hangar and field where more than a dozen planes are being restored. The whole setup provides a refreshing contrast to the nearby high-tech attractions: There are no neon signs, no buttons to push, and the refreshment stand consists of a soft-drink machine, a box filled with candy, and (maybe) coffee brewing on a card table in the corner; it's like dropping in on a neighbor who's tinkering in the backyard.

A small, hand-painted sign directs visitors from the unpaved parking lot to the entrance through a gate. Once inside, it's best to go straight to the barrackslike building and sign up for the tour, though there's no charge to just wander around. Mechanics always seem willing to answer questions. Among the planes displayed are a 1941 Ryan PT22 Trainer; two Boeing B-17 Flying Fortresses; and two North American B-25J Mitchells, a medium-size bomber used on the Doolittle

Raid on Tokyo in 1942. Planes take off regularly on test flights or for the fun of it, but there is no set schedule at "Bombertown, USA," as the museum is sometimes called. Finding the museum is tricky; Hoagland Boulevard is also known as Airport Road south of Highway 192. ◆ Fee for a guided tour. Daily. 231 Hoagland Blvd (south of W Hwy 192). 933.1942

19 Days Inn Downtown $ Another good value with a pool, the 226-room motel features efficiency units with kitchenettes. There's no restaurant. ◆ 4104 W Hwy 192 (at Airport Rd). 846.4714, 800/647.0010; fax 932.2699; www.daysinn.com ௸

19 Airboat Rentals U-Drive For an unusual Central Florida experience, pilot your own boat through miles of unspoiled Florida wilderness. You can rent a canoe, electric boat, or airboat (airboats by the hour; canoes and electric boats by the hour or all day) for an adventure on Shingle Creek, which meanders through a large cypress swamp. Alligators, blue herons, otters, and other Florida wildlife have been spotted. ◆ Admission. Daily. 4266 W Hwy 192 (between Airport and Bass Rds). 847.3672; fax 847.3141

20 Tropicana Motel $ An economical choice, this 54-room motel is quite suitable if you're going to be out all day and just want a place with a clean bed, a laundry room, and a pool. There's no on-site restaurant, but many are in the area and free coffee is always available. ◆ 4131 W Hwy 192 (between Hoagland Blvd and Yates Rd). 847.4707, 800/333.6044; fax 847.0980 ௸

21 192 Flea Market In four bright-blue buildings under big oak trees, more than 400 vendors sell everything from Nintendo games to athletic gear to Florida souvenirs. There's also a food court. ◆ Daily. 4301 W Hwy 192 (at Yates Rd). 396.4555

21 EconoLodge Maingate East $ Since it's set back from the tourist hotel strip, this 173-room motel offers peace and quiet. Ask for a room in the rear by the large, heated pool for a taste of tranquillity at last. The property has a children's pool, a video gameroom, shuffleboard and volleyball courts, and a horseshoe-pitching area. Another smart touch: a do-it-yourself laundry. There's no restaurant. ◆ 4311 W Hwy 192 (between Yates and Old Vineland Rds). 396.2000, 800/365.6935; fax 239.2636; www.econolodge.com ௸

22 Pirate's Island Adventure Golf Offering two wildly landscaped, 18-hole forays among waterfalls, caves, and streams, this is one of the area's many themed miniature golf courses. ◆ Admission. Daily. 4330 W Hwy 192 (between Airport and Bass Rds). 396.4660

23 River Adventure Golf With all its bridges, ponds, streams, and waterfalls, this miniature golf course seems like a small version of the real thing. Breaks in the greens make it particularly challenging. ◆ Admission. Daily 9AM-11PM. 4535 W Hwy 192 (between Yates Rd and Four Winds Blvd). 396.4666 ௸

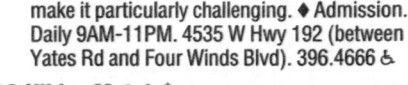

23 Viking Motel $ You can't miss its turreted tower and castlelike appearance. A family-owned and -operated establishment, it has 49 rooms (some efficiencies), all facing the parking lot. There's a little Viking playhouse for kids, a miniature golf course, a pool, and an area for outdoor grilling, but no restaurant. ◆ 4539 W Hwy 192 (between Yates Rd and Four Winds Blvd). 396.8860; fax 396.2088 ௸

23 Ramada Inn $ The 114 rooms at this motel are tropically decorated. Each has two extra-long double beds and HBO; some have kitchenettes. Also on-site are a restaurant, a swimming pool, a playground, and a laundry. ◆ 4559 W Hwy 192 (between Yates Rd and Four Winds blvd). 396.1212, 800/544.5712; fax 396.7926; www.disneyramada.com ௸

24 Medieval Times Dinner, Tournament & Living Museum Considering everything else you see on Highway 192, this replica of an 11th-century European castle doesn't seem out of place. As you enter the castle across a drawbridge, you're given a colorful cardboard crown—to get into the spirit of things. On display in the **Hall of Arms** are authentic shields, a 350-year-old carved oak bench, and several suits of armor. **Medieval Times** features jousting knights and other tournaments as well as a falconry show. Guests feast on a tasty four-course meal consisting of an appetizer, vegetable soup, roasted chicken, spareribs, herb-roasted potatoes, and dessert. And you eat just as they did in the olden days—with your fingers! Beer, wine, and soft drinks are included in the dinner tab (there's also a cash bar). Naturally, everyone is in costume, including the serfs and serving wenches. This is one of the best of Central Florida's dinner shows. Before and after the show, guests can tour the museum, a re-created village of the Middle Ages. Blacksmiths, weavers, carpenters, architects, glassblowers, potters, coppersmiths, and enamelists demonstrate their crafts throughout the village, and visitors also can tour a medieval kitchen, a wine cellar, and a dungeon complete with instruments of torture, including an interrogation chair covered with iron spikes. There's also a gift shop. ✦ Admission for dinner show, village, and museum. Daily; show times vary according to the season. 4510 W Hwy 192 (between Oren Brown Rd and Four Winds Blvd). 396.1518, 800/229.8300

24 Gator Motel $ The two-story motel next to **Jungleland** provides basic and clean accommodations, with a pool out front and 38 rooms equipped with two double beds, cable TV, and in-room refrigerators. There's no restaurant, but free coffee is always available. ✦ 4576 W Hwy 192 (between Oren Brown Rd and Four Winds Blvd). 396.0127, 800/254.2867; fax 396.6262 ♿

24 Jungleland Zoo A big alligator statue sits in the parking lot, but don't confuse this attraction with **Gatorland** (see page 60). Walk through the gift shop to buy admission tickets. The petting zoo is to the right as you enter, but save it for the end unless you want to smell like a farm throughout your visit. There are hundreds of animals in the zoo, which opened in 1977 as a refuge for abused, injured, and unwanted animals. Among the more exotic are Vietnamese pot-bellied pigs, and endangered species such as Bengal tigers. And, of course, there are plenty of gators. ✦ Admission. Daily. 4580 W Hwy 192 (between Oren Brown Rd and Four Winds Blvd). 396.1012 ♿

25 Casa Rosa Inn $ Popular with families, this small, pink Mediterranean-style motel has a small pool and 56 rooms, including suites, efficiencies, and units with adjoining doors. There's free coffee, but no restaurant. ✦ 4600 W Hwy 192 (at Four Winds Blvd). 396.2020, 800/432.0665; fax 396.6113; www.hotel4you.com ♿

25 Gemini Motel $ There are 85 rooms, including two efficiencies, here. A restaurant is next door, and free doughnuts and coffee are offered on the premises. ✦ 4624 W Hwy 192 (between Four Winds Blvd and Siesta Lago Dr). 396.2151; fax 396.7418 ♿

26 The Haunted Mansion This interactive horror-house adventure includes a museum with one of the world's largest collections of Halloween antiques and memorabilia. On view are porcelain collectibles, metallic and brass items from the turn of the century, tin toys, candy containers from the 1950s through the 1970s, and thousands of science fiction and horror figurines. In addition, there is an expanded arcade area and a 2,500-square-foot costume shop. ✦ Admission. Daily noon–11PM. 4710 W Hwy 192 (between Siesta Lago and Lake Cecile Drs). 396.6661 ♿

·ₒCAPONE'S

27 Capone's Dinner and Show $$ The Italian food is plentiful but just average; the show is lively. Guests sit in an old-fashioned ice-cream parlor that turns out to be Al Capone's hideout circa 1931. Handsome mobsters and their beautiful molls put on a song-and-dance revue with comic touches. ✦ Italian ✦ Daily dinner. Reservations recommended. 4740 W Hwy 192 (between Lake Cecile and Lawton Drs). 397.2378, 800/220.8428 ♿

28 Congo River Golf & Exploration Co. With so many miniature golf courses in the area, all with mountains, waterfalls, and caves, new gimmicks are rare. But this one features an exploration game in which clues on the scorecard lead players to six treasures on the course. Collect them all and win a prize. ✦ Admission. Daily. 4777 W Hwy 192 (between Seven Dwarfs La and Rte 535). 396.6900. Also at: 6312 International Dr (between Universal and Carrier Drs), Orlando. 352.0042

28 Orlando Maingate DoubleTree Guest Suites $$ A cut above the competition, this pretty, tile-roofed hotel has 150 spacious one-, two-, and three-bedroom villas, each with a family-size living and dining area, a fully equipped kitchen, and two color TVs with cable. A convenience store, a restaurant, and air-conditioned racquetball courts are on the property. It's a good value for the money. ✦ 4787 W Hwy 192 (between Seven Dwarfs La and Rte 535). 397.0555, 800/292.9765; fax 397.0553; www.doubletreehotels.com

29 Best Western on Lake Cecile $$ The 159 rooms in this sprawling complex are spacious and suitable for families, with queen-size beds and free HBO. There's a nice pool, and complimentary continental breakfast is served, but there's no restaurant. ✦ 4786 W Hwy 192 (between Lake Cecile and Lawton Drs). 396.2056, 800/468.3027; fax 396.2909; www.bestwesternhotelfl.com ♿

30 Golden Link Motel $ The two-story, 84-room motel is on Lake Cecile and has a fishing pier and a pool (but no restaurant). The rooms are clean, with two double beds and in-room safes, as well as satellite TV. You can rent jet skis or water-ski on the lake. ✦ 4914 W Hwy 192 (between Lake Cecile and Lawton Drs). 396.0555, 800/654.3957; fax 396.6531 ♿

30 Quality Inn Lake Cecile $ This futuristic-looking pink-and-turquoise 222-room motel has some nice touches: a VCR and video library in every room, free HBO, and balconies. Ask for a room overlooking the lake. The pool in back is beside Lake Cecile, where there's a private beach and jet-ski and paddleboat rentals. There's no restaurant, but a complimentary continental breakfast buffet is set up daily. ◆ 4944 W Hwy 192 (between Lawton and Pine Haven Drs). 396.4455, 800/864.4855; fax 396.4182; www.thhotels.com &

31 Magic Castle $ A well-run, three-story motel, it has 107 rooms with two double beds and cable TV. Complimentary continental breakfast is included in the rate, but there's no restaurant. ◆ 5055 W Hwy 192 (at Hart Ave). 396.2212, 800/446.5669; fax 396.0253; www.magicorlando.com

32 Ramada Fountain Park Resort $ Well managed and with an exceptionally friendly and helpful staff, this hotel boasts 400 oversize rooms, a heated pool with saunas and a hot tub, a lighted tennis court, a restaurant, a lounge, and lakeside picnic grounds and paddleboats. There's also a nine-hole putting green, shuffleboard courts, and a playground. Transportation to Disney parks is provided. ◆ 5150 W Hwy 192 (at Poinciana Blvd). 396.1111, 800/327.9179; fax 396.1607; www.ramadaeastgate.com

33 Green Meadows Petting Farm Families who want to take a break from long lines at the theme parks or just spend time outdoors communing with all kinds of animals will enjoy this shady setting off the beaten path. Friendly guides take you on a two-hour tour that includes activities such as milking a cow, riding a pony, and cuddling baby ducks. There are more than 200 farm animals in all. The experience ends with an old-fashioned tractor-drawn hayride. ◆ Admission. Daily; closed Thanksgiving Day and Christmas Day. 1368 S Poinciana Blvd (south of Oren Brown Rd). 846.0770; fax 870.8644

34 Days Inn Eastgate $ Many amenities found at the more expensive properties nearby also are offered at this 200-room, two-story hotel. The lounge often features live entertainment, and there's a restaurant, gameroom, playground, and large pool. A complimentary shuttle takes guests to Disney theme parks. ◆ 5245 W Hwy 192 (between Hart Ave and Polynesian Isles Blvd). 396.7700, 800/922.2302 in FL, 800/423.3864; fax 396.0293; www.daysinn.com &

Cypress Gardens and Beyond: More Fun in the Orlando Area

Forty minutes southwest of Orlando, **Cypress Gardens** (2641 South Lake Summit Dr, off Rte 540, 941/324.2111, 800/282.2123 in FL, 800/237.4826) is the highlight of the otherwise quiet community of **Winter Haven**. A major theme park, it's one of the state's oldest tourist attractions.

Something is always in bloom in the park's botanical gardens, which feature more than 8,000 varieties of plants from 75 countries. Many consider the fall Chrysanthemum Festival to be the year's most special event. The largest display of its kind in North America, it features more than 2.5 million brilliant blooms. Southern belles promenade through the gardens wearing plantation-style dresses.

Cypress Gardens is also considered the waterskiing capital of the world. The first waterskiing show took place here in 1942 and international championships are held here each summer. Among the park's many daily performances is a fast-paced waterskiing show featuring variations on the park's legendary four-tier human pyramid, as well as huge stunt kites that soar as high as 50 feet at speeds up to 30 mph.

Among the park's other highlights are a butterfly conservatory and an electric boat ride through a cypress swamp. Special events take place throughout the year. **Cypress Gardens** is open daily; there's an admission charge.

A few miles southeast is another of Florida's oldest attractions, **Bok Tower Gardens** (Burns Ave and Tower Blvd, Lake Wales, 941/676.1408). This majestic 57-bell carillon tower plays host to visiting musicians, moonlight recitals, and other special programs. More than 150 acres of gardens and nature trails surround the bell tower. The gardens are open daily; there's an admission fee.

Also of interest to visitors in the area is **Chalet Suzanne** (★★★★ $$$) 3800 Chalet Suzanne Dr, between Starr Ave and Rte 17A, Lake Wales, 941/676.6011, 800/433.6011 in FL), which is approximately 10 miles southeast of **Cypress Gardens** and about a 45-minute drive from Orlando. The slightly ramshackle, brightly painted country inn features 30 rooms and suites, all uniquely decorated, but what attracts most people to this out-of-the-way spot is the food. The dinner menu is limited—baked chicken, lamb chops, or lobster, accompanied by broiled grapefruit and rum pie—but the fare is simply unforgettable. The soups are renowned; their signature spinach, mushroom, and herb soup even made it to the moon on one of the *Apollo* flights. (Since then it's been known as "moon soup.") Breakfast, lunch, and dinner are served daily.

Old Town

35 Wild Bill's Wild West at Fort Liberty
The main draw at this re-creation of an 1876 stockade is the dinner show, but there are also shops and a Miccosukee Indian village that visitors can explore during the day. The entertainment complex has doubled in size to 22 acres since it opened in 1987. ♦ 5260 W Hwy 192 (between Poinciana and Scott Blvds). 351.5151, 800/883.8181

Within Wild Bill's Wild West at Fort Liberty:

Wild Bill's Wild West Dinner Show ★$$
Tables for 12 on two tiers surround center stage in this 600-seat arena, where Wild Bill and Miss Kitty entertain. The show features can-can dancing, singing, lariat roping, square dancing, and good humor for adults and youngsters alike. The four-course meal consists of hearty Western vittles: chicken and ribs, corn, and pork and beans, as well as beer, soft drinks, and wine. ♦ American ♦ Daily 7PM, 9PM. Reservations recommended. 351.5151, 800/883.8282 &

Liberty Village and Trading Post Twenty stores, most with Old West themes, surround a courtyard with the dinner theater at one end. There's no admission fee for the village, which is decked out with suitable props—tepees, totem poles, horses, and the like. On occasion cowboys and Indians give crafts demonstrations. ♦ Free. Daily

36 Movie Rider Orlando A giant screen and digital surround-sound put moviegoers right in the middle of all the excitement at this theater, where the seats move from side to side and back and forth along with the action of the film. Films change about every six months; recent showings have included *Super Speedway,* about car racing, and *Secrets of the Lost Temple,* an Indiana Jones–inspired

adventure. ♦ Admission. M-Th, Su 11AM-11PM; F-Sa 11AM-midnight. 5390 W Hwy 192 (between Scott and Florida Plaza Blvds). 352.0050 &

37 Best Western Eastgate $ Fronted by a small pond, this 403-room motel is set back from the road and features a whirlpool, a gameroom, tennis courts, a playground, a gift shop, and a restaurant. It's about two miles from the entrance to **Walt Disney World**'s **Magic Kingdom.** ♦ 5565 W Hwy 192 (between Polynesian Isles and Seralago Blvds). 396.0707, 800/223.5361; fax 396.6644 &

38 Holiday Inn Hotel & Suites Maingate East $ Here's a child-friendly hotel with a particularly good attitude and several notable features. First, there are more than 100 certified clowns on staff. (Management believes that clown training makes for better customer service.) Second, the hotel has an extensive kids' program. There's licensed child care and activities for children ages 3 to 12 from 2 to 10PM daily (for a nominal fee). Kids even have their own special check-in desk and are greeted with a bag of treats. There's a merry-go-round in the lobby and the hotel also boasts a food court. All 670 rooms are equipped with microwave ovens, refrigerators, and coffee/tea makers. Two-room suites include a Super Nintendo.There are two Olympic-style swimming pools, a heated children's pool, two playgrounds, two lighted tennis courts, a video gameroom, and a free scheduled shuttle to **Walt Disney World.** Another plus for families: Kids under 12 eat free in the restaurant. ♦ 5678 W Hwy 192 (at Florida Plaza Blvd). 396.4488, 800/FON KIDS; fax 396.8915; www.familyfunhotel.com &

38 Old Town A new **Century Ferris Wheel** with 3,000 multicolored lights is the landmark of this four-block, 75-store dining/entertainment/shopping complex with distinctive turn-of-the-century Florida architecture. Although shopping is the main attraction here, there are more than a dozen rides, notably the **Windstorm,** a new 60-foot blue-and-white steel roller coaster designed in Munich. Other attractions include the original **Scrambler** carnival ride from 1946; an upside-down ride called the **Mixer;** the **Wave Swinger,** with rotating swings; the **Dragon Wagon** mini–roller coaster; **Mine Train,** a kiddie train on an electric track; spinning teacups, consisting of giant teacups revolving on a circular floor; **Moon Walk;** a **Haunted House** that takes about 20 minutes to explore; and go-karts and various bungee rides. The newest addition is **Happy Days Family Attractions,** with four go-kart tracks, bumper cars, laser tag, virtual reality games, and a 180-foot human slingshot experience.

Among the emporia along the redbrick pedestrian mall are a Disney souvenir store, a magic shop, a candle store with candle-making demonstrations, a place selling music boxes and cuckoo clocks, another spot featuring gifts and jewelry from Eastern Europe, and an old-time general store where you can get a 25-cent Pepsi. One particularly popular place features all types of movie-character merchandise—great *Wizard of Oz* T-shirts, MGM shot glasses, and coffee mugs bearing stars' portraits. There are also eight food and beverage outlets. On Saturday nights, up to 20,000 people show up for a free rock 'n' roll concert. Also on Saturday nights (and also free) is a parade of 300 vintage cars that has achieved national renown among automobile buffs. At other times, a variety of street performers keep visitors entertained. ♦ Fee for individual rides and attractions. Daily. 5770 W Hwy 192 (between Florida Plaza Blvd and Central Florida Greeneway). 396.4888, 800/843.4202

38 Days Suites $ This motel has 604 suites, three pools, and a restaurant. ♦ 5820 W Hwy 192 (between Florida Plaza Blvd and Central Florida Greeneway). 396.7900, 800/327.9126; fax 396.1789; www.thhotels.com ♦

38 Days Inn East of Magic Kingdom $ If you don't need a suite, save a couple of bucks and stay here. Each of the 404 rooms has two double beds. Facilities include a lounge, pool, restaurant, gift shop, and gameroom. ♦ 5840 W Hwy 192 (between Florida Plaza Blvd and Central florida Greeneway). 396.7969, 800/327.9126; fax 396.1789; www.daysinn.com

39 Quality Suites $ Looking like a freshly painted European village, this 225-suite hotel stands out from the rest along Kissimmee

Highway. The beautifully landscaped pool area features a children's pool and whirlpool, and **Kokomos,** a poolside bar serving drinks and snacks. In-room amenities include a coffeemaker and microwave oven. Also on the premises are gamerooms and a restaurant. Rates include continental breakfast and free beer, wine, and sodas in the evening. ♦ 5876 W Hwy 192 (between Florida Plaza Blvd and Central Florida Greeneway). 396.8040, 800/848.4148; fax 396.6766; www.thhotels.com ♦

40 Water Mania It doesn't offer as many thrills as **Wet 'n Wild** on International Drive, and it isn't as lushly landscaped as **Typhoon Lagoon** at **Walt Disney World,** but this 36-acre park has its own faithful following and is a great place for families. The **Wave Pool** is always popular, and thrill seekers like the white-water adventure on **Rip Tide,** the free-falling **Screamer** and **Double Berzerker,** and the 380-foot drop on the **Abyss.** Tamer attractions are the twisting **Anaconda** and the two-passenger **Banana Peel.** The **Rain Forest** is a children's water playground. Behind the water slides is a wooded picnic area and a sandy beach. Visitors may bring their own food, but alcoholic beverages and glass containers are not allowed. Dry off while playing miniature golf. Concerts are often held on the stage in front of the **Wave Pool** (enjoy the music while floating on rafts during the show). ♦ Admission. Parking fee. Daily. 6073 W Hwy 192 (between Central Florida Greeneway and Parkway Blvd). 396.2626, 800/527.3092 outside FL

40 Larson's Lodge Main Gate $ You may need reservations during peak seasons, as this 128-room family-owned lodge has a loyal following. Tall folks appreciate the extra-long double beds. There's a bright and airy dining room, a heated pool, a Jacuzzi, and a gameroom. A branch of the **Shoney's** restaurant chain is on the premises. Children under 18 stay free in rooms with their parents. ♦ 6075 W Hwy 192 (between Central Florida Greeneway and Parkway Blvd). 396.6100, 800/327.9074; www.flausa.com ♦

Arabian Nights

41 Arabian Nights ★$$ The chariot race is the hit of this show, which also features the Royal Lipizzaners, more than 60 beautiful and well-trained dancing and prancing horses. Twenty-five acts are loosely held together by the story of a princess searching for her true love with the help of a genie. A four-course dinner with unlimited drinks is served in the 1,200-seat arena. Choose between prime rib or a vegetarian dish. A low-cholesterol meal is available but must be requested when making reservations. ♦ American ♦ Daily (show times vary). Reservations recommended. 6225 W Hwy 192 (between Central Florida Greeneway and Parkway Blvd). 239.9221, 800/533.3615 in Canada, 800/553.6116; fax 239.9622 &

42 Hampton Inn Maingate $ The 164-room motel boasts a fine location on tranquil Parkway Boulevard, far from busy, crowded Highway 192. There's no restaurant but a free continental breakfast is offered in the lobby. There's a pool as well as tennis, shuffleboard, and basketball courts. ♦ 3104 Parkway Blvd (north of W Hwy 192). 396.8484, 800/243.8440; fax 396.7344; www.hamptoninn.com &

42 Homewood Suites $ Designed for businesspeople, for families enjoying a longer-than-average vacation, or for folks who just want to spread out, the 156 handsome suites feature king-size beds, fully equipped kitchens, and plenty of work space, including computer hookups. Some suites even have wood-burning fireplaces. There's also an up-to-date business center with personal computers, typewriters, calculators, copiers, and a fax machine. Breakfast and weekday (Monday-Thursday) Happy Hours are free, and the 24-hour **Suite Shop** is stocked with snacks, videos, and microwave meals. There's also a fitness center with a Jacuzzi, pool, children's pool, basketball court, and play area. ♦ 3100 Parkway Blvd (north of W Hwy 192). 396.2229, 800/255.4543; fax 396.4833; www.homewoodsuites.com &

43 Hyatt Orlando $ Convenient to **Walt Disney World,** this 922-room hotel has all the special touches the upscale Hyatt chain is known for, including well-appointed rooms in four major courts, each with its own heated pool, whirlpool, and kids' pool. Two of the courts have a playground. There are jogging trails and three lighted tennis courts. The restaurant's food is generally much better than average, though pricey; a huge breakfast buffet is offered each morning. ♦ 6375 W Hwy 192 (between Parkway Blvd and I-4). 396.1234, 800/331.2003 in FL, 800/233.1234; fax 396.5090; www.hyatt.com &

Each week, 269 new businesses are established in Orlando.

Restaurants/Clubs: Red   **Hotels:** Blue
Shops/🌳 **Outdoors:** Green   **Sights/Culture:** Black

Within the Hyatt Orlando:

Fio Fio ★$$$ Located in the hotel lobby, this upscale restaurant serves northern Italian food, including fettuccine Alfredo and chicken parmigiana. Patrons dine by candlelight at white-linen–draped tables. ♦ Italian ♦ Daily dinner. 396.1234

44 Holiday Inn Nikki Bird Resort $ Across from the entrance to **Walt Disney World,** this sprawling, two-story motel boasts 529 rooms, three pools, three restaurants, a whirlpool spa, three lighted tennis courts, two playgrounds, and a gameroom. Children 12 and under eat free in the restaurant. ♦ 7300 W Hwy 192 (between I-4 and Old Lake Wilson Rd). 396.7300, 800/465.4329; fax 396.7555; www.holiday-inn.com &

45 Ramada Plaza $ Here you'll find 500 rooms (including six one-bedroom suites) with either king- or queen-size beds; remote-control TV with HBO and, of course, the Disney Channel; and telephones equipped to accommodate personal computers. There's the **Palms Restaurant** and a lounge serving deli goodies. Two pools, a gameroom, miniature golf, and an outdoor fitness center round out the picture. ♦ 7470 W Hwy 192 (between I-4 and Old Lake Wilson Rd). 396.4400, 800/327.9170; fax 396.4320; www.ramada.com &

45 EconoLodge Maingate Hawaiian Resort $ One of the larger non-Disney lodgings close to the **Magic Kingdom,** the hotel has 445 rooms, each equipped with two double beds, cable TV with in-room video movies, and a safe. There's also a restaurant and a large pool. Family-friendly features include a kids-eat-free program and a free shuttle to **Walt Disney World.** ♦ 7514 W Hwy 192 (between I-4 and Old Lake Wilson Rd). 396.2000, 800/365.6935; fax 396.1295 &

46 A World of Orchids This popular attraction claims to be the world's largest permanent orchid display under one roof. The orchids, including some rare and unusual varieties, are in garden settings.

From the 1,000-foot nature walk visitors also may view exotic birds, Far East chameleons, South American frogs, and thousands of fish. At the fishing hole stocked with catfish, a fishing competition entertains the non-horticulturists in the crowd. Plants may be purchased in the gift shop. ♦ Admission; free for children 16 and under. Daily. 2501 Old Lake Wilson Rd (south of W Hwy 192). 396.1887 &

47 Ramada Resort Maingate $ The location is great if you want to get away from **Walt Disney World** crowds. This 384-room motel has two pools, a kiddie pool, and two tennis courts, plus a restaurant, a lounge, and a gameroom. ♦ 2950 Reedy Creek Blvd (just north of W Hwy 192). 396.4466, 800/365.6935; fax 396.6418 ♿

47 Wilson World Hotel Maingate $ From the road this looks like just another large motel, but the interior is a pleasant and unexpected surprise. The four-story atrium of the 442-room property features an indoor heated swimming pool with a waterfall. There's also a large outdoor pool with a sandy beach, an indoor whirlpool, a cafeteria, a gameroom, and a gift shop. The lounge generally features live entertainment. ♦ 7491 W Hwy 192 (between High Point Blvd and Sherberth Rd). 396.6000, 800/669.6753; fax 396.7393 ♿

47 Inn at Maingate $ A nice 580-room motel, it offers great prices. Rooms feature cable TV and free movies. There's a heated outdoor pool, a tennis court, a whirlpool, a gameroom, a restaurant, a take-out deli, **T.J.'s Lounge,** and a pool bar. Laundry facilities are available. ♦ 7501 W Hwy 192 (between High Point Blvd and Sherberth Rd). 396.1400; fax 396.0660 ♿

48 Comfort Inn Maingate $ A step above your average motel, this well-maintained property has 280 rooms, a restaurant, a pool, a gameroom, and a gift shop. ♦ 7571 W Hwy 192 (between High Point Blvd and Sherberth Rd). 396.7500, 800/432.0887 in FL, 800/223.1628; fax 396.7497; www.hotelchoice.com/hotel/FL400/ ♿

49 Howard Johnson Maingate West $ Each of the 206 large rooms features a color TV, a double vanity, and a patio or balcony. Also on the premises are two swimming pools, shuffleboard courts, a putting green, a restaurant, a gameroom, and a gift shop. ♦ 7600 W Hwy 192 (between Old Lake Wilson Rd and Entry Point Blvd). 396.2500, 800/432.4335 in FL, 800/654.2000; fax 396.2096; www.hojo.com

The Town of Celebration

When Walt Disney announced plans in 1965 to build his Florida project, a "city of the future" was among the myriad ideas. Walt died a year later, before construction on **Walt Disney World** had even begun. Many plans were shelved when his brother, Roy, took charge to get the **Magic Kingdom** open in 1971, on time and on budget.

Fast-forward to 1982 and the opening of **Epcot (Experimental Prototype Community of Tomorrow)** with an entire area, called **Future World,** dedicated to future technologies. This park touched on Walt's original ideas, but his vision went much further.

By the end of the 1980s, Disney had created a strong development team, which, building on Walt's words, put the first thoughts about a "new town" on paper—a town that would embrace new technology but also would have many of the values of small-town life before World War II. They called it **Celebration** (407/566.4663).

The Celebration Company studied towns all across the US and distilled thousands of ideas to create the design for Celebration. The new town, 16 miles southwest of Orlando, is master-planned for 8,000–10,000 residents, 3.1 million square feet of office space, 2.1 million square feet of retail space, a 60-bed hospital, a school, and a golf course designed by Robert Trent Jones Sr. and Jr. Children started attending the public school (kindergarten to 12th grade) in the fall of 1996, shortly after the first residents moved in.

Downtown Celebration, the focus of the community, is a showcase for some of the world's foremost architects, including **Robert A.M. Stern** (health-care facility), **Michael Graves** (post office), **Philip Johnson** (town hall), **Charles Moore** (preview center), **Cesar Pelli** (cinema), and **Robert Venturi (SunTrust Bank).** Visitors who want to take an **Architectural Walking Tour** can pick up a free brochure at the **Celebration Preview Center** (100 Celebration Ave, at Market Street, 407/566.4663). Downtown also features a lakeside promenade and weekend and holiday entertainment, and family bicycling events. For information on events, call 407/566.3448.

You can cover the downtown area in 30 minutes, or make it a leisurely stroll. Shops and restaurants are doing a brisk business with visitors and residents alike (ask for a map at the **Celebration Preview Center,** above). Among shops on **Market Street** are **Village Mercantile,** stocking trendy sportswear; **Soft As A Grape,** carrying women's casual clothing; **Amélie & Mélanie, La Provence,** purveying French soaps and potpourris; **Market Street Gallery,** featuring fine art; **Zirbes' Antiques;** and **Wood, Stone & Steel,** a home accessories shop. Locally owned **Gooding's** is the town grocery. Just around the corner on **Front Street** you'll find **Chambers Jewelers** and **Celebration Cycle.** And nearby **Bloom Street** is home to **Downeast—An Orvis Store** for sportswear and **White's Books & Gifts.**

Restaurants include **Max's Cafe & Coffee Shop** and **Max's Grille,** both owned by renowned South Florida chef Dennis Max; **Café D'Antonio** for Italian food; and **Columbia** restaurant for Cuban/Spanish cuisine. **Wm. J. Sweet's** sells ice cream, and **Bread Alone,** tucked next to **Max's Cafe,** offers fabulous loaves baked on the premises.

50 Holiday Inn Maingate West No. 2 $ Put this at the top of your list of moderately priced hotels near the **Magic Kingdom**'s main gate. Set on a small road far from the crowds along busy Highway 192, the 287-room property is well maintained and has a pretty pink exterior. An attractive pool and a restaurant are on-site. ♦ 7601 Black Lake Rd (just north of W Hwy 192). 396.1100, 800/365.6935; fax 396.0689; www.enjoyfloridahotels.com &

51 Sheraton Inn Lakeside $ The grounds of this 651-room property are lushly landscaped and feature a small lake with paddleboats. Also here are four lighted tennis courts, three heated pools, and a children's pool. For dining there's a lakeview restaurant, buffet restaurant, deli, and lounge. Most of the rooms have double beds (though king-size beds are available) and small refrigerators. The coin-operated laundries are a plus, especially for families. There's free transportation to **Walt Disney World** and free breakfast and dinner for children ages 10 and under. ♦ 7769 W Hwy 192 (between Sherberth Rd and Orange Lake Blvd). 396.2222, 800/848.0801; fax 396.1399; www.orlandosheraton.com &

51 Quality Inn $ On a private lake, this 200-room hotel has an attractive pool and patio area, a restaurant, a laundry room, and a gameroom. ♦ 7785 W Hwy 192 (between Sherberth Rd and Orange Lake Blvd). 396.1828, 800/846.4253; fax 396.1305; www.thhotels.com &

52 Chinatown and Splendid China This $100-million attraction embraces 5,000 years of Chinese history and evokes a 10,000-mile journey through China's countryside. Covering 76 acres and located just two miles from **Walt Disney World**'s main gate, the park is basically a walk among more than 60 miniature replicas of China's most notable landmarks, including the **Great Wall** and the **Imperial Palace/Forbidden City** (see map on page 71). Perhaps most impressive of all are the replicas of a good number of the 8,000 terra-cotta warriors uncovered near Xian in 1974. Similar to the actual full-size figures that guard the burial tomb of the Qinshihuang emperor, the miniatures all have very lifelike expressions. The skilled workmanship that went into constructing the park, which required two years and 120 artisans, is truly staggering. One section of the **Great Wall** replica, for example,

took more than six million one- and two-inch blocks. Small porcelain figures with individually painted faces accompany all of the building replicas—there are tens of thousands throughout the park. You can explore **Splendid China** in several ways. Start in **Chinatown** (no admission charge) at the park's entrance, where you're immersed in the Chinese culture, including crafts, foods, shops, and entertainment. Once you're inside the theme park, an hour-and-a-half guided walking tour and an hourlong guided golf-cart tour are available for an additional charge; also, a free tram runs around the perimeter of the beautifully landscaped grounds. Those who choose to explore on foot should be prepared to walk two to three miles—the main path is a mile and a half, but you'll want to see the exhibits on the side paths, too. Exhibits have both audio commentaries and explanatory signs, but information on the different sites is sketchy, and if you go it alone you'll probably come away wanting to know a great deal more. The park map marks the must-see exhibits. As there are no rides and the atmosphere is peaceful and rather sedate, the park has more appeal for teens and adults than for young children (although there is a playground).

Demonstrations and performances are a major part of the experience here: The 800-seat **Golden Peacock Theater** hosts *The Mysterious Kingdom of the Orient*—presented by a cast of 80—every day except Monday. Acrobats perform in the **Pagoda Garden** and films are shown in **Harmony Hall**. Souvenir seekers will find handicrafts from all over China at surprisingly good prices. There are also several restaurants, including several casual eateries offering either Chinese or American fare, and the **Suzhou Pearl,** an elegant dining spot serving Cantonese, Mandarin, Mongolian, Hunan, and Szechuan dishes. Far more interested in promoting Chinese culture than in addressing political issues, this theme park glosses over some of the troublesome aspects of China's history. It created a minor political stir and attracted a handful of protestors when it first opened because of its affiliation with the Chinese government and its replica of Tibet's Potala Palace, from which the Dalai Lama was forced to flee following a Tibetan revolt against the Chinese in 1959. Park officials responded in a characteristic theme-park fashion: Instead of closing off the Potala Palace replica, they simply took away the identifying sign, which essentially removed the protestors' rallying point. The Orlando park is a near-duplication of a popular one near Hong Kong, conceived by Ma Chi Man, the general manager of China Travel Services. In a way, **Splendid China** serves as a clever marketing gimmick to attract tourists to China: Now that you've seen the miniatures, come see the real thing! **China Travel** even has an on-site office where visitors can pick up brochures and arrange for a real trip to China. ◆ Admission. Free parking. Daily. 3000 Splendid China Blvd (north of Formosa Gardens Blvd). 396.7111, 800/244.6226; fax 396.7392 ♿

53 Orange Lake Country Club $$ Kemmons Wilson, the man who brought you **Holiday Inn** and **Wilson World,** has built a time-share complex with 27 challenging holes of golf designed by renowned golf-course architect Joe Lee, 16 lighted tennis courts, racquetball courts, and a variety of water sports, all centered around an 80-acre lake with a sandy beach. Two-bedroom, fully equipped town homes line the fairways. The clubhouse features hotel-type rooms, a restaurant, lounge, coffee shop, pool bar, pizza parlor, video gameroom, miniature golf course, and 155-seat movie theater. ◆ 8505 W Hwy 192 (at Orange Lake Blvd). 239.0000, 800/877.6522; www.orangelake.com ♿

53 Raccoon Lake Camp Resort These campsites have full water and electric hookups. There's also miniature golf, a pool, and many planned activities throughout the day and evening. ◆ 8555 W Hwy 192 (between Orange Lake Blvd and Rte 545). 239.4148

Within Raccoon Lake Camp Resort:

J. T.'s Prime Time $ Housed in a large log cabin with a screened-in porch, this restaurant serves standard-issue prime rib and barbecue. There's also a bar, and the general store next door is equipped with supplies and liquor. ◆ American ◆ Daily lunch and dinner. 239.6555

54 Sleep Inn Maingate $ This 104-room motel has the advantage of being far enough from the highway to be insulated from the noise. It has free HBO, plus a small outdoor pool. A **McDonald's** is within walking distance. ◆ 8536 W Hwy 192 (between Formosa Gardens and Lindfields Blvds). 396.1600, 800/225.0086; fax 396.1971 ♿

54 Best Western Maingate $ One of many hotels on the quiet side of I-4, it offers free shuttle service to **Walt Disney World.** Each of the 299 rooms has two double beds and cable TV with free HBO, and there's a restaurant on-site. Kids under 13 stay and eat free. ◆ 8600 W Hwy 192 (between Formosa Gardens and Lindfields Blvds). 396.0100, 800/327.9151; fax 396.6718; www.bestwestern.com ♿

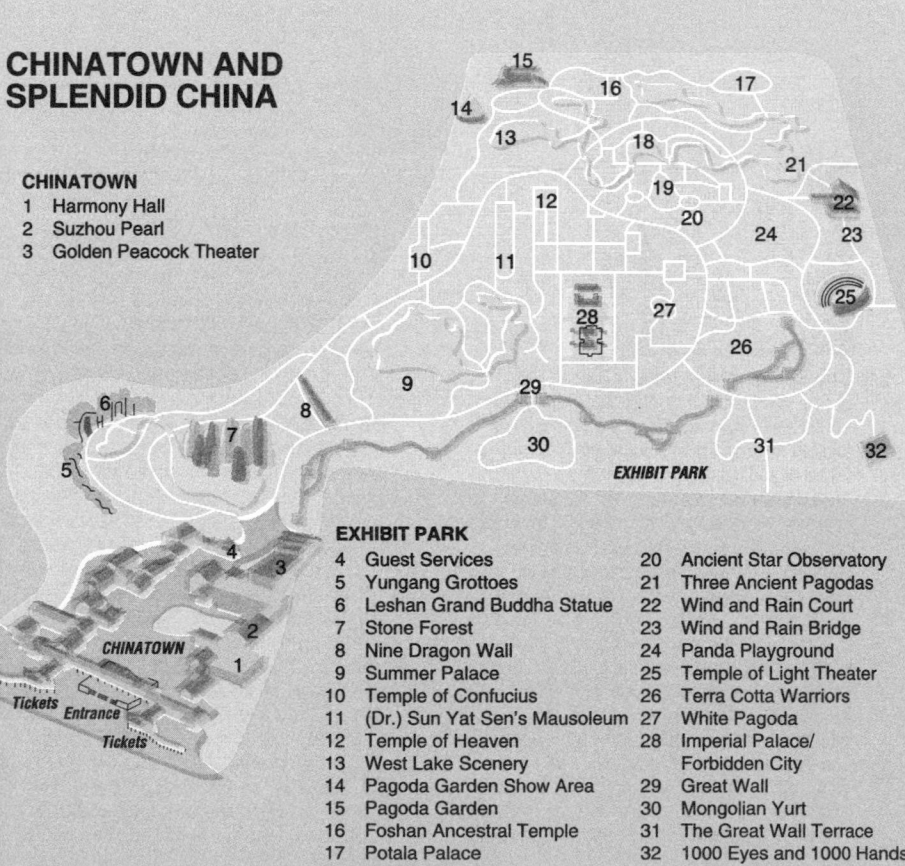

CHINATOWN AND SPLENDID CHINA

CHINATOWN
1   Harmony Hall
2   Suzhou Pearl
3   Golden Peacock Theater

EXHIBIT PARK
4   Guest Services
5   Yungang Grottoes
6   Leshan Grand Buddha Statue
7   Stone Forest
8   Nine Dragon Wall
9   Summer Palace
10   Temple of Confucius
11   (Dr.) Sun Yat Sen's Mausoleum
12   Temple of Heaven
13   West Lake Scenery
14   Pagoda Garden Show Area
15   Pagoda Garden
16   Foshan Ancestral Temple
17   Potala Palace
18   Yueyang Pavilion
19   Shaolin Temple
20   Ancient Star Observatory
21   Three Ancient Pagodas
22   Wind and Rain Court
23   Wind and Rain Bridge
24   Panda Playground
25   Temple of Light Theater
26   Terra Cotta Warriors
27   White Pagoda
28   Imperial Palace/Forbidden City
29   Great Wall
30   Mongolian Yurt
31   The Great Wall Terrace
32   1000 Eyes and 1000 Hands Guanyin Buddha Statue

Walt Disney World

For years, **Cape Canaveral** was the best-known area in Central Florida. But even NASA couldn't compete with Mickey, the world's most famous mouse. When **Walt Disney World** opened in 1971, more than 10 million visitors flocked to the park that year. These days it attracts more than 37 million people annually, making it *the most popular tourist spot in the world.* And why not? This city-size world of fantasy (nearly 43 square miles) offers spectacular rides and attractions, extravagant hotels, plenty of opportunities for golf, tennis, and swimming, and a working movie studio that takes you behind the scenes and sometimes puts you in front of the camera.

All this came about because of the vision of Walt Disney, the man who created Mickey Mouse. Disney first began snatching up acre after acre of swampy pine scrub in Central Florida in 1965. By the time he had finished, he had amassed more than 27,000 acres. Today, **Walt Disney World** consists of four major theme parks—**Magic Kingdom, Epcot, Disney's Animal Kingdom,** and **Disney-MGM Studios**—and several other "minor" parks, including **Disney's Wide World of Sports,** a multimillion-dollar complex for

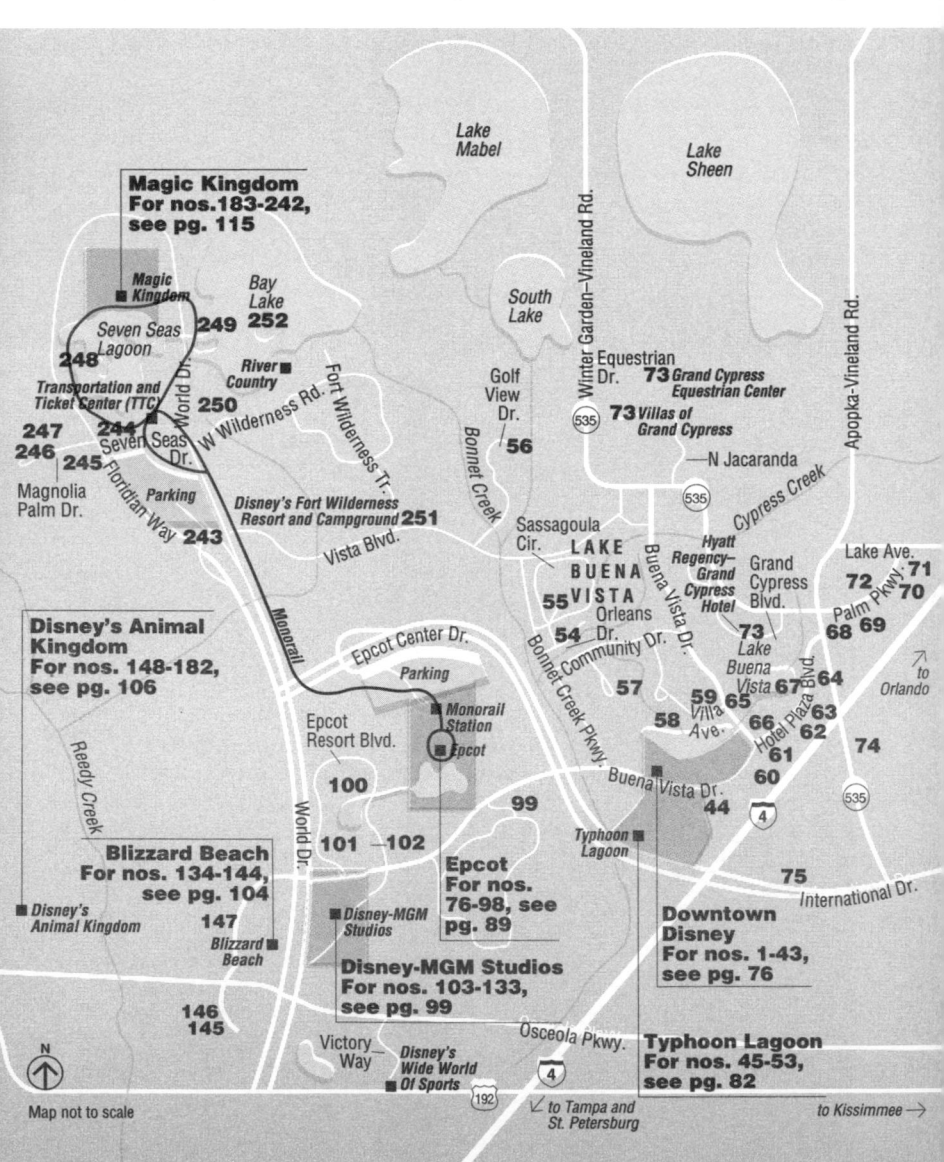

Magic Kingdom
For nos. 183-242,
see pg. 115

Disney's Animal Kingdom
For nos. 148-182,
see pg. 106

Blizzard Beach
For nos. 134-144,
see pg. 104

Epcot
For nos. 76-98, see
pg. 89

Disney-MGM Studios
For nos. 103-133,
see pg. 99

Downtown Disney
For nos. 1-43,
see pg. 76

Typhoon Lagoon
For nos. 45-53,
see pg. 82

Map not to scale

training and competition in more than 30 sports (see "Disney's Wide World of Sports," page 100); **Pleasure Island** and **Downtown Disney West Side**, with shopping, dining, and nightclubs; **Discovery Island**, a zoological park and nature preserve; and three water parks—**Typhoon Lagoon, River Country**, and **Blizzard Beach**. There are also more than 24,000 hotel rooms; one executive and five championship golf courses; and various shopping plazas, including **Downtown Disney Marketplace**. Disney today covers 30,000 acres, with just 7,100 acres developed, leaving plenty of room for more attractions—and *more* is exactly what's coming.

Walt himself expressed the desire that his vacation kingdom remain fresh, in a state of perpetual growth—and apparently that's a wish his successors intend to make come true. Recent new attractions include theme park thrillers like **Test Track** at Epcot; **Buzz Lightyear Space Ranger Spin** at **Magic Kingdom; Countdown to Extinction** at **Disney's Animal Kingdom**; and **Fantasmic!** at the **Disney-MGM Studios. Disney's Fairy Tale Wedding Pavilion**, on the banks of the **Seven Seas Lagoon**, is the site of several ceremonies every week. **Disney's BoardWalk** features a 200-yardlong boardwalk with two hotels, clubs, and restaurants. **Disney's Coronado Springs Resort**, themed to the Old Southwest, is Disney's first moderately priced resort to include a convention center. And the first **Disney Cruise Line** sailed in the summer of 1998, featuring Disney-themed shows and special events that can be combined with an extended stay at **Walt Disney World**.

In response to the need for less expensive hotel rooms within **Walt Disney World, Disney's All-Star Sports Resort** and **Disney's All-Star Music Resort** opened in 1994, and a third location—**Disney's All-Star Movies Resort**— was set to open as we went to press. Inexpensive by Disney standards, they're pricey compared to many of those found at such places as **Kissimmee's Highway 192** and **Lake Buena Vista**, not far from the gates of **Walt Disney World**. Staying on Disney property, nevertheless, does confer some privileges. A Disney Resort ID means there's no need to carry cash. You can enter the four major parks earlier than the general public, and you can get the best golf tee times. What's more, there's guaranteed park admission on the most popular days, when the park is filled to capacity and gates may be closed. All guests staying on Disney property have free use of the bus, boat, and monorail transportation systems to get to different areas of the park. Visitors staying off the property have to pay a parking fee for each day's visit.

Disney hotels also offer an in-room baby-sitting service, day-care centers, and a variety of children's activity programs (although the **Polynesian Resort's Never Land Club** has an evening program that's also open to non-resort guests). For young and old alike, there are more than a dozen tennis courts at selected resorts, plus golf, bicycling, health clubs, fitness trails, swimming pools, marinas, and horseback riding. Most of these activities are open to Disney resort guests only, although all visitors to **Walt Disney World** can rent boats at the **Downtown Disney Marketplace** marina, go horseback riding, and play on the Disney golf courses. Those staying at a Disney hotel are given preferential treatment on the links, however; Disney hotel guests may reserve a tee time up to 60 days in advance; others may reserve 30 days in advance (407/824.2270).

In addition to the Disney-owned hotels, there are also seven Disney-associated hotels on **Walt Disney World** property in the area. "Disney-associated" means that while Disney does not operate them, they meet Disney standards and offer most of the privileges of the Disney resorts. For information on staying at a Disney-owned or -associated hotel, call the central hotel reservations number, 407/W.DISNEY (407/934.7639).

Each of the major and minor parks that make up **Walt Disney World** have separate admission fees; a one-day ticket to the **Magic Kingdom**, for example, allows entrance to that park only. However, a variety of money-saving packages and multi-day passes are available.

In addition to admission fees, there are parking fees at all the **Walt Disney World** parks except **Downtown Disney Marketplace, Pleasure Island, Downtown Disney West Side, Typhoon Lagoon,** and **Blizzard Beach.** However, the parking sticker from one Disney lot is valid elsewhere in **Walt Disney World** on the same day.

A few tips about visiting **Walt Disney World:** The best advice is *arrive early,* especially during school vacation times (Easter week, the week between Christmas and New Year's Day, and the summer months). Each of the Disney parks has its own hours of operation and they vary from season to season, so call ahead to find out the exact schedule and be at the gate at least a half hour before the park opens. Those without the restrictions of children's holiday times might opt to visit when school is in session. To minimize time waiting in line, eat lunch early or in the mid-afternoon, or come after an early dinner.

Disney no longer books dining "reservations" but instead offers "priority seating" times for all table-service restaurants. (Priority seating means that your party will be seated at the next available table that will accommodate it.) Priority seating is also imperative for the popular breakfasts with Disney characters (even those held in cafeterias). Reservations for priority seating can be made 60, 30, or seven days in advance (a certain number of seats are released 60 days in advance, more seats are released 30 days in advance, and the rest are released seven days in advance). It's also possible to make same-day reservations at the individual parks, but some restaurants may be fully booked at that point. Special dinner shows, including the popular *Hoop-Dee-Doo Musical Review* at **Fort Wilderness,** also use the priority seating systems. **Walt Disney World**'s central restaurant reservations number is 407/WDW.DINE (407/939.3463). The general **Walt Disney World** information number is 407/824.4321.

Disney Cruise Line Sails

In 1998, Disney launched its first cruise ship, the 2,400-passenger *Disney Magic,* a megaship with remarkable amenities: 875 spacious staterooms (75 percent with ocean views), nearly an entire deck of kids' activities, original Disney theatrical productions, an adults-only nightclub district (but no casino), a full-service spa and fitness center, and four dining rooms.

The ship is the centerpiece of a land-and-sea vacation that combines three or four days onboard with three or four days at **Walt Disney World.** The trip begins at Disney, then a private motor coach takes you to nearby **Port Canaveral.**

Designed by notable architects and interior design firms and built in Italy, the *Disney Magic*'s streamlined sculptural form is inspired by the *Queen Mary* and other great ships of the 1930s and 1940s. The elegant public spaces are Art Deco–inspired but unmistakably Disney, with playful touches like the colorful 15-foot sculpture of Goofy painting the finishes on the ship's stern.

The highlight of the cruise is a day at Castaway Cay, Disney's private Bahamian island, where you can play all day—snorkeling, bicycling, sailing, volleyball—or just take it easy. Adults have their own beach with open-air massage cabanas.

The children's programs, both onboard and at Castaway Cay, are superior, with up to 50 counselors offering age-specific activities. Teens enjoy an area just for them (no parents allowed).

A day in the port of Nassau is part of every cruise, with snorkeling, diving, and sightseeing excursions offered.

The *Disney Wonder,* sister ship to the *Magic,* was set to sail as we went to press.

For reservations, call 407/566.7000.

Downtown Disney/ Typhoon Lagoon

This area of **Walt Disney World** includes Downtown Disney—the new name for the entertainment-shopping-dining district encompassing **Downtown Disney Marketplace, Pleasure Island,** and **Downtown Disney West Side**—and **Typhoon Lagoon,** a water park. In addition, there are three Disney golf courses in this vicinity: the **Lake Buena Vista Golf Club,** and the **Eagle Pines** and **Osprey Ridge Golf Courses** at the **Bonnet Creek Golf Club.**

For those who would like to stay in this part of the Disney universe, the **Downtown Disney** area offers several Disney-owned properties. Also nearby is **Hotel Plaza Boulevard,** site of seven Disney-affiliated hotels. There are also several hotels in the nearby town of **Lake Buena Vista.**

Area code 407 unless otherwise noted.

Downtown Disney Marketplace

If you need a breather from the theme park hustle and bustle, consider a stop at **Downtown Disney Marketplace.** A few pleasant hours spent roaming through shops, lingering over a meal, or even boating on **Buena Vista Lagoon** might provide just the break you were looking for. There are more than 20 shops and eateries (note that none of the **Marketplace** restaurants takes reservations). The marketplace also features demonstrations by artisans; performances by musicians, dancers, storytellers, and comedians; and special events, including holiday festivals, art exhibits, and boat shows. **Downtown Disney Marketplace** connects with **Pleasure Island,** a specialty shopping and restaurant center by day and a nightclub complex after 7PM (see page 77), and **Downtown Disney West Side,** home of the newest shops and eateries (see page 79). There's free parking and bus and water taxi transportation to and from Disney hotels. All shops are open daily from 9:30AM to 11PM. For information call 824.4321. ♦ Buena Vista Dr and Hotel Plaza Blvd

1 2R's Reading and Riting This large bookstore sells tomes covering all topics, not just Disney stories. Pick up a best-seller to peruse by the pool or some children's books for the trip home. Greeting cards and stationery are also sold. Shoppers are welcome to sip coffee as they browse.

1 The Art of Disney You'll find Disney animation cels and unique collectibles in this upscale gallery.

2 Rainforest Cafe ★$$$ Crowned by a 65-foot volcano and featuring cascading waterfalls, thunder, lightning, and tropical birds, this giant eatery is like a mini–theme park. Eight animated gorillas chatter from the treetops, bats fly about inside a cave, and two elephants shower each other with water. Diners are further entertained by jungle-size fluttering butterflies and enormous fish tanks in this fascinating re-creation of a tropical rain forest. The food is so-so, but every serving is enough to feed two and is cleverly named, like Rasta Pasta, a bowtie pasta in a creamy garlic sauce with grilled chicken and fresh spinach; and Rumble in the Jungle, pita bread filled with turkey and Caesar salad. This environmentally friendly restaurant will not buy beef raised on deforested land, and it serves only line-caught fish. On the way out, stop in the 5,000-square-foot retail shop, where you'll find artifacts, gardening accessories, and handmade wood products among the logo-infused merchandise.
♦ American ♦ Daily lunch and dinner

3 Wolfgang Puck Express ★★★★$
World-renowned chef Wolfgang Puck offers a variety of quick-service specialties here, including pizza, focaccia sandwiches, soups, and fresh salads. The restaurant, which was designed by Puck's partner and wife, Barbara Lazaroff, immerses diners in a kaleidoscope of colors, with brilliantly colored mosaic tiles and rich woodwork. The exhibition kitchen adds a high-energy buzz to this 228-seat cafe. ♦ Italian-American. ♦ Daily lunch, dinner, and snacks

3 Disney's Days of Christmas Open 365 days a year, this shop features a variety of Christmas collectibles, ornaments, animated figurines, and other accessories for the holiday season, including a wide selection of Hanukkah merchandise.

> The world's largest sundial is located in Central Florida—in the Team Disney Building at Walt Disney World, according to the Guinness Book of World Records.

Restaurants/Clubs: Red	**Hotels:** Blue
Shops/ ♦ Outdoors: Green	**Sights/Culture:** Black

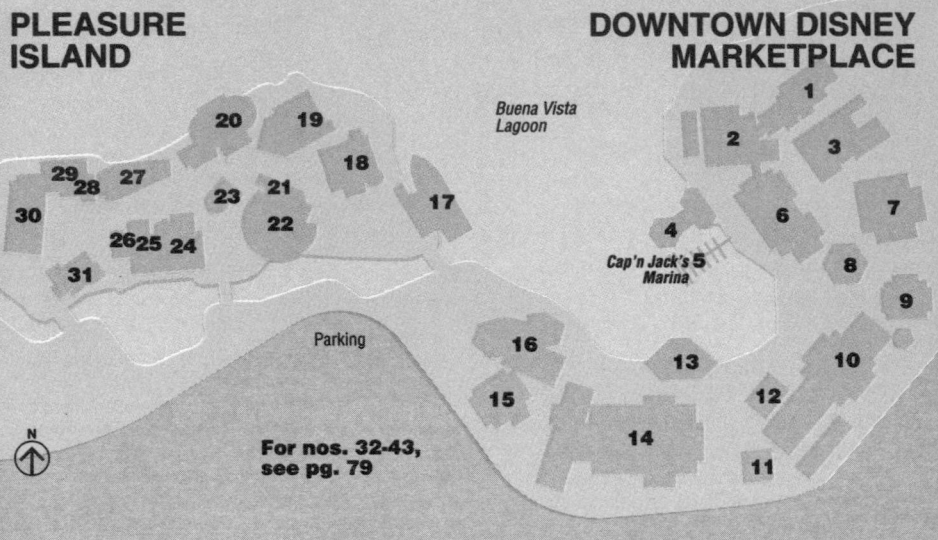

PLEASURE ISLAND

DOWNTOWN DISNEY MARKETPLACE

Buena Vista Lagoon

Cap'n Jack's Marina

Parking

For nos. 32-43, see pg. 79

4 Cap'n Jack's Oyster Bar ★★$$
This restaurant and bar overlooks the Buena Vista Lagoon. The bar, a pleasant place in which to sip a cocktail (it's known for its frozen margaritas), rarely gets too crowded, and the view is lovely. This is also a wonderful spot for a meal; the menu features lobster, crab, and fresh fish daily. Favorite dishes include seafood salads packed with smoked fish, marinated scallops, and shrimp, and a spicy conch chowder. Finish off with a big slice of Key lime pie. ♦ Seafood ♦ Daily lunch and dinner

5 Cap'n Jack's Marina Rent a small motorboat, pontoon, or paddleboat for an excursion on Buena Vista Lagoon. Fishing excursions leave from here; equipment is available for rent. ♦ Daily. 828.2204

6 Resortwear Unlimited This women's sportswear shop is just the place to pick up an extra swimsuit or a new set of tennis togs.

6 Pooh Corner This store is dedicated to Disney's honey-loving bear and the rest of his friends—Tigger, Eeyore, Kanga, Roo, and Piglet.

6 Summer Sands Browse this great place for extra-nice souvenirs. Choose from a selection of sun-care products, straw hats and bags, jewelry, and other gifts, all reminiscent of Florida.

Walt Disney World is the largest employer in Central Florida, with about 48,000 employees.

Mickey Mouse has more than 150 sets of clothes to choose from when he gets dressed, but Minnie Mouse has him beat—she selects from a closet of more than 175 different ensembles.

7 Gourmet Pantry If you love being in the kitchen you'll want to stop in here. Cookbooks and irresistible household gadgets are featured, along with gourmet coffee, imported candy, and fine wines and liquors.

7 Gourmet Pantry Deli and Treat Shop For a quick, tasty lunch to go, order a sandwich or a salad, a cup of coffee or cappuccino, and fresh-baked cake or cookies for dessert.

8 Captain's Tower The two-story octagonal structure is a **Downtown Disney Marketplace** landmark; it houses a gift shop featuring merchandise related to the latest Disney celebration.

9 Harrington Bay Clothiers Fashion-conscious men will appreciate the sportswear and accessories here.

10 Team Mickey's Athletic Club This colorful store is filled with sports attire, footwear, and equipment, most of which is adorned with Disney characters.

10 Guest Services Stop in for helpful information, stroller and wheelchair rental, film and two-hour express photo service, batteries, and gift wrapping. You can also buy tickets for Disney theme parks here.

10 Toys Fantastic This shop carries mostly Mattel toys, but you'll also find kiddie merchandise inspired by the latest Disney films.

10 Eurospain There's almost always a crystal cutter at work in this unusual shop, demonstrating the age-old art of glass sculpting and custom engraving. And all of the interesting merchandise is hand-crafted by European artists.

10 Studio M If you miss the Disney characters at the theme parks, you can head to this shop and have them "magically" appear in a family portrait. Also available is custom-designed apparel decorated by robots, which "paint" the clothes as patrons watch.

11 Disney at Home Mickey Mouse is everywhere in this home-furnishings shop—on linens, towels, dishware, blankets, shower curtains, even furniture.

12 Ghirardelli Soda Fountain and Chocolate Shop $ This old-fashioned soda fountain reflects a turn-of-the-century look and serves old-fashioned ice-cream sundaes, shakes, root beer floats, and malts. You'll also find wall-to-wall chocolates from San Francisco's Ghirardelli Chocolate Company. ♦ Soda fountain ♦ Daily

13 Dock Stage A venue for a variety of performances, this stage is used primarily in the summer. ♦ Check the entertainment schedule for show times

14 World of Disney If you want to make only one stop for Disney souvenirs, this is the place. It's the biggest Disney shopping experience on earth, with 12 Disney-themed areas. There's even a wall of plush toys stacked with more than 8,000 huggable characters. The children's area, themed to *Alice in Wonderland,* is a fantasyland of toys, clothes, and other merchandise. As you enter through a Queen of Hearts archway, there's a larger-than-life Alice. Furniture themed to the film gives kids a place to rest—and watch Disney videos, of course. You name it, you probably can find it here, with a Disney character or logo. Among the departments are luggage, housewares, photo albums and stationery, jewelry, men's and women's apparel, infants', toddlers', and children's clothing, heroines' costumes, children's sleepwear, and even adults' sleepwear.

15 Ronald's Fun House $ Typical McDonald's fare is served here in such locales as **Ronald's Dining Room,** with a 20-foot dining table; **Birdie's Music Room,** with a giant french-fry "organ"; and **Grimace's Game Room,** with videos for children. ♦ American ♦ Daily breakfast, lunch, and dinner

16 LEGO Imagination Center Inside, it's an ordinary LEGO store, with toys, puzzles, clothing, computer games, and watches, but outside it's a 3,000-square-foot hands-on play area filled with hundreds of thousands of LEGO, PRIMO, and DUPLO blocks. Also, there are larger-than-life LEGO models, including a 30-footlong sea serpent in Buena Vista Lagoon, a dinosaur family, and an entire human family with a snoring grandpa—all built of LEGO.

Pleasure Island

The one thing that **Walt Disney World** lacked for many years was a place that catered to grown-ups. When adults wanted a break from cartoon characters, thrill rides, and lifelike Audio-Animatronics, they usually left the Disney universe entirely and headed to **Church Street Station** in downtown Orlando. To compete, **Walt Disney World** added this complex of retail shops, nightclubs, and restaurants next to **Downtown Disney Marketplace.**

It was a good idea, but the complex wasn't a big hit until Disney came up with a clever gimmick: Every night is New Year's Eve on **Pleasure Island.** There's a countdown to midnight every night, and the "New Year" is greeted with booming cannons that shower everyone with confetti. By day, tourists can browse in the shops and eat at the restaurants. But the real fun begins at 7PM, when the island's eight theme nightclubs switch into high gear.

Pleasure Island is open to everyone, free of charge, from 10:30AM to 7PM; starting at 7PM there's an admission charge, and those under 18 years old must be accompanied by an adult. Visitors over age 18 but not yet 21 (Florida's drinking age) are admitted to all clubs except **Mannequins Dance Palace** and **BET SoundStage Club** but are not served alcohol. There are no admission fees or age requirements for restaurants. Parking is free at all times. For information about any **Pleasure Island** restaurant or club, call 934.7781.

A reminder for folks traveling with kids ages 3 to 12: If you're staying at a **Walt Disney World** hotel and want a night out on your own, Disney baby-sitting services will keep your youngsters happy and entertained while you dance the night away. ♦ Buena Vista Dr (between Hotel Plaza Blvd and Bonnet Creek Pkwy)

17 Fulton's Crab House ★★★$$$ Eating at this seafood extravaganza is not exactly an intimate experience—six themed dining rooms provide seating for 700. But the food is varied and excellent, and the location—on the triple-deck stern-wheeler riverboat that's permanently moored on the edge of the Buena Vista Lagoon—is delightful. Levy Restaurants, proprietor of **Pleasure Island's** popular **Portobello Yacht Club** restaurant (see 78), operates this establishment. The menu boasts more than 50 seasonal selections from ports around the world—including seven varieties of crab, six varieties of oysters, Great Lakes walleyed pike, Copper River king salmon, and whole Florida yellowtail snapper.

Signature dishes include spicy cioppino and a melt-in-your-mouth peppered tuna fillet served rare. The wine "cellar" (actually the second-floor hallway) holds more than 2,000 bottles. ♦ Seafood ♦ Daily lunch and dinner. 934.2628

18 Portobello Yacht Club ★★★$$$
The Northern Italian fare at this 326-seat restaurant run by Levy Restaurants of Chicago is wonderful, if pricey. Even if you're not a pizza fan, try a small one as an appetizer; with their thin crusts and perfect spices, they redefine the dish. The Pizza Verdure, with sun-dried tomatoes, eggplant, mushrooms, zucchini, and provolone cheese, makes a fine starter, as does the velvety baked garlic on bread. For an entrée, forget your diet and try *salsiccia e polenta* (homemade Italian sausage served over creamy polenta, with caramelized onions). Though the fare is Italian, the decor is nautical, with photos of yachts and pennants on the walls. ♦ Italian ♦ Daily lunch and dinner

19 Wildhorse Saloon
If you enjoy country music, you'll love this restaurant/nightclub. **Wildhorse** features live bands seven nights a week and a concert hall where country recording artists perform. There's also a 1,500-square-foot dance floor where dance lessons are given nightly. The fare is basic barbecue. ♦ Cover included in fee to complex. Admission charge for special concerts. Daily 11:30AM-1:30AM

20 Rock N Roll Beach Club The biggest hits of the 1950s and 1960s—with a few current Top 40 tunes mixed in—are played by live bands seven nights a week. A large dance floor is on the bottom level; games and billiards tables are on levels two and three. The club includes a small retail shop called **Island Depot.** ♦ Cover included in fee to complex. Daily 7PM-2AM

21 D-Zertz ★$ Order a slice of fresh chocolate cake or cheesecake and a cup of cappuccino or espresso in this cozy little shop. Everything is made fresh each day. ♦ Desserts ♦ Daily 10:30AM-1AM

22 Pleasure Island Jazz Company
This is the only place in **Walt Disney World** that offers live jazz performances; bands play nightly. Lighting is subdued, the noise level bearable, and the seating comfortable. The lounge serves appetizers and desserts. ♦ Cover included in fee to complex. Daily 8PM-2AM

23 Music Legends Here you can purchase just about anything from T-shirts to coffee mugs bearing the likeness of your favorite rock star.

24 Changing Attitudes Trendy, youthful fashions—mostly in black, white, or a combination thereof—are sold here.

24 Mannequins Dance Palace Open to the over-21 crowd only, this dance club for the young, Lycra-clad set has a post-Industrial look that was all the rage in New York some years back. Still, it's a fine place for people watching. There's Top 40 music and a revolving dance floor. If you no longer look so great in skin-tight duds, stop in anyhow—Disney will thrill you with some great special effects. There are several themed shows nightly. ♦ Cover included in fee to complex. Daily 7PM-2AM

25 8TRAX Complete with bean-bag chairs and revolving mirrored balls hanging from the ceiling, this disco dance club takes you back to the 1970s. If you still like Grand Funk Railroad and Donna Summer, you'll want to check it out. ♦ Cover included in fee to complex. Daily 7PM-2AM

26 Superstar Studios Ever long to strap on a guitar and swivel your hips like Elvis? For a fee, you can star in your own rock video and take it home to show friends.

27 Avigators Supply This trendy shop has some pricey but tempting goods. It's Disney's version of Banana Republic.

28 Adventurers Club Styled as a 1930s-era private club for eccentric world travelers, this place has some clever touches, including old photographs of hunting and fishing safaris and "talking" African masks on the walls. There are stage shows, and the actors interact with guests during the shows. There are five different rooms with continuous entertainment. ♦ Cover included in fee to complex. Daily 7PM-2AM

29 BET SoundStage Club Black Entertainment Television often brings live performers to this high-energy hot spot that features soul, rhythm and blues, jazz, and hip-hop music. Music videos and **BET**'s own dancers keep the crowd on the dance floor. This club is for patrons 21 years of age and older. ♦ Cover included in fee to complex. Daily 8PM-2AM

30 West End Stage New Year's Eve is celebrated nightly with confetti, lasers, and fireworks at this outdoor stage area. The action starts at 11:45PM, but arrive earlier to secure a good space. The stage also hosts a collection of live performances by top-name artists and music groups.

31 The Comedy Warehouse A very entertaining improvisational comedy troupe performs five times nightly. The later it gets, the more crowded things become, so try to arrive early. The room is tiered, making every seat in the house a good one (though the stools aren't the most comfortable things to sit on for extended periods). ◆ Admission charge in addition to the Pleasure Island admission when headliners appear. Daily 7:30PM-2AM

Downtown Disney West Side

Adjacent to **Downtown Disney Marketplace** and **Pleasure Island, Downtown Disney West Side** expands **Downtown Disney** with exciting restaurants, nightclubs, and shopping—65 acres featuring celebrity tenants like Gloria Estefan, Dan Aykroyd (one of the owners of the **House of Blues**), and superchef Wolfgang Puck.

Two of Disney's giant new attractions are here: **DisneyQuest,** an interactive family entertainment center, and **Cirque du Soleil,** a show that blends circus art and theatrics. A 24-screen movie complex also draws big crowds.

There's an eclectic collection of little shops that sell mostly non-Disney merchandise, everything from sculpture and jewelry to hand-rolled cigars. Shopping is most enjoyable during the day, when the crowds are lighter. After dark, the street gets jammed with revelers strolling over from **Pleasure Island** or coming out of the movie theater.

Downtown Disney West Side, unlike **Pleasure Island,** charges no admission after dark (though you pay for **DisneyQuest, Cirque du Soleil,** and concerts at the **House of Blues**). Parking is free, and there's bus and water taxi transportation to and from Disney hotels. Shops open daily at 9:30AM and close at 10PM; restaurants are open from 11:30AM until midnight or later. For more information, call 824.4321. ◆ Buena Vista Dr (between Hotel Plaza Blvd and Bonnet Creek Pkwy)

32 Planet Hollywood ★$$ Part of the international chain co-owned by Demi Moore, Arnold Schwarzenegger, Sylvester Stallone, and Bruce Willis, this eatery features movie memorabilia, tasty but fairly standard fare,

and the (slim) chance of seeing a real-life movie star. The sphere-shaped, three-level building seats over 400 and is scattered with such big- and little-screen artifacts as Tom Hanks's costume from *Forrest Gump,* a Klingon battle cruiser from TV's "Star Trek," and the pistol brandished by Clint Eastwood in *The Good, the Bad and the Ugly.* Food is pizza, turkey burgers, salads, pasta, and the like. ◆ American ◆ Daily lunch and dinner (until 1AM). 827.7827

33 AMC 24 Theatres Complex This is an expansion of the original **AMC Theatres** built several years ago, so you'll feel lucky if the movie you want to see is in one of the 14 new or 2 remodeled theaters with roomy, stadium-style seats. All theaters have a new sound system and listening devices for the hearing impaired. This is a good place to go on a rainy day. ◆ 298.4488

34 Starabilias There are more than 1,000 pieces of original memorabilia on the shelves here at any given time, all restored and guaranteed authentic. There are autographed items dating from 1700 to the present, Hollywood costumes from 1939 to the present, autographed guitars from 1956 to the present, and nostalgic gifts.

34 All Star Gear An extension of the **Official All Star Cafe,** this shop sells items of apparel for several different sports— tennis and golf polo shirts, hockey and football jerseys, and basketball tank tops, to name just a few. There are also logo pins, watches, golf balls, footballs, coffee mugs, and more.

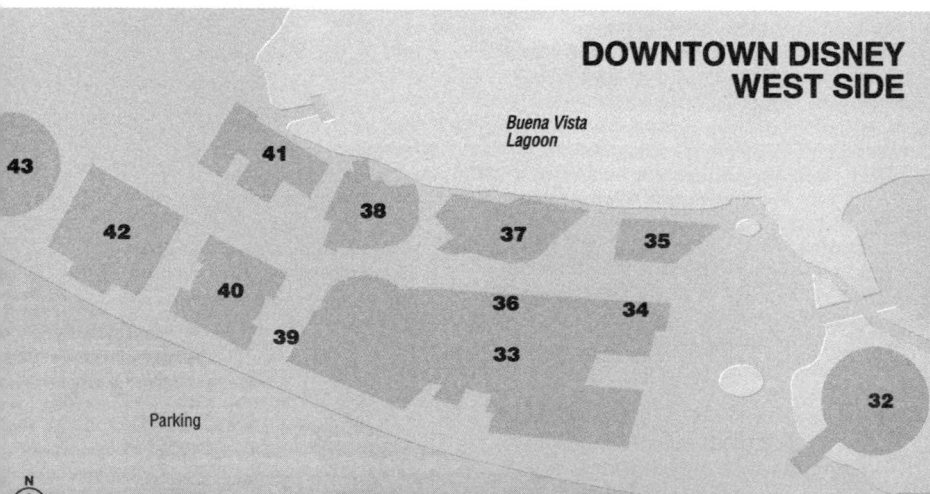

DOWNTOWN DISNEY WEST SIDE

Buena Vista Lagoon

43

41

42

38

40

39

37

36

33

35

34

32

Parking

N

34 Magnetron More than 20,000 collector-quality magnets line the steel walls in this 1,400-square-foot specialty shop. You name it, you'll find it on a magnet—magnets that talk, sing, ring, and beep; magnets that light up, change color, and glow in the dark; magnets in the shape of food, animals, and everyday objects like telephones. The shop also carries the world's largest selection of magnetic space aliens.

34 Disney's Candy Cauldron This shop is themed as the dungeon of the Wicked Queen from *Snow White and the Seven Dwarfs,* but there are friendly cooks in the open kitchen stirring the fudge, making candy apples, and dipping strawberries and marshmallows in chocolate. There are more than 200 sweets in all, from decadent truffles to cotton candy.

35 Forty Thirst Street $ This tiny cafe with walls of windows serves some of the freshest coffee you'll ever sip—ground and brewed within two minutes of roasting. Though there are a few tables inside, most guests order their coffee to go. Also served are cappuccino, espresso, fresh juices, smoothies, and desserts. ♦ Cafe ♦ M-Th, Su 9:30AM-11PM; F-Sa 9:30AM-midnight. 827.0100

36 Celebrity Eyeworks Studio You can gaze at autographed photos of celebrities and see the eyewear that actors wore in films in this hip eyeglasses shop. Only high-end brands, like Revo, Oakley, Gucci, Donna Karan, Calvin Klein, and 22-karat-gold–plated Boucherons, are for sale.

36 Hoypoloi Gallery High ceilings and exposed brick walls are part of the Zen-like ambience of this gallery of one-of-a-kind pieces created by artists from across the US. Water falls over Japanese river stones in Zen fountains; the subtle fragrance of incense is in the air, along with lilting music. The shop offers light sculpture, accent furniture, and small decorative accessories. This is one of the best shops at **Downtown Disney.**

36 Sosa Family Cigars The Sosa family has been rolling cigars for generations, and every week there's an experienced *torcedor* (cigar roller) showing off his handiwork. Cigars from around the world are for sale, with the most expensive ones stored in a 150-square-foot walk-in humidor.

36 Wildhorse Store If you need a country-western outfit to wear to the **Wildhorse**

Saloon at **Pleasure Island,** this is the place to get it. The shop features a mix of traditional and contemporary clothes.

37 Bongos Cuban Cafe ★$$ Bongos brings Cuban cuisine and Latin rhythms to this tropical-themed restaurant created by superstar Gloria Estefan and her husband and producer, Emilio. It's one of the prettiest restaurants at **Walt Disney World,** a perfect place to go for an authentic *mojito* (a rum, lime juice, and sugar cocktail) and live music. Service can be slow, but the food is good, though not spectacular. ♦ Cuban ♦ Daily lunch and dinner (until 2AM). 828.0999

38 Wolfgang Puck Cafe ★★★$$$ World-renowned chef Wolfgang Puck brings his artfully edible West Coast creations to this colorful cafe designed by his wife and partner, Barbara Lazaroff. The cafe has four different concepts: quick service in a small eatery with a separate entrance; a sushi bar at the front; a downstairs dining room; and a fancier upstairs dining room. Don't miss Puck's pizzas, or his spicy Chinois chicken salad. ♦ American ♦ Daily lunch and dinner (until midnight). 938.9653

39 Guitar Gallery by George's Music More than 150 custom, collector, rare, and unique guitars from the top manufacturers in the world are for sale—prices range from $199 to $25,000. There are also books and educational videos.

40 Virgin Megastore This is the largest music and entertainment store in Florida—49,000 square feet of music, video, interactive media, and books. There are more than 150,000 music titles on CD and cassette, and more than 300 listening stations for sampling CDs. And there are about 20,000 music and movie titles on video, laser disc, and DVD, including new releases and classics, many of which can be sampled at the 20 video/laser disc preview stations. Outside, an elevated stage is used for live performances.

41 House of Blues ★$$ This restaurant, with its distressed wood and rusted metal exterior, is modeled after an old-time Mississippi juke joint. Inside, the walls are covered with folk art from founder Isaac Tigrett's unusual collection, most of which was created by outsider artists in the Mississippi Delta region. The menu offers eclectic cuisine from the bayou, including jambalaya, étoufée, and bread pudding, but there's also a wide selection of salads and sandwiches. Adjacent to the 500-seat restaurant is a 2,000-person-capacity music hall featuring world-class and local artists from the worlds of blues, rock 'n' roll, hip-hop, alternative, country, gospel, and jazz music; the concert hot line is 934.2222. An energetic Gospel Brunch takes place in the concert hall on Sundays, featuring regionally and nationally recognized artists and a Southern-style buffet. The **House of Blues Company Store** carries everything from rare books and videos about blues art and culture to T-shirts, hats, and jackets. ♦ American ♦ Daily lunch and dinner (until 2AM). 827.0112

42 DisneyQuest You can climb aboard a real river raft, buckle into a motion simulator to ride a roller coaster of your own design, or fly a magic carpet at this high-tech playground housed in a giant five-story building. Each of the four entertainment zones—**Explore,** where guests discover exotic locales; **Score,** where guests match their game-playing skills against superheros; **Create,** a studio for artistic self-expression; and **Replay,** a carnival on the moon where guests experience classic games in a new way—has its own interactive challenges, from the relatively simple (like skeeball) to the amazingly sophisticated (**CyberSpace Mountain,** where you ride your own creation in a simulator). You can happily spend an afternoon or evening here, and the concept is pay-as-you-play, with a debit card that's purchased at the entrance for unlimited play; simply swipe the card at attractions. ♦ Daily 10:30AM-midnight.

CIRQUE DU SOLEIL

43 Cirque du Soleil Just opening at press time, this extraordinary show features a stunning blend of circus art and street entertainment, with outrageous costumes and original sets and music. There are 64 artists from all over the world performing two live shows a day in a brand-new 1,671-seat theater. ♦ Admission. W-Sa 5:30, 8:30; Su 2:30, 5:30. 934.7639

44 Team Disney Building Although the Walt Disney Company is based in Burbank, California, it obviously has sizable operations in Florida. About a thousand employees moved into this 401,000-square-foot office building constructed by Tokyo-based **Arata Isozaki & Associates** in 1991. Many have joked that the rose-and-green cone that rises from the center of the building makes it look

like a nuclear power plant. Actually, the hollow cone houses an ingenious, eight-story sundial, complete with a viewing platform. The atrium is open to the public. ♦ 1375 Buena Vista Dr (between Hotel Plaza Blvd and Epcot Center Dr)

Typhoon Lagoon

So thoroughly landscaped is this 56-acre water park (see map on page 82) that you feel as if you're on a tropical island. **Mount Mayday,** the world's largest man-made watershed mountain, is the park's centerpiece; it houses **Typhoon Lagoon's** water gathering/pumping system. A shrimp boat teetering atop its peak testifies to the terrible (imaginary) typhoon that once blew through this "tropical village," leaving the buildings in their present rickety shape. A geyser periodically bursts through the boat. It's possible to climb the 85 feet to the top of the mountain for an excellent overview of the water park. Two inexpensive restaurants, **Leaning Palms** and **Typhoon Tilly's Galley & Grog,** serve salads, burgers, fries, and other snacks (**Leaning Palms** has the more extensive menu). There's also **Let's Go Slurpin',** a full-service bar, and **Lowtide Lou's,** a hot-dog stand. Or bring your own lunch—there are a few picnic tables. Changing rooms and coin lockers are available. **Typhoon Lagoon** is open daily from 9AM to 8PM during June, July, and August and from 10AM to 5PM the rest of the year—weather permitting—except in January and February, when the park is usually closed for refurbishment. Children under 10 must be an accompanied by an adult. There's an admission charge, but parking is free. For additional information call 824.4321. ♦ Buena Vista Dr (between Hotel Plaza Blvd and Epcot Center Dr)

45 Typhoon Lagoon Surf Pool The 2.75-million-gallon wave pool—the world's largest inland surfing lagoon—gives the park its name and contains a monster wave machine that creates breakers up to six feet high. If you have small children, watch them carefully. These waves will definitely be over their heads.

46 Ketchakiddee Creek On the tamer side, this creek is geared to smaller children and features slides, a raft ride, and bubbling jets.

47 Keelhaul Falls This ride aboard oversize inner tubes whips you through a triple vortex (a twisting slide).

48 Gangplank Falls A family ride, it features four-passenger rafts that navigate the falls.

49 Mayday Falls Board an oversize inner tube for a don't-miss ride down a 460-foot slide through white water.

50 Storm Slides: Jib Jammer, Rudder Buster and Stern Burner These three body slides take you zooming through waterfalls, rock formations, and caves before plunking you down into one of several lagoons. With a top speed of only 20 mph, the ride is far more genteel than the **Kowabunga** (see page 82).

TYPHOON LAGOON

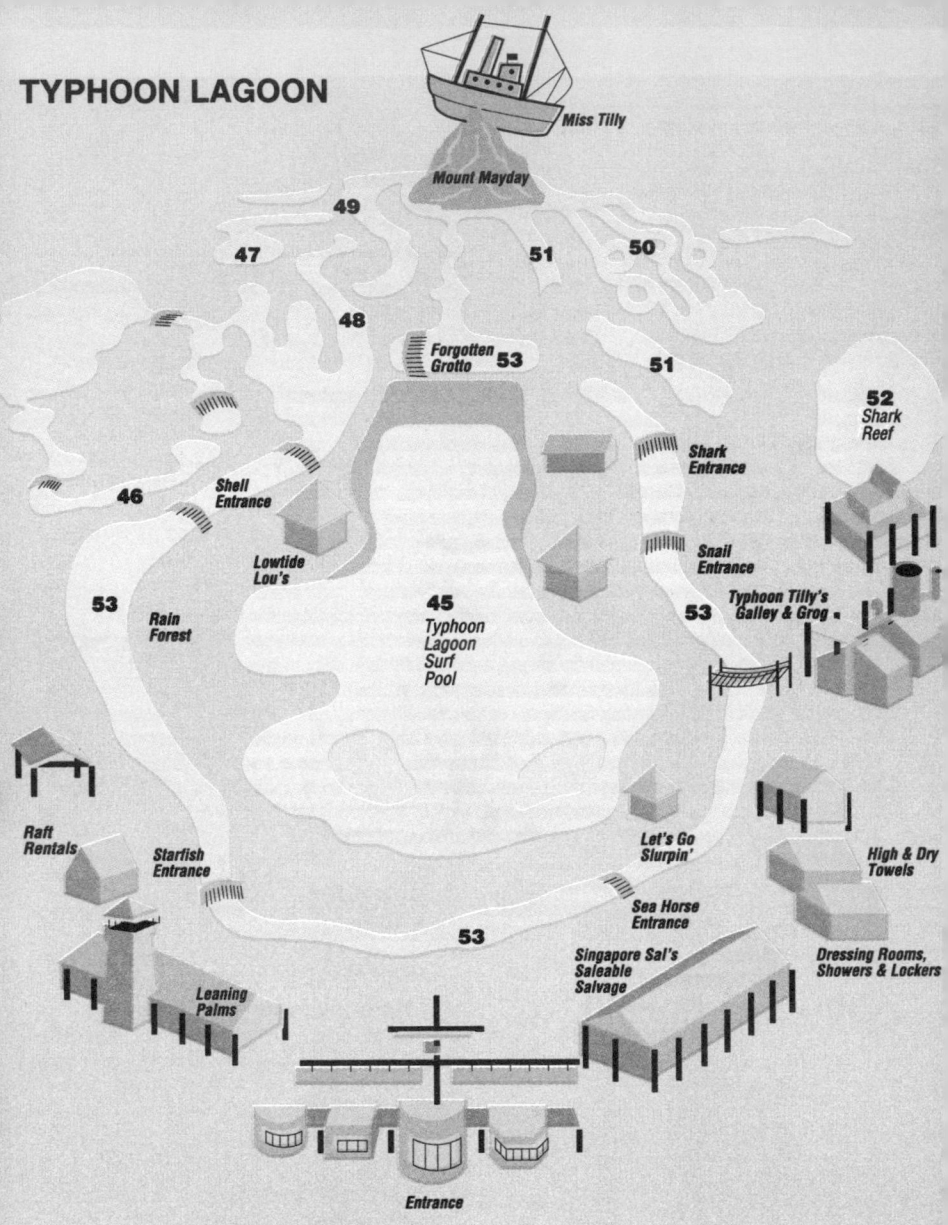

Miss Tilly

Mount Mayday

49

47   51   50

48

Forgotten
Grotto   53   51

52
Shark
Reef

Shell
Entrance   Shark
Entrance

46   Snail
Entrance

Lowtide
Lou's   45
Typhoon
Lagoon
Surf
Pool   Typhoon Tilly's
Galley & Grog

53   53
Rain
Forest

Raft
Rentals

Let's Go
Slurpin'   High & Dry
Towels

Starfish
Entrance   Sea Horse
Entrance

53   Dressing Rooms,
Showers & Lockers

Leaning
Palms   Singapore Sal's
Saleable
Salvage

Entrance

51 Humunga Kowabunga Speed Slide
There are actually two water slides that
send you plunging down a man-made
mountain, through a cave, and out again
at 30 mph. The 214-foot slide drops you
51 feet so fast that the ride is over before
you know it.

52 Shark Reef In a hurry? Skip this. Yes,
the lure of swimming in a 362,000-gallon
saltwater pool among real fish (including
small, nonbiting sharks) and alongside a
wrecked (albeit fake) ship is mighty tempting,
but if it's a particularly busy day, hordes of
other swimmers make it less than fun. First,
you must wait in line to get snorkel gear, then
wait in line to be instructed on how to use
it (even if you already know how), all for a
five-minute swim at best. You must swim in
one direction only, then you're outta there to
make room for others. At that point, the thrill
is gone.

53 Castaway Creek All the other rides may
be brief, but this one is a relaxing, leisurely
30-minute float in an inner tube on a creek
that conveys you around the whole water
park. You can continue floating for as long
as you like, stopping at points along the
way—don't miss **Rain Forest,** a picturesque
section in which you get sprayed with a
gentle, cooling mist as you pass through.

Disney Village Resort Area

Two moderately priced hotels, a resort consisting of more expensive villas and town houses, and a time-share development are the Disney-owned lodging options closest to **Downtown Disney** and **Typhoon Lagoon**. This area also boasts three Disney golf courses, the **Lake Buena Vista Golf Club,** and the **Eagle Pines** and **Osprey Ridge Golf Courses** at the **Bonnet Creek Golf Club.** Those staying at a Disney hotel may reserve a tee time up to 60 days in advance; others may reserve 30 days in advance (824.2270).

Though many **Walt Disney World** resorts and restaurants list separate telephone numbers, there are just four you need to remember: 824.2222 is for the Disney operator, who can connect you anywhere on Disney property; 824.4321 is the general information number for basic questions; W.DISNEY (934.7639) is the number for hotel reservations; and WDW.DINE (939.3463) is the number to dial for dining reservations for priority seating.

54 Disney's Port Orleans Resort $$ Disney has done a good job making its "moderate" hotels attractive, welcoming, and efficient. Although this complex is enormous (1,008 guest rooms in seven three-story structures), its wings are cleverly arranged around a beautifully landscaped square. The rooms have 18th-century accents, such as ornate sinks, brocade-patterned wallpaper, and ceiling fans. The hotel's courtyard has a New Orleans look; wrought-iron balconies look down on courtyards lined with azaleas and magnolias. The main pool, **Doubloon Lagoon,** has a water slide; there's also a kiddie pool. ♦ 2201 Orleans Dr (between Bonnet Creek Pkwy and Sassagoula Cir). 934.5000; www.disneyworld.com ♿

Within Disney's Port Orleans Resort:

Sassagoula Floatworks and Food Factory ★$$ Decorated with real Mardi Gras floats, this informal dining area does a credible job of preparing a spicy chicken jambalaya. Food is served in a trendy food court, which offers a broad selection of dishes, including the New Orleans–style doughnuts called beignets. There's good ice cream, and baked goods are made on the premises. ♦ Fast Food ♦ Hours vary at the various counters, but something is always open from 6AM to midnight

Bonfamille's Cafe ★★$ This smallish, 156-seat cafe is the hotel's only sit-down restaurant. The menu includes excellent cuts of steak and spicy Creole crawfish entrées. A fountain adds a bit of splash to the pleasant, shaded courtyard dining area. ♦ American ♦ Daily breakfast and dinner. 934.5412

Scat Cat's Club It doesn't quite have the funky feel of a real New Orleans bar, but you'll appreciate the beautiful photographic prints of jazz stars adorning the walls. Hors d'oeuvres and specialty drinks are served. ♦ Daily 4:30PM-midnight

55 Disney's Dixie Landings Resort $$ A meandering river connects **Disney's Port Orleans Resort** with this 2,048-room establishment, another of Disney's moderately priced hotels. The vast, sprawling complex has an Old South ambience and offers lodging in buildings designed to resemble either a stately plantation home or a tin-roofed bayou dwelling. Rooms are all the same size and well outfitted; most have two double beds, a few have one king-size bed. The complex also has two restaurants, five pools, two lounges, a themed play area, a swimming pool with a water slide, and an old-time fishing hole. Watercraft are available for rent. ♦ 1251 Dixie Dr (just east of Sassagoula Cir). 934.6000; www.disneyworld.com ♿

56 Bonnet Creek Golf Club This is home base for two championship courses. There's a pro shop, and lessons are available. Golf View Dr (north of Vista Blvd). 824.2270

At the Bonnet Creek Golf Club:

Eagle Pines Golf Course Designed by Pete Dye, this 18-hole layout (par 72, 6,309 yards) features undulating greens and low-profile, dishlike fairways. ♦ Greens fee. Daily. Reservations required

Osprey Ridge Golf Course This 18-hole course (par 72, 6,680 yards) is the work of Tom Fazio. It offers large greens and rolling fairways surrounded by high ridges and scrub oaks. ♦ Greens fee. Daily. Reservations required

57 Disney's Old Key West Resort $$$$ This vacation-ownership complex features Old Key West architecture and one-, two-, and three-bedroom villas. To become a member, you must pay a one-time purchase price plus annual dues. Membership lasts until the year 2042 and includes reciprocal exchanges with more than 200 resorts worldwide (not just other Disney theme park properties). Some villas are available for nightly rentals as well. Each unit has a full kitchen, TV and VCR, porch, laundry room, and a whirlpool in the master bath. The complex has four pools, a fitness center, a playground, an arcade, and a marina; it overlooks the **Lake Buena Vista Golf Club.** ♦ Community Dr (between Treehouse La and Bonnet Creek Pkwy). 827.7700; www.disneyworld.com

58 Lake Buena Vista Golf Club Joe Lee designed this 18-hole, 6,391-yard, par-72 course. It has small, well-bunkered greens and meanders through dense pine forests and residential resort areas. There's a clubhouse with a pro shop, and lessons are available.

♦ Greens fee. Daily. Reservations required. Club Lake Dr (south of Fairway Dr). 824.2270

59 Disney Institute $$$ Staying at this unique resort is really a whole new way for Disney fans to vacation. No two stays are alike, because guests design their own schedules, choosing from hands-on programs. You might spend the morning in a cooking class, the afternoon learning about photography. A family can take a program together or everyone can choose a different one and meet at the end of the day. Children must be at least age 10 to take a program. Note that a stay at **Disney Institute** doesn't preclude visiting the theme parks; you can create a vacation that allows time for both. The resort looks like an intimate college campus, and you're within walking distance of all of the classrooms. Accommodations are cozy bungalows or town houses. **Seasons,** the resort restaurant, is open daily for breakfast, lunch, and dinner. The **Disney Institute Spa** is first class, with dozens of treatments available. And the adjacent **Sports and Fitness Center** offers aerobics, swimming aerobics, fitness consultations, and a state-of-the-art exercise room. Because the "institute" concept can be a bit confusing, it's best to call for a free video, which shows all that the resort offers. And Disney has a staff of "vacation consultants" to help you plan a stay. ♦ 1960 Magnolia Way (off Villa Ave). 827.1100, 800/496.6337; www.disneyworld.com

60 Casting Center You've visited **Walt Disney World** as a tourist and now you want to work here; this is the place to submit your resume. The center's bold gold letters have been an eye-catching sight from Interstate 4 since the **Robert A.M. Stern**–designed structure was built in 1988. If you decide to file an application, you'll hire into a small rotunda, then up a broad ramp—where whimsical murals depict great moments from Disney history—to the receptionist's desk. Disney has always referred to every one of its employees, from street sweepers to on-stage performers, as members of its "cast," because everyone is part of the ongoing show. ♦ M-F, 7:30AM-5PM. 1515 Buena Vista Dr (between Hotel Plaza Blvd and Bonnet Creek Pkwy). 934.6944

Disney Village Hotel Plaza

Seven Disney-associated hotels are found on **Walt Disney World** property in this area. Disney-associated means that while Disney does not operate them, they meet Disney standards and offer some of the privileges of the Disney-owned resorts. The advantage these hotels have over the Disney properties is that they provide transportation to and tickets and package deals for the non-Disney theme parks in the area, as well as discounts within **Downtown Disney.** The seven hotels are within

walking distance of **Downtown Disney Marketplace, Pleasure Island,** and **The Crossroads of Lake Buena Vista,** a shopping and entertainment center outside **Walt Disney World.** You may be steered to one of the hotels if you call Disney's reservations number and the Disney-owned resorts are full or too pricey for your budget (though the rates at the Disney-affiliated hotels are still generally higher than those at comparable hotels off Disney property). **Downtown Disney Resort Area** hotels are linked by Disney's efficient shuttle bus to its theme parks; none are on the monorail.

61 The Hilton Disney World Resort $$$ The most elegant property in **Hotel Plaza,** this 814-room hotel has a pink marble lobby, four restaurants, two pools—one with a poolside bar—and a health club. ♦ 1751 Hotel Plaza Blvd (at Buena Vista Dr). 827.4000, 800/782.4414; fax 827.6380; www.hilton.com

Within The Hilton Disney World Resort:

Benihana ★$$$ A branch of the well-known chain, it features light but satisfying Japanese food cooked with flair by dextrous chefs right at your table in the simple, contemporary-style dining room. ♦ Japanese ♦ Daily dinner. 827.4000

62 Courtyard by Marriott $$$ Most of the 323 rooms have private balconies, and those in the 14-story tower circle an unspectacular atrium with a bar on the ground floor. There are two heated pools and a cafe/grill. ♦ 1805 Hotel Plaza Blvd (between Buena Vista Dr and Apopka-Vineland Rd). 828.8888, 800/654.2000 in FL, 800/223.9930; fax 827.4623; www.courtyard.com/mcolb &

63 Hotel Royal Plaza $$$ A solid choice for families, this 394-room hotel has a Bermuda-inspired decor. Each room has a private balcony and the grounds offer four lighted tennis courts, a swimming pool, a sauna, and a whirlpool. There's also a restaurant, pool lounge, and snack bar. If you're feeling flush with cash, the hotel has two celebrity suites, with decorative appointments lent by Burt Reynolds and Barbara Mandrell. A glass elevator services the concierge units, which offer such special amenities as continental breakfast, turndown service, and a lounge. ♦ 1905 Hotel Plaza Blvd (between Buena Vista Dr and Apopka-Vineland Rd). 828.2828, 800/248.7890; fax 827.6338; www.royalplaza.com &

64 DoubleTree Guest Suites $$$ There are 229 spacious suites in this pretty hotel, each

with a bedroom and a vanity dressing area; a dining area; and a living room furnished with a sofa bed. Suites are packed with amenities, including three remote-controlled TVs (one in the bathroom), a wet bar, and a small refrigerator. There's a hotel restaurant. ◆ 2305 Hotel Plaza Blvd (between Buena Vista Dr and Apopka-Vineland Rd). 934.1000, 800/222.8733; fax 934.1015; www.doubletreehotels.com &

65 Wyndham Palace Resort & Spa $$$ A European-style spa, the only one of its type in Central Florida, is one of the star attractions of this 1,300-room hotel. The spa offers à la carte services and half- and full-day packages, plus spa cuisine. Spa guest rooms are ecologically friendly, featuring upgraded bathroom amenities, special air- and water-purifying systems, undyed linens, and allergy-free pillows. Its well-trained staff, three swimming pools, lighted tennis courts, and a health club, are some other perks. A separate wing houses 200 roomy suites. The hotel has standout restaurants, too (see below). ◆ 1900 Buena Vista Dr (between Hotel Plaza Blvd and Winter Garden–Vineland Rd). 827.2727, 800/327.2990; fax 827.6034

Within the Wyndham Palace Resort & Spa:

Arthur's 27 ★★★★$$$$ Intimate, romantic, sophisticated, and elegant, this 27th-floor restaurant provides a striking panoramic view and serves fabulous four-, five-, or six-course feasts. Diners select each course from a number of specials, including lobster bisque, red snapper, Black Sea scallops with mango salsa, loin of lamb, and Amaretto mascarpone cheesecake. This place is popular among local residents because the food and atmosphere are so wonderful. ◆ American ◆ Daily dinner. Reservations for priority seating recommended; jacket requested. 827.3450

Outback Restaurant ★$$$ A touch of Australia in Central Florida, this casual, attractive establishment is decorated with photos of Australian wildlife and landscapes. Choice, tender steaks, prepared in the brick-lined grill area in the middle of the restaurant, are the house specialty, and some 99 brands of beer are served. A glass elevator takes diners from the third-floor lobby to the restaurant on the first floor. Note: This place is

not affiliated with the Outback Steak House chain. ◆ Australian ◆ Daily dinner. 827.3430

66 Grosvenor Resort $$$ Two heated swimming pools, a hot tub, two lighted tennis courts, two racquetball courts, and a video gameroom are among the facilities at this 628-room hotel. Standard room amenities include TV sets and VCRs. The property has a cozy, wood-paneled British look and, in keeping with that theme, there's a restaurant called **Baskerville's,** a pub called **Moriarty's,** and a Sherlock Holmes dinner show. ◆ 1850 Hotel Plaza Blvd (between Buena Vista Dr and Apopka-Vineland Rd). 828.4444, 800/624.4109; fax 828.8120; www.grosvenorresort.com

67 Travelodge Walt Disney World $$ One of the smallest and least expensive hotels in **Hotel Plaza,** it has 325 spacious rooms (the largest in this area) with two queen-size beds; some units come equipped with a hair dryer, coffeemaker, safe, and mini-bar. **Toppers,** a nightclub on the 18th floor, has a splendid view, and there's also a lobby cocktail lounge, a restaurant, and a cafe. A pool, gameroom, playground, two gift shops, and laundry facilities complete the picture. ◆ 2000 Hotel Plaza Blvd (between Buena Vista Dr and Apopka-Vineland Rd). 828.2424, 800/423.1022 in FL, 800/348.3765; fax 828.8933

Lake Buena Vista

The following hotels and shops are not on **Walt Disney World** property, but you'd never know it by looking at a map because they're so close to the Disney "border." Keep in mind that since they're officially outside the **World,** they don't have access to the Disney transportation system and do not offer the other benefits available to those staying at a Disney property.

68 The Crossroads of Lake Buena Vista More than two dozen stores and restaurants can be found at this shopping and entertainment center. Spend a few hours on the miniature golf course, then grab a bite to eat at one of the many fast-food joints, including **McDonald's.** There's even a nice bookstore. ◆ Apopka-Vineland Rd (between I-4 and Palm Pkwy)

At The Crossroads of Lake Buena Vista:

Pebbles ★★$$ This pleasant restaurant, one of Central Florida's most popular, boasts a creative menu and a large variety of wines and imported beers. The daily specials are normally terrific, as are the pasta dishes, salads, and chicken sandwiches. Don't be afraid to bring the kids; they serve burgers, too. The Key West–style dining room features lots of plants and pastel colors and overlooks a small lake. ◆ American ◆ Daily lunch, dinner, and late-night snacks. 827.1111

Pirate's Cove Adventure Golf Climb mountains, walk under waterfalls, and hit through caves on this 18-hole miniature golf course. ◆ Admission. Daily. 827.1242

White's Bookstore You'll find great vacation and poolside reading here. There's a nice magazine selection. ◆ Daily. 827.1268

Gooding's This grocery store is open all day and all night. ◆ Daily 24 hours. 827.1200

Jungle Jim's $ The diverse menu and funky decor, including walls lined with movie posters and jungle paraphernalia, may be just what you're looking for after a round of miniature golf at **Pirate's Cove.** The specialty here is the gourmet burger, and there's a children's menu. ◆ American ◆ Daily lunch and dinner. 827.1257

69 Radisson Lake Buena Vista $$ This attractive, 200-room hotel offers free transportation to **Walt Disney World** attractions, a beautiful outdoor pool with water slide and waterfall, a kids' play area, a restaurant and bar, a snack shop, and a whirlpool. Most rooms have balconies and small refrigerators. ◆ 8686 Palm Pkwy (between Apopka-Vineland Rd and Lake Ave). 239.8400, 800/333.3333; fax 239.8025; www.radisson.com ♿

69 RIU Orlando $ So close you hardly notice it's not on Disney property, this small, upscale lodging (formerly the **Wyndham Gardens** hotel) offers free shuttle-bus service to **Walt Disney World.** The 167 spacious rooms come equipped with TV sets, coffeemakers, and hair dryers. There's a pool, sundeck, health club, sauna, and whirlpool. ◆ 8688 Palm Pkwy (between Apopka-Vineland Rd and Lake Ave). 239.8500, 800/228.2846; fax 239.8591; www.RIUhotels.com ♿

70 Comfort Inn Lake Buena Vista $ Owned by Orlando hotelier Harris Rosen, who offers some of the lowest rates in town, the 640 basic rooms at this sprawling hotel face he street or the interstate. On the plus side, children age 11 and under eat free at the hotel restaurant. There are two pools and a gift shop. ◆ 8442 Palm Pkwy (between Apopka-Vineland Rd and Lake Ave). 239.7300, 800/999.7300, 800/221.2222; fax 239.7740; www.comfortinn.com ♿

71 Embassy Suites Lake Buena Vista Resort $$$ Painted a wild combination of pink, tangerine, and aqua, this all-suite resort features 280 two-room suites that, while smallish, are packed with amenities. There's a TV in the bedroom and another with a VCR in the living room; the kitchen is equipped with a coffeemaker and a microwave oven. A free breakfast, including eggs made to order, is served in a sunny atrium, where the **Tropix Grille,** which serves dinner, is also located. Other perks include a pool with a small indoor section, a children's pool, a tidy health club with up-to-date equipment, a sauna, a whirlpool, and a poolside bar and grill. ◆ 8100 Lake Ave (at Palm Pkwy). 239.1144, 800/25.SUITE; fax 239.1718; www.embassy-suites.com ♿

72 Howard Johnson Park Square Inn & Suites $ With 86 two-room suites, two pools, a whirlpool, a playground, and shuffleboard courts, it's a good value for families. Suites have two double beds, a pullout queen sofa bed, two color TVs, and a kitchenette area with a microwave oven. There's also a small restaurant. ◆ 8501 Palm Pkwy (between Apopka-Vineland Rd and Lake Ave). 239.6900, 800/635.8684; fax 239.1287; www.hojo.com ♿

73 Grand Cypress Resort This 1,500-acre luxury playground on the border of Disney property has become a local landmark, attracting both an international and domestic clientele. The complex includes two lodging choices—the **Hyatt Regency–Grand Cypress Hotel** and the **Villas of Grand Cypress**—plus 45 holes of Jack Nicklaus–designed golf. The courses have been ranked among the 25 best resort golf courses in the US by *Golf Digest.* In addition, there is a lavish equestrian center, the **Racquet Club** (with 12 tennis courts, an open-air racquetball court, an instruction program, and a 150-seat grandstand for tournaments), and the **Grand Cypress Academy of Golf,** featuring top instructors and the "CompuSport" video teaching technique. ◆ 239.4700, 800/835.7377; fax 876.5880; www.grandcypress.com

Within the Grand Cypress Resort:

Hyatt Regency–Grand Cypress Hotel $$$$ The hotel lobby is so special that even if you don't stay overnight you might want to stop by for breakfast, lunch, dinner, or drinks in the lobby bar, which has live entertainment on Saturday and Sunday nights. The Asian art in the lobby is exceptional, as are the furnishings, flowers, and stream alive with goldfish. Gorgeous palm trees and live parrots add to the luxurious tropical ambience—this place really makes you feel like you're on vacation. The 750 rooms have balconies, TV sets, and hair dryers; some have a wet bar. There's also a health club with a sauna, steam room, and massage area, and a thousand-foot sandy beach on a 21-acre lake, where you can rent paddleboats, canoes, and small sailboats. ♦ Grand Cypress Blvd (south of Winter Garden–Vineland Rd). 239.1234, 800/233.1234; fax 239.3800; www.grandcypress.com

Within the Hyatt Regency–Grand Cypress Hotel:

La Coquina ★★★$$$ This place is famous in these parts for its lavish Sunday champagne brunch, perhaps one of the best culinary experiences in Central Florida. The meal begins with a buffet of fruit, cheese, breads, seafood, pâtés, meats, and more. Return to the buffet table as many times as you like, then order a main course (perhaps the tender lobster in champagne sauce). Afterward, a buffet table brimming with desserts beckons. Count on spending at least two very relaxing, satisfying hours for brunch. At dinner, the menu features rack of lamb, glazed shrimp, and red snapper. The elegant dining room has a view of the lake and its swans. ♦ American ♦ M-Sa dinner; Su brunch. Reservations recommended; jacket requested. 239.1234

Hemingway's ★★$$$ Perfectly cooked seafood dishes such as Maryland crab cakes, paella, coconut shrimp, and Maine lobster are served in this airy, Key West–style dining room overlooking the garden and pool. ♦ Seafood ♦ M-Sa lunch and dinner; Su dinner. 239.1234

Cascade ★★$$ A 92-foot waterfall dominates this lovely dining room, which also features floor-to-ceiling windows and six cypress trees. It's the hotel's most casual dining room and a relaxing place for families. ♦ Continental ♦ M-Sa breakfast, lunch, and dinner; Su brunch and dinner. 239.1234

White Horse Saloon ★$$$ You feel transported to an elegant Old West restaurant when you dine here—there's lots of carved wood and dark marble accented with antique mirrors, old-fashioned lamps, and brass rails. The T-bone steaks are tasty and juicy; the menu also features barbecued beef ribs and free-range chicken. A thoroughly professional band of singing cowboys entertains Monday through Saturday nights. ♦ American ♦ Daily dinner. 239.1234

Villas of Grand Cypress $$$ Built along the Jack Nicklaus–designed golf course, these rooms are among the most elegant in Central Florida. Some of the one- to four-bedroom villas have fireplaces and whirlpools; all have full kitchens, dining rooms, and living rooms, as well as private patios or verandas. You're never too far away from the resort's swimming pool and whirlpool, and you can't

beat the twice-daily housekeeping service. There's also room service. ♦ 1 N Jacaranda (north of Winter Garden–Vineland Rd). 239.4700, 800/835.7377; fax 239.7219; www.grandcypress.com

Grand Cypress Equestrian Center
This luxurious riding stable has a professional staff. The center offers private lessons as well as trail riding with guides. ♦ Equestrian Dr (east of Winter Garden–Vineland Rd). 239.1234

74 Holiday Inn SunSpree Resort $$ This hotel served as the prototype and testing site for Holiday Inn's family-friendly SunSpree Resorts line of properties. The 507-room hotel, less than a half-mile from **Walt Disney World** property, goes out of its way to cater to families. Guest rooms all have two queen-size beds and an ironing board, a VCR, refrigerator, microwave oven, coffee and tea maker, and hair dryer. Children are welcomed at a kid-size check-in desk, where they're given a gift. Max the Raccoon, the resort's life-size cartoon character mascot, tucks them in at night. In addition, children 12 and under eat free from the hotel restaurant's special kid's menu when accompanied by a parent. Most attractive to families with young children is **Camp Holiday,** a fully supervised, state-licensed child-care and activity program available for a nominal fee. The hotel has a pool, whirlpool, and fitness center. Waterskiing and jet skiing are available on the nearby lake. ♦ 13351 Apopka-Vineland Rd (between Lake Bryan Dr and I-4). 239.4500, 800/FON.MAXX, 800/HOLIDAY; fax 239.7713; www.kidsuites.com

75 Marriott's Orlando World Center Resort and Convention Center $$ There's so much to do here, you might be tempted never to venture out of this 1,503-room luxury hotel, one of Florida's largest. A health club with whirlpools and saunas, two pools (one indoor and one outdoor), nine restaurants and lounges, 12 tennis courts, a sand volleyball court, and a basketball court are just some of the facilities. Also on the property is an 18-hole golf course—with a clubhouse, pro shop, instruction program, and driving range. The **Lollipop Lounge** has video games, arts and crafts, and certified child care daily. An international currency exchange desk, a car-rental desk, and a hair salon are also on-site. ♦ World Center Dr (just north of International Dr). 239.4200, 800/621.06389; fax 238.8991; www.marriott.com &

Epcot

Walt Disney World's **Epcot** (the name stands for **Experimental Prototype Community of Tomorrow**) is like a grand world's fair, a celebration of human progress, imagination, and culture. The park is divided into two seemingly unrelated areas: **Future World**, featuring ever-changing displays of the world's most advanced technology, and **World Showcase**, with live entertainment, shops, restaurants, movies, and attractions representing 11 countries. What ties the two areas together is a view of the world as a community where science, culture, and education interact. In keeping with this idea, the park not only provides visitors with an entertaining and at times educational vacation experience, but also sponsors a number of serious scientific and cultural programs for students from around the globe.

More than the other Disney theme parks, this one requires a lot of walking because of its unusual figure-eight layout. (A double-decker bus provides transport for the weary.) The main entrance immediately places visitors in the heart of **Future World**, right beneath the giant golf ball known as **Spaceship Earth**. And since **World Showcase** doesn't open until late morning (usually 11AM), it's preferable to spend the early morning hours at **Future World** attractions. Note that most visitors immediately get in line for **Spaceship Earth**, so if it seems crowded, start at one of the other pavilions—the attraction is always less busy later in the day. And don't forget to pick up *Disney's Entertainment Schedule* along with a park map as you enter. The entertainment, featuring performers from around the world, is one of the best aspects of this park. **Epcot** also is home to the springtime Flower and Garden Festival, and the Food and Wine Festival in the fall.

World Showcase, besides featuring the culture, foods, and art of 11 countries, is a shopping mecca (remember, you can have your purchases delivered to the **Package Pickup** for retrieval on your way out, or delivered to your room if you're staying in a Disney resort).

Plan on having at least one meal at **World Showcase**, where the food of the different nations is prepared by native chefs; several of these restaurants are among the best in Central Florida. Lunch and dinner "priority seating" reservations are recommended at all **Epcot** restaurants that offer table service. The Disney "character breakfasts" attended by Mickey Mouse and friends also require priority seating. To avoid disappointment, reserve in advance; priority seating may be booked up to 60 days ahead of time by calling WDW.DINE (939.3463). To make same-day reservations, go to one of the **WorldKey** interactive information service kiosks, located at the front of the park, at the bridge at **World Showcase Plaza**, at the **Germany Showcase**, and at **Innoventions East**. Alcohol is available at all full-service restaurants in **Epcot** (the drinking age is 21). Picnicking inside the park is not allowed.

As at other Disney parks, it's best to arrive early, especially during school vacation times (Easter week, the week between Christmas and New Year's Day, and the summer months). If you run counter to the usual dining patterns by eating lunch early or in the mid-afternoon, or come to the park after an early dinner, you can minimize time spent waiting in line. Try to stay until closing for *IllumiNations*, an impressive show of lasers and lights, fountains and fireworks, all dancing to music over the lake.

Epcot is open daily, generally from 9AM to 9PM, but sometimes the park opens an hour earlier and closes an hour later. There's an admission charge and a parking fee. For information, call the main **Walt Disney World** information number (824.4321). Most **Epcot** attractions, restaurants, and shops are wheelchair accessible.

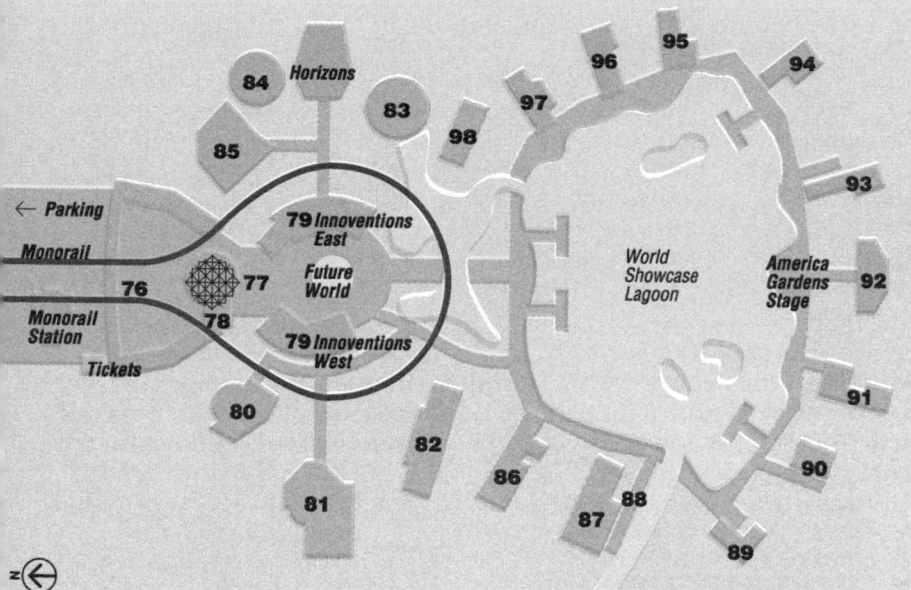

Area code 407 unless otherwise noted.

Future World

The future doesn't seem so far away in this section of **Epcot,** which emphasizes new technologies coming soon to your home and workplace. Advancement and innovation are extolled, although several exhibits sound a cautionary environmentalist note against unbridled progress.

76 Entrance Plaza A **Guest Relations** window is located on the right side of the plaza (there's another in **Innoventions East**). Here you can make same-day dining reservations, exchange foreign currency, find out about various Disney special guest programs, and receive information on guided tours, personal translators, behind-the-scenes educational and personal development programs, and services for visitors with disabilities (taped narrations for the sight-impaired, written descriptions for the hearing-impaired, and the *Guidebook for Guests with Disabilities*). Nearby is the **Package Pickup/Lost and Found.** On the east side of the plaza is the pet kennel, where you can stash Fido for a nominal fee. (Pets are not allowed in the park, and it's not only too hot in Florida to keep your pet in the car—it's also against the law.) East of the ticket booths lies an automatic teller machine that accepts major bank network cards; there's also a window for renting strollers and wheelchairs (including motorized ones).

77 Spaceship Earth Epcot's signature pavilion looks like a giant golf ball or a dimpled geodesic dome. But unlike a dome, this 180-foot-high geosphere, encompassing 2.2 million cubic feet of space, is completely round. Inside, little cars take passengers through the 30,000-to-40,000-year history of human communication, from early cave drawings to satellites. As is the case throughout **Epcot,** much effort has been made to keep things as authentic as possible here. For example, the page of the Bible that Johannes Gutenberg is shown examining is an exact replica of the *Gutenberg Bible* on display in San Marino, California. In recent years the ride has been updated to include 15 new scenes, a new soundtrack, and new special effects. Narrated by actor Jeremy Irons, the presentation now includes a section on interactive and digital communications, including virtual reality classrooms of the future. At the end of the ride, visitors can experience the new "global neighborhood" by testing the latest in communication technology—you can explore the information highway, play a video-telephone game, or use computers to translate idioms from one language to another. The **Spaceship Earth** pavilion introduces and complements **Innoventions** (see page 90), **Epcot's** ever-changing exposition of new products for the near future. Don't wait in a long line here; come back at a mealtime or late in the day, when lines are likely to be much shorter.

78 Camera Center Here you can buy film, get your snapshots processed in two hours, or rent a camera or video camcorder (you'll have to leave a deposit for rentals). Employees will assist you with camera problems and suggest the best photo spots. Kodak has also put up markers around the park to point out prime picture-taking locations.

Restaurants/Clubs: Red
Shops/ Outdoors: Green

Hotels: Blue

Sights/Culture: Black

79 Innoventions East and West Here's what Walt said: "**Epcot** . . . will never be completed, but will always be introducing and testing and demonstrating new materials and systems." This is the demonstration part. Formerly **Communicore East and West,** the **Innoventions** pavilions feature high-tech products of the near future. In **Innoventions East,** visitors can explore the **House of Innoventions,** where all the latest gadgets for the home are featured; a virtual reality exhibit sponsored by Motorola, an interactive display of the latest electronic consumer products, a science show starring Bill Nye. The **Discovery Center,** in **Innoventions West,** is a two-story educational resource center in which visitors can get answers to technical questions about any Disney or **Epcot** exhibit; it's also the site of a resource center for teachers. **Innoventions** exhibits allow you to test wrist telephones, surf the Web, play the latest video games, and much more. Products aren't sold here but you can arrange to receive information by mail; this attraction is intentionally commercial and entrepreneurial because the Disney folks believe that a competitive marketplace drives innovation. And, they promise, as technology changes, so will **Innoventions.** There's also a **Guest Relations** information center at **Innoventions East.**

Within the Innoventions East and West pavilions:

Restaurants at Innoventions Since the mind works best on a full stomach, there are several eateries here. At **Innoventions East,** the **Electric Umbrella Restaurant** serves burgers, sandwiches, and salads daily for lunch and dinner. **Innoventions West** is the site of **Pasta Piazza Ristorante,** where breakfast includes omelettes, Danish, and (on occasion) a visit with Disney characters. Pasta, pizza, and salads are on the menu at this counter-service eatery the rest of the day. For coffee and fresh pastry, visit **Fountain View Espresso and Bakery,** also at **Innoventions West.** Explore a refreshment research station—**Ice Station Cool**—and sample beverages from around the world for free.

80 The Living Seas
Probably the most technologically complex pavilion at Epcot and reputed to have cost more than $90 million, this is the world's largest man-made saltwater aquarium, holding 5.7 million gallons of seawater. The realistic-appearing coral reef is artificial, but the more than 8,000 sea creatures—representing some 70 varieties of fish and other marine animals, including sharks, dolphins, and manatees—are not. When you enter the pavilion, take time to examine the exhibit that chronicles the many advances made in undersea exploration. Then begin your trip aboard a "hydrolator" that feels as if it's plunging into the depths of the sea. (Actually, the hydrolator doesn't drop a single fathom; it just shakes you around a bit while the view through the glass simulates your descent.) Visitors disembark at **Sea Base Alpha,** where they can view the coral reef and its inhabitants. There are also special displays of sea life, including one that houses the endangered manatee.

Within The Living Seas pavilion:
Coral Reef Restaurant ★★$$ Dine on seafood as you watch it swim by—one wall of the restaurant consists of the specially engineered acrylic panels of **The Living Seas** aquarium. Beef, chicken, and pasta dishes are also served. ◆ Seafood ◆ Daily lunch and dinner. Reservations for priority seating required

81 The Land Updated in 1995, this pavilion now features *The Circle of Life,* a motion picture that addresses the delicate balance between human progress and the environment, incorporating scenes from 30 nations and animated characters from the Disney film *The Lion King.* Also added was *Food Rocks,* a concert about good nutrition featuring giant Audio-Animatronic cartoon figures of famous rock stars. The updated **Living with the Land** boat ride focuses on the future of agriculture. It explains actual research on the management of resources being conducted at Disney greenhouses, and focuses on alligator farming as an example of a viable aquaculture industry. Visitors can learn more about sustainable agriculture—using agricultural practices to satisfy human food and fiber needs while minimizing harm to land and water resources—by scheduling an hour-long **Greenhouse Tour** (reservations required; 824.4321). The tour includes a stop at Disney's updated **Biotechnology Lab,** twice as large as the old one.

Within The Land pavilion:
Garden Grille Restaurant $$ Mickey Mouse and friends greet diners at this revolving restaurant, where family-style breakfasts feature eggs, ham steak, grits, and biscuits. Lunch and dinner platters include chicken, steak, and fish. ◆ American ◆ Daily breakfast, lunch, and dinner. Reservations for priority seating required

Sunshine Season Food Fair $ A good bet if your kids need immediate feeding, this food court (with counter service) offers a little of everything, including pasta, sandwiches, beer, and wine. ◆ American ◆ Daily breakfast, lunch, and dinner

82 Journey Into Imagination After Michael Eisner and the late Frank Wells became the heads of Walt Disney Company in 1984, they paid big bucks to rework this pavilion, with stunning results. Among the most recent changes is the replacement of the old *Captain EO* 3-D movie, featuring the frenzied antics of Michael Jackson, with *Honey, I Shrunk the Audience*. The 15-minute presentation features Rick Moranis and the other stars of the hit movies *Honey, I Shrunk the Kids* and *Honey, I Blew Up the Kid*, and is filled with visual effects and sensory shocks. The audience, wearing 3-D goggles, is "reduced" to the size of a bread box, surprised by a herd of scurrying white mice, and caught in a shower of breaking glass. Get ready to squeal at the top of your lungs. Elsewhere in the pavilion there's an appealing ride showing the power of the imagination, starring Dreamfinder and his devilish companion, Figment, who charmingly illustrate how one little spark of imagination can trigger a world of innovation. Dreamfinder and Figment occasionally can be seen in person at the pavilion's courtyard. There's also a creative kiddie's playground.

83 Test Track This all-new attraction, presented by General Motors, is the first high-speed ride for **Epcot,** taking guests behind the scenes of automobile testing—acceleration, braking, hill climbs, and negotiating curvy roads. Cars hit speeds up to 65 mph on a nearly milelong track. Sections even loop outside the pavilion. And everyone loves to sit behind the wheel in the latest, greatest *real* General Motors cars that are on display as you exit the ride.

84 Wonders of Life The big attraction here is **Body Wars,** a thrill ride that pairs a flight simulator (basically a fancy platform whose pneumatically controlled motion mimics that of an airplane) with a film. Once strapped into your seat, you're taken on a fast-moving trip through the human body. Veering and swooping, the simulator is real enough to induce motion sickness, but most people love it. After the ride, the pavilion's participatory exhibits soon have visitors taking stock of their diet and exercise programs and testing their senses. Note the 75-foot tower in front of the pavilion—it's an artistic representation of a DNA molecule.

Inside the Wonders of Life pavilion:

Cranium Command In this clever show, the audience sees what happens inside the head of a 12-year-old boy as he negotiates his way through a typical day. Audio-Animatronic figures representing different parts of the body argue in lively fashion with Cranium Commando, his brain.

The Making of Me It's hard to believe, but this endearing film about pregnancy and birth was criticized by people who felt it was out of character for Disney when the pavilion first opened. But Walt Disney Company chairman Michael Eisner backed it from the start. The film manages to deal with the mysteries of human reproduction in a charming way.

Coach's Corner Swing a golf club, baseball bat, or tennis racket, and you'll get a videotaped comment from a sports pro. An instant replay also compares your swing, captured on videotape, with that of a pro.

Met Lifestyle Revue Embarrass yourself in front of your friends by punching your health habits into a computer. You'll get a printout telling you how to live a more healthy life.

AnaComical Players A troupe of actors presents skits on various health-related topics. ◆ Check the entertainment schedule for show times

Pure & Simple ★★$ A good place for a healthful, low-fat snack, this counter-service restaurant serves salads, sandwiches, and waffles with fruit toppings. Fruit drinks are a smart substitute for the ubiquitous sodas. ◆ American ◆ Daily breakfast, lunch, and dinner

85 Universe of Energy Visitors board solar-powered cars for an entertaining and informative ride through this pavilion. First they see a film introducing the story, starring Ellen DeGeneres and Bill Nye "the Science Guy." The cars then move into an area with Audio-Animatronic figures of Ellen and Bill. Each of several ensuing scenes has a little twist, a little surprise to make the subject of energy fun. And the wonderful dinosaurs—part of the pavilion since it opened in 1982—are still there, in a scene that takes visitors back to a primeval jungle. The roof of this Exxon-sponsored pavilion contains a photovoltaic array of some 2,200 modules, each containing 36 individual silicon solar cells; the entire array can produce up to 70,000 watts of DC power.

World Showcase

After glimpsing the future, **Epcot** visitors enter this section of the park, which celebrates the world's varied cultures, past and present.

86 Canada Showcase *O Canada!,* a 17-minute, 360° Circlevision film, doesn't seem to dazzle most visitors, although it is certainly well worth seeing. There are the usual shots of Canadian mounties on horseback, but the movie also depicts the many magical ways this nation celebrates winter. The images of snowy, icy Canadian cities are enchantingly beautiful. Other shows staged here include bagpipe and folk music concerts (check the entertainment schedule for show times).

At the Canada Showcase:

Northwest Mercantile For sale here are Indian and Eskimo clothing, moccasins, and luxurious sheepskin rugs that look perfect for dozing near an open hearth. ◆ Daily

LeCellier Steakhouse ★$$$ When all the other **World Showcase** restaurants are full, it's often possible to get a seat in this eatery that's tucked away on the lowest level of the pavilion—partly because of its location, but also because the menu is not as interesting as some of the other **Epcot** restaurants. Steaks and roast prime rib are the mainstays, but the maple-glazed Canadian salmon is a tasty alternative to meat. Or you can try the pasta with fresh basil pesto and vegetables if you're going vegetarian. The restaurant was recently renovated, brightening the interior and giving it a wine-cellar feel. ◆ Canadian-American ◆ Daily lunch and dinner. Reservations for priority seating recommended

La Boutique des Provinces This shop offers more Canadian merchandise, but with a French flair. ◆ Daily

87 United Kingdom Showcase When **Epcot** first opened, this showcase was often bypassed because it doesn't have a glitzy travelogue film on Great Britain. But that was before people discovered the **Rose & Crown Pub and Dining Room** (see below). Now the cozy pub is always packed. American tourists delight in the British accents of the convivial pub employees, many of them British students working in a special Disney employment program. Visitors also can enjoy a brew on the outdoor terrace overlooking World Showcase Lagoon, an excellent place to watch the nighttime *IllumiNations* show. Some lively entertainment takes place here from time to time. For a flashback to the 1960s, catch the British Invasion, a group similar to the mop-topped Fab Four. The showcase buildings are examples of several British architectural styles and regions—Victorian, London, Yorkshire, Manor, Tudor, Georgian, Hyde Park, Regency, and Shakespearean cottage. There's also an herb garden and maze.

At the United Kingdom Showcase:

Rose & Crown Pub and Dining Room ★ $$ Americans who have crossed the Atlantic often come back grousing about the British food, but the fare at this full-service restaurant is both authentic and first-rate (try the meat pies). Stop In for a full meal, afternoon tea, or a pint in the pub—Bass and Harp ales and Guinness stout are on tap. Tables are inside and on the terrace. ◆ British ◆ Daily lunch, afternoon tea, and dinner. Reservations for priority seating required

Pringle of Scotland It's hard to get excited about wool sweaters in balmy Florida, but these are the real thing. The shop also sells traditional tartan kilts and ties. ◆ Daily

88 International Gateway Here, between the **United Kingdom** and **France** buildings, you can catch trams and boats to Disney hotels and to the **Disney-MGM Studios** theme park. Visitors who've already purchased **Epcot** passes at one of the resort ticket booths can enter the park here. Strollers and wheelchairs are available for rent.

89 France Showcase You'll be ready to book a trip to France after watching the 18-minute *Impressions de France,* the favorite show of many **Epcot** aficionados. Enhanced by a ravishingly beautiful soundtrack with snippets of Debussy and Saint-Saëns, the film takes you on a quick tour of present-day France, through a lively marketplace, past stately châteaux, and into the countryside. Unlike at Circlevision movies, you get to watch this film sitting down in comfortable, theater-style seats. Don't miss it. The showcase's park, by the canal, was inspired by post-Impressionist artist Georges Seurat's famous painting *A Sunday Afternoon on the Island of La Grande Jatte.* There's also a replica of a French rural street circa 1600. Magic, music, mime, and comedy are performed in the streets (check the entertainment schedule for show times).

At the France Showcase:

Chefs de France ★★$$$ Resembling a Parisian bistro, this eatery serves traditional French cuisine, although some dishes have lighter sauces than you might find in the City of Light. Start with baked oysters in Champagne sauce. For a main dish try the roast duck with prunes and wine sauce, fillet of grouper baked in a puff pastry, or coq au vin. ◆ French ◆ Daily lunch and dinner. Reservations for priority seating required

Shops at the France Showcase
Boulangerie Patisserie is an excellent bakery where you can indulge in a delectable almond croissant. Stop at **Plume et Palette** for delicate Limoges porcelain items and mementos. Next door, **Les Vins de France** sells wine, including many vintages that are hard to find in Central Florida. **Tout pour le Gourmet,** as the name suggests, has

everything for the gourmet cook, including exotic foodstuffs. ♦ Daily

90 Morocco Showcase The winding entrance into this pavilion evokes the ambience of a Middle Eastern bazaar, which is fitting since the main emphasis here is on shopping. Along the way, **Casablanca Carpets** sells handmade rugs and wall hangings and **Tangier Traders** offers leather goods and Moroccan clothing. Take note of the architecture, especially at the **Fez House.** Islam prohibits artistic depiction of live objects, hence Muslim artists developed a unique, abstract decorative design style. Geometric patterns are seen in tile walls and carved plaster on the buildings. The tower at the entrance to the showcase is a replica of the Katoubia Minaret in Marrakesh. Traditional music and dance in the courtyard entice people into the bazaar (check the entertainment schedule for show times). But the main reason to come here is **Restaurant Marrakesh,** one of **Epcot's** best.

At the Morocco Showcase:

Restaurant Marrakesh ★★★$$$
Start with the fragrant bread dusted with poppy seeds and move on to a Middle Eastern favorite, couscous. For an entrée try the roast lamb or a sampler platter. The lunch sampler consists of broiled chicken brochette, chicken *bastila* (chopped chicken, almonds, and cinnamon wrapped in phyllo), beef *brewat* (similar to a meat-filled egg roll), and couscous; a similar platter is available at dinner. Palatial surroundings and traditional belly-dancing and music add to the exotic ambience (check the entertainment schedule for show times). This is probably the most unusual food to be found in Central Florida, so be adventurous. ♦ Moroccan ♦ Daily lunch and dinner. Reservations for priority seating required

91 Japan Showcase The most popular show here is at the **Teppanyaki Dining Rooms** (see below), where food is prepared at your table. Also featured is a replica of the pagoda Horyuji at Nara. Each story of the structure represents one of the five elements—earth, water, fire, wind, and sky—which, according to Buddhist teachings, produced everything in the universe. There's also traditional music and dance (check the entertainment schedule for show times) and **Bijutsu-kan Gallery,** which features both traditional and modern Japanese art.

At the Japan Showcase:

Tempura Kiku ★$$ It's a cozy spot, but the quality of the batter-fried meats, seafood, and vegetables varies here. Real Japanese-food aficionados may be disappointed—but the Kirin beer is always cold. ♦ Japanese ♦ Daily lunch and dinner. Reservations for priority seating required

Teppanyaki Dining Rooms ★★$$$
If you're craving stir-fry, plan on a meal in one of the many small dining rooms here. With great panache, the chef will chop and cook your steak or seafood entrée on the grill at your table. Kirin beer and sake are served. ♦ Japanese ♦ Daily lunch and dinner. Reservations for priority seating required

Matsu No Ma Lounge ★$$ Providing respite from the Florida heat, this bar serves exotic mixed drinks, sushi, and other small appetizers. ♦ Japanese ♦ Daily snacks

Yakitori House $ Broiled chicken and Japanese beef are among the selections at this self-serve eatery. ♦ Japanese ♦ Daily

Mitsukoshi Department Store The Japanese came up with the department store concept during the feudal Tokugawa Shogun era, making this an appropriate attraction for the **Japan Showcase.** It's fun to browse here, but it seems that the giant Tokyo department store—this one's parent—has stocked it only with typical souvenirs. There are some pretty Japanese dolls, though, as well as beautiful fine porcelain and unusual stationery items.

92 The American Adventure There's hardly anything adventurous in the politically correct, 29-minute sermon presented here. But if you consider yourself a real patriot, you won't mind waiting to see the show, billed as the "dramatic and inspirational story of America and its people" told through motion pictures and Disney's famous Audio-Animatronic figures. The presentation was updated in 1993, adding events of the last decade, and the resulting show is much improved, with more exciting multimedia effects. Some of the most advanced of Disney's Audio-Animatronic characters—including Ben Franklin, Mark Twain, and Susan B. Anthony—can be seen here. The showcase's architectural elements are drawn from such classic Georgian-style buildings as Independence Hall and Jefferson's Monticello. Notice the clock tower, typical of the style, where "IIII" instead of "IV" is used on the face to represent four o'clock, as was the practice during that period. An a capella singing group performs regularly, as does a colonial fife and drum corps (check entertainment schedule for show times).

At The American Adventure:

Liberty Inn $ Appropriately, the bill of fare at this counter-service eatery features

hamburgers, hot dogs, and apple pie.
♦ American ♦ Daily lunch and dinner

America Gardens Stage Across from, but part of, **The American Adventure** and overlooking World Showcase Lagoon, this open-air stage features live entertainment throughout the year, most notably Disney's legendary *Christmas Candlelight* every December. ♦ Shows several times daily; check the entertainment schedule for times

93 Italy Showcase There's no film on Italy and its wonders here, but there are amusing shows in which audience members are drafted to play roles in humorous folktales, and an Italian quartet entertains in the courtyard. Make sure to check out the Living Statues (consult the entertainment schedule for show times). There's also a replica of St. Mark's Square in Venice, authentically re-created right down to the marble (actually painted fiberglass) in the Doge's Palace. There's not much else, except **Epcot**'s favorite restaurant, **L'Originale Alfredo di Roma Ristorante** (see below).

At the Italy Showcase:

L'Originale Alfredo di Roma Ristorante
★★★$$$ This trattoria serves a creamy, delicious fettuccine Alfredo and a variety of other pasta, veal, and seafood dishes. Italian wine makes your meal even more like the real thing. In the evening, waiters belt out arias from favorite operas as they serve you. ♦ Italian ♦ Daily lunch and dinner. Reservations for priority seating required

Shops at Italy Showcase Perugina chocolate, cookies, and candies can all be found at **Delizie Italiane. Il Bel Cristallo's** features pretty leather and straw purses, belts, and ties. **La Gamma Elegante's** specialties are inlaid music boxes and alabaster figures.

94 Germany Showcase Here's another showcase devoted mostly to shopping and lacking both a travelogue and a ride. There is, however, a statue of St. George and the dragon, and a replica of Elz Castle, which appears on the 500–deutsche mark note. Further contributing to the authentic ambience are a singing trio and a strolling accordionist playing traditional polkas and waltzes (check the entertainment schedule for show times). The **Biergarten** restaurant, serving hearty German fare, can be a lot of fun.

At the Germany Showcase:

Biergarten ★★$$ An oompah band plays from a bandstand while patrons dine on chicken, salads, sausages, and other German specialties served buffet style in a large indoor beer garden. Seating is banquet style, and Beck's beer and H. Schmitt Sohne wines make the meal merrier. Some diners choose to join the yodelers, dancers, and musicians

on stage. Oktoberfest is celebrated daily here. ♦ German ♦ Daily lunch and dinner. Reservations for priority seating required

Sommerfest $ Soft pretzels, bratwurst, desserts, and beer can be purchased at this snack bar. ♦ German ♦ Daily

Glas und Porzellan This is the place for the Hummel figurine lover. Goebel gifts are sold here as well. ♦ Daily

Die Weihnachts Ecke Nutcrackers and German Christmas items are featured at this charming shop. ♦ Daily

Der Teddybär Traditional German toys, including dolls and that perennial favorite, the teddy bear, are found here. ♦ Daily

95 China Showcase The enchanting *Land of Beauty, Land of Time,* a 360° Circlevision film, manages in less than 20 minutes to impart a sense of the vastness and diversity of the huge nation. Audience members stand while images of breathtaking scenery and impressive monuments unfold all around them. The movie at the **Chinatown and Splendid China** theme park comes nowhere near matching this magnificent travelogue. The showcase also features a replica of the Hall of Prayer for Good Harvests, and *Dragon: Ruler of the Wind and Waves,* an exhibit of royal cabinets, thrones, pottery, robes, and other artifacts from Si Zhu, on loan from the Beijing Museum. Shows feature Asian music and Chinese acrobats (check the entertainment schedule for show times).

At the China Showcase:

Yong Feng Shangdian Shopping Gallery Items from all over China—handicrafts, clothing, toys, and expensive furniture— are on sale in this one convenient place. The selection is great and the merchandise is without a doubt the most colorful in **Epcot**.

Nine Dragons Restaurant $$ Food from many different regions of China can be sampled at this very casual, family-oriented place. The fare isn't bad, but some dishes are bland and uninspired. Chinese wine and beer are available. ♦ Chinese ♦ Daily lunch and dinner. Reservations for priority seating required

Lotus Blossom Cafe ★$ The sweet-and-sour chicken is fine, and the egg rolls are always good for a quick snack. ♦ Chinese ♦ Daily lunch, dinner, and snacks

96 Norway Showcase A thrill ride instead of a film makes this showcase a standout. Children and adults love the **Maelstrom,** a boat ride through Norse mythology; it includes a nasty encounter with a three-headed troll and ends with a North Sea storm. Also interesting is the **Stave Church,** which contains Norwegian artifacts. The church is a replica of one found in the Norwegian Folk Museum in Oslo; the architectural style is common to Norwegian churches. Additional showcase buildings are examples of four other Norwegian styles: Setesdal, with its grassy roofs and thick logs; Bergen, marked by gabled windows on close-set, wooden buildings; Oslo, seen in the walls of Akershus Castle; and Alesund, typified by white stucco and stone trim.

At the Norway Showcase:

Restaurant Akershus ★★$$$
Norwegian food isn't something that Americans are particularly attracted to and that's too bad, because this restaurant offers much more diversity than most. The varied buffet includes authentic cold dishes such as herring and salmon as well as hot and hearty meatballs and roast chicken. Don't forget to try the wonderful bread. There's Ringnes beer, too. ♦ Norwegian ♦ Daily lunch and dinner. Reservations for priority seating recommended

Kringla Bakerl og Kafe ★★$ For a nice change from hot dogs, try a Norwegian pastry. Scandinavians practically wrote the book on open-faced sandwiches, and these are splendid. Enjoy your selection with a cold beer. ♦ Norwegian ♦ Daily snacks

Puffin's Roost Porcelain, glass, pewter, and wood knickknacks are on this shop's shelves. ♦ Daily

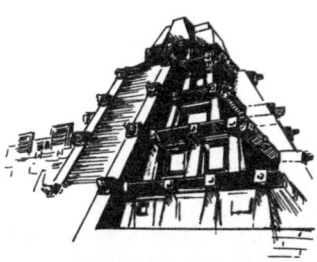

97 Mexico Showcase The ride here, **El Rio del Tiempo,** takes visitors on boats down the River of Time, providing a wholly inadequate glimpse of Mexican history. Unless you're with a small child, skip it and enjoy a meal at the excellent **San Angel Inn Restaurante** (see below) instead. The pyramid here is modeled after the Aztec Temple of Quetzalcoatl, the god of life, represented by large serpent heads along the entrance stairs. Marimba Mayalandia and Mariachi Cobre perform the traditional music of Mexico (check the entertainment schedule for show times).

Within the Mexico Showcase:

San Angel Inn Restaurante ★★★$$$
A sister to the renowned San Angel Inn in Mexico City, this is one of the most outstanding restaurants at **Epcot.** The

ambience is unmatched: The dining room, decorated in traditional Mexican style, looks out over the **Mexico Showcase**'s re-created Mexican street, which has a realistic high-tech backdrop of the still-active Popocatepetl volcano. Order the tender chicken enchiladas or anything with mole (a sauce with a touch of chocolate). Dos Equis and Sol beers are served; they also mix a mean margarita. ♦ Mexican ♦ Daily lunch and dinner. Reservations for priority seating required

Plaza de Los Amigos Buy that sombrero you need to protect yourself from the Florida sun. ♦ Daily

Artesanias Mexicanas The colorful ceramics make attractive souvenirs. There are occasional glass-blowing demonstrations. ♦ Daily

Cantina de San Angel ★$ Mexican fast food and a patio on the World Showcase Lagoon are the attractions at this self-serve cantina. It's also a good place to view *IllumiNations.* ♦ Mexican ♦ Daily lunch, dinner, and snacks

98 Lost Children Office You can get help in finding your lost child here (or by calling 560.7928). There's also a **Baby Care Center** and a **First Aid Station.**

Epcot Resort Area

With the addition of **Disney's BoardWalk,** there are now five Disney hotels near **Epcot,** one moderately priced and four in Disney's (and our) most expensive category. The **Epcot Resort Area** also boasts several fine restaurants.

99 Disney's Caribbean Beach Resort $$
This was Disney's first venture into hotel rooms that are moderately priced (that is, for Disney), and the sprawling 2,112-room complex was an instant success. Each of the five lodges is painted a different pastel color, and all borrow heavily from Caribbean architecture—windows look shuttered (but aren't really) and the peak roofs are reminiscent of the tin-roofed structures prevalent in mild Caribbean climes. Each of the five "island villages" has its own sandy beach, pool, and laundry facilities. There's also a main pool and a marina with boats that can be rented for excursions on 42-acre Barefoot Bay, a man-made lake. Bicycles can be rented too, and there's a 1.4-mile trail for cycling or jogging. ♦ 900 Cayman Way (just southeast of Buena Vista Dr). 934.3400; www.disneyworld.com ♿

Within Disney's Caribbean Beach Resort:

Old Port Royale $$ This food court has six counter-service snack bars offering a range of fast food. ♦ Snack bar ♦ Daily breakfast, lunch, and dinner

100 Disney's Yacht & Beach Club Resorts
$$$$ Designed by **Robert A.M. Stern** in 1990 to look like two distinctly different turn-of-the-century oceanside inns, these sister hotels have a combined 1,213 rooms set around a 25-acre lake. The **Yacht Club** is a five-story, oyster-gray clapboard cottage and the **Beach Club** is a stately blue-and-white hotel. Rooms have private balconies and one king-size or two queen-size beds. The concierge level, with 200 rooms, offers special services and amenities. The hotels share a health club, laundry facilities, a day-care center, a grass croquet court, a sand volleyball court, a tennis court, three heated pools, a game arcade, and a marina offering boat rentals. **Stormalong Bay**, a three-acre mini-waterpark for hotel guests only, lies behind the dual resorts. It features water slides from the deck of a shipwrecked vessel and two of Disney's niftiest pools: one has a sandy bottom and the other has a racing current. **Epcot** is within walking distance of both hotels and a water taxi provides transportation to **Disney-MGM Studios.**
◆ 1700 and 1800 Epcot Resort Blvd (north of Buena Vista Dr). Yacht Club 934.7000, Beach Club 934.8000; www.disneyworld.com &

Within Disney's Yacht & Beach Club Resorts:

Yachtsman Steakhouse ★★$$$ Prime cuts of beef are displayed in a glass-enclosed aging room; diners also can watch the chefs cook over hardwood-fired grills. Fish, pasta, and chicken dishes are also available, but the emphasis here is on beef (despite the fact that the decor has a seagoing flair, with nautical prints adorning the dark-wood paneled walls). ◆ American ◆ Daily dinner. Reservations for priority seating required

Yacht Club Galley $$ Economically priced meals are served here all day. Breakfast is buffet style or à la carte; there are hearty soups, salads, and tasty sandwiches for lunch; and dinner entrées range from tender fried clams to prime rib. The ambience is casually nautical, with lots of brass, dark wood, and nautical prints. ◆ American ◆ Daily breakfast, lunch, and dinner. Reservations for priority seating recommended

Cape May Cafe ★$$$ What would an oceanside resort—even a mock one—be without a clambake? With Disney's usual scrupulous attention to detail, an indoor clambake is offered here every night. The meal features clams, shrimp, chicken, and pasta; lobster is available at an extra charge. In the morning there's a breakfast buffet. ◆ Seafood ◆ Daily breakfast and dinner

Beaches & Cream Soda Shop ★$ An original Wurlitzer jukebox pumps out hits from the 1940s, 1950s, and 1960s as diners enjoy juicy "Fenway Park burgers" or dig into ice-cream concoctions. ◆ American ◆ Daily breakfast, lunch, and dinner

101 Walt Disney World Dolphin Hotel $$$$ Some critics are put off by the look of this hotel, operated by Sheraton, and its sister, the **Walt Disney World Swan,** operated by Westin (see below). But others think the fanciful touches are perfect, given the hotels' location within the world's most magical and popular theme park. When Walt Disney Company chairman Michael Eisner commissioned Princeton architect **Michael Graves** (with New York architect **Alan Lapidus**) to design the hotels, he told them he didn't want the structures to be boring. With such whimsical (some might say outrageous) embellishments as chandeliers that look like monkeys and hallway benches sprouting giant palm trees, boring they definitely are not. The hotel's namesake dolphins—actually two mythical, funny-looking fish—rise 55 feet above the hotel roof. A pattern of waves and banana leaves decorates the exterior, and inside, the walls are hung with beautifully framed but inexpensive prints by Matisse, Chagall, and Australian artist Ken Done. The 1,510-room property, with 140 suites, is one of the largest hotels in Florida. Rooms aren't cheap, but they are filled with extras, and the location is excellent: Hotel guests can walk or take a tram or water taxi from the hotel to **Epcot** or the **Disney-MGM Studios** theme park. ◆ 1500 Epcot Resort Blvd (north of Buena Vista Dr). 934.4000, 800/227.1500, 800/325.3535; fax 934.4099; www.swandolphin.com &

Within the Walt Disney World Dolphin Hotel:

Juan & Only's Cantina $$ A restaurant with an international flair, this colorful place is decorated with Mexican hats and posters. Standard Tex-Mex fare is served. ◆ Mexican ◆ Daily dinner. Reservations for priority seating recommended. 934.4000

Fantasia Gardens Two 18-hole mini–golf courses and a 22,000-square-foot covered outdoor pavilion (available for meetings) carry the theme of Disney's classic *Fantasia,* with lively fountains and animated statues. One course is just for fun; the other is a serious 18 holes that emphasize skill—exaggerated contours, menacing water hazards, and diabolical sand traps. ◆ Admission. Daily

101 Walt Disney World Swan Hotel $$$$ Designed by **Michael Graves** in 1989, this hotel is half the size of its sister **Walt Disney World Dolphin Hotel,** containing 758 rooms and suites, with 54 concierge rooms on the top two floors. Two 47-foot-high, 56,000-pound swans grace the crown of the hotel, which is painted in a colorful pattern of aquamarine-and-coral waves. The 12-story building has two seven-story wings and overlooks Crescent Lake, where there's a beach, playground, and wading area. West of the hotel is a free-form grotto pool with water slides, three Jacuzzis, and a patio bar. Next to the grotto is a tennis center with eight hard courts, four of them lighted. Guests can walk, take a tram, or ride a water taxi to **Epcot** or **Disney-MGM Studios.** ♦ 1200 Epcot Resort Blvd (just north of Buena Vista Dr). 934.3000, 800/248.SWAN, 800/228.3000; fax 934.1399; www.swandolphin.com &

Within the Walt Disney World Swan Hotel:

Palio ★★$$$ Fine Italian specialties, from antipasto and salads to pizzas prepared in a wood-fired brick oven and pasta dishes topped with veal, shrimp, or calamari, are the stars here. The extensive Italian wine list is another plus. As you enter the restaurant, in the lobby of the east wing, watch chefs at work in the open kitchen. Hand-painted porcelain plates line the walls, and flags representing different regions of Italy hang from the ceiling. The Tuscan scene on the enormous mural was painted by Ani Rosskam. ♦ Italian ♦ Daily dinner. Reservations for priority seating recommended. 934.3000

Kimonos ★★$$ Order a full dinner or just hors d'oeuvres at this posh lounge, with touches of rich teakwood and authentic kimonos on display. Teriyaki dishes and other Japanese fare are served, and there's a sushi bar. ♦ Japanese ♦ Daily dinner and hors d'oeuvres. 934.3000

102 **Disney's BoardWalk** $$$$ This charming resort designed by **Robert A.M. Stern** sits across the lake from the **Yacht & Beach Club Resorts,** the architect's other **Walt Disney World** creation. The two hotels, inspired by turn-of-the-century Atlantic seaboard towns, paint a lovely picture on the shores of Crescent Lake. **BoardWalk Inn** has 378 rooms, many overlooking the boardwalk that stretches along the lakefront. The attention to detail is startling, right down to the original postcards from seaside towns that were used to create the pattern in the curtains. The 532 **BoardWalk Villas** are part of the **Disney Vacation Club** and are available when they're not being occupied by members. The villas include complete kitchens, laundry facilities, and almost all the comforts of home— even a VCR. The resort's themed swimming area, **Luna Park,** has a 200-foot coaster slide. There's also a health club, video arcade, and tennis courts. ♦ 2101 Epcot Resort Blvd (just north of Buena Vista Dr). 939.5150; www.disneyworld.com &

Within Disney's BoardWalk:

Spoodles ★★★$$ Distinct Mediterranean flavors distinguish the food at this attractive restaurant, where the open kitchen is a beehive of activity in a spacious dining room. Dark wood floors, warm Mediterranean colors, and casual table settings create a fun atmosphere. Tapas are the specialty here, with an interesting array of the appetizer-size creations listed on the menu. Kids love "making" their own pizzas: The chef brings the bare pie to the table, where the kids select and add the toppings. ♦ Mediterranean ♦ Daily breakfast, lunch, and dinner. Reservations for priority seating recommended

Flying Fish ★★★$$$ The dining room is a real showstopper, a trendy creation of well-known interior designer Martin Dorf that conjures up visions of the sea. Giant shimmering fish scales hug the walls, delicate lights dangle from oversize fish hooks, and sleek, golden fish sculptures arc overhead. The fancy food matches the decor—such as the potato-wrapped striped bass with leek fondue and a Cabernet Sauvignon sauce. The chef vows to serve only the freshest fish from "native American waters" and fruits and vegetables in season. Save room for the chocolate lava cake with a liquid white chocolate center. ♦ American ♦ Daily dinner. Reservations for priority seating recommended

ESPN Club $$ It's the 70 TV screens, not the food, that makes this a hot spot. (They're even in the bathrooms so that you won't miss a minute of the action.) You can try the spinach and black bean dip, or the Bloody Mary chili, but sports are the draw here. There's a noisy arcade if you want to test your skills. ♦ American ♦ Daily lunch and dinner

Atlantic Dance This spacious club is the best place in Central Florida to experience the swing dancing craze. There's swing dancing seven nights a week, with swing lessons five nights a week and occasional dance competitions. For information about featured bands and competitions, call 939.2444. ♦ Admission. Daily 8PM-2AM

Big River Grille & Brewing Works ★$$ The food is ordinary, but the fun is the freshly brewed ale—three flagship beers are brewed right on the premises. The menu features filling stuff like lobster potpie, veal loaf with mashed potatoes, and burgers. ♦ American ♦ Daily lunch and dinner

Jellyrolls It's dueling pianos, and it's good, clean fun. You're likely to be part of a singalong here, with the piano players pounding out everything from 1970s standards to current hits. ♦ Admission. Daily 7PM-2AM

Disney-MGM Studios

Disney's 110-acre version of Hollywood, the **Disney-MGM Studios** theme park features actual working television and movie studios in addition to rides, attractions, and a selection of shops and restaurants. Since its 1989 opening, the studio has been the site of dozens of entertainment and sports productions for network and cable television stations, from soap operas to golf events. Major films and a great deal of radio programming also have been produced here. With luck, you might catch the taping of a movie or TV show.

Thanks to the presence of the Muppets and the blockbuster success of such Disney animated movies as *The Lion King, Aladdin, Beauty and the Beast, Pocahontas, The Hunchback of Notre Dame,* and *Hercules,* **Disney-MGM Studios** has strong kiddie appeal. Older kids and adults may find the attractions a bit tame, except for the **Twilight Zone Tower of Terror, The Magic of Disney Animation Tour, Fantasmic!,** and the **Indiana Jones Stunt Spectacular.**

Near **Disney-MGM Studios** and also covered in this chapter are **Blizzard Beach,** Disney's newest and largest water park, which opened in 1995 and occupies 66 acres; **Disney's All-Star Resorts** area, with **Walt Disney World's** two least expensive hotels; and **Coronado Springs,** Disney's first moderately priced convention resort, with 1,900 rooms surrounding a 15-acre lake.

Area code 407 unless otherwise noted.

Disney-MGM Studios

If you arrive at **Disney-MGM Studios** early in the day, head straight for the **Twilight Zone Tower of Terror,** which always has long lines; **Star Tours,** one of Disney's best flight-simulator rides; and **The Magic of Disney Animation Tour,** perhaps the most enjoyable and interesting attraction in the entire park. Save the souvenirs for the end of your visit.

If you plan to attend a "character breakfast" or to have lunch or dinner at one of the park's four full-service restaurants (**50's Prime Time Cafe, Mama Melrose's Ristorante Italiano, Sci-Fi Dine-In Theater Restaurant,** and **The Hollywood Brown Derby**), be sure to reserve priority seating in advance; restaurant reservations may be made up to 60 days ahead of time by calling WDW.DINE (939.3463). Same-day reservations also can be arranged at **Guest Relations** or at the **Hollywood Junction** (as you turn onto Sunset Boulevard from Hollywood Boulevard).

Most attractions in the park are accessible to guests with disabilities, but not **Star Wars** or **Twilight Zone Tower of Terror,** where you have to transfer from your wheelchair to a seat on the attraction. There are age, size, and health boarding restrictions for **Twilight Zone Tower of Terror** and **Star Tours. Disney-MGM Studios** is generally open from 9AM to 7PM, although hours change depending on the season. There is a parking fee in addition to the admission charge. For more information, call 824.4321.

At 199 feet, The Twilight Zone Tower of Terror at Disney-MGM Studios is Disney's tallest theme park attraction. Any structure taller than that is required to incorporate airplane warning signals into its design.

103 Crossroads of the World Located at the entrance to the park, this small plaza is the place to get information, purchase souvenirs, and check the times for live performances, parades, and the spectacular evening fireworks display. Pick up an entertainment schedule at **Guest Services** here (it's also available at the **Guest Information Board** at the corner of Hollywood and Sunset Boulevards). If you're keen on seeing a real TV show taping, be sure to arrive early at either **Guest Services** or the **Production Information Window** (also located here). Tickets are available on a first-come, first-served basis.

104 Hollywood Boulevard Similar in concept to the **Magic Kingdom's Main Street,** this boulevard behind the statue of Mickey Mouse greets visitors with shops and street theater. You may be approached by a character such as the "autograph hound" or the "flimflam man." Patterned after Los Angeles's Hollywood Boulevard as it was in the 1930s and 1940s, Disney's Hollywood Boulevard is filled with nostalgic architecture. **Oscar's Super Service,** an old-time gas station with a 1947 Buick parked out front, has lockers, strollers, and wheelchairs for rent and plenty of automotive memorabilia for sale, including vanity license plates, key chains, mugs, and models. Nearby are the **Hospitality Building (First Aid, Lost and Found, Guest Relations, Baby Services); Movieland Memorabilia,** selling souvenirs; and **Sid Cahuenga's One-of-a-Kind,** with authentic old costumes, movie posters, and promotional photos for sale. Also on Hollywood Boulevard: **The Darkroom,** selling cameras and film; **Cover Story,** where they'll put your picture on the cover of a magazine; **Celebrity 5 & 10,** featuring non-Disney movie memorabilia in

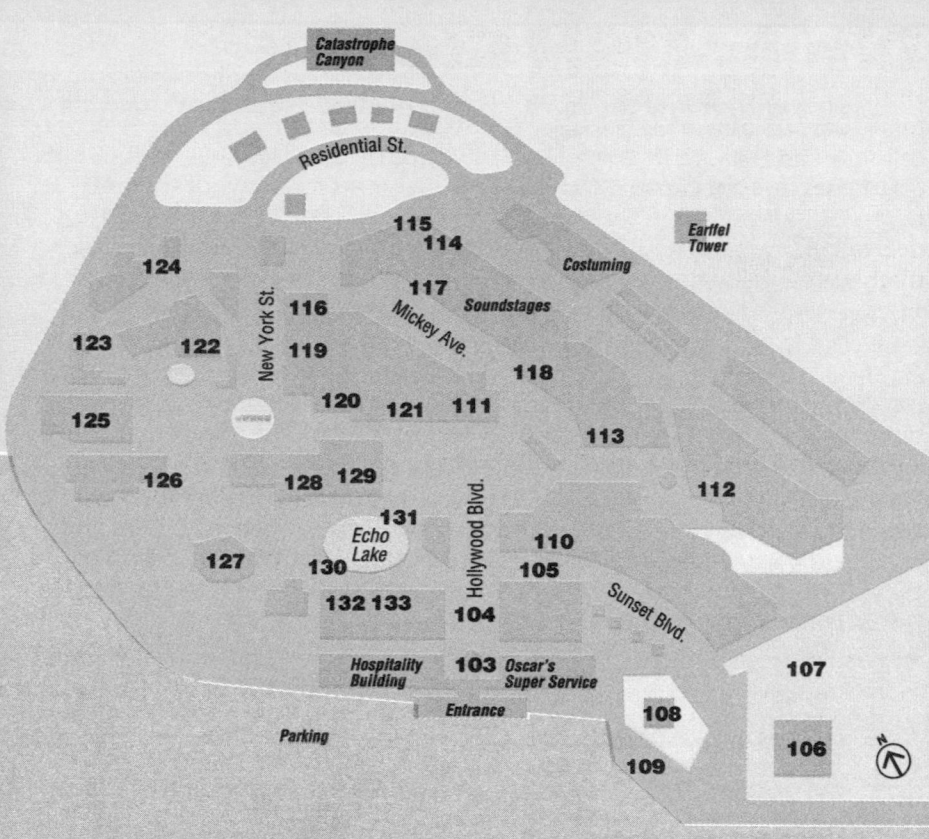

what looks like an old five-and-dime store; **Sweet Success,** purveyors of fancy candy, including postcards made of chocolate; and **L.A. Prop Cinema Storage,** with children's clothing emblazoned with characters from Disney's most recent animated films. In addition, there's **Mickey's of Hollywood,** this park's one-stop Disney merchandise mart, and **Keystone Clothiers,** where it's possible to buy just about any article of clothing you can think of with Mickey or Minnie emblazoned on it. Celebrities appear regularly in "star" motorcades down Hollywood Boulevard. They place their handprints in cement and participate in photo, autograph, and interview sessions with park guests. A daily parade also travels down Hollywood Boulevard, usually based on the latest Disney animated feature. At press time, this was **Disney's Mulan Parade,** filled with colorful floats celebrating the characters of *Mulan,* Disney's 36th animated feature film. The parade also features a 150-footlong Chinese dragon.
♦ Check the entertainment schedule for times

105 Sunset Boulevard A re-creation of another of Tinseltown's most famous streets, Sunset Boulevard has a number of fake storefronts and several real shops. **Once Upon a Time** is a replica of the Carthay Circle Theater, where *Snow White and the Seven Dwarfs* premiered in 1937; items for sale include kitchenware and collectibles. **Legends of Hollywood**

features merchandise from Disney's latest theatrical releases. Disney books, videos, and CDs are also for sale. Also on Sunset is **Sunset Ranch Market,** patterned after an old-time farmers' market and featuring numerous snack stands; there's also the **Starring Rolls Bakery, Planet Hollywood Super Store,** with logo merchandise, and **Sunset Club Couture,** featuring watches, jewelry, and upscale clothing. A posted schedule announces when the "Star of the Week" will be at Sunset Boulevard to perform or just chat with visitors. Visiting celebrities have included actors Warren Beatty, Charlie Sheen, Bruce Willis, Demi Moore, and Arnold Schwarzenegger, and Olympic figure skater Tara Lipinski.

106 Twilight Zone Tower of Terror The mysterious and decrepit "Hollywood Tower Hotel," which looms at the end of Sunset Boulevard, is the setting of this thrill ride. Visitors enter the spooky "hotel"—struck by lightning on Halloween night in 1939, you're told—on foot. Once you're in the cobweb-covered lobby, the voice of the late Rod Serling, creator of the "Twilight Zone" television series, introduces the hotel staff. The tour of the hotel includes encounters with ghostly apparitions and an exciting elevator ride; it shoots up 10 times faster than regular elevators, then plunges 130 feet—twice. There are age, height, and health restrictions on this ride. **Tower Hotel Gifts,** stocked with T-shirts, towels, and other items with the hotel's logo, is on the way out.

107 Rock 'n' Roller Coaster This thrilling new attraction was scheduled to open as we went to press. A roller coaster housed in a building, Rock 'n' Roller Coaster will make you scream as it loops and races around sloping curves. The twists and turns of the ride are synchronized to a rock music sound track that resonates from speakers mounted in each car.

108 Theatre of the Stars This open-air, 1,500-seat theater features a Broadway-style, 25-minute production of highlights from the *Beauty and the Beast* musical show. The costuming is wonderfully detailed and clever, and the Beast's transformation into a handsome prince is pulled off with super special effects. ♦ Check the entertainment schedule for show times

109 Fantasmic! Join Mickey Mouse as he battles the forces of evil in this must-see, all-new nighttime extravaganza. The 25-minute show incorporates water fountains, animation, lasers, and fireworks and takes place at the **Hollywood Hills Amphitheater,** which seats 6,500 with room for an additional 2,500 standing guests. To ensure a good seat, arrive 15 to 20 minutes before the show.

♦ Check the entertainment schedule for show times

110 The Hollywood Brown Derby ★★$$$ From the pictures of stars on the walls to the derby-shaped brass lamps, this 235-seat restaurant is a faithful reproduction of the famous Brown Derby in Hollywood. The menu includes steak, seafood, and chicken dishes, as well as the restaurant's signature Cobb salad. Although the fairly formal dining room is usually filled with adults, a children's menu is available. ♦ American ♦ Daily lunch and dinner. Reservations for priority seating required

111 The Great Movie Ride Head for the replica of Grauman's (now Mann Corporation's) Chinese Theater to board this "moving theater" attraction. A 50-passenger vehicle moves along as you view film clips on large screens; the ride includes 60 Audio-Animatronic figures that look like they are part of some of the scenes. Old-time movie buffs love it, as do youngsters, who get a kick out of the interaction between the live and Disney-engineered actors even if they haven't seen the flick. Highlights include a Gene Kelly figure dancing in the rain, John Wayne fighting bank robbers, and scenes from *Casablanca* and *The Wizard of Oz.*

Disney's Wide World of Sports

If you're a sports fan, it might be worth checking the schedule at **Disney's Wide World of Sports** to see who's in town. The **Atlanta Braves** baseball team comes here for spring training, playing exhibition games in a 7,500-seat baseball stadium, and the **Harlem Globetrotters** basketball team trains here, packing fans into the 5,000-seat field house for their games. Tennis spectators head for the 2,000-seat center court stadium every spring for the US Men's Clay Court Championships.

Nearly every day of the year there's something going on at the 200-acre, multimillion-dollar sports complex, from amateur sports to professional competitions. Along with baseball, basketball, and tennis, there's a track and field complex, football/soccer fields, and volleyball courts.

If you want to get some exercise, the **NFL Experience** has a permanent home at the complex, giving armchair quarterbacks and casual football fans a chance to test their football skills in a series of challenges.

Professional events, like the Braves exhibition games, sell out early, so be sure to order tickets ahead of your vacation.

The only restaurant here is the **Official All Star Cafe,** located at the entrance to the complex. Celebrity owners include Tiger Woods, Shaquille O'Neal, Joe Montana, Wayne Gretzky, Ken Griffey Jr., Andre Agassi, and Monica Seles. The restaurant features a main dining room lined with baseball mitt–shaped booths and huge video screens, upon which diners can view sports highlights and live-action games. The food is mediocre—soups, salads, and sandwiches.

Disney's Wide World of Sports is at 800 Victory Way, south of Osceola Pkwy half a mile east of World Drive; call 407/939.1500 for more information.

112 The Magic of Disney Animation Tour
Many folks consider this self-guided tour
through a real animation studio to be by far
the most enjoyable attraction at **Disney-MGM
Studios.** To avoid long lines, come here first
thing in the morning; if you opt to wait, keep
in mind that the animation artists here are
real, and they don't usually stick around
after working hours. After viewing *Back to
Neverland,* a short introductory film featuring
the unlikely duo of Robin Williams and Walter
Cronkite, visitors proceed to the new **Walt
Disney Feature Animation Florida** building,
where they can observe artists involved
in each step of the process of creating an
animated film—from drawing characters and
developing backgrounds to the final edit. An
explanation of what you are seeing is provided
by a Disney host or hostess. The tour ends
with highlights of Disney's best animated
movies in the **Disney Classics Theater. The
Animation Gallery** gift shop is adjacent to the
building.

113 Voyage of the Little Mermaid
This 20-minute presentation is one of the
park's most popular. The show follows the
continued adventures of Ariel, star of *The Little
Mermaid,* and features both live and animated
performers, puppetry, lasers, and other special
effects. The best seats are in the back. ♦ Check
the entertainment schedule for show times

114 Studio Backlot Tour If you hit this 35-
minute attraction early, lines shouldn't be too
long. The tour starts at the **Special Effects
Water Tank** with a six-minute lesson in how
battle scenes at sea are created on a studio
set. Next, you board the tram; let the children
sit on the left side for a surprise along the
way. The tram first rolls past an area where
trees and shrubbery are grown and sculpted
for use on the set, then proceeds to the
costume and crafts shops. Cruising down
"Residential Street," you'll see the "Golden
Girls" home and the *George of the Jungle* set.
Things are pretty tame up to this point, but
after winding around some more props, the
tram comes to **Catastrophe Canyon,** where
you experience some special effects firsthand.
There's a rainstorm, then an explosion in
which you feel the heat of the flames, and
finally a flash flood (passengers sitting on
the left get sprayed with water). Afterward,
the tram goes behind **Catastrophe Canyon**
so that you can see the water cannons and

sophisticated machinery that created the
realistic disaster. The tram then shuttles you
to a New York street scene, and exits through
the **American Film Institute Showcase.**

115 American Film Institute Showcase
Displayed here are props and sets from
recent popular television shows and movies.

116 Studio Catering Company $$ This is a
good place to refuel after the **Studio Backlot
Tour** (see above). Snacks, desserts, soft
drinks, and beer are served. ♦ Snack bar
♦ Daily

117 Backstage Pass A spotted puppy named
Wizzer and 100 of his pals join the evil Cruella
de Vil in this attraction, with special effects,
authentic costumes, and sets from the live-
action film *101 Dalmatians.* The 20-minute
tour begins in **Jim Henson's Creature Shop,**
where barking puppies, spraying skunks,
and other hidden surprises start the show.
Handmade mechanical puppies are on
display, so you can see how latex foam
and synthetic fur are transformed into
some of the dalmatians featured in the film.
One guest from the audience will be part of a
scene in which Pongo (a dalmatian) drags the
bicycle-riding participant through the streets
of London, thanks to "blue screen" cinema
magic. Next, you get a peek at the three
working soundstages, and, if you're lucky,
there'll be a taping going on. Otherwise,
looking at empty rooms gets dull fast,
but overhead monitors explain how the
soundstages are used. Finally, you see props
and sets from the movie, including Cruella de
Vil's mansion and office, as well as original
costumes worn by Glenn Close. Even her
$500,000 car is on stage.

118 Lights! Camera! Action! Theater The
walking tour offered here starts with a look at
the post-production facilities at **Disney-MGM
Studios.** Guests get a chance to see actual
film editing and other post-production tasks,
observing through walls of glass. Throughout
the tour, video monitors show how the
work creates the featured movie (recently,
Armageddon, which stars Bruce Willis as a
scientist who must try to save Earth from a
huge asteroid collision). The tour ends with
clips from the film and displays of sets and
props. The features shown here change about
twice a year to keep up with current Disney
releases. The tour runs continuously during
park hours.

119 Honey, I Shrunk the Kids! Movie Set Adventure Children ages four and up can play among 30-foot blades of grass and cereal loops that are nine feet in diameter in this 11,000-square-foot playground, which lets youngsters imagine they've been "shrunk" like the kids in the popular movie. Tree stumps are slides, a giant mushroom houses three levels of interconnecting tunnels, and there's a multilevel spiderweb that has a pretty good view from the top. Kids are always amazed when they climb the fern sprouts, which emit sounds as they get stepped on.

120 Sci-Fi Dine-In Theater Restaurant ★★★$$$ This 250-seat restaurant is set up as a 1950s drive-in movie theater. Enter through the ticket lobby and slide into a re-creation of a vintage car. Once seated, you are served really good popcorn. Club sandwiches and salads are popular items, but the grouper sandwich and the vegetable sandwich are the best bets. A children's menu is available. While you munch, you can watch old science-fiction films on the large screen; the sound is delivered through drive-in speakers mounted next to each car. Or you can lean back and look at the fiber-optic "stars" twinkling in the Hollywood Hills "night sky." ◆ American ◆ Daily lunch and dinner. Reservations for priority seating required

121 ABC Commissary Restaurant $$ Burgers, chicken breast sandwiches, salads, and chicken nuggets are among the choices at this large fast-food restaurant with counter service. A children's menu is available. ◆ Fast food ◆ Daily lunch and dinner

122 Jim Henson's MuppetVision 3-D A 12-minute Muppets video keeps the crowd amused while you're waiting for the theater doors to open. The theater itself is a replica of the one used for TV's "The Muppet Show"—old Statler and Waldorf are in their usual mezzanine seats to your right, and behind you, high on the wall, sits the Swedish Chef, who is the projectionist. Live and Audio-Animatronic characters interact seamlessly with the 3-D movie, creating a new dimension Disney calls "4-D." One mischievous character, Waldo C. Graphic, interacts directly with the audience. Kids love the fireworks, and everyone is astonished when they're squirted by a boutonniere. This is the best 3-D movie you'll see at any of the theme parks. An added bonus: When it's hot and sunny outside, this attraction offers 30 blissful minutes of air-conditioned comfort. ◆ Check the entertainment schedule for show times

123 Mama Melrose's Ristorante Italiano ★$$ This fine pizza palace bakes its pies in wood-burning ovens. Other options include grilled fish and steaks, veal chops, chicken dishes, and various types of pasta. A full-service dining spot, it's the quintessential "little Italian restaurant," with brick walls, white tablecloths, soft music, and candles. ◆ Italian ◆ Daily lunch and dinner. Reservations for priority seating required

124 "Disney's Hunchback of Notre Dame—A Musical Adventure" This elaborate stage show brings a taste of Broadway to **Disney-MGM Studios,** with a cast of more than 20 and the powerful music of Academy Award–winning composer Alan Menken and Broadway lyricist Stephen Schwartz. Exquisite costumes and stage sets and a miniature cast of medieval puppets re-create 15th-century Paris. ◆ Check the entertainment schedule for show times

125 Star Tours Although still very popular, this flight-simulator ride is now considered a bit tame in comparison to newer attractions elsewhere in **Walt Disney World.** Try to sit up front or near the middle, and remember that you can take your eyes off the screen and focus them elsewhere if the rocking and rolling make you queasy. The story line involves a rookie pilot flying off to the "Moon of Endor" when trouble occurs. People with back problems or heart conditions, pregnant women, and children under three are warned not to go on this ride; children under age seven must be accompanied by an adult.

126 Backlot Express ★$$ This 600-seat cafeteria is disguised as a workshop. The left side is filled with props, and the right side is set up like a paint shop, complete with drips and spatters. There are salad bars in both sections and in the glass-enclosed, air-conditioned patio. Hot dogs, salads, burgers, chocolate chip cheesecake, beer, and wine are sold at the counters. ◆ American ◆ Daily lunch, dinner, and snacks

127 Indiana Jones Stunt Spectacular Several scenes from *Raiders of the Lost Ark* are played out before your eyes, with the stunts explained during the action. A number of extras are chosen from the audience to participate in the demonstrations. The extras are never in any real danger, but not so the stunt people, who fall from buildings and escape from an exploding overturned truck. No Audio-Animatronics here—this is the real thing. Note: The lines may look daunting, but the outdoor covered theater holds 2,000 people; still, try to arrive at least 15 minutes before the show. ◆ Check the entertainment schedule for show times

128 The ABC Sound Studio In this attraction that features scenes from Disney's Saturday morning ABC television show "One Saturday Morning," audience members will be selected to supply sound effects and voices to videos of Saturday morning cartoons, including "101 Dalmatians: The Series," with humorous results. The show runs continuously throughout the day; sit near the front or in the middle if you want to be selected.

128 **Golden Age Souvenirs** Gifts for sports fans, featuring ESPN and ABC Sports merchandise, are showcased here.

129 **"Disney's Doug Live!"** This musical stage show stars Doug, one of the popular characters from Disney's ABC television program "One Saturday Morning." The story follows Doug Funnie, his dog, Porkchop, his best friend, Skeeter, his secret crush, Patty, and the class bully, Roger, through the ups and downs of preteen life. ♦ Check the entertainment schedule for show times

130 **Dinosaur Gertie's Ice Cream of Extinction** Seek out this dinosaur-shaped shop for ice cream, yogurt, or some other frozen treat to ease those long waits in line. ♦ Daily

131 **Min and Bill's Dockside Diner** $$ This old tub doesn't leave its dock on Echo Lake, but serves tacos, ice cream, and other snacks, plus beverages. ♦ Snack bar ♦ Daily

132 **50's Prime Time Cafe** ★★$$$ Step into a TV sitcom from the 1950s. Diners sit at kitchen table alcoves that have all the period trimmings, right down to meals on Fiesta Ware or TV dinner trays served by a waitress dressed up as dear old "Mom." Be sure you wash your hands before you're seated because she's likely to ask you and will be cross if you haven't. Old-fashioned television sets showing clips of 1950s sitcoms are visible from wherever you sit—unfortunately, it's often the same clips over and over. You can opt for a burger, but most

of the menu is "comfort food" straight out of Mom's kitchen: meat loaf, pot roast, chicken salad, and numerous terrific desserts. Beer and wine are available. While you wait for a seat, relax in the **Tune In Lounge.** ♦ American ♦ Daily lunch and dinner. Reservations for priority seating required

133 **Hollywood & Vine Cafeteria of the Stars** ★$$$ You've probably never been in a 1950s diner this big—368 seats. Meals are served "buffeteria-style"—help yourself at the buffet, then pay at the cashier. Breakfast is hearty and filling here, with scrambled eggs, potatoes, bacon, and other traditional choices. Lunch is heavy on salads and seafood, but roasted chicken and baby back ribs are also available. The dinner buffet includes lunch offerings, plus grilled pork chops, prime rib, veal chops, and other entrées. A children's menu is available. Disney characters join guests for breakfast, lunch, and dinner. Beer and wine are sold. ♦ American ♦ Daily breakfast, lunch, and dinner

Blizzard Beach

Disney's third "water adventures" park, which was three years in the making, is by far its most extensive (see map on page 104). With lots of thrill rides aimed at teenagers, **Blizzard Beach** is in head-to-head competition with the venerable **Wet 'n Wild.** As with all Disney theme parks, this one comes complete with a scene-setting story. It seems a freak storm dropped such a mountain of snow on the site that plans were immediately made for Florida's first snow ski resort, complete with chairlifts, a ski jump, and slalom and bobsled courses. But wouldn't you know it, all the snow started melting, and soon the ski resort was all washed up—until some resourceful soul realized that the slalom and bobsled runs could make great water slides. . . . The rest is Disney-generated history.

The ski resort theme is carried throughout this watery playground. Slalom gates and flags adorn various slides, and the **Mount Gushmore Ski Lift** transports visitors to what is the tallest (and possibly the fastest) water slide in the world. (Women are advised to wear one-piece bathing suits.) There are 19 water slides and "icy" bobsled runs (actually, they stay warm), as well as white-water rafting and toboggan racing rides, wave pools, and play areas.

Changing rooms and rental lockers are available. Pack your own picnic lunch or opt for snacks and soft drinks at the **Avalunch** or **The Warming Hut.** **Lottawatta Lodge** near the entrance offers the most complete menu but is still limited to hot dogs, burgers, and fruit salads. Like **Typhoon Lagoon** and **River Country,** this park has a separate admission charge, plus fees for lockers and towels; parking is free, however. For more information, call 824.4321.

Restaurants/Clubs: Red	**Hotels:** Blue
Shops/♦ **Outdoors:** Green	**Sights/Culture:** Black

BLIZZARD BEACH

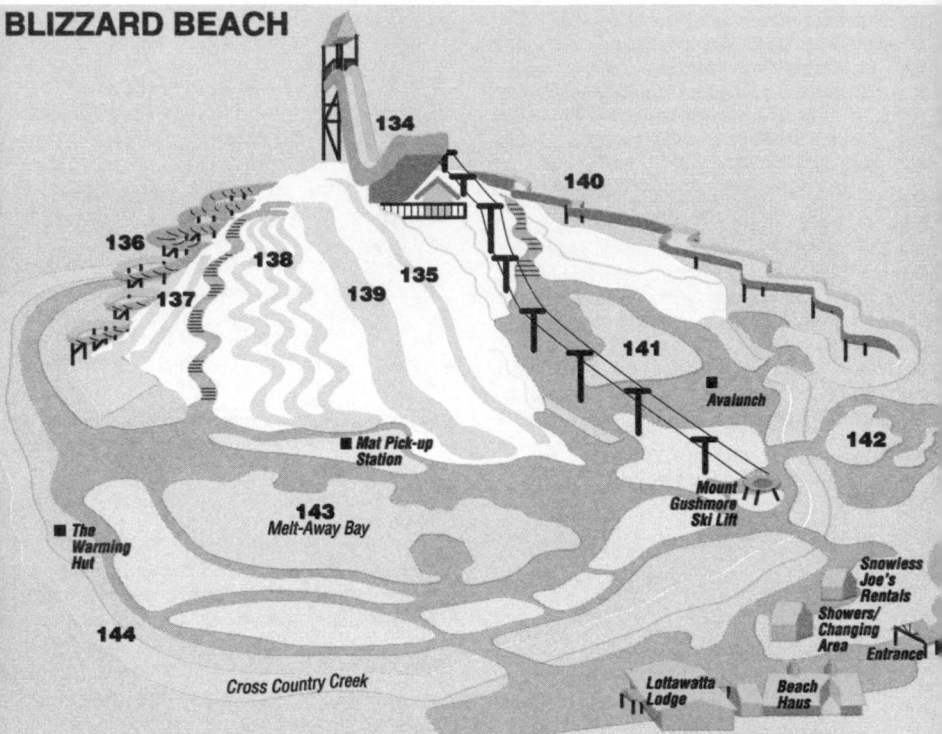

134

136

137

138

139

135

140

141

142

■ **Mat Pick-up Station**

Avalunch

Mount Gushmore Ski Lift

■ **The Warming Hut**

143
Melt-Away Bay

144

Snowless Joe's Rentals

Showers/ Changing Area

Entrance

Cross Country Creek

Lottawatta Lodge

Beach Haus

134 Summit Plummet This is the park's star attraction. A lift takes you to the top of Mount Gushmore, and a 500-footlong slide takes you to the bottom—at speeds of up to 55 mph.

135 Slush Gusher If the **Summit Plummet** seems too extreme, here's a slower and shorter version of the slide.

136 Runoff Rapids An inner-tube ride down Mount Gushmore, this one takes you into complete darkness.

137 Downhill Double Dipper Side-by-side tube slides are the draw here; an Olympic-style clock measures the time of your run.

138 Snow Stormers Another headfirst mat ride, this one sends you through the flags and gates of a "slalom course."

139 Toboggan Racers Lie on a mat and plunge headfirst down the 250-foot slide. With eight lanes, it's perfect for racing other family members.

140 Teamboat Springs This raft ride is mild enough for the whole family, despite the waterfalls.

141 Ski Patrol Training Camp This activity area is a hit with teenagers. They love trying to walk across broken icebergs without getting wet or sliding down an old pipe and dropping into eight feet of water.

142 Tike's Peak This area features slides and pools scaled down for little splashers.

143 Melt-Away Bay The wave pool at the foot of Mount Gushmore is ideal for swimming or just bob-bob-bobbing along.

144 Cross Country Creek A more sedate attraction, this mild inner-tube ride circles the perimeter of **Blizzard Beach**. The creek current is only 2.5 mph, except for one section with rushing water.

Disney's All-Star Resorts

When it comes to thinking up unusual and outlandish themes—for theme parks or hotels—nobody does it better than Disney. Assisting in the fun in this case was **Arquitectonica,** a Miami-based architectural firm. The motel-like buildings of **Disney's All-Star Music Resort** and **Disney's All-Star Sports Resort** (and, as we went to press, a new **All-Star Movies Resort** that was scheduled to be unveiled) have a cartoonish feel; they're painted in a variety of bright colors and are adorned with giant icons reflecting their respective themes.

The playful approach is carried out in the hotel interiors, which feature bright colors and a skewed sense of proportion; everything is larger or smaller than normal, adding to the goofy, surreal ambience. The music and sports themes are reflected on the furniture, the bedspreads, even the towels.

The two resorts have a total of 3,840 rooms divided among 10 buildings. Rooms at both resorts sleep up to four persons and at only 260 square feet are the smallest at **Walt Disney World** (in contrast, rooms at the moderately priced **Caribbean Beach, Port Orleans,** and **Dixie Landings** resorts are 314 square feet). But then, the room rates here are also the lowest of all the Disney properties. Each room is furnished with two double beds, a single-sink vanity area, a separate bathroom, a closet, a table with two chairs, and an armoire.

Designed with budget-conscious families in mind, both hotels feature play areas, video arcades, and food courts with inexpensive food stands that are open daily for breakfast, lunch, dinner, and snacks. Pizza, pasta, ribs, chicken, salads, burgers, and lots of baked goods are available; if you're too tired to go out after a long day at the Mouse House, pizza can be delivered to your room. For an economical meal, a new McDonald's restaurant has opened less than a quarter mile from the resort.

145 Disney's All-Star Music Resort $
The five buildings here celebrate five American music styles—calypso, country, rock, jazz, and Broadway. Larger-than-life icons illustrating the music theme include three-story cowboy boots and a neon-lit walk-through jukebox. There are two swimming pools—one in the shape of a grand piano and the other in the shape of a guitar. ♦ 1801 W Buena Vista Pkwy). 939.6000; www.disneyworld.com &

146 Disney's All-Star Sports Resort $
Football, baseball, basketball, tennis, and surfing are the themes of the five buildings here, which are decorated with huge football helmets, baseball bats, surfboards, and the like. At one building, palm trees are arranged to look like a basketball team at tip-off; at another, an interior courtyard resembles a football field. One of the pools is shaped like a baseball diamond; the other is supposed to be a surfing lagoon. ♦ 1801 W Buena Vista Dr (south of Osceola Pkwy). 939.5000; www.disneyworld.com &

More films are produced in Florida than any other state except California and New York.

Walt Disney World has 8,300 acres that are designated as a permanent wildlife conservation area and will never be developed.

Every day, as many as 400 pairs of sunglasses are turned in to Walt Disney World's lost and found, as well as about 300 hats and 4 or 5 sets of dentures.

147 Coronado Springs $$ This 1,900-room hotel is Disney's first moderately priced resort with convention facilities. Palm-shaded courtyards and lake views are part of the "old Southwest" ambience, with rooms and suites situated in three Spanish-style villages. Meeting space in the resort's 95,000-square-foot convention center includes a 60,214-square-foot ballroom, the largest in the Southeast. There's a white sand beach and a fitness center, swimming in five themed pools, and boat and bike rentals. Restaurants include a lakeside eatery, a food court, and a 200-seat lounge. ♦ 1000 W Buena Vista Dr (between Osceola Pkwy and World Dr). 934.7639; www.disneyworld.com

Bests

Charles Stovall
Theme Parks/Attractions Producer, *Orlando Sentinel Interactive*

Best attraction—"The Magic of Disney Animation Tour" at **Disney-MGM Studios.** It doesn't get more behind-the-scenes than this. Art and animation come alive in this tour of the actual Disney animation studio. **MGM** visitors see the artists in their workspace, interact with them, and get a sneak peek at upcoming animated films. And what's more, it's included in **Disney-MGM's** admission price.

Best ride—**Back to the Future** at **Universal Studios Escape.** Combining the thrill of movie shaker rides with spectacular visual effects and a cute story line, this ride definitely delivers on **Universal's** promise to "ride the movies." You get to blast through time and space to help Doc Brown save the future from Biff Tannen. This ride holds the best bang for the action buff in town.

Best theme park combo—Lunch at **Finnegan's** and the **Blues Brothers** show at **Universal Studios Escape.** In **Universal Studios'** downtown New York setting, **Finnegan's** offers great, reasonably priced food in a "Cheers"-type atmosphere. Right outside **Finnegan's** door is one of the best performances around, the **Blues Brothers** spectacular, a singing and dancing extravaganza, which employs some of the best performers at the parks.

Best place to sample the Orlando music scene—**Sapphire Supper Club.** Live blues, jazz, folk, rock, and alternative music fill the dark club, while regulars chow down on a rather eclectic menu and sample the latest martini creations.
Local musicians such as Blue Meridian, Von Ra, and My Friend Steve grace the stage most nights, with national acts coming in on a regular basis.

Best garage sale area—**College Park.** A quaint shopping district at the northeastern corner of downtown Orlando, College Park is a place where locals love to wheel and deal. The city's best and brightest can be found searching for bargains Friday mornings on their way to work and sometimes all day Saturday and Sunday.

Disney's Animal Kingdom

Disney's Animal Kingdom, the fourth and newest theme park at **Walt Disney World,** features breathtaking shows, thrilling attractions, and more than 1,000 animals in habitats replicating those found in the wild. Every inch of the colorful park is about wild and whimsical creatures: from extinct dinos to real rhinos to such popular Disney characters as Mickey and Minnie Mouse, Goofy, Donald Duck, and Pocahontas.

Disney's Animal Kingdom is divided into five distinct "lands": **Safari Village, Camp Minnie-Mickey, Africa, Asia,** and **DinoLand U.S.A.** At 500 acres, this is by far the largest Disney theme park, but nearly 25 percent of the park (110 acres) is taken up by **Africa,** home to the wild animals.

Unlike the other Disney theme parks, where the landscaping complements the buildings, in many areas at **Disney's Animal Kingdom** it is the landscaping itself that is the stage and set. More than 2.3 million plants from around the globe—plants from every continent except Antarctica—create a unique botanical garden. The 260 species include 850 species of trees—40 species of palm trees alone. The plants come from places like Madagascar, Botswana, Tasmania, and Nepal. In **DinoLand U.S.A.,** for example, there are 20 species of magnolia. The cycad collection in **DinoLand U.S.A.** is the third largest such collection in North America.

Park your car and board a tram for the **Main Entrance,** where you can pick up a park map and entertainment schedule. Strollers and wheelchairs are for rent in **Garden Gate Gifts.** A giant **Rainforest Cafe** is just to the left of the entrance, open for breakfast, lunch, and dinner.

There are don't-miss attractions in every "land," so rest often and wear comfortable walking shoes. The experience begins in **The Oasis,** a tropical garden filled with real animals, lush plants, and cool waterfalls. Most guests quickly head for **Kilimanjaro Safaris** in **Africa,** but take a few moments to enjoy this lovely setting.

Like humans, animals prefer to avoid the intense midday heat, so morning and late afternoon hours are the best times to ride Kilimanjaro Safaris, the star

167 Pangani Forest Exploration Trail

166

165

168

164

162

163

AFRICA

Discovery River

156

169

170

152

155

ASIA

Maharajah 171 Jungle Trek

154

172

SAFARI VILLAGE

150

151

153

The Oasis
149

Discovery River

173

Oldengate Bridge

174

Garden Gate Gifts

DINOLAND USA

180

181

182

175

179

177 Cretaceous Trail

178

176

attraction. During the morning hours, the action-packed thrill ride **Countdown to Extinction** in **DinoLand U.S.A.** and the 3-D spectacular **It's Tough to Be a Bug** at **The Tree of Life** have minimal wait times. Bear in mind that there are certain health, age, and size restrictions at **Countdown to Extinction**.

Festival of the Lion King anchors a strong entertainment lineup at **Disney's Animal Kingdom**. Music and characters from the animated Disney classic flood the stage during this spectacular show that combines the pageantry of a parade with the excitement of an African celebration. Other shows include **Journey into Jungle Book, Colors of the Wind: Friends from the Animal Forest, Flights of Wonder,** and the whimsical daily parade **March of the ARTimals**.

Although a majority of the restaurants at **Disney's Animal Kingdom** offer quick service only, there's a wide variety of choices and the food is generally very tasty. There is only one Disney "character breakfast" at the park: "Donald's Prehistoric Breakfastosaurus" at **Restaurantosaurus** in **DinoLand U.S.A.** Reservations for the character breakfast are recommended, and may be made ahead of time by calling WDW.DINE (939.3463).

Disney's Animal Kingdom is open daily, generally from 8AM to dusk. There is an admission fee and a parking charge. Try and pace yourself and make sure to drink plenty of liquids. For more information, contact **Walt Disney World** Guest Information at 824.4321. For a visual tour of **Disney's Animal Kingdom**, visit **Walt Disney World's** home page at www.disneyworld.com. Most attractions, restaurants, and shops are wheelchair accessible.

Area code 407 unless otherwise noted.

Main Entrance

A **Guest Relations** window is located on the left side of the **Entrance Plaza,** along with rest rooms, telephones, a mail drop, and lockers. At **Guest Relations,** you can pick up a free guide map, exchange foreign currency, find out about special programs, and receive information on guided tours. Additional services are available for guests with visual or hearing disabilities (you can request the *Guidebook for Guests with Disabilities,* which provides details on all services, including transportation, parking, and attraction access). You should also report lost children at **Guest Relations** (or alert a Disney employee). **The Outpost,** a shop selling Disney T-shirts, hats, and other merchandise, is also on the left. Pet kennels are located to the right, as well as additional lockers and an automatic teller machine. **Garden Gate Gifts,** also to the right as you enter the park, is where you can rent strollers and wheelchairs. This is also a good place to stock up on film and sun-care products. Purchases made throughout the park can be transferred to this location at no extra charge. Just ask for the package-pickup option when you make your purchase.

148 **Rainforest Cafe** **$$$** You'll see this restaurant on your left before you even reach the entrance to the theme park. Billed as "A Wild Place to Shop and Eat," this is the only full-service restaurant at the park. It is much larger than the **Rainforest Cafe** at **Downtown Disney Marketplace,** although the interior design is very similar. The menu features a wide variety of entrées—burgers, sandwiches, salads, and pastas—and the portions are plentiful. Theme park admission is not required to dine here. ♦ American ♦ Daily breakfast, lunch, and dinner

149 **The Oasis** This tropical garden, with dozens of exotic plants and wildlife just inches from the walkway, sets the stage for the rest of **Disney's Animal Kingdom.** Easily viewed animals include Reeve's muntjac, hyacinth macaws, Chinese tufted deer, and military macaws. With a careful eye you should be able to spot a Parma wallaby, a rhinoceros iguana, a two-toed sloth, and a Southern giant anteater. We recommend a leisurely stroll, but if you're in a hurry to see the rest of the park, this is a great area to explore later in the day, after you've been to some of the park's bigger attractions.

Safari Village

Cross the **Discovery River** bridge to **Safari Village,** the central hub of **Disney's Animal Kingdom.** This area is home to the magnificent 145-foot-tall **Tree of Life,** which has the images of 325 animals carved into its roots, trunk, and branches. The village itself is a blend of architecture from Africa, Latin America, and the South Pacific, with Balinese sculpture, stone carvings, and splashes of vibrant color—orange, turquoise, pink, and red—decorating the artful buildings. The shops showcase crafts from around the world along with the usual Disney souvenirs and are open daily during park hours.

There are several live animal attractions, like the otter pool and the tiny monkeys that live in the trees. This area also hosts one of the park's premier attractions, **It's Tough to Be a Bug.** Ethnic musical groups can be heard around every corner of **Safari Village,** so take some time to enjoy the sights and sounds.

Safari Village is also the starting point for the **March of the ARTimals,** which proceeds along the edge of **Asia** and past **DinoLand U.S.A.** (at 2PM and 4PM). It's a vivid pageant of fanciful creatures—human-sized bumblebees, 11-foot-tall spiders, and giant praying mantises—celebrating the world of animals. There are 55 artist-performers and five rolling stages in the parade, including musicians, acrobats, and dancers. The art pieces worn as costumes are the creation of the European artist Rolf Knie, who designed them with color, modern style, and unlimited imagination. Ant costumes, for example, include bangles, cymbals, bells, and other instruments that create the rhythm as the creatures bounce along to "La Cucaracha"; beaded, embroidered, and mirrored fabrics create the costumes for the elephants, apes, tigers, and lions in the band of beasts.

150 **Island Mercantile** This is the place for **Disney's Animal Kingdom**–themed merchandise.

151 **Disney Outfitters** This shop sells upscale clothing and accessories as well as collectible gifts and a variety of **Disney's Animal Kingdom** logo merchandise. There is also a ring carver on the premises.

152 **The Tree of Life** This man-made tree was crafted by Disney Imagineers into a stunning, 14-story icon that forms the centerpiece of the entire park. The base of the "tree" is actually an oil rig; the 50-foot-wide trunk is made of a concrete-like material and spreads 170 feet in diameter. A team of 11 sculptors spent 12 months standing on scaffolding to carve more than 325 animals into the tree's roots, trunk, and branches—giraffes, chimpanzees, lions, dolphins, eagles, even Mickey Mouse. The man-made leaves were all attached by hand to more than 8,000 of the tree's branches. In all, it took more than 18 months and a crew of thousands to complete the exterior construction. Around the tree live real Galápagos tortoises, South American capybaras (rodents that weigh up to 150 pounds), and green-winged macaws.

Within The Tree of Life:

It's Tough to Be a Bug Inside the roots of the massive **Tree of Life** is a humorous eight-minute show, featuring a computer-animated 3-D film, Audio-Animatronic figures, and amazing in-theater effects. If you've experienced *Honey, I Shrunk the Audience* at **Epcot**, you'll get the general idea, but **It's Tough to Be a Bug** takes the technology even further—this is one of the most innovative theatrical experiences ever created. You'll squeal in your seat when a giant Chilean tarantula lets his poisonous quills fly or when a solider termite mistakes you for an intruder (and even these pale in comparison to the stinkbug). Be ready to squirm when the maggots, cockroaches, and bedbugs prepare to leave the theater. The show runs continuously during park hours.

153 **Flame Tree Barbecue** ★★$ Walk up to the window and place your order for some of the best barbecued chicken, pork, and beef you'll find in Central Florida. All seating is outdoors in vividly colored pavilions that are decorated with folk-art carvings from Bali. It also offers kid's meals and fresh fruit plates. ♦ American ♦ Daily breakfast and lunch

154 **Beastly Bazaar** This shop sells T-shirts, name mugs, hats, and merchandise from around the globe.

155 **Pizzafari** $ This cleverly designed restaurant features animal murals and figurines lining the walls and ceiling. As the name suggests, the specialty here is oven-baked pizza. Also included on the menu is a selection of hot sandwiches and calzones. Save room for dessert: The chocolate mousse cake is delicious. ♦ Italian ♦ Daily breakfast, lunch, and dinner

156 **Creature Comforts** Gifts for children are sold here, including clothing, stuffed animals, and conservation-themed merchandise.

Camp Minnie-Mickey

Camp Minnie-Mickey was inspired by the cool green Adirondack Mountains, and was designed just so that the Disney characters would have their own space to "vacation" in this wild animal park. Indeed, it's the only place at **Disney's Animal Kingdom** where you can meet Disney characters (except for the morning "character breakfasts" at **Restaurantosaurus**). It also features one of the best stage shows at **Walt Disney World, Festival of the Lion King**, as well as the warm and fuzzy **Colors of the Wind: Friends from the Animal Forest**.

157 **Colors of the Wind: Friends from the Animal Forest** Children will love this show, held at **Grandmother Willow's Grove**. Pocahontas, along with a cast of furry animal friends, takes the stage to discover the secrets of saving the forest from destruction. The 12-minute show is performed numerous times throughout the day, so plan to see this show in between some of the bigger shows at the park. ♦ Check the entertainment schedule for show times

158 **Chip 'n' Dale's Cookie Cabin** This open-air cart sells fresh-baked cookies and ice cream treats. Try the chocolate-chip cookie ice-cream sandwich.

159 **Forest Trail Funnel Cakes** Visit this food cart for funnel cakes, the delicious theme-park treat made from deep-fried dough and dusted with powdered sugar, plus corn dogs (batter-dipped hot dogs) and drinks.

Orlando is the number one city in which to vacation with grandchildren, according to a survey by the Orlando/Orange County Convention & Visitors Bureau. Other cities ranking in the top ten were Washington DC, San Francisco, and New York City.

Restaurants/Clubs: Red   **Hotels:** Blue
Shops/ Outdoors: Green   **Sights/Culture:** Black

160 Festival of the Lion King Staged at the **Lion King Theater**, a rustic, open-air amphitheater, this don't-miss show puts you right in the middle of the excitement. The 28-minute performance stars Simba and other animal heroes from *The Lion King,* along with singers, dancers, and acrobatic performers dressed in elaborate costumes. If you sit near the front, a lucky family member may be selected to join the show. Plan to arrive 30 minutes before the performance begins.
♦ Check the entertainment schedule for show times

161 Character Greeting Areas This is the place to find Mickey, Minnie, Winnie the Pooh, Tigger, Timon, Rafiki, and many of the other Disney characters. They pose for pictures, sign autographs, and give out plenty of hugs.

Africa

Natives of Africa say they are amazed by this realistic re-creation of their homeland. **Africa** is the largest of the "lands" in **Disney's Animal Kingdom.** Guests walk over a bridge across **Discovery River** and down the bustling main street of the "village," called **Harambe** (which means "coming together" in Swahili), to begin their African adventure. While this area is inspired by actual African towns, Disney chose not to copy a specific street or marketplace but to try to capture the essence of a busy coastal city. Careful "aging" makes new structures look old. For realism, Disney brought 13 Zulu thatchers to Florida to create the roofs for the thatch huts throughout the village. And though the Zulus have returned home, about 80 Africans continue to work in the park.

Outside of the village, you'll feel as though you've been transported across the continent when you board **Kilimanjaro Safaris** and begin your trek over the majestic savannah. You can also hike along the **Pangani Forest Exploration Trail** or take the **Wildlife Express to Conservation Station.**

162 Dawa Bar This casual, outdoor bar is inspired by those in small African villages. There are a few tables and live Caribbean-African music. You can order any cocktail imaginable, and their margaritas and piña coladas are especially popular. The bartender recommends the Sundowner Punch, a stiff rum concoction, or Safari Red, a micro-brewed beer. There's no food, but pretzels are served with drinks. ♦ Daily

163 Tamu Tamu Refreshments This stand sells frozen yogurt, ice cream, and sundaes.

164 Tusker House Restaurant ★★$ One of the best quick-service restaurants at **Walt Disney World,** its specialties include a roasted vegetable sandwich and tender rotisserie chicken. The menu also has a good selection of beef, chicken, and turkey sandwiches. Indoor seating is limited, but the restaurant has plenty of seats in a covered outdoor pavilion. ♦ American ♦ Daily breakfast, lunch, and dinner

164 Kusafiri Coffee Shop & Bakery This walk-up window, which is in the same building as the **Tusker House Restaurant,** sells fresh cookies, pastries, coffee, cappuccino, and espresso. Just inside the door to the building is the bakery, where you may also purchase coffee and baked goods at the inside counter. Guests may sit at tables in **Tusker House** or outdoors.

165 Mombasa Marketplace/Ziwani Traders Filled with safari supplies, this shop offers a unique collection of African-themed souvenirs and accessories, including apparel, decorative objects, and stuffed toys.

166 Kilimanjaro Safaris There are no Audio-Animatronic animals on this safari—they're all real. A 32-passenger open-air vehicle takes you over rutted roads and through overflowing pools. Throughout your 20-minute journey you'll encounter elephants, hippopotamuses, giraffes, zebras, gazelles, elands, okapis, rhinoceroses, wildebeests, and even fierce predators such as lions and cheetahs. The animals get so close to the vehicles that the driver will sometimes have to stop and wait for them to cross the road. Like all Disney attractions, this ride has a story line. Halfway through your adventure you're enlisted to join a daring chase to capture poachers who are preying on elephants for their ivory. Make sure to have your cameras ready and loaded with plenty of film.

167 Pangani Forest Exploration Trail *Pangani* means "place of enchantment" in Swahili, and this attraction lives up to its name. Along this walking trail located near the exit from **Kilimanjaro Safaris,** you'll see hippopotamuses as they swim (which you can view from under water), meerkats, tropical birds (in the **Avian Research Center**), and the honeycombed world that the naked mole rat creates by tunneling through the dirt. Farther along the path you'll come upon a group of lowland gorillas. The viewing area here is spectacular. At one point the only thing separating you from the gorillas is a thin pane of Plexiglas.

168 Wildlife Express to Conservation Station The 19th-century–style train that takes you to **Conservation Station** may be exciting for railroad buffs, but the 1.2-mile ride is fairly dull. Along the way you'll see the "backstage areas" where the park's animals are housed and fed. At **Conservation Station,** however, things get a little more interesting. There, visitors explore the challenges that face animals worldwide through fascinating, innovative, and colorful exhibits. One such exhibit allows you to watch as Disney veterinarians perform routine checkups and other medical procedures on some of the animals who live at the park. Another popular spot is the animal nursery, featuring the park's newest arrivals. Find out about the shrinking natural habitat at **Rafiki's Planet Watch,** an interactive video that connects guests to information about endangered animals, or about conservation efforts around the world via the **EcoWeb.** Also, animal experts showcase rare or endangered animals during 15-minute presentations throughout the day.

At Conservation Station:

Affection Section This is the only place at **Disney's Animal Kingdom** where children can touch live—albeit domesticated—animals, such as sheep, goats, miniature donkeys, and rabbits. Children will love the "elephant" hand-wash station.

Asia

Asian themes from Nepal, India, Thailand, and Indonesia are carried out through architecture, animal carvings, and ruins scattered throughout the re-created fictional "village" of **Anandapur.** Prepare yourself for adventure on the **Kali River Rapids** water ride. **Flights of Wonder** offers an entertaining look at some exotic birds, and the **Maharajah Jungle Trek** will lead to animal habitats among ancient ruins.

169 Mr. Kamal's Burger Grill This open-air stand near the Discovery River boats between **Africa** and **Asia** serves decent broiled burgers with potato chips. There are a few seats nearby.

Jewels of the Real Florida

The Florida Park Service has recognized a handful of state parks throughout Florida as "gems"—special, sometimes out of the way, and worth your visit. There are four of these jewels in Central Florida.

Tranquil **Faver-Dykes State Park** near **St. Augustine** is quiet, peaceful, relaxing, and unhurried—752 acres alongside **Pellicer Creek** where you may spot deer, turkeys, hawks, bobcats, and river otters. Fishing, picnicking, nature walks, and camping are favorite activities, and canoes are for rent. The park is 18 miles south of St. Augustine near the intersection of Interstate 95 and Highway 1; call 904/794.0997 for information.

Tomoka State Park in **Ormond Beach** offers scenic oak trees and camping in a spot where Native Americans once lived off the fish-filled lagoons. A nature trail, canoeing, fishing, boating, and picnicking are also available. It is located three miles north of Ormond Beach on Beach Street; call 904/676.4050 for information.

Hontoon Island State Park was first inhabited by Timucuan Indians, whose mounds can be viewed on the park's nature trail. Accessible only by private boat or by the free passenger ferry, which operates daily from 8AM until one hour before sundown, the park offers camping (six rustic cabins for rent), boating, picnicking, and fishing. It is located six miles southwest of De Land, off Route 44; call 904/736.5309 for information.

South Central Florida was the heart of Florida's frontier cattle country, and the life of early Florida cowboys is interpreted with a living history demonstration at the **Lake Kissimmee State Park** "cow camp." Located on the shores of **Lakes Kissimmee, Tiger,** and **Rosalie,** the park also offers outstanding fishing, bird watching, and boating, and 13 miles of nature trails that are home to white-tailed deer, bald eagles, sandhill cranes, turkeys, and bobcats. The park is off Route 60, 15 miles east of Lake Wales; call 941/696.1112 for information.

170 Flights of Wonder A winged cast of dozens of rare birds lead an American student (Luke) on a treasure-seeking journey across southern Asia. The highlight of this 25-minute outdoor show, presented at the **Caravan Stage,** is a parrot who sings show tunes. Birds of prey also take part in this demonstration, including a Harris hawk who swoops down and grabs Luke's hat. ♦ Check the entertainment schedule for show times

171 Maharajah Jungle Trek This is **Asia**'s version of the **Pangani Forest Exploration Trail,** except the featured animals here are Bengal tigers and not lowland gorillas. Cutting through thick jungle, you'll see Komodo dragons, Malayan tapirs, and a family of bats that can be viewed at close range through huge glass windows. The ruins of a maharajah's palace will set the scene for a dramatic view of a group of Bengal tigers as they peer across a lotus-filled pool at a family of blackbuck, an antelope species, and Elds deer.

172 Kali River Rapids A 12-person raft will takes you on the ride of your life. Drifting along the **Chakranadi River,** you'll glide through a lush jungle filled with flowering shrubs under a dense green canopy. Then the raft picks up speed. Suddenly the smell of burning wood catches your attention and the raft comes upon a massive logging operation. Danger abounds as a giant truck slips down a rain-soaked embankment and flaming trees threaten the raft's safety. The raft careens down a massive waterfall into a rocky canyon filled with white-water rapids. Be prepared to get wet. If the waterfall and rapids don't soak you, the two "elephant showers" near the ride's conclusion will.

DinoLand U.S.A.

Start your journey here by walking under the **Oldengate Bridge,** a 50-foot-tall steel Brachiosaurus skeleton that straddles the entrance. This is the wackiest "land" at **Disney's Animal Kingdom,** designed with tongue in cheek as a working archaeological dig overrun by college interns. The detail is incredible. No bones about it—kids will love uncovering a mammoth dinosaur skeleton at **The Boneyard.** Special Disney magic brings dinosaurs back to life for the most thrilling of all attractions, **Countdown to Extinction,** and lighthearted fun for the whole family awaits at **Journey into Jungle Book.**

DinoLand has the only Disney character breakfast at **Animal Kingdom—Donald's Prehistoric Breakfastosaurus** (starring Donald Duck and friends), featuring an all-you-can-eat buffet.

173 Dino Diner Stop at this take-out window for a giant turkey leg to munch on as you stroll. Soft drinks and breakfast breads are also available.

174 The Boneyard Although designed as a children's play area, adults have been known to get into the action, too. Swirling slides, bouncing bridges, and giant dinosaur bones will thrill the children. Hot stops with neat special effects include the xylophone bones (a musical note sounds when a bone is struck) and dinosaur footprints, which release a ferocious roar when stepped upon. Across the way sits a sand-filled dig site. Here kids can uncover dinosaur bones buried beneath the sand. This is a great place for adults to relax and take a breather while the children play.

175 Restaurantosaurus $ This quick-service restaurant offers typical theme-park fare, such as hot dogs and hamburgers. They do carry McDonald's french fries, Chicken McNuggets, and Happy Meals (with exclusive **Disney's Animal Kingdom** toys). Every morning this is the site of "Donald's Prehistoric Breakfastosaurus," starring Donald Duck. ♦ American ♦ Daily breakfast, lunch, and dinner. Reservations for priority seating recommended. WDW.DINE (939.3463)

176 Countdown to Extinction If you're looking for a heart-stopping, edge-of-your-seat thrill ride, this is it. You'll rocket back 65 million years to the age of the dinosaurs aboard a "time rover." Your mission: Locate an iguanodon and bring it back through the time portal before a massive asteroid slams into the earth. One major obstacle stands in your way—a monstrous, meat-eating carnotaurus. It's an exhilarating ride. Your time rover speeds and swerves to avoid the carnotaurus's razor-sharp teeth and giant claws, along with hundreds of small meteors spun off by the approaching asteroid. There are height and health restrictions on this ride and it may be too intense for young children.

177 Cretaceous Trail Slow down and take a hike on this little trail that takes you past plant and animal species that have survived since dinosaur times, such as cycads, palms, ferns, and soft-shelled turtles.

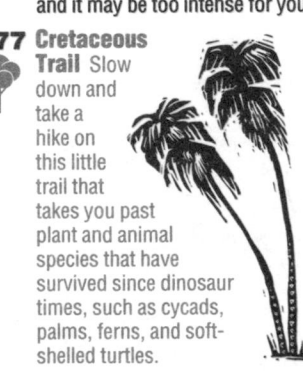

178 Chester and Hester's Dinosaur Treasures Even if you don't enjoy shopping, you'll love this store, which carries an amazing collection of weird and humorous dinosaur souvenirs. Lining the ceiling and walls are countless wacky knickknacks.

179 Dinosaur Jubilee After narrowly escaping the jaws of the carnotaurus at **Countdown to Extinction,** guests can explore the fossilized remains of real prehistoric creatures along with replicas of several gargantuan dinosaurs at this exhibit.

180 Fossil Preparation Lab See the preparation of the largest and most complete Tyrannosaurus rex skeleton ever found, which researchers have named Sue. Discovered in 1990, the full skeleton will go on permanent display at the Field Museum in Chicago in September of 2000. Before that, however, selected bones will be shipped to **Disney's Animal Kingdom,** where Field Museum staffers will conduct the painstaking work of preparing the dinosaur for display.

181 DinoLand Snacks If you're feeling faint from hunger and need something to tide you over, stop at this take-out window for McDonald's french fries and soft drinks.

182 Journey into Jungle Book This show, held at **Theater in the Wild,** a 1,500-seat covered outdoor ampitheater, features all of the lively music and characters portrayed in Disney's classic film *The Jungle Book.* Join Mowgli, Baloo, King Louie, Bagheera, and other characters during this enjoyable 30-minute romp combining costumed performers with colorful puppets. It will delight the kids and make you step to the beat. ♦ Check the entertainment schedule for show times

Bests

James A. Madison
Editor, *Florida Sun Review*

Wandering along **International Drive,** enjoying the sights, the sounds, and tourists from all over the world.

Visiting the **Orlando Science Center** and taking in a film at the **CineDome.**

Strolling around **Lake Eola,** either early in the morning or at twilight.

Visiting **Epcot** at night.

Having afternoon tea at **Disney's Grand Floridian Resort & Spa.**

Visiting **Pointe★Orlando.**

Visiting **Disney's Animal Kingdom.**

Taking in a **University of Central Florida** football game at the **Citrus Bowl** on an autumn afternoon.

Having breakfast on the weekend at **Max's Cafe & Coffee Shop** in downtown **Celebration.**

Visiting **Universal Studios Escape.**

Looking out over the **Buena Vista Lagoon** while having coffee and dessert at **Forty Thirst Street** in **Downtown Disney West Side.**

Visiting downtown **Winter Park,** with its quaint shops.

Taking in an **Orlando Magic** game at the **"O-Rena."**

Spending an afternoon at the **192 Flea Market** in **Kissimmee.**

Visiting **Disney-MGM Studios** in November to talk to television stars.

Enjoying the carnival-like atmosphere of **Church Street** at night in downtown Orlando.

Visiting the **Magic Kingdom.**

Jay Porcher
Jay Porcher, Marketing and Public Relations Consultant

The Arboretum at the **University of Central Florida**— In the midst of the bustle of one of the country's fastest growing universities (just 30 years old, the **University of Central Florida**'s enrollment is rapidly approaching 30,000!) is this 80-acre oasis of shaded paths and colorful and fragrant blooms. Strolling along the paths is peaceful and relaxing—it has yet to be discovered by most locals, much less visitors.

Sushi at **Ichiban**—Central Florida's best sushi is tucked into a cozy brick-walled restaurant on downtown **Orlando**'s main drag **(Orange Avenue).** The bento box dinners offer a delicious variety of sushi, tempura, and other Japanese delights.

Art collection at **Hyatt Regency–Grand Cypress Hotel**—One of the area's most impressive private art collections is on public view in the lobbies and hallways at this hotel in **Lake Buena Vista.** Don't miss the massive carved-jade ship. While you're there, have a drink or dinner at **Hemingway's** and stroll around the exotic pool, with waterfalls and grottoes.

Dinner and fireworks at **California Grill**—Even locals are willing to battle crowds of tourists to vie for a table at this place, located on the top floor of a **Walt Disney World** resort and one of the best restaurants in town. The food is adventurous and delicious, and the wine list is quite extensive (although a little pricey). If you time dinner right, you can enjoy the panoramic view of fireworks over the **Magic Kingdom**—the lights are dimmed in the restaurant during the display, and they play the same dramatic music park visitors hear. Be forewarned: Like most other tourist-area restaurants, families with children abound and therefore the restaurant is more casual and louder than you might expect.

Magic Kingdom

Established in 1971, the **Magic Kingdom** holds the distinction of being the first of the four major theme parks to open at **Walt Disney World**. For that reason, some people still refer to **Walt Disney World** as the **Magic Kingdom**, which can confuse things at times. For many longtime Disney devotees, this park is not only the Disney oldie, it's also the Disney goodie. Nothing else in Central Florida captures the imagination of youngsters like the **Magic Kingdom**—still regarded as an innocent, special place for children. (Alcohol is permitted in many parts of **Walt Disney World**, but never here.) What's more, it's astounding how many adults without kids and how many honeymooners frequent this children's playland

The 78-acre park is divided into **Main Street, U.S.A.** and six "lands": **Adventureland, Frontierland, Liberty Square, Fantasyland, Mickey's Toontown Fair**, and **Tomorrowland**. Each has at least one favorite attraction with long, long lines even during the slow season. As always, the best strategy is to eat breakfast early and arrive just as the park opens, or as an alternative, get to the park late in the afternoon when crowds thin. Before you get here, pick out the one can't-miss ride and be prepared to bolt for it once the minor logistical details are taken care of. Bear in mind, there are certain health, age, and size restrictions at **ExtraTERRORestrial Alien Encounter, Splash Mountain, Space Mountain, Big Thunder Mountain Railroad**, and **Grand Prix Raceway**.

In addition to myriad fast-food places, there are four table-service restaurants in the park—**Tony's Town Square Restaurant, Liberty Tree Tavern, Cinderella's Royal Table**, and **The Plaza Restaurant**. Advance reservations for priority seating for lunch and dinner at these restaurants, and for the popular breakfasts with Disney characters, are highly recommended; reservations may be made up to 60 days ahead of time by calling WDW.DINE (939.3463). Same-day reservations are taken at the door. Disabled visitors should note that most **Magic Kingdom** rides and attractions are wheelchair accessible; consult Disney's *Guidebook for Guests with Disabilities*.

Trams whisk visitors from the parking lot to the **Transportation and Ticket Center (TTC)**, from which you can take either the monorail or a ferry across **Seven Seas Lagoon** to get to the **Magic Kingdom**. A tip for first-timers: The monorail zips through the 15-story, A-frame **Disney's Contemporary Resort** hotel, and drivers have, on occasion, invited a guest to sit up front with them—something children will talk about long after they've forgotten Dumbo the Flying Elephant. The monorail circles the **Magic Kingdom** and runs whenever the park is open. Take the more leisurely ferry ride on your return trip.

Once you've gone through the turnstiles, head directly to **City Hall** at the entrance to **Main Street, U.S.A.** Obtain here, or at any shop, the day's schedule of events—parades, live performances, and the fireworks display. Now you're ready to come up with a game plan. You might want to proceed immediately to the ride you designated as "a must," especially if it's **Splash Mountain** in **Frontierland**, the always-popular **Space Mountain**, or the **ExtraTERRORestrial Alien Encounter** in **Tomorrowland**. After that, work your way around the park, keeping in mind that lines are shortest during lunch and dinner hours.

If you're with small children who want to meet Mickey Mouse, start your day by boarding the **Walt Disney World Railroad** and get off at **Mickey's Toontown Fair**. This part of the park can be a madhouse at times. Other characters also appear pretty regularly outdoors at **City Hall** in **Town Square** and near the **Pirates of the Caribbean** in **Adventureland**.

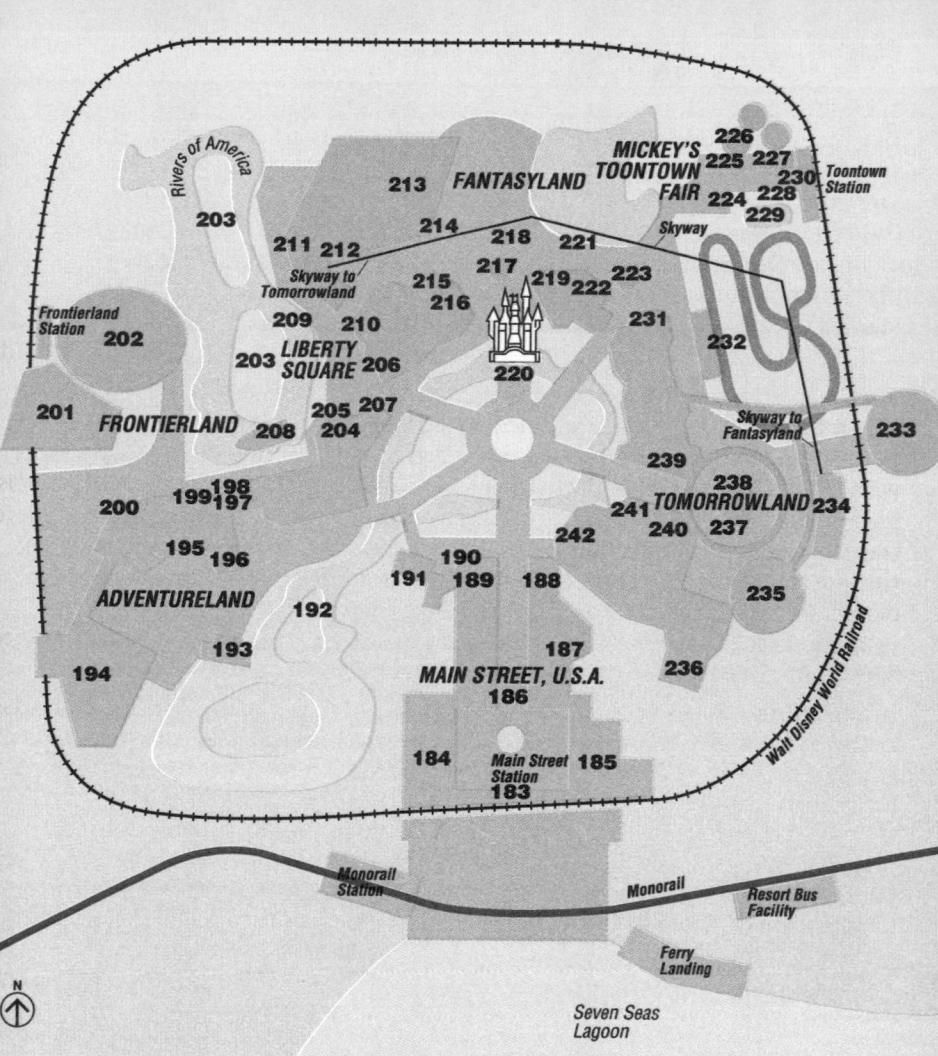

Live shows change throughout the year but usually include the Dapper Dans, a barbershop quartet that performs along **Main Street,** a Dixieland band, the Walt Disney World Band, the **"Disney's Magical Moments"** Parade at 3PM daily, fireworks and another parade at night, and more. Gospel and classic rock are sometimes featured. Consult the daily entertainment schedule. *Disneymania,* starring Mickey and friends, takes place in front of **Cinderella Castle.**

The **Magic Kingdom** is open daily; hours vary, but the park generally opens at 9AM and closes at either 6PM, 7PM, 9PM, or midnight. Keep in mind that if it's the time of year when the park stays open late, you might want to return to your hotel for a nap and perhaps a swim in the afternoon and head for the park again around 5PM or 6PM, when other folks are on their way out. In summer, the most pleasant time weatherwise is after dark; also, frequent summer afternoon rains typically end by 5PM or 6PM. If you do leave the park, don't forget to hold on to your passport and get your hand stamped at the turnstile when you exit; it's the only way you can get back in without paying a second admission fee. Also, hang on to your parking ticket to avoid paying that fee again.

Adjacent to the **Magic Kingdom,** but actually separate parks (with separate admission fees), are **River Country,** a water theme park, and **Discovery Island,** a zoological park and nature preserve. Both are located in **Disney's Fort Wilderness Resort,** which offers a broad range of lodging options, including campsites. Hotels in the **Magic Kingdom Resort Area,** which borders the **Seven Seas Lagoon,** provide the most convenient access to the park since you can take the monorail. For information, call 824.4321.

Area code 407 unless otherwise noted.

Main Street, U.S.A.

You won't find any rides in this portion of the theme park, just information, reservations windows, and souvenirs. Main Street is an idealized version of small-town USA in the late 1800s. Each building is different in design and decor, from wallpaper to chandeliers. The Dapper Dans, a barbershop quartet, add to the 19th-century ambience.

If you visit when park hours are extended (during the summer and on holidays), you might consider doing your shopping in the afternoon, when the lines at the attractions are longest. Purchase Mickey Mouse ears and other gifts and then store them in the conveniently placed lockers under the **Main Street Station.**

Main Street, U.S.A. empties onto an island hub directly in front of **Cinderella Castle,** which is 100 feet taller than Sleeping Beauty Castle at California's Disneyland. As you walk clockwise around this hub, the first path to the left leads to **Adventureland,** the next one goes to **Liberty Square** and **Frontierland,** and the path through **Cinderella Castle** leads to **Fantasyland.** The next walkway goes to **Fantasyland** and **Mickey's Toontown Fair,** and the final path stretches all the way to **Tomorrowland.** If you want to bypass one "land" to get to another, it's faster to cut through the hub.

183 Walt Disney World Railroad There are four trains in the **Magic Kingdom** roundhouse, all built in the early 1900s as steam engines but now running on diesel fuel. The trains circle the park clockwise, with stops at **Frontierland** and **Mickey's Toontown Fair.** Hop on a train to get the lay of the land at the start of your day. The ride takes just 21 minutes. Passengers can also board at **Mickey's Toontown Fair** and **Frontierland,** both of which have access for the physically disabled; the **Main Street** stop doesn't. For parade enthusiasts, the **Main Street** train station platform is the optimum spot for viewing the daily 3PM parade or the evening "Spectro Magic" parade. But seats are limited so plan on a long wait.

184 City Hall Free transportation up Main Street begins here. Choose from horse-pulled trolleys, a fire truck, vintage cars, and a double-decker bus. You can pick up an entertainment schedule at **City Hall,** as well as lost items (and lost children); maps in

French, German, Japanese, Spanish, Portuguese, and Braille; information for guests with disabilities (taped narrations for the sight-impaired, written descriptions for hearing-impaired); and information on programs, Disney character appearances, and all that goes on in The Kingdom. **Main Street Gallery,** stocking cels from Disney movies and hard-to-find memorabilia, is located next door.

185 Tony's Town Square Restaurant ★$$$
If you've ever seen *Lady and the Tramp,* you'll feel right at home in this Victorian-style restaurant inspired by the movie. Primarily a pasta place, they also make good burgers. This is also a popular breakfast spot for those who arrive before 9AM; order the waffles in the shape of Mickey Mouse. ♦ Italian ♦ Daily breakfast, lunch, and dinner. Reservations for priority seating recommended

186 Shops on Main Street, U.S.A. Hats of all kinds, including Goofy hats and Mickey Mouse ears, can be monogrammed at **The Chapeau;** the **Kodak Camera Center** offers film, photography tips, two-hour processing, and rentals. Gifts, snacks, and tobacco products are for sale at **Main Street Market House.** Other stores along Main Street include **Disney & Co.** (souvenirs), **The Shadow Box** (silhouettes created and framed while you wait), **Crystal Arts** (glass cutting, blowing, and engraving), **Disney Clothiers** (clothing featuring Disney characters), **Main Street Athletic Store,** and **Uptown Jewelers.** In **Emporium,** a Disney merchandise store, find **Harmony Barber Shop,** where you can get a shave and a haircut and buy shaving bowls and brushes and moustache cups.

187 Main Street Cinema Now a retail shop, this old movie house features merchandise from the latest Disney theatrical releases. It also shows previews of upcoming films.

188 The Plaza Restaurant $$$ This eatery with a turn-of-the-century theme has a good location for viewing fireworks in the evening, but the sandwiches and burgers aren't as memorable as the desserts available next door at **Main Street Bake Shop** and **Plaza Ice Cream Parlor.** ♦ American ♦ Daily lunch, dinner, and snacks. Reservations for priority seating recommended

189 Casey's Corner $ A shady place to grab a hot dog or a soda and listen to the pianist playing an antique upright. ♦ Snack bar ♦ Daily

190 First Aid Center This and **The Magic Kingdom Baby Center** (a good place for mothers to nurse, stocked with disposable diapers and other infant items) are located on the way to **Adventureland,** just before you get to **The Crystal Palace.**

191 The Crystal Palace $$ The **Magic Kingdom**'s only buffet, this Victorian-style restaurant is one of the few that serve a full breakfast. Winnie the Pooh and friends are there for every meal. Sit near the windows for a view of **Cinderella Castle.** ♦ American ♦ Daily breakfast, lunch, and dinner

Adventureland

Jungle Cruise and **Pirates of the Caribbean** are the big attractions here. If the sign in front of the **Jungle Cruise** indicates a wait of 45 minutes or longer, you might want to come back in the early evening, when the lines are usually shorter (but don't wait until after dark, when you may not be able to see all the animals).

192 Swiss Family Treehouse Scramble up, around, and through an elaborate tree house. Children like the climb, but many adults find this prop pretty boring, although it is indeed amazing that 300,000 plastic leaves are affixed to 1,400 branches.

193 Jungle Cruise Both children and adults enjoy this 10-minute boat ride through tropical jungles, complete with many Audio-Animatronic wild animals. The captain's corny jokes seem fresh to the kids, who strain to see what awaits around each bend.

194 Pirates of the Caribbean Keep your eyes open to catch all the clever Disney details. The drunken, brawling pirates are the best Audio-Animatronic figures in the entire park. People sitting in the front of this ride may get splashed at one point.

195 El Pirata y el Perico Restaurante $$ The name of this snack stand means "the Pirate and the Parrot." Across from the **Pirates of the Caribbean,** it features hot dogs and tacos with a variety of toppings. ♦ Snack bar ♦ Daily lunch and snacks

196 The Enchanted Tiki Room This refreshing and humorous nine-minute show, starring more than 225 singing birds, flowers, and tiki statues, blends an original cast of characters with cleverly choreographed musical numbers. The plot is that the show's newest stars, Iago (Jafar's partner in crime in *Aladdin*) and Zazu (from *The Lion King*), want to change the long-running show, but the lovable tiki birds have other plans. The show runs continuously during park hours.

196 J.P. and the Silver Stars This steel drum band performs the authentic music of the Caribbean. Steel band music originated on the island of Trinidad as part of the Caribbean's largest carnival celebration. ♦ Check the entertainment schedule for show times

197 Sunshine Tree Terrace Lots of yummy citrus-based drinks (try the citrus swirl) plus frozen yogurt shakes, cappuccino, espresso, and soft drinks are on tap. ♦ Daily

Frontierland

Splash Mountain and the **Big Thunder Mountain** rides are the favorites here, incongruously high-tech attractions for a place designed to recall the days of Davy Crockett and Tom Sawyer.

198 Frontierland Shootin' Arcade Lasers and electronics, not bullets, are used, though the replicas of old buffalo rifles are very realistic. Moving tombstone targets and good sound effects make this test of skill a lot of fun. ♦ Nominal fee

199 Country Bear Jamboree The song-and-dance routine, performed by a pack of Audio-Animatronic bears, stars Henry, but it's Big Al who steals the show. Another showstopper is Teddi Beara, lowered from the ceiling on a swing while belting out "He Doesn't Know the Heart He's Breakin'." The lines can be long, but the show is definitely worth waiting for.

Former US President Richard Nixon made his famous "I am not a crook" speech at Walt Disney World on November 17, 1973, while visiting a meeting of Associated Press managing editors at Disney's Contemporary Resort.

Restaurants/Clubs: Red   **Hotels:** Blue
Shops/ ⊺ Outdoors: Green   **Sights/Culture:** Black

200 Pecos Bill Cafe $$ This place is good for chili or chicken, and the burgers aren't bad. There's counter service and seating is both inside and out. ♦ American ♦ Daily lunch and dinner

201 Splash Mountain This charming attraction, with Audio-Animatronic characters based on Disney's 1946 film *Song of the South,* is one of the world's steepest flume rides. In eight-person boats, guests pass through caves and hollowed-out trees, watching as Brer Rabbit is pursued by Brer Fox and Brer Bear. At the end, riders plunge down 87-foot-high **Splash Mountain** at more than 40 mph. Don't miss it—and expect to get wet. There are health, age, and size boarding restrictions.

202 Big Thunder Mountain Railroad Here's a roller-coaster ride for those who thought they didn't like roller coasters. It's sort of a roller coaster with training wheels, although there are plenty of dips, twirls, and surprises to make it exciting. Keep your eyes open so you won't miss any of the dandy details, including floods, tumbleweeds, and waterfalls. One trip isn't enough to appreciate it. Come back in the evening, when you will get a different view of the scenery and won't have to wait an hour for a three-minute ride. There are health, age, and size boarding restrictions.

203 Tom Sawyer Island When you find your energy level flagging, mosey on back here. At the entrance, which is near **Big Thunder Mountain,** take a raft to the island and then, keeping **Rivers of America** to your right, follow the path to **Aunt Polly's Landing.** While you sit sipping lemonade, let the kids explore the island's cave, bridges, dirt paths, and fort. **Fort Sam Clemens** has guns to fire on the upper level, and you can make your escape through a secret passageway. Nothing extraordinary, just a nice change of pace.

On Tom Sawyer Island:

Aunt Polly's Landing $$ A two-story wooden structure with a covered patio protruding out into the water, this is one of the least-known eateries at the park. You can get a sandwich, cookies, or a piece of pie, accompanied by iced tea, lemonade, or a soft drink. ♦ American ♦ Daily lunch and snacks

204 Diamond Horseshoe Saloon Revue
This big Old West–style dance revue features songs, dances, and corny jokes from an energetic cast. Guests may stay for the entire

hour or just stop by for a few minutes. Fast food is available during performances.

Liberty Square

Sandwiched between **Frontierland** and **Fantasyland, Liberty Square** makes visitors feel as though they are in a small colonial village, with saltbox homes, stores with brick fronts, and plenty of American flags. In the center is the **Liberty Tree,** a giant live oak that is more than 130 years old. From its branches hang 13 lanterns in honor of the original 13 states. The big draws are the **Haunted Mansion, Hall of Presidents,** and the **Liberty Belle Riverboat.**

205 Liberty Tree Tavern $$$ Built to look like a 200-year-old tavern, this full-service restaurant has a fireplace, colonial-style furniture, and hardwood floors. You can easily make a filling lunch of New England clam chowder and a salad. Minnie Mouse and Chip 'n' Dale stop by the dining rooms after 4PM each day. At dinner, the fare shifts to pot roast, turkey, and seafood pasta dishes. ♦ American ♦ Daily lunch and dinner. Reservations for priority seating recommended

206 The Hall of Presidents The 17-minute, updated show is narrated by the celebrated author and poet Maya Angelou and focuses on the evolution of the president's role in protecting the ideals set forth in the Declaration of Independence. The highlights here are the Audio-Animatronic figures of the US presidents. President Clinton has a speaking part, as does the updated Abraham Lincoln.

207 Liberty Square Shops On both sides of a little passageway to the island hub is a cluster of shops: **Heritage House** (presidential and Civil War memorabilia), **Ye Olde Christmas Shoppe, Umbrella Cart** (rain gear and parasols), and **Silhouette Cart** (silhouette drawings done on the spot). Grab a snack at **Sleepy Hollow.**

208 Liberty Belle Riverboat This triple-decker is a real steamboat, although it glides through **Rivers of America** via rail. The ride doesn't hold much amusement for children because it is slow and the only action comes from fake figures on shore, but it does offer a few relaxing moments for grown-ups. If your time is limited, skip it.

209 Mike Fink Keelboats If you saw Disney's original *Davy Crockett,* you'll recall the memorable episode when Crockett and Mike Fink have a keelboat race. This ride isn't as memorable. It goes down the same **Rivers of America** as the low-key **Liberty Belle Riverboat.**

210 Columbia Harbour House ★$$ This nautical-themed fast-food favorite serves fish, clam chowder, and sandwiches. ◆ Seafood ◆ Daily lunch, dinner, and snacks

211 The Haunted Mansion Disney special effects are showcased here. The walkway up to the mansion is lined with tombstones that set the tone: funny, not scary. The ride takes you through the house, which is inhabited by all sorts of ghosts and goblins. The suit of armor that moves is predictable, but try to figure out how the floor you're standing on in the portrait gallery sinks.

Fantasyland

It's a Small World is the attraction kids want to ride over and over. Still, **Peter Pan's Flight** and **Mr. Toad's Wild Ride** are probably the best. **Fantasyland** shops include **Fantasy Faire** (another place to get monogrammed Mickey Mouse ears), the **Kodak Kiosk** (photography supplies), **Tinker Bell's Treasures** (toys and Disney-themed clothes for kids), **Sir Mickey's** (miscellaneous souvenirs), and the **Seven Dwarfs Mine** (candy and sundries).

There are lots of fast-food and snack spots in **Fantasyland,** including **Enchanted Grove** (lemonade, soft ice cream, and slushes), **Hook's Tavern** (lemonade and hot cocoa), **Lumière's Kitchen** (primarily a kid's menu), **Scuttle's Landing** (sodas and shaved ice), and **Mrs. Pott's Cupboard** (ice cream).

212 Skyway Taking a gondola ride in the sky is a pleasant way to get from **Fantasyland** to **Tomorrowland,** but not if there's a long line. If you want to ride the **Skyway** just for fun, board it in **Tomorrowland,** where lines are shorter.

213 It's a Small World The first time through you'll enjoy watching all the early Disney Audio-Animatronic dolls perform and sing the catchy tune. On your second trip, it's fun to watch the bright-eyed delight on small children's faces as the boat drifts past hundreds of dolls that all look the same except for their costumes. It's more than a little saccharine, but the ride's message— we're all alike no matter what our skin color is

or how we dress—is still an important one. Warning: If you go more than twice, the song will haunt you for at least the rest of the day, if not the entire week. Arnold Schwarzenegger was quoted by the *Orlando Sentinel* as saying that **It's a Small World** was his favorite Disney ride; it's one of ours, too.

214 Pinocchio Village Haus $$ Beef or turkey burgers, sandwiches, and pasta salads are served up at this fast-food stop decorated with clocks and murals telling the story of the puppet who wanted to be a boy. ◆ Fast food ◆ Daily lunch, dinner, and snacks

215 Peter Pan's Flight The nighttime journey over London in a flying pirate ship is sure to make you fall in love with this ride. It hits the highlights of the *Peter Pan* story, including an encounter with the Indians and Captain Hook's meeting the clock-ticking crocodile.

216 Legend of The Lion King Based on the top-grossing film of 1994, *The Lion King,* this stage show at the **Fantasyland Theater** uses a combination of special effects, puppetry, film footage, and animation to deliver a message about protecting the world's environment. Some of the puppets are so elaborate they require four people to work them. During the show, Simba grows from a 2.5-foot cuddly cub to a 7-foot full-grown lion. Naturally, there's plenty of the film's music, written by Elton John and Tim Rice. Rafiki, the wise baboon (whose voice is provided by actor Robert Guillaume), is the show's narrator. ◆ Check the entertainment schedule for show times

217 Cinderella's Golden Carousel Built in 1917, this authentic carousel has been refurbished. Young kids and preteens love it.

218 Dumbo, the Flying Elephant Six more elephants and bright colors have been added to this kids' favorite. Climb aboard Dumbo and spin around and around and around, controlling how high or low he flies.

219 Snow White's Adventures This ride through the dark forest to meet the Seven Dwarfs has been toned down in recent years. It's not as scary as it was in the past, but the Wicked Witch may give little ones a fright.

220 Cinderella Castle Most visitors to the **Magic Kingdom** use the castle as a landmark to navigate by but don't realize that it also houses one of the park's restaurants. The mostly fiberglass structure was patterned after King Ludwig's castle at Neuschwanstein in Germany. Across from the entrance on the island hub is the **Castle Forecourt Stage,** where there's often live entertainment featuring singing and dancing.

Within Cinderella Castle:

Cinderella's Royal Table ★$$$$ The furnishings and costumes of the persons staffing the great hall are true to the 13th century. Roast beef sandwiches and seafood salads are served at lunch; prime rib, chicken, and seafood at dinner. Cinderella always puts in an appearance and Suzy and Pearla mouse join her for a character breakfast daily. ♦ American ♦ Daily breakfast, lunch, and dinner. Reservations for priority seating required

221 Ariel's Grotto This photo-autograph stop is set near the former **20,000 Leagues Under the Sea** attraction, and it's where you'll find Ariel, the star of the hit animated film *The Little Mermaid*. She signs autographs and holds court with an audience of mostly girls.

222 Mr. Toad's Wild Ride The mild intensity here comes from sudden turns and near disasters, such as a close call with an oncoming train and the slamming through a barn door. Kids love it. There are two lines, one going to the left, one to the right. If possible, take the right one: It's a little different and slightly more fun.

223 Mad Tea Party Climb into the Mad Hatter's teacups for a ride. You control how fast the cup spins by turning a wheel in the center. Not recommended soon after eating.

Mickey's Toontown Fair

Mickey and all his Toon pals greet their fans in this village, with kid-friendly attractions in a country fair setting. One of the biggest attractions is the chance for a one-on-one photo with Mickey Mouse.

224 Wiseacres Farm Classic red barns and farm buildings are the setting for **The Barnstormer,** a tame, kid-size roller coaster. Kids of all ages board the coaster for a quick spin that ends as it "crashes" through a barn.

225 Minnie's Country House Disney created a charming pastel bungalow for Mickey's sweetheart. Kids can turn on the oven to bake an inflatable cake, open the refrigerator for a blast of cool air, and listen to her answering machine. Fun for the under-seven set.

226 Toontown Hall of Fame Don't waste time looking for Disney characters elsewhere in the **Magic Kingdom**—this is the place you'll find them all day, every day. Great for photos.

Ever wonder how many stones are in the 185-foot-tall Cinderella Castle in the Magic Kingdom at Walt Disney World? Not one. The entire facade is made of fiberglass.

Anyone who enters the Magic Kingdom at Walt Disney World can walk right into Harmony Barber Shop on Main Street, U.S.A., to get a haircut—at very reasonable prices. The shop's 2 barbers clip about 20 manes a day. No appointments are necessary.

---

227 Mickey's House You can peek into Mickey's bedroom, living room, kitchen, and home office on your way to a one-on-one meeting with Mr. Mouse. As you exit the back door through the garden, you'll enter a tent where Mickey extends a personal greeting to each family (remember, he can't talk, but will answer your questions with a nod). There's generally a line, but it's worth the wait for a personal moment with the Big Cheese.

228 Toon Park Let the kiddies loose here while you sit and relax. The ground is spongy and there are foam topiaries in the shapes of goats, cows, pigs, and horses. Kids can jump onto interactive lily pads to hear the animal topiaries moo, bleat, and whinny.

229 Donald Duck's Boat, Miss Daisy A cross between a tugboat and a leaky ocean liner, Donald's yacht is really a giant playhouse for pint-size seafarers. Kids can blow the whistle, clang the bell, or squirt water on anyone who's in the line of fire. Down below, lily pads spout jumping streams and spray without warning. Most kids don't want to leave.

230 Walt Disney World Railroad Toontown Station is one of three stops on the line.

Tomorrowland

Except for the **Space Mountain** ride, **Tomorrowland** was already somewhat outdated when it opened. Man had already walked on the moon, but you never would have known it here. By trying to present a realistic vision of the future, **Tomorrowland** was destined always to be on the brink of becoming behind the times. With this in mind, **Walt Disney World** took a different approach for the $100 million makeover that was completed in 1995. The present **Tomorrowland** is an imaginary city of the future, a space-age metropolis as it might have been envisioned 60 years ago. Drawing from science fiction and comic books of the 1920s and 1930s, Disney created a whimsical cityscape that would make Buck Rogers feel right at home. The **Tomorrowland** renovation also included the addition of the **ExtraTERRORestrial Alien Encounter,** far scarier than any other Disney attraction.

231 Cosmic Ray's Starlight Café $$
The largest fast-food outlet in the **Magic Kingdom,** it serves big salads, soup, and sandwiches. ♦ American ♦ Daily lunch and dinner

232 Grand Prix Raceway Little gas-powered go-karts putt-putt along on tracks, amusing the little ones on board. This isn't a very exciting ride for older kids or adults, since the cars don't go faster than seven mph. There are age and size boarding restrictions.

233 Space Mountain This roller-coaster ride in the dark is the one that everybody will ask you about when you return home. Lines are long, and as you wait for a place in an eight-seat rocket, you hear screams as the coaster screeches along the rails. The apprehension isn't lessened by the well-posted warning signs and restrictions. Try to keep your eyes open during the two-and-a-half-minute ride so you can fully enjoy the shooting stars—and don't tell your friends back home that this roller coaster never even reaches 30 mph. If you chicken out once you're in line, a moving walkway will lead you out past the *RCA 1 Dream of a New World,* an exhibit exploring electronic media of the future. There are health, age, and size boarding restrictions.

234 Skyway A gondola sweeps you into the air and transports you to **Fantasyland.**

235 Carousel of Progress The popular musical comedy show in a revolving theater traces the impact of technological progress on the daily life of an Audio-Animatronic family through the 20th century. The pre-show tells about the original Carousel show, which debuted at the **1964 World's Fair.** The final scene offers a glimpse at such innovations as virtual reality, voice activation, and high-definition television.

236 Galaxy Palace Theater *Galaxy Search,* a live stage show starring Mickey Mouse and friends and featuring an array of singing and dancing space aliens, is presented several times a day. ♦ Check the entertainment schedule for show times

237 Tommorowland Transit Authority Small trains take you on an aboveground, 10-minute tour of **Tomorrowland,** including an inside look at **Space Mountain.** The motors of the magnetic-powered trains have no moving parts, nor do they emit pollution.

238 Astro Orbiter Board your personal Buck Rogers–styled rocket for a trip through space, passing orbiting planets on the way. Formerly **Star Jets,** this revamped ride offers a good aerial view of **Tomorrowland.**

239 ExtraTERRORestrial Alien Encounter This attraction, a "sensory thriller" from Disney and George Lucas, is a remarkable departure from the typical family-oriented ride. You enter a "convention hall" of the future, where a mysterious corporation from a distant planet is demonstrating its line of high-tech products. Things go awry and an alien is set loose on the unsuspecting audience; the ensuing mayhem involves numerous and elaborate special effects. Young children may find this too intense.

240 Buzz Lightyear's Space Ranger Spin In this attraction, inspired by characters from the Disney film *Toy Story,* guests join Buzz on an intergalactic mission to defeat the evil emperor Zurg. You can fire infrared lasers throughout the attraction, causing targets to spring to animated life.

241 The Timekeeper Stand in this Circlevision 360° theater and wait for the sounds and sights to surround you. In-theater effects create the illusion that you are traveling backward and forward in time to meet famous inventors and visionaries of the machine age.

242 Plaza Pavilion $$ Located at the edge of **Tomorrowland** near the **Plaza,** this self-serve eatery offers Italian specialty sandwiches, pizza, and pasta salads.
♦ Italian ♦ Daily lunch, dinner, and snacks

Magic Kingdom Resort Area

The three hotels in the **Magic Kingdom Resort Area** are the most convenient to the **Magic Kingdom** because they're right on the monorail, which circumnavigates the park and also goes to the **Transportation and Ticket Center (TTC),** where you can catch another monorail to **Epcot.**

This area also boasts the new **Walt Disney World Speedway** and three Disney golf courses: the **Palm,** the **Magnolia,** and the nine-hole **Oak Trail** course. (Those staying at a Disney hotel may reserve a tee time up to 60 days in advance; others may reserve 30 days in advance by calling 824.2270.) The **Disney Fairy Tale Wedding Pavilion** is also located here, on an island in the **Seven Seas Lagoon.**

243 Walt Disney World Speedway Continuing to diversify, Disney constructed, in 1995, one of the most unusual attractions at the resort: a one-mile, tri-oval, motor sports race track. Events have included the annual Indy 200, featuring Indy 500 cars and drivers, and the Chevy Trucks Challenge, a **NASCAR** Craftsman Truck Series event. Drive a genuine race car around the track at speeds up to 145 mph at the **Richard Petty Driving Experience.** For the timid fan, there is a ride-along program in which a professional driver whisks you around the track. ♦ Track is open daily 9AM-5PM; lessons are given daily at 8AM; driving begins daily at 1PM. Reservations required for Driving Experience. 3450 World Dr (at Floridian Way). 939.0526

244 Disney's Polynesian Resort $$$ The first hotel to be built at **Walt Disney World,** the **Polynesian** looks a bit dated but has a loyal following. Not everyone finds the lushly landscaped lobby hokey; called the "Great Ceremonial House," it has three-story-high palms and a waterfall cascading over lava rock. Eleven two- and three-story "longhouses" feature 853 comfortable and well-equipped rooms and suites, most with a balcony or patio, two queen-size beds, and a daybed. There's a three-level concierge lounge with special check-in, 7AM to 10PM buffet, a library, and other services. The hotel also has an efficient staff, two heated swimming pools, a child-care program (ages 3-12), and a sandy beach with a marina that rents boats. It's on the monorail. ◆ 1600 Seven Seas Dr (between World Dr and Floridian Way). 824.2000, 800/647.7900; fax 824.3174; www.disneyworld.com ♿

At Disney's Polynesian Resort:

'Ohana ★★$$$ It's a South Pacific all-you-can-eat feast. Shrimp, beef, chicken, and pork are cooked in a 16-foot-long open fire pit, then served at the tables in giant portions on long skewers, accompanied by salads, vegetables, and homemade bread. Servers dressed in Hawaiian garb entertain diners with South Pacific folklore. It's fun for the family, but the dining room gets rather noisy. ◆ International ◆ Daily breakfast and dinner. Reservations for priority seating recommended. WDW.DINE (939.3463)

245 Palm Golf Course Designed by Joe Lee, this 18-hole championship layout (par 72, 6,461 yards) features fairways that are densely lined with trees. ◆ Greens fee. Daily. Reservations required. Magnolia/Palm Dr (west of Floridian Way). 824.2270

246 Oak Trail Golf Club This nine-hole, par-three 3,000-yard executive course is perfect for beginners or those looking for a quick round. ◆ Greens fee. Daily. Reservations required. Magnolia/Palm Dr (west of Floridian Way). 824.2270

247 Magnolia Golf Course Another championship course, this 18-holer (par 72, 6,642 yards) with elevated tees and greens and rolling fairways is also the creation of Joe Lee. And true to its name, there are more than 1,500 magnolia trees on the course. The par three, number six hole has a bunker shaped in the outline of Mickey's head. ◆ Greens fee. Daily. Reservations required. Magnolia/Palm Dr (west of Floridian Way). 824.2270

248 Disney Fairy Tale Wedding Pavilion Reminiscent of a Victorian summer home, this glass-enclosed structure on a private

island in **Seven Seas Lagoon** accommodates wedding parties from 2 to 250. Ceremonies take place in an elegant solarium with a view of **Cinderella Castle;** there are also dressing rooms for the bridal party, planning offices, and a shop offering wedding-related merchandise. Fantasy wedding receptions—including a Cinderella Ball complete with a glass carriage, fairy godmother, and wicked stepsisters—can be held at Disney resort hotels. ◆ 828.3400

248 Disney's Grand Floridian Resort & Spa $$$$ Conceived as Disney's top-of-the-line hotel when it was built in 1988, this luxurious establishment doesn't disappoint. Patterned after the landmark turn-of-the-century Hotel Del Coronado in California, it has sweeping verandas and an enormous atrium with crystal chandeliers. Many of the 905 rooms have balconies, and the "dormer rooms" make guests feel as if they're staying in a cozy attic in a rich aunt's mansion. Providing plenty of fun is the on-site marina with rental boats, and the white, sandy beach along **Seven Seas Lagoon.** The 8,000-square-foot swimming pool is a beauty. The spa is staffed with knowledgeable personnel. There's plenty for kids to do (including an activities program for children ages 4 to 12), and lawn croquet adds a special touch. Suites and concierge rooms with restricted access, special amenities, and free continental breakfasts are available. The Disney monorail stops on the hotel's second level. ◆ 4401 Floridian Way (north of Seven Seas Dr). 824.3000; fax 824.3186; www.disneyworld.com ♿

Within Disney's Grand Floridian Resort & Spa:

Victoria & Albert's ★★★$$$$ Standards at this small, sumptuous restaurant probably are among the most exacting at **Walt Disney World.** You're seated in an elegant, dome-topped room and waited upon by two servers, Victoria and Albert. This seems a bit silly, since neither Queen Victoria nor her prince consort ever served anyone a meal, but that doesn't mean you won't enjoy your prix-fixe dinner. The menu changes daily to take advantage of the freshest ingredients. Entrées might include mushroom-crusted veal steak over black truffle risotto, or blood-orange–marinated wild boar with herb polenta. For dessert, try one of the signature soufflés. For a truly special treat, reserve the Chef's Table right in the kitchen. ◆ Continental ◆ Daily dinner. Reservations for priority seating required; jacket and tie required. 824.2383

Citrico's ★★★$$$ Light, flavorful French cuisine is served here, emphasizing a variety of local produce and seafood. The restaurant borrows the sun-drenched colors of the Mediterranean, South America, and the Caribbean to create a dramatic space, at once sophisticated and casual. Meals are orchestrated in an open kitchen, where the cooks are clearly visible from the 190-seat dining room. The veal shank is a house specialty; also try the refreshing snapper carpaccio served with melon-pepper salsa. Desserts, all made on the premises, get an artful flourish in the "finishing kitchen" that's part of the dining room. ♦ French ♦ Daily dinner. Reservations for priority seating recommended. 824.2383

Narcoosee's ★★$$$ This octagon-shaped restaurant, with its big windows and exposed beams, has a marvelous view of **Seven Seas Lagoon.** Steamed, sautéed, smoked, or broiled seafood is served, as well as a variety of steaks. ♦ Seafood ♦ Daily lunch and dinner. Reservations for priority seating recommended. 824.2383

249 Disney's Contemporary Resort $$$
You can't beat the convenience or the pure pizzazz of having the Disney monorail zipping through the center of your hotel. This ultramodern triangular structure has a primarily purple interior decorated with contemporary furnishings and artwork. It's perennially popular with 15 stories and 1,041 rooms, some of which have a view of the **Magic Kingdom**'s nightly fireworks. Facilities include a marina with rental boats, three heated swimming pools, a child-care program (for ages 4 to 12), a health club, a hair salon, and laundry facilities. ♦ 4600 World Dr (north of Timberline Dr). 824.1000; fax 824.3539; www.disneyworld.com ♿

Within Disney's Contemporary Resort:

Chef Mickey's ★★$$ This place is the best choice for breakfast or dinner with Mickey and Minnie Mouse (and a few other Disney characters), but even with priority seating, the wait can be long. Mickey and Goofy stop by the dining rooms after 4PM each day. Recently remodeled, this restaurant in the **Contemporary Concourse** gives guests an audience with Mickey (he stops by every table), and kids love to watch the monorail as it whizzes by on its elevated track. ♦ International ♦ Daily breakfast and dinner. Reservations for priority seating required

California Grill ★★★$$$ Situated high atop the resort, this trendy restaurant with a stylish and spacious dining room is the culinary star at **Walt Disney World,** offering "market-inspired" cooking, California wines, and a spectacular view of the **Magic Kingdom.** The on-stage kitchen is the centerpiece of this lively place, allowing guests to watch the chefs preparing such specialties as grilled tuna, brick-oven–baked pizzas, and sushi, as well as unique vegetarian fare. The service can be slow when it gets busy, but this is the one Disney dining

experience you won't want to miss. ♦ International ♦ Daily 5:30PM-10PM. Reservations for priority seating required

Disney's Fort Wilderness Resort Area

Adjacent to the **Magic Kingdom,** this section of **Walt Disney World** has the feel of a national park. It's home to **Disney's Wilderness Lodge; Disney's Fort Wilderness Resort and Campground; Pioneer Hall,** venue for the popular **Hoop-Dee-Doo Musical Revue;** the **River Country** water park; and **Discovery Island,** a nature preserve.

250 Disney's Wilderness Lodge $$$ Located between **Disney's Contemporary Resort** and the **Fort Wilderness Campground,** this property, opened in mid-1994, is reminiscent of the grand National Park Service lodges of the early 1900s. Designed by **Urban Design Group of Denver,** headed by architect **Peter Dominick Jr.,** the structure evokes the great Northwest at the turn of the century while at the same time possessing a new, modern flair. The lodge's main lobby is eight sun-drenched stories high and contains two huge authentic Northwest Coast totem poles, a stone fireplace, and a hot spring that feeds into the hotel's swimming pool. Actual Indian artifacts and maps from Western survey teams are on display, and artwork showcases the culture and beauty of the Northwest. The lodge is tucked away on the shores of Bay Lake and surrounded by towering pine, cypress, and oak trees, and you can sometimes see free-roaming deer (wild, non–Audio-Animatronic) on or near the property. There are 728 guest rooms, most with two queen-size beds and a writing table and chairs. **Cub's Den** is the kid's recreation and dining club. Swimming, biking, boating, fishing, and in-line skating (bring your own Rollerblades) are among the sports you can enjoy on-site. The tennis and golfing facilities at **Disney's Contemporary Resort** are also available to guests here. Boats take you to the **Magic Kingdom,** or you can hop aboard a bus to **Fort Wilderness.** ♦ 901 Timberline Dr (just north of W Wilderness Rd). 824.3200; www.disneyworld.com

---

More than 360 kinds of trees are found in Florida.

Four poisonous snakes are indigenous to Florida: the copperhead, the coral snake, the cottonmouth, and the rattlesnake.

Disney washes about 246,000 pounds of linens in a single day—to accomplish that at home would take 342 days of continuous washing in an extra-large–capacity washing machine.

Within Disney's Wilderness Lodge:

Artist Point ★★$$$ In keeping with the hotel's theme, this upscale restaurant serves Pacific Northwest specialties and boasts an award-winning regional wine list. ♦ American ♦ Daily breakfast and dinner. Reservations for priority seating required for dinner

Territory Lounge This bar pays homage to trappers, explorers, and survey parties who led the westward movement. The all-wood lounge sports a map of the Lewis and Clark expedition on the ceiling; a display case filled with guns, riding boots, and compasses of the period; and six-foot-tall carved bears standing on the bar. Look closely at the ceiling: You may find a rendering of "Mickey" among the pioneers. ♦ Daily 11AM-1AM

Whispering Canyon Cafe ★$$ Meals are served family style and it's all-you-can-eat, with oven-roasted and wood-smoked meats, vegetables, and homemade desserts. ♦ American ♦ Daily breakfast, lunch, and dinner

251 **Disney's Fort Wilderness Resort and Campground** Located in one of the most heavily wooded and prettiest parts of **Walt Disney World**'s 43 square miles, the 785 campsites at this 700-acre resort are among the more economical lodging options on **Walt Disney World** property. Campsites have full hookups for recreational vehicles, and there are rest rooms, showers, ice machines, laundry facilities, grills, picnic tables, and telephones. No more than 10 people per campsite are allowed. This is a popular place, so book early. "Wilderness Homes" (mobile homes) are also available here; far more costly than the campsites, they come equipped with a double bed in the bedroom, a bunk bed, a pull-down double bed in the living room, a fully equipped kitchen and bath, TV, telephone, picnic table, and grill. An extra bonus: A housekeeper stops in daily.

Fort Wilderness offers guests plenty of activities and sports facilities. There are two heated swimming pools, two lighted tennis courts, biking and jogging paths, a petting farm, pony rides, bicycle rental, nightly movies, and a marina with boats for rent. You can also rent horses and ride the trails (age nine and up), or play volleyball, tetherball, or basketball. Fishing for largemouth bass on **Bay Lake** or in the canals can be excellent; it's strictly catch and release, though. Best of all, there's no admission fee for people staying elsewhere to enter, walk around, or enjoy the beach. If you drive, you will have to pay to park in the Day Guest Parking Lot and take a bus to the resort. An evening campfire program features Chip and Dale greeting the kids at 8PM, followed by a Disney cartoon and such

feature films as *The Little Mermaid* and *Angels in the Outfield.* Call or pick up a copy of the *Gazette,* the resort's own newspaper, to find out what's playing, and bring marshmallows to roast over the fire. The program is open to guests of any Disney resort. ♦ 4510 Fort Wilderness Tr (north of Vista Blvd). 824.2900

At Disney's Fort Wilderness Resort and Campground:

Trail's End Buffet ★★$$ The all-you-can-eat breakfast buffet features the usual choices. You can also chew until you're blue at lunch and dinner. Midday choices include barbecued chicken and ribs, fish, and a taco bar. Evenings, it's a soup-and-salad bar, a dessert bar, and such country-style dinners as chicken and dumplings. The Hoe Down Supper on Saturday from 4:30 to 9:30PM features all the lasagna, spaghetti, and fried chicken you can eat. The informal atmosphere fits the Davy Crockett–themed pioneer decor. ♦ American ♦ Daily breakfast, lunch, and dinner

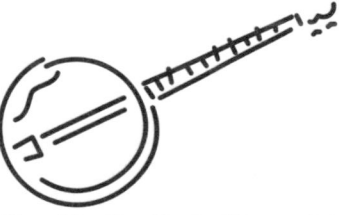

Hoop-Dee-Doo Musical Revue ★★$$$ Held nightly in **Pioneer Hall,** this is probably the best of all the Disney dinner shows, with lots of audience participation. As a result, everyone wants to come, and reservations can be difficult to get. Every evening here is like the Fourth of July, with a barbecue dinner of ribs, fried chicken, corn on the cob, and more, plus lots of beer or sangria. The actors are incredibly energetic and keep the crowd laughing and entertained for a solid two hours. It's sometimes corny but always fun for both kids and adults. ♦ Daily. Seatings at 5PM, 7:15PM, and 9:30PM. ♦ Reservations required. WDW.DINE (939.3463)

River Country Conceived as an updated version of Tom Sawyer's swimming hole, it doesn't have the plethora of thrill rides found at its sister parks **Typhoon Lagoon** and **Blizzard Beach,** but the slides here are plenty of fun. There's also a swimming pool with a rock grotto and slide, and a sandy beach with scores of lounge chairs to soak up some sun. **Pop's Place** serves up big burgers, hot dogs, salads, beer, and soft drinks; or bring your own picnic. ♦ Admission (reduced after 3PM); there are also fees for parking, towels, and lockers. Ticket sales stop when the crowd reaches capacity levels. ♦ Daily. ♦ 824.4321

252 Discovery Island Don't let your children miss this chance to see free-roaming animals and rare waterfowl. A short boat ride across Bay Lake from **Fort Wilderness, Disney's Contemporary Resort,** and several other locations ends at this 11.5-acre island nature preserve, an accredited zoological park. You can wander at your leisure and see more than a hundred types of birds, walk through a large aviary featuring a breeding colony for scarlet ibis, and see daily parrot shows. The animals include Galápagos tortoises, alligators, and some small primates. Pack a lunch and stay here for the day as a refuge from the amusement park circuit. The **Thirsty Perch** snack bar sells sandwiches, hot dogs, beer, and soda. There's no swimming from the sand beach, but you can bask or build sand castles. ♦ Admission; parking fee. Daily 10AM-5PM. 824.2875

Bests

Sara Van Arsdel
Director, Orange County Regional History Center

Best window shopping—**Park Avenue** in **Winter Park.**

Best shopping (cheap stuff)—**Belz Factory Outlet World.**

Best antiques—**Renninger's Twin Markets** in **Mount Dora,** expecially during extravaganza weekends.

Best art festival—Mount Dora, in early February.

Best farmer's market—Winter Park on Saturday morning. Great coffee and salsa.

Best art museums—**Charles Hosmer Morse Museum of American Art** and **Cornell Fine Arts Museum** in Winter Park.

Favorite activity—going to yard sales on Saturday.

Joanie Schirm
President, GEC, Inc./Chairman, World Cup Orlando 1994

Evening lectures on astronomy and the **CineDome** at the **Orlando Science Center.**

Drink beer and munch while watching foreign movies at the **Enzian Theater.**

Stroll down **Park Avenue** in **Winter Park** (stay at **Park Plaza Gardens**).

Stay at **The Courtyard at Lake Lucerne** and walk to **City Hall.**

Ride the swan boats at **Lake Eola.**

Ben Van Hook
Photographer

Catch a band at the **Sapphire Supper Club** on **Orange Avenue.**

Lunch or dinner at **Dexter's of Thorton Park.** While you're downtown, check out **Chez Jose** for great, inexpensive Mexican food. For dessert, visit its neighbor, **Moos Brothers Ice Cream.**

Canoe trip on the **Wekiva River** (it's a state park).

Have Chinese food at **The Forbidden City** on Mills Avenue.

For high-end dining, go to **Enzo's on the Lake** (Italian) or **Le Coq au Vin** (country French), the two best restaurants in Central Florida.

Take your kids to the **Orlando Science Center,** just north of downtown.

Walk around **Lake Eola.**

Harris Rosen
President, Tamar Inns, Inc.

SeaWorld Orlando. Never any lines, always a fresh show. The children love the arcade and the children's play area.

Jack's Place, a restaurant at the **Clarion Plaza Hotel.** I just love the food, service, and the caricatures!

Everglades restaurant at the **Omni Rosen Hotel.** Love everything about it. Great menu. Fantastic ambience.

Cocoa Beach. By far the best beach and surf anywhere!!!

Karen Plunkett
Vice President/Co-owner, Stephen Plunkett Studios

Orlando Science Center. Great place to take children/family.

Touring backstage at the **Bob Carr Performing Arts Centre,** home of the **Southern Ballet.** Great historic building as their home.

Take the free **LYNX** shuttle throughout downtown Orlando.

Sip a cappuccino or café mocha at **La Venezia Cafe** on Park Avenue in **Winter Park.**

Timothy's Gallery in Winter Park. Great place to get gift ideas.

Reading *Orlando* magazine's reviews of local homes of celebrities.

Fred Griffin
Director, Grand Cypress Academy of Golf

Taking a canoe trip down the **Wekiva River.**

Jazz in the park on Sunday afternoon in **Winter Park.**

Having dinner at **Hemingway's** at the **Hyatt Regency–Grand Cypress Hotel.**

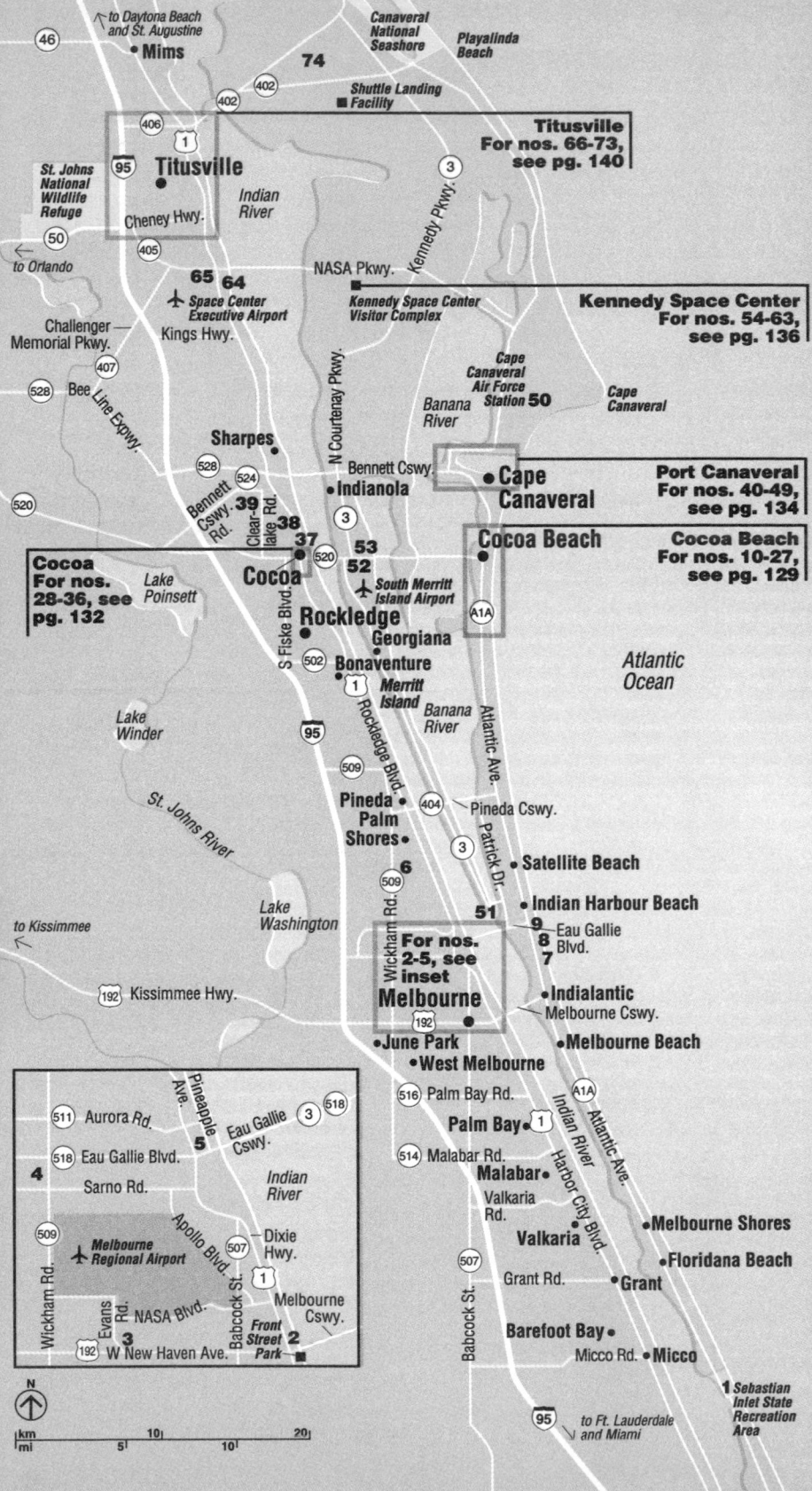

46

↗ to Daytona Beach
and St. Augustine

Mims

402
402
74

Canaveral
National
Seashore

Playalinda
Beach

Shuttle Landing
Facility

406
1

95
Titusville

Titusville
For nos. 66-73,
see pg. 140

St. Johns
National
Wildlife
Refuge

50

← to Orlando

Cheney Hwy.

Indian
River

405

3

Kennedy Pkwy.

65 64

Space Center
Executive Airport

NASA Pkwy.

Kennedy Space Center
Visitor Complex

Kennedy Space Center
For nos. 54-63,
see pg. 136

Challenger
Memorial Pkwy.

407

Kings Hwy.

528

Bee Line Expwy.

520

Cape
Canaveral
Air Force
Station 50

Banana
River

Cape
Canaveral

Sharpes

528

524

Bennett Cswy. Rd.

Clearlake Rd.

39

38

37

Bennett Cswy.

Indianola

3

53

52

520

Cape
Canaveral

Port Canaveral
For nos. 40-49,
see pg. 134

Cocoa Beach

Cocoa Beach
For nos. 10-27,
see pg. 129

Cocoa
For nos.
28-36, see
pg. 132

Lake
Poinsett

Cocoa

South Merritt
Island Airport

Rockledge

Georgiana

A1A

Atlantic
Ocean

Lake
Winder

502

Bonaventure

1

Merritt
Island

Banana
River

95

Rockledge Blvd.

509

Pineda
Palm
Shores

404

Pineda Cswy.

Satellite Beach

Patrick Dr.

St. Johns River

Lake
Washington

3

6

509

51

Indian Harbour Beach

9 — Eau Gallie
8   Blvd.
7

Atlantic Ave.

to Kissimmee

Wickham Rd.

For nos.
2-5, see
inset

Melbourne

192

Indialantic
Melbourne Cswy.

192

Kissimmee Hwy.

June Park

West Melbourne

Melbourne Beach

516

Palm Bay Rd.

A1A

514

Malabar Rd.

Palm Bay

1

Indian River

Valkaria
Rd.

Malabar

Harbor City Blvd.

Melbourne Shores

Valkaria

Floridana Beach

507

Grant Rd.

Grant

Babcock St.

Barefoot Bay

Micco Rd.

Micco

1 Sebastian
Inlet State
Recreation
Area

95

to Ft. Lauderdale
and Miami

N

km
mi

10

20

5

10

Melbourne inset

511 Aurora Rd.

Pineapple Ave.

3

518

5

Eau Gallie
Cswy.

518 Eau Gallie Blvd.

4

Sarno Rd.

Indian
River

509

Melbourne
Regional Airport

Apollo Blvd.

Dixie
Hwy.

507

Wickham Rd.

Evans Rd.

Babcock St.

1

3

192

NASA Blvd.

W New Haven Ave.

Front
Street
Park

2

Melbourne
Cswy.

The Space Coast/ Kennedy Space Center

In 1807 young Douglas Dummitt noticed a delightful fragrance as he sailed up the coast of Florida from Barbados to his family's new sugarcane plantation near St. Augustine. Learning that it was the scent of orange blossoms, he vowed one day to have his own orange grove. As it turned out, the perfume of orange blossoms became the sweet smell of success for Dummitt, who in 1825 settled on **Merritt Island** in eastern **Brevard County** and began planting citrus trees. Three years later, his first harvest was shipped up the **Indian River.** Dummitt is now credited with establishing Indian River citrus fruits, a brand that has become world famous. His efforts led to the development of the citrus industry for which the entire state of Florida has become renowned.

Brevard County is still home to Indian River citrus, but space exploration is what puts it on the map these days. The tourist office even markets it as "The Space Coast." **Titusville, Cocoa, Cocoa Beach, Melbourne,** and **Indialantic** are home to the thousands of employees of the **Kennedy Space Center,** and its **Visitor Center** (formerly **Spaceport USA**), an elaborate indoor and outdoor space museum within the center, is one of Florida's most popular tourist destinations. An added attraction right next door to **Kennedy Space Center** is **Cocoa Beach,** which has long lovely stretches of sand. This combination of sun, sea, and educational entertainment—all less than an hour's drive from **Walt Disney World**—makes the Space Coast a popular family vacation spot.

Area code 407 unless otherwise noted.

1 Sebastian Inlet State Recreation Area
One of Florida's most popular state parks and a favorite with surfers, this 576-acre recreational area stretches between the Atlantic Ocean and the Indian River. There are separate beaches for surfers and for swimmers, a fishing pier, a lagoon for snorkelers, a boat ramp, campgrounds, and a concession stand. The **McLarty State Museum and Visitor Center,** two miles south of the Sebastian Inlet Bridge on Route A1A, features treasures from a 1715 shipwreck and other historic exhibits. Nighttime walks to see nesting loggerhead turtles take place in June and July (see "Blinded by the Light" on page 141). ♦ 9700 S Hwy A1A (south of Long Point Rd). 984.4852

Melbourne

In the 1880s, Melbourne's main thoroughfare was Front Street, a bustling place with dry-goods and grocery stores and a fish house with a brothel upstairs. In 1919, fire engulfed Front Street; all the shops burned to the ground and the area was reduced to rubble. Today Melbourne's main street is **New Haven Avenue,** and a lovely park is on the site where the buildings of Front Street once stood. Visitors enjoy strolling through the town's small arts center, shopping in the mall, and risking a few dollars at the race track. The town also boasts two charming eateries.

2 The Strawberry Mansion ★★$$ Wide brick walkways beneath towering oaks lead to this restaurant in a charmingly restored house. Owners Bob and Susan Brown offer diners an array of delicious choices, including fresh fish, pasta, steak, quiche, soups, and specials such as conch chowder and crab thermidor. The fresh seafood sampler is broiled to perfection. ♦ American ♦ Daily lunch and dinner. 1218 E New Haven Ave (east of Dixie Hwy). 724.8627

Within The Strawberry Mansion:

Mister BeauJean at The Strawberry Mansion ★★$ This casual cafe and grill is a popular place for breakfast and lunch. Breakfast specialties include Belgian waffles, eggs Benedict, and vegetarian omelettes. Homestyle dishes such as prime rib, fish platters, burgers, and sandwiches are served at lunch and dinner. ♦ American ♦ Daily breakfast, lunch, and dinner. Reservations recommended. 724.8627

3 Melbourne Square Mall Mall aficionados should find what they're looking for here. There are 132 specialty shops, plus such larger stores as **Belk Lindsey, Burdine's, Dillard's,** and **JCPenney.** ♦ Daily. 1700 W New Haven Ave (between Piney Branch Way and Evans Rd). 727.2000

4 Melbourne Greyhound Park There's racing here from the start of November to the start of April; horses run in the daytime, dogs at night. The rest of the year there's televised simulcast racing and jai alai. Minors aren't allowed to place wagers, but the track tries to foster a family atmosphere and parents are encouraged to bring the kids. During the live races, there's dining in the air-conditioned clubhouse, which has TV monitors on the tables for a close-up look at the action. ♦ Admission. Call for post times and days. 1100 N Wickham Rd (between Sarno Rd and Eau Gallie Blvd). 259.9800

5 Brevard Museum of Art and Science Six galleries, a museum shop, and an auditorium can be found in this large, modern complex that's both a museum and an educational facility where arts and crafts classes and workshops are held. The galleries feature works by national, regional, and local artists; exhibits change every few months. ♦ Admission. Daily. 1463 Highland Ave (between Eau Gallie Blvd and St. Clair St). 242.0737 ♿

6 Maxwell C. King Center for the Performing Arts Small-scale touring versions of Broadway shows as well as dance performances, chamber music concerts, and community theater productions are staged here. The 2,000-seat theater is located on the **Brevard Community College** campus. ♦ 3865 N Wickham Rd (between Parkway Dr and Post Rd). 242.2219

Indialantic

In 1918 Ernest Kouwen-Hoven, one of the many land developers who flocked to Florida in the early part of this century, founded this beach resort community on the barrier island that parallels the Central Florida coast. The first bridge linking Indialantic to the mainland was constructed in 1921; the original narrow, wooden structure was replaced by a concrete-and-steel bridge 26 years later. The town remains a quiet community that few travelers ever see.

7 Oceanfront Quality Suites $ A heated outdoor pool with an underwater sound system is this hotel's highlight. All 208 two-room suites have ocean views, two TV sets, VCRs, cassette players, two telephones, and private balconies. A breakfast buffet is included in the rate, and **Atlantic Jack's Restaurant** serves lunch and dinner. ♦ 1665 N Hwy A1A (between Ocean Oaks and Shores Drs). 723.4222, 800/876.4222; fax 768.2438; www.qualityinn.com ♿

8 Holiday Inn Melbourne Oceanfront Resort $ A good choice, this 295-room chain hotel boasts ocean views and fine beach access—the sand is just steps away down a wooden staircase. An activities director plans adventures for children and groups, and there are four tennis courts, a Jacuzzi, a big sundeck, and outdoor pools. Vacationers who feel like splurging can book the 4,000-square-foot penthouse suite. The **Ocean Terrace Restaurant** is open for breakfast, lunch, and

dinner. ♦ 2605 N Hwy A1A (at Paradise Blvd). 777.4100, 800/465.4329; fax 773.6132; www.holiday-inn.com ♿

9 Melbourne Beach Hilton $$ All 118 rooms and 10 suites at this glitzy hotel have ocean views. Right on the beach, the property has a private boardwalk. The **Seaside Terrace** serves breakfast, lunch, and dinner; the outdoor pool bar is a great place to relax during the day; and night owls can whoop it up at **Encore**, a high-energy nightclub. ♦ 3003 N Hwy A1A (between Atlantic Ave and Eau Gallie Blvd). 777.5000, 800/445.8667; fax 777.3713 ♿

9 Radisson Suite Hotel Oceanfront $$ Right on the beach, this hostelry offers 168 suites, all with ocean views. It has 551 feet of secluded sand, along with an outdoor pool and two spas. There's also **The Bistro**, a reasonably priced restaurant; **La Bistro Lounge**; and a pool bar. ♦ 3101 N Hwy A1A (between Atlantic Ave and Eau Gallie Blvd). 773.9260, 800/777.7800; fax 777.3190; www.radisson.com ♿

Cocoa Beach

Cocoa Beach became a municipality in 1925, just a month after developer Gus Edwards sold it to a New York syndicate for $1.3 million. The city's population at that time isn't known, but it must have been small because 14 years later there were only nine houses on today's jam-packed **South Atlantic Avenue.**

It was the nation's space program that eventually brought Cocoa Beach to its current population of 13,000 people. When the program took off in the late 1950s, dozens of large missile contractors began moving to the **Cape Canaveral** and Cocoa Beach areas, and houses, apartments, and hotels couldn't be built fast enough. Newspaper accounts of the day say that people coming to look for jobs often had to sleep in their cars, and a few even slept in the huge water pipes waiting to be installed along **Route 520** as part of Cocoa Beach's first public water system.

These days Cocoa Beach is extremely popular with the young crowd because the surfing conditions are among the best on Florida's **Atlantic Coast.** An 800-footlong fishing pier is another major draw.

10 Coconuts on the Beach ★★$$ Food, beer, and the patrons' tanned and toned bodies are the draws at this après-beach singles spot. The restaurant and bar are air-conditioned, but it's more fun to sup and sip on the large patio overlooking the beach, where volleyball games and bikini contests are often held. There's live music most nights and a brunch on Sunday. The menu offers fancy sandwiches (crab salad, "French dip" roast beef) and pasta dishes. ♦ American ♦ M-Sa lunch and dinner; Su brunch and dinner; late-night snacks daily. 2 Minutemen Cswy (east of S Atlantic Ave). 784.1422

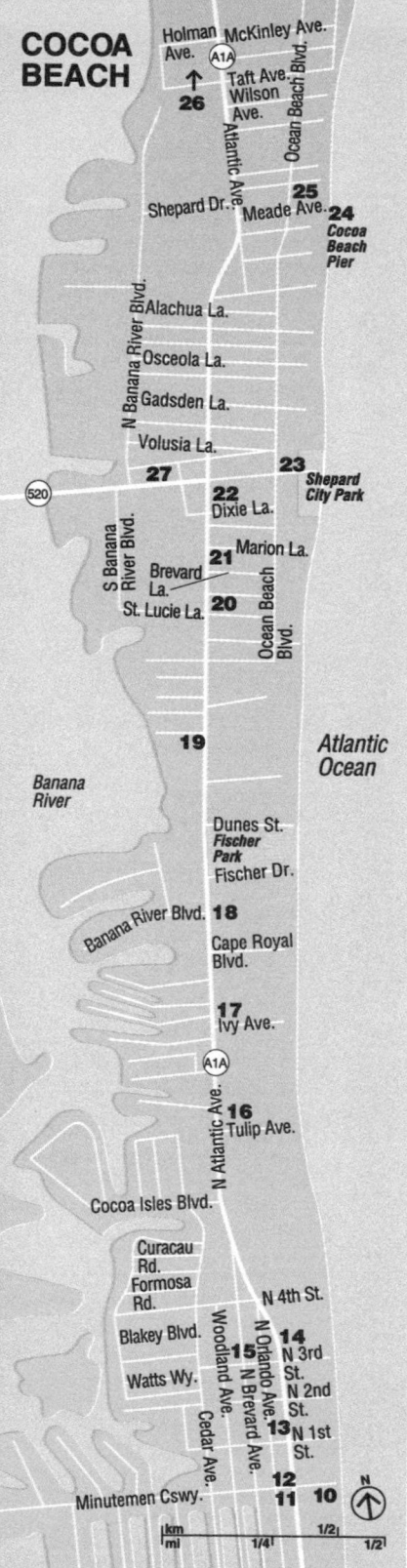

COCOA BEACH

Holman Ave.
McKinley Ave.
Taft Ave.
Wilson Ave.
Atlantic Ave.
Ocean Beach Blvd.
Shepard Dr.
Meade Ave.
Cocoa Beach Pier
N Banana River Blvd.
Alachua La.
Osceola La.
Gadsden La.
Volusia La.
Shepard City Park
S Banana River Blvd.
Dixie La.
Marion La.
Brevard La.
St. Lucie La.
Ocean Beach Blvd.
Atlantic Ocean
Banana River
Dunes St.
Fischer Park
Fischer Dr.
Banana River Blvd.
Cape Royal Blvd.
Ivy Ave.
N Atlantic Ave.
Tulip Ave.
Cocoa Isles Blvd.
Curacau Rd.
Formosa Rd.
Blakey Blvd.
Watts Wy.
Woodland Ave.
N Orlando Ave.
N Brevard Ave.
Cedar Ave.
N 4th St.
N 3rd St.
N 2nd St.
N 1st St.
Minutemen Cswy.

km
mi
1/4
1/2
1/2

11 Bernard's Surf ★★$$$ You might think they're joking when they hand you the menu—it's almost three feet across and just as long—but the food is no laughing matter. Few places in this area prepare seafood in as many ways or as imaginatively. The restaurant opened in 1948 with Bernard Fischer serving fish caught by his fleet of boats. His nephew Rusty Fischer now supplements the family's catch with such delicacies as lobsters from Maine and oysters from the Chesapeake Bay. **Rusty's Raw Bar** is a popular annex, decorated with sports photos and colorful pennants and serving less-expensive seafood dishes and hamburgers. The main entrance to **Rusty's Raw Bar** is on the west side of the restaurant. ♦ Seafood ♦ Daily lunch and dinner. Reservations recommended for dinner. 2 S Atlantic Ave (at Minutemen Cswy). 783.2401. Also at: 628 Glen Cheek Dr (between Flounder St and George King Blvd), Port Canaveral. 783.8732

12 Heidelberg $$ A variety of savory German wursts served with rye or Bavarian black bread make a tasty lunch, and the dinner menu is German through and through: Specialties include roast duckling with potato dumplings and melt-in-your-mouth sauerbraten (marinated beef served with a potato dumpling and tangy red cabbage). ♦ German ♦ M-Sa lunch and dinner. Reservations recommended. 7 N Orlando Ave (between Minutemen Cswy and First St). 783.6806

13 Mango Tree ★★ $$$ Betty Price and her son Bob own this charming restaurant, whose wooden-frame exterior behind a brightly painted picket fence seems a bit out of place among the more ordinary buildings lining North Atlantic Avenue. Inside, a waterfall splashes gently into a lily pond and palms crowd the ceiling. The setting is comfortable but elegant, with straight-backed wooden chairs at tables swathed in starched white linen. Among the wonderful creations on the menu are juicy roast Long Island duckling in orange sauce with macadamia nuts; flaky Florida grouper grilled with olive oil, garlic, and fresh herbs; and a fine pasta primavera. The vegetables are always fresh and perfectly prepared. ♦ American ♦ Daily dinner. Reservations recommended. 118 N Atlantic Ave (between First and Second Sts). 799.0513

The Mormon Church owns 316,000 acres of land, called the Desert Ranch, just west of Melbourne on Florida's east coast.

14 Desperados $ Drink your tequila or *cerveza* atop the outdoor deck or at the beachside cantina behind the main restaurant. Find some other place to dine, though; while the enchiladas are passable, some meat dishes are woefully shy of *carne,* and the quesadillas are more worthy of a fast-food restaurant than of a place that bills itself as having "fine Mexican food." ♦ Tex-Mex ♦ Restaurant daily lunch and dinner; cantina daily breakfast and lunch. 301 N Atlantic Ave (at Third St). 784.3363

15 Alma's Italian Restaurant ★$$ Instead of knocking down walls to make large dining rooms, the restaurateurs who purchased this old house left it pretty much intact. As a result the dining areas are small but cozy. Good pasta dishes are served, and there's an excellent wine cellar. A children's menu and early-bird specials are available. ♦ Italian ♦ Daily lunch and dinner. 306 N Orlando Ave (between Third and Fourth Sts). 783.1981

16 Holiday Inn Cocoa Beach Resort $$ Located right on the Atlantic Ocean and about a 20-minute drive from the **Kennedy Space Center,** this 523-room hotel has an Olympic-size pool, 625 feet of sandy beach, a wading pool for kids, a Jacuzzi, two lighted tennis courts, shuffleboard courts, and a gameroom. A plus for parents: There's an activities program for children run by a qualified recreation pro. There's also **Willard's** restaurant and **Plum's Lounge,** which has live entertainment every night. ♦ 1300 N Atlantic Ave (at Tulip Ave). 783.2271, 800/465.4329; fax 784.8878; www.holiday-inn.com

Florida has more than 8,000 miles of shoreline, giving it the longest tidal coast of any of the contiguous United States.

The three-story Coca-Cola sign that dominates Times Square in New York City was manufactured in Central Florida, as well as the security system that protects the Hope Diamond. The containers for Heinz ketchup, Gatorade, and Wilson tennis balls also are fabricated in Central Florida.

Restaurants/Clubs: Red   **Hotels:** Blue
Shops/♥ **Outdoors:** Green   **Sights/Culture:** Black

17 Cocoa Beach Hilton and Towers $$ Sleek and modern, this property has all you need in a resort hotel. There are 300 rooms, including 11 suites; amenities include hot and cold whirlpools, a heated outdoor pool, **Sea Shells** oceanfront restaurant, **Coco's Lounge,** and a pool bar. From the hotel's expansive pool deck, a wooden bridge crosses dunes to the sandy beach. The seventh floor has a concierge and other special services; another floor is for nonsmokers only. ♦ 1550 N Atlantic Ave (between Ivy Ave and Cape Royal Blvd). 799.0003, 800/526.2609; fax 799.0344; www.hilton.com ♦

18 DoubleTree Oceanfront Hotel $$ This upscale establishment has something for everyone, including a beachfront location, one big swimming pool, a nice pool deck, and a tiki bar (an outside patio bar) for those who want only to sit and sip a tropical drink. There are 148 rooms, all with views of the Atlantic Ocean. A concierge floor offers special services. Visit **3 Wishes Restaurant and Lounge,** a casual dining spot with an ocean view and live entertainment. ♦ 2080 N Atlantic Ave (between Cape Royal Blvd and Fischer Dr). 783.9222, 800/654.2000; fax 799.3234 ♦

At the DoubleTree Oceanfront Hotel:

3 Wishes Restaurant and Lounge $ A casual restaurant, it features tasty Mediterranean cuisine—nothing extraordinary, but the food is well prepared. We suggest the grilled portobello mushroom appetizer, served with cool slices of mozzarella cheese. You can't go wrong with a thin-crust pizza from the brick oven, served with your choice of toppings. There are daily fish and pasta specials, like linguine with shrimp, scallops, and sun-dried tomatoes, or grilled mahimahi with capers and roasted garlic. ♦ Mediterranean ♦ Daily breakfast, lunch, and dinner. 783.9222

18 Howard Johnson Express $ This 62-room hotel used to be the courtyard lodge in the **Howard Johnson Plaza Hotel Cocoa Beach** (now the **DoubleTree Oceanfront Hotel**). There are not many perks, but the no-frills rooms all have kitchenettes (there is no restaurant). The hotel offers beachfront access, a pool, and a children's pool. ♦ 2082 N Atlantic Ave (between Cape Royal Blvd and Fischer Dr). 783.8855, 800/654.2000; fax 784.1008

19 Luna Sea Bed and Breakfast $ It's not your classic bed-and-breakfast inn, but this two-story motel is a pleasant, reasonably priced lodging spot with a pretty pink exterior, meticulously maintained rooms, and a small pool ringed with palms. The beach is about a 10-minute walk away, across a busy highway. There's no restaurant. ♦ 3185 N Atlantic Ave (between Banana River Blvd and Seminole La). 783.0500

20 Motel 6 $ The econo-chain is okay if you're searching for a bargain near the beach. It has 150 basic rooms, an outdoor pool, and shuffleboard. ◆ 3701 N Atlantic Ave (at St. Lucie La). 783.3103; fax 868.0875 ♿

21 Comfort Inn $ There are a total of 144 units at this property, which is across a two-lane street from the beach. The ground-level rooms with kitchenettes face an interior courtyard with a pool, charcoal grills, a shuffleboard court, and a sand volleyball court. Mini-suites are located in a tower, where ocean views are partially blocked by a condo building, although you can still appreciate sea breezes from your balcony. The homey suites are equipped with two TVs, two queen-size beds, and a sofa bed. There's a bar, but no restaurant. ◆ 3901 N Atlantic Ave (between Brevard and Marion Las). 783.2221, 800/247.2221 in FL, 800/327.2224; fax 783.0461; www.comfortinn.com

22 Ron Jon Surf Shop A vast retail establishment, this department store–like surf shop is a testament to the great staying power of T-shirts and the enduring appeal of bikinis. Even if you don't plan to hit the sand, this landmark is a must-see. Bronzed youths wearing tiny headsets attached to walkie-talkies will direct you to your parking place. A glass elevator zips from a grotto near the back of the store up to the mezzanine level. The two-story, pseudo–Art Deco structure is painted purple, pink, and blue and features turrets, glass blocks, and miles of computer-controlled lights that can be programmed to any one of 16 lighting options. In addition to casual beachwear (including every type of flip-flop known to mankind), the store stocks fancy sporting goods, including in-line skates, surfboards, diving equipment, and cycling gear. You also can buy or rent any kind of water-related equipment here, from boogie boards to beach bikes. ◆ Daily 24 hours. 4151 N Atlantic Ave (between Dixie La and E Cocoa Beach Cswy). 799.8888

23 Inn at Cocoa Beach Bed and Breakfast $ Perhaps the nicest hostelry on the beach, this place has 50 rooms with ocean views. Ground-floor units feature patios; upper-floor units have balconies; and the honeymoon suite comes complete with a Jacuzzi. The inn is small enough to give guests plenty of personal attention, but it really feels more like a hotel than a cozy bed-and-breakfast. Continental breakfast (included in the rate) is served in a room decorated with French country furniture, Oriental rugs, and tile floors. There's also complimentary wine and cheese in the lobby at sunset. ◆ 4300 Ocean Beach Blvd (at E Cocoa Beach Cswy). 799.3460, 800/343.5307; fax 784.8632; www.theinnatcocoabeach.com

24 Cocoa Beach Pier A dining, entertainment, and shopping complex that stretches 840 feet out into the Atlantic, the pier is home to three restaurants, an open-air bar with an ocean view, a T-shirt store, and a bait shop. It's a hangout for all ages and is a good spot to sit back, quaff a brew, and watch surfers skim the waves. Fishing from the pier is allowed from 6AM to 1AM. ◆ Parking fee. 401 Meade Ave (east of Ocean Beach Blvd). 783.7549 ♿

On the Cocoa Beach Pier:

Oh Shucks $ A casual outdoor raw bar at the beginning of the pier, it specializes in oysters on the half shell. Munchies such as burgers and hot dogs also are served. ◆ Oyster bar ◆ Daily lunch, dinner, and late-night snacks. 783.4050

Ocean Notions Walk up the boardwalk and past the showers to get to this tropical gift shop. All you need for the beach is right here—sunglasses, hats, and the Panama Jack T-shirts that seem to have become requisite Florida beachwear. ◆ Daily. 783.7552

Boardwalk Set over the ocean, this outdoor bar is a good spot to watch beach volleyball. It usually has live music, too. ◆ Hours vary according to the weather. 783.7549

Atlantic Ocean Grill ★★$$$ Behind the outdoor tables of the **Boardwalk** is the entrance to this upscale establishment, which has floor-to-ceiling windows overlooking the ocean. The seafood selections are solid but predictable for the most part, and the catch of the day is always a good choice. ◆ American ◆ M-Sa dinner, Su brunch. Reservations recommended. 783.7549

Marlin's ★$$ Shorts—but not swimsuits—are okay at this casual restaurant with laminated wood booths, a beamed ceiling, and Atlantic views from three sides. On the menu are good, basic burgers and lighter fare, including tuna and chicken salads. Look for the daily specials. ◆ American ◆ Daily lunch and dinner. 783.7549

Bait & Tackle You can rent fishing equipment here, near the end of the pier. ◆ Daily 6:30AM-5PM

25 Ocean Suite Hotel $ It's a good bet if you want to be near the surfing action at **Cocoa Beach Pier**, but the ocean views from some of the 50 suites in this five-story building are somewhat obscured by the **Oceanside Inn** (see below). Each unit has two rooms, a wet bar, a refrigerator, and two TVs. The property also offers a heated pool, **Jennifer's** restaurant, and a lounge. ◆ 5500 Ocean Beach Blvd (at Meade Ave). 784.4343, 800/367.1223; fax 783.6514 ♿

25 Oceanside Inn $ Many area hotels tout their ocean views, but the ones here are the real thing—straight-on and unobstructed. All 76 rooms face the Atlantic, and each has a balcony and either two double beds or a king-size bed. A low wall separates the pool area from the beach, offering a bit of privacy. There is no restaurant. ◆ 1 Hendry Ave (at Ocean Beach Blvd). 784.3126 ♿

26 Funntasia Family Fun Center The mini-golf course here is made all the more challenging by its waterfalls. There's also an arcade. ◆ Hours vary according to season. 6355 N Atlantic Ave (between Holman Ave and Cape Shores Dr), Cape Canaveral. 799.4856

26 Sunseed Food Co-op You don't have to be a member of the food co-op to shop at this natural foods store. In addition to all types of yogurt, organic produce, exotic teas, and other goodies, you'll find Birkenstock sandals, yoga videos, and one of the best T-shirt collections in Central Florida—everything from tie-dyed designs to shirts bearing Gary Larson's *Far Side* cartoons. ◆ Daily. 6615 N Atlantic Ave (between Cape Shores Dr and Cape Shores Blvd), Cape Canaveral. 784.0930

27 Old Fish House Restaurant ★$$ A convenient place to stop for a meal as you leave Cocoa Beach, this casual family restaurant serves fried or steamed oysters, shrimp, and crab. Another plus: It doesn't attract the large crowds that pack the **Cocoa Beach Pier** restaurants. ◆ Seafood ◆ Daily lunch and dinner. 249 Rte 520 (between Bay St and N Banana River Blvd). 799.9190

Cocoa

Pioneer families put down roots in Cocoa around 1860, and the area's first commercial building, a general store built by B.C. and C.A. Willard, opened some 20 years later. The town was known as **Indian River City**, until—as local lore would have it—postal authorities declared the name too long. The decision to change the town's name was announced at the Willard store, where (so the story goes) one Mrs. James, a poor woman known for her charitable deeds, suggested the name "Cocoa" after spotting a box of Baker's Cocoa on a store shelf. Today the city of Cocoa is primarily a bedroom community for employees of **Cocoa Beach** resorts and the nearby **Kennedy Space Center.**

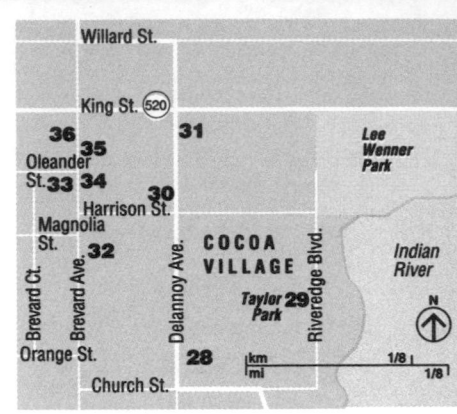

28 Cocoa Village The heart of Cocoa is contained in this charming four-square-block area of cobblestone streets, shade trees, patios, parks, and restored turn-of-the-century buildings. Here you'll find restaurants, a historical house, a theater, and plenty of craft shops and other stores to explore. ◆ Bounded by Riveredge Blvd and Brevard Ave, and Church and Willard Sts

28 Porcher House An example of 20th-century Classic Revival architecture, this structure is made primarily of local coquina (concrete made of limestone and shells). It was built in 1916 by Edward Postell Porcher and his wife, Byrnina, who was the first postmistress of Merritt Island. Byrnina loved to play bridge so much that she had playing-card symbols worked into the coquina rock around the front entrance of the house. During a renovation, this feature was incorporated into the new stonework at the rear entrance. One of the founders of Cocoa, Edward Porcher established the Deerfield Citrus Groves on Merritt Island in 1883; they soon grew to be the largest in the county. Porcher was also co-founder of the Florida Citrus Commission, and he is credited with being the first Florida citrus grower to inspect, wash, and grade his fruit. ◆ Admission. M-F. 434 Delannoy Ave (between Church and Harrison Sts). 639.3500

29 Taylor Park Shuffleboard courts now stand on the land settled in 1886 by Albert A. Taylor. The Taylors were one of many area families that took advantage of the Homestead Act of 1862, which gave land away for free to those who agreed to live on it. The Taylor estate burned down in 1940, but the family's furniture (which had been removed before the fire) can be seen at the **Brevard Museum of History and Natural Science** (see page 132). ♦ 421 Riveredge Blvd (between Church and Harrison Sts)

30 **Collectible Corners** A pack rat's dream come true, this small store is filled with old magazines, antique jewelry, sports cards, and racing memorabilia. ♦ Daily. 100 Harrison St (at Delannoy Ave). 632.9924

31 **The S.F. Travis Company** The Travis family still runs a one-block-square hardware store in the 1885 building that Colonel Fred S. Travis Jr. bought in 1900. Step in to see the tin ceiling and the track ladders (just like those used in libraries). Before the creation of Commodore Plaza, Riveredge Boulevard, and **Lee Wenner Park** on landfill behind the building, ships used to pull up to the Travis docks to unload supplies. The Mutual Moving Picture House, where traveling vaudevillians performed, also was located behind the store at one time. ♦ M-Sa. 300 Delannoy Ave (at King St). 636.1441

32 **Patty's Boutique** An eclectic combination of women's clothes and accessories, including antique and estate jewelry, is sold here. ♦ M-Sa. 404 Brevard Ave (between Church and Harrison Sts). 635.8718

33 **Bath Cottage** This little shop features Crabtree & Evelyn and Caswell-Massey bath and beauty products. It also assembles gift baskets and sells wallpaper and window furnishings. ♦ Daily. 301 Brevard Ave (at Oleander St). 690.2284

34 **Cocoa Village Playhouse** Built in 1924 and originally the **Aladdin Theatre,** a leading vaudeville house of its time, this stately redbrick building was restored in 1988 and now is the venue for children's and community theater performances. The stage also is used for a rock 'n' roll festival, the Miss Cocoa High pageant, and ballet productions. ♦ Box office Tu-F. 300 Brevard Ave (between Harrison and King Sts). 636.5050

35 **Cafe Margaux** ★$$ Tucked away in the corner of a little courtyard next to the **Cocoa Village Playhouse,** this cafe is a good place for an afternoon break from shopping or a pretheater dinner. The homemade pasta dishes make for inexpensive but tasty meals; try the fettuccine Alfredo or the pasta primavera. Another specialty is roast duckling with mango relish. ♦ French/Italian ♦ Daily lunch and dinner. 220 Brevard Ave (between Harrison and King Sts). 639.8343

The Black Tulip

36 **The Black Tulip** ★★$$$ A very good choice for fresh fish, this eatery serves seafood in many different ways: in pastry, with an unusual banana and lemon butter sauce, or simply grilled or baked. The espresso is strong, as it should be. The semiformal dining room is adorned with mirrors and silk flowers. ♦ American ♦ M-Sa lunch and dinner. 207 Brevard Ave (between Oleander and King Sts). 631.1133

37 **Village Plate Collector** Fine china, miniature figurines, and delicate bells make this shop a good stop for gifts. ♦ M-Sa. 120 Forrest Ave (between Center and Peachtree Sts). 636.6914

38 **Byrd Plaza** The largest mall in the Cocoa-Rockledge area, it has about 15 stores, including the **Belk Lindsey** department store. ♦ Daily. Dixon Blvd (between Hwy 1 and N Fiske Blvd)

39 **Astronaut Memorial Planetarium and Observatory** One of the 10 largest planetariums in the nation, this facility houses Florida's largest public-access telescope. It also contains the only Minolta Infinium star projector currently in the Western Hemisphere. Visitors can view large-format films at the three-story IWERKS theater. The building is located on the campus of **Brevard Community College.** ♦ Admission. Tu, F-Sa 6:30-9PM for the planetarium show, movie, telescope viewing (weather permitting); Sa 1:30-4PM for the planetarium show and movie. 1519 Clearlake Rd (between Rosetine St and Michigan Blvd). 634.3732

39 **Brevard Museum of History and Natural Science** The museum is worth a quick visit to see the vast chart on the fish that inhabit the Brevard reef, and the possessions (furniture, clothing, and children's toys) of the family of Albert A. Taylor, one of the region's pioneers. Kids will be fascinated by the live bee colony in the small children's activity center. There are also 22 acres of nature trails, all wheelchair accessible. ♦ Admission. Tu-Su. 2201 Michigan Blvd (between Clearlake Rd and Mercer Dr). 632.1830 &

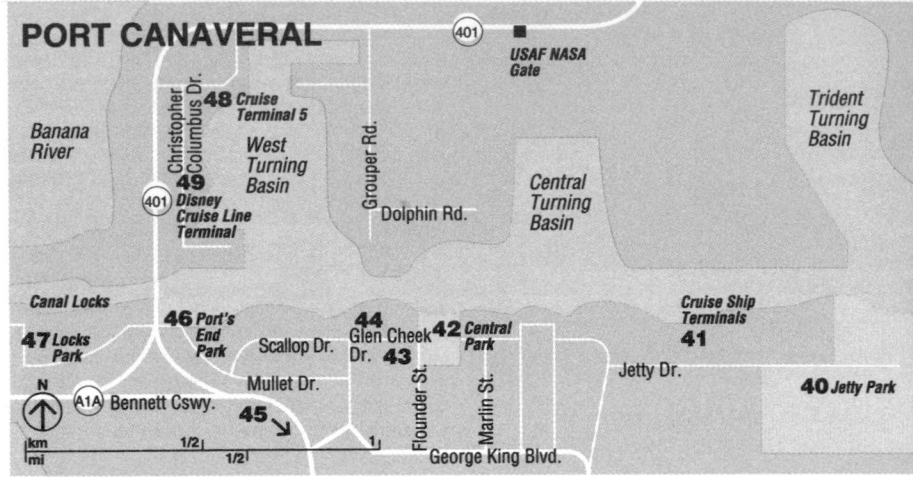

Port Canaveral

In addition to being the home of the **Kennedy Space Center** (which is covered in a separate section page 136), **Cape Canaveral** is the site of Florida's fastest-growing cruise port. Already the third-largest in the United States, Port Canaveral is undergoing a multimillion-dollar expansion that will add more cruise and cargo berths. At press time three cruise lines operated out of the port, **Carnival Cruise Lines** (783.2049, 800/327.9501), **Premier Cruise Lines** (783.5061, 800/327.7113), and the new **Disney Cruise Line** (566.7000; www.disneycruise.com); all offer three- and four-night cruises to the Bahamas.

Sharing the port with the cruise ships are private boats, small commercial operations, and the military (a ship that tracks underwater test missiles launched from submarines is often docked at the port's north end). Several public parks, great for picnicking, fishing, and watching NASA launches, also are located here. For information about **Port Canaveral**, call 783.7831.

40 Jetty Park On the eastern tip of the cape, this 35-acre park offers swimming, fishing, surfing, and camping, and provides bathrooms, shower facilities, and barbecue grills. It's also a popular place to watch the cruise ships and to view shuttle launches. A boardwalk and dunes are hidden from the road. Call ahead for campsite reservations. ♦ Jetty Dr (north of N Atlantic Ave). 868.1108

41 Cruise Ship Terminals 2, 3, and 4 These 9,000-square-foot geodesic domes are filled with tropical plants, giving those departing on cruises a taste of the islands before they leave port. Cruise passengers walk through the terminals to get to the docks. Non-passengers may enter the terminals, but are not allowed on board the cruise ships. ♦ Jetty Dr (north of N Atlantic Ave)

42 Central Park The three double-wide boat-launching ramps, boat-wash stations, fish-cleaning tables, pavilions, picnic tables, rest rooms, and parking lot (that accommodates vehicles hauling trailers) make this a popular hangout. At most times the 10-acre park is full of people playing softball, flying kites, or working on their golf game. Its big playing field is home to the **Space Coast Rugby Association** (matches are free and open to the public). ♦ Flounder St and Glen Cheek Dr

43 Frankie's Wings & Things $ A cozy restaurant specializing in "finger foods," it has a cute gimmick: nine "levels" of sauces for its chicken wings, ranging from "mild" to "call 911." Warning: They start getting fiery at about level four. ♦ American ♦ M-F lunch and dinner, Sa-Su dinner. 555 Glen Cheek Dr (between Flounder St and George King Blvd). 799.4349

44 Rusty's ★★$$$ This branch of **Bernard's Surf** (named for the owner's nephew), one of the most famous restaurants in town, is a good choice for a casual evening. Decorated with sports pictures and pennants, the eatery has a lively ambience, outstanding seafood dishes, and a great view of the water. ♦ Seafood ♦ Daily lunch and dinner. 628 Glen Cheek Dr (between Flounder St and George King Blvd). 783.2033. Also at: 2 S Atlantic Ave (at Minutemen Cswy), Cocoa Beach. 783.2401

45 Jungle Village This playland features a jungle-themed miniature golf course, batting cages, and three go-kart tracks. ♦ Daily. 8801 Astronaut Blvd (at W Central Blvd). 783.0595

45 Radisson Resort at the Port $$ The 200 rooms at this pretty, pink hotel have plenty of amenities, but unfortunately ocean views are not among them. Children love the 90-foot, twisting water slide that empties into a big outdoor pool. **Flamingos** restaurant is on the premises, and free coffee is available in the lobby. ♦ 8701 Astronaut Blvd (at Commerce St). 784.0000, 800/333.3333; www.radisson.com

46 Port's End Park This four-acre park is perfect for fishing enthusiasts. You can fish from a seawall or launch your own boat from a double-wide launching ramp. There are covered picnic tables, rest rooms, and an observation tower. The park also offers a view of NASA's launch pads five miles away. ♦ Mullet Dr (west of Scallop Dr)

47 Locks Park The newest of the four port parks, this one is at the far west end of **Port Canaveral,** where the locks connect the port to the Banana River and the Intracoastal Waterway. The park has picnic tables, pavilions, and rest rooms, but it's hard to find. There's talk of creating a road from Route 528 to the park. Until then, go through the main entrance to the port and bear left until you have gone past **Port's End Park** and under Route 401. The road dead-ends at the park. ♦ Mullet Dr (west of Scallop Dr)

48 Cruise Ship Terminal 5 Designed by **Post Buckley, Schuh & Jernigan,** the 42,000-square-foot triangular building holds 2,500 passengers and can accommodate the large cruise ships. ♦ Snapper Rd (east of Rte 401)

49 Disney Cruise Line Terminal Home of the **Disney Cruise Line**'s first ship, the *Disney Magic,* this Art Deco–inspired terminal features a glass entranceway. Approximately 19,000 passengers pass through this facility every month. ♦ Christopher Columbus Dr (south of Snapper Rd)

50 Air Force Space and Missile Museum This outdoor museum looks like an aerospace graveyard, filled with skeletons of military defense missiles, rockets, and other obsolete space hardware, including *Gemini* and *Mercury* capsules used in practice sessions by land and water rescue teams. More than 70 missiles and space launch vehicles are on display. An exhibit hall provides information about rockets, space achievements, and space technology. A National Historic Landmark, the museum is at **Launch Complex 26,** where the first US satellite, *Explorer I,* was launched. Also on the grounds is the site where Alan Shepard and Virgil "Gus" Grissom blasted off on the first two-man space flight. Note: This is the only part of **Cape Canaveral Air Force Station** that can be visited by people not on the **Kennedy Space Center Cape Canaveral Tour** (see page 137); you can obtain a museum pass from the guard inside **Cape Canaveral Air Force Station.** ♦ Free. M-F 10AM-2PM; Sa-Su 10AM-4PM (closed on some launch days). 853.3245

Merritt Island

Situated between the mainland and the barrier island that contains **Cocoa Beach,** with the **Banana River** to the east and the **Indian River** to the west, Merritt Island is 43 miles long and only seven miles across at its widest point. Samuel Field and his family settled here in 1868, creating a community called **Indianola.** Field donated land for the first community building, the first school, and the first church; he opened the first store and post office; and he even became the town's first minister.

The southern part of the island is home to a handful of beach resorts, restaurants, and related attractions; north of the town of **Merritt Island**—but still on the island itself—are the **Visitor Center** and the **Merritt Island National Wildlife Refuge/Canaveral National Seashore,** which are covered in separate sections below.

51 Merritt Island Dragon A 100-foot dragon made of more than 20 tons of concrete and steel is perched at the southern tip of Merritt Island, where the Banana and Indian Rivers converge. Created by artist and self-described warlock Lewis Vandercar, it was installed on the site in 1971; a few years later four hatchling dragons were added. The sculpture, inspired by Vandercar's "prophetic" dreams, has survived a "Ban-the-Dragon" campaign by locals who consider it an eyesore and officials who said it violated zoning laws. It since has been blessed by a Catholic priest and rigged so that it breathes fire on the Fourth of July. The dragon is on private property and can be viewed closely only from a boat. ♦ S Tropical Tr (south of Mathers Bridge)

52 Merritt Square Mall If you're in a hurry and need a place to go for one-stop shopping, stop here. There are about a hundred stores, including **Burdine's, JCPenney, Dillard's,** and **Sears.** ♦ Daily. 777 Rte 520 (between S Sykes Creek Pkwy and S Plumosa St). 452.3270

The Sunshine State is a little larger than England, a little larger than Greece, and can fit into the state of California a little more than two and one-half times.

The Florida Canoe Trail System offers nearly three dozen scenic pathways through 950 miles of waterways. For information on access points, as well as the mileage between starting and finishing points, call 850/488.9872.

Within the Merritt Square Mall:

Ruby Tuesday $ This noisy, casual chain restaurant serves ample portions of American favorites—ribs and fried chicken wings are their specialties. The pasta is a decent alternative to meat dishes, or you can create an entire meal at the salad bar. Just save room for a generous slab of the Oreo cookie cake. ♦ American ♦ Daily lunch and dinner. 458.6340

Outback Steakhouse ★★$$ There's usually a wait for a table, but it's worth it if you're hungry. This isn't a fancy steak house— there's no carpet, just wood floors, and the tables don't have linens—but you won't be disappointed in the steaks. Most everyone starts with the "bloomin' onion" appetizer— a giant whole onion sliced so that it opens like a blossom when it's deep fried. A wide variety of steak cuts—filet mignon, porterhouse, New York strip, prime rib—are all on the menu. Though most diners go for the beef, we can also recommend the grilled fish. ♦ Steak house ♦ Daily lunch and dinner. 454.4450

53 Holiday Inn of Merritt Island $ Set off the highway a bit, this is a standard 128-room member of the chain, complete with a tennis court and a pool. **Austin's Sports Bar & Grille** serves lunch and dinner and features sporting events on large TVs. ♦ 260 E Merritt Island Cswy (between N Plumosa St and N Courtenay Pkwy). 452.7711, 800/465.4329; www.holiday-inn.com &

Kennedy Space Center/Visitor Complex

When the federal government decided in the late 1940s that it needed a long-range missile testing site, it chose **Cape Canaveral,** a relatively unpopulated Florida peninsula jutting out into the **Atlantic Ocean.** The region was mostly rural, and at the time all of **Brevard County** had a population of only 16,142 people. In 1958 the National Aeronautics and Space

Administration (NASA) began operations at Cape Canaveral, where it launched scientific, meteorological, and communications satellites. A few years later, when President John Kennedy accelerated the space exploration program, things changed dramatically in this region. NASA hired thousands of employees, significantly boosting the local population, and rocket launches attracted thousands of tourists to the area. Today, Cape Canaveral remains the home of the **Kennedy Space Center** and its **Visitor Complex,** formerly **Spaceport USA** (NASA Pkwy, west of Kennedy Pkwy, 452.2121).

A visit to this extensive space museum and attraction may end up being one of your favorite—and least expensive—experiences in Central Florida. Except for three IMAX films and a two-hour bus tour of the **Space Center** or **Cape Canaveral Air Force Station,** everything—even the parking—is free at the **Kennedy Space Center Visitor Complex.** The **Kennedy Space Center** lies within a 140,000-acre wildlife sanctuary on **Merritt Island,** managed for NASA by the US Department of the Interior. It's open daily from 9AM to dusk (except some launch days). Get here early and go straight through the entrance of the **Kennedy Space Center Visitor Complex** (shown on the map below) to the **Ticket Pavilion,** where you can get theater and bus tour tickets. You'll probably want to spend close to a full day here. For the most current shuttle launch information, call 452.2121 or, in Florida, 800/KSC.INFO (800/572.4636).

54 Kennedy Space Center Visitor Complex Main Building On the left as you enter the space center's hub is a small kiosk with tourist information on Brevard County. **Spaceport Theater,** featuring a number of short films, is also located in this building, and there are telephones, rest rooms, drinking fountains, mailboxes, and snacks as well.

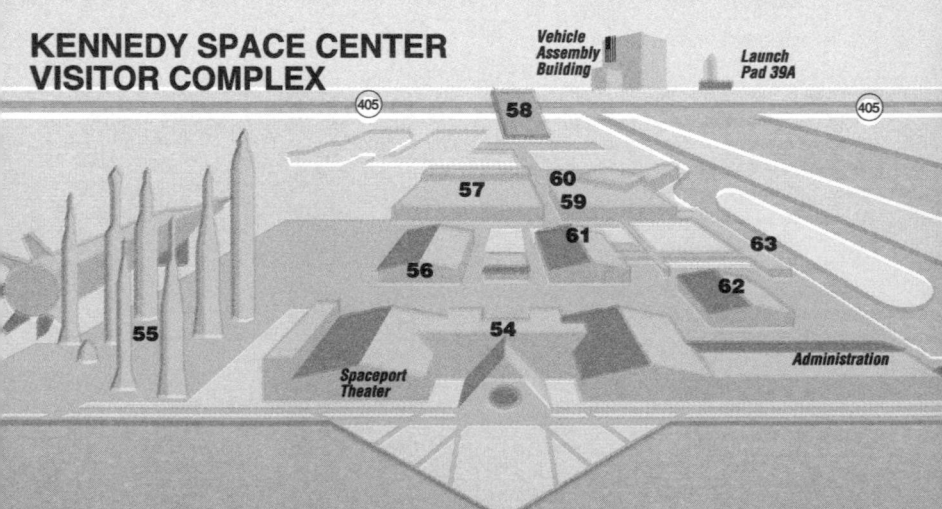

KENNEDY SPACE CENTER VISITOR COMPLEX

Vehicle Assembly Building

Launch Pad 39A

Spaceport Theater

Administration

55 Rocket Garden Outside the **Spaceport Theater** side of the **Kennedy Space Center Visitor Complex** is the "garden" where NASA displays many of its rockets. In the front of the garden is an *Apollo* spacecraft access arm and a lunar excursion module.

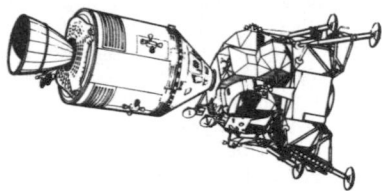

56 Gallery of Space Flight Near the **Rocket Garden** is this museum, where spacecraft actually used on missions, as well as models, space clothes, and photographs, are on display.

57 Galaxy Center Along with the **Galaxy** and **IMAX Theaters,** the center houses more than 250 paintings and sculptures commissioned by the NASA Art Program. The **IMAX Theater** features *L5: First City in Space,* a 3-D film that depicts a future space city; *The Dream is Alive,* photographed from space by astronauts and narrated by Walter Cronkite; and *Mission to Mir,* featuring firsthand accounts by US astronauts aboard the Russian space station *Mir.* ♦ Admission. Call 449.4411 for film times

58 Astronauts Memorial A magnificent 42-by-50-foot polished granite monument is carved with the names of the 16 American astronauts who have lost their lives in the line of duty. The memorial is actually a rotating space mirror, which tracks the sun throughout the day. Funded largely by the sale of *Challenger* license plates in Florida, the $6-million memorial is located on six acres of land at the back of the **Kennedy Space Center Visitor Complex,** overlooking a pristine lagoon. Adjacent to the memorial is a full-scale model of a space shuttle that you can explore firsthand.

59 Orbit Restaurant $ Step up to a rotating serving wheel and grab what you want to eat at this air-conditioned cafeteria. ♦ American ♦ Daily lunch

60 MILA's Roadhouse $ Themed to look like a 1960s diner with Formica tables and early space memorabilia on the walls, this table-service restaurant dishes up such home-style specialties as Salisbury steak, fried chicken, and Yankee pot roast. The eatery's name comes from the acronym for **Merritt Island Launch Area** (the original name of the **Kennedy Space Center**). ♦ American ♦ Daily lunch

61 Gift Gantry Souvenirs ranging from clothes with NASA insignias to space food and postcards are sold here. ♦ Daily. 800/621.9826

62 Lunch Pad $ The fare is one small step above cafeteria food—ribs, chicken, and fish are served. ♦ American ♦ Daily breakfast, lunch, and early dinner

63 Bus Tours Two tours are offered; the **Kennedy Space Center Tour** (formerly the **Red Tour**) is the more exciting of the two because visitors get to see sights familiar from TV coverage of the space-shuttle program, including the launch pads and the large **Vehicle Assembly Building.** This tour also includes the new **Apollo/Saturn V Center,** featuring dramatic you-are-there theatrical presentations; an actual 363-foot Saturn V rocket; a look at the **International Space Station Center;** and an intergalactic hands-on gallery to tell the story of NASA's historic Apollo program. The **Cape Canaveral Tour** (formerly the **Blue Tour**) covers the **Cape Canaveral Air Force Station** and includes the old **Mission Control;** a monument to the seven original Mercury astronauts; launch pads used for the Mercury and Gemini missions; launch pads currently used for satellite launches; and the **Air Force Space and Missile Museum** (see page 135). A walkway between the **Orbit Restaurant** and the **Lunch Pad** (see above) leads to the bus boarding area. ♦ Fee. Kennedy Space Center Tour leaves every 15 minutes beginning at 9:45AM (last tour departs two hours before dusk). Cape Canaveral Tour departs at various times based on demand. 452.2121

Titusville and Environs

The county seat of **Brevard County,** Titusville was named for Colonel Henry T. Titus, who made his fortune selling supplies to the Confederate Army during the Civil War. After the war, Titus became a saloon-keeper and hotelier in Sand Point, a small town on Florida's east coast. He later became postmaster and had the name of the post-office station changed from Sand Point to Titusville.

Titusville is now one of the best places for viewing launches at the **Kennedy Space Center,** located just across the **Indian River.** It is also a major access point to **Merritt Island National Wildlife Refuge/Canaveral National Seashore.**

64 US Astronaut Hall of Fame Though it's not actually part of the **Kennedy Space Center,** this high-tech warehouse is just outside the center's mainland gate. Filled with NASA memorabilia and videotapes, it's basically a tribute to the original Mercury Seven, America's first astronauts. The museum collection includes Virgil "Gus" Grissom's Congressional Space Medal of Honor and a checklist that was strapped to the arm of Alan Shepard when he made his famous moon walk. There's also a replica of *Sputnik,* the world's first satellite, which was launched by the Soviet Union in 1957. Also look for a copy of President John Kennedy's pledge to put a man on the moon by the end of the 1960s. A gift shop offers all the usual T-shirts, mugs, and postcards, as well as dinners just like the ones the astronauts ate in space: freeze-dried chicken, rice, peas, peaches, and ice cream in a plastic envelope. ♦ Admission. Daily. 6225 Vectorspace Blvd (between Hwy 1 and Rte 405). 269.6100 &

Within the US Astronaut Hall of Fame:

United States Space Camp The camp offers five-day programs for children in grades four to seven from March through December. It isn't cheap, but where else can kids wear flight suits, eat freeze-dried food, experience one-sixth gravity, and perform simulated shuttle missions? A single-day camp, which lasts about four hours, is available year-round to both adult and youth groups; preregistration is required. ♦ Fee. 800/63.SPACE (800/637.7223) &

65 Valiant Air Command Warbird Air Museum Vintage aircraft are the pride of this place. Since its formation in 1977 the Valiant Air Command, an organization dedicated to

finding and preserving historic aircraft, has obtained more than 350 historic warbirds at various locations around the world. At any one time, 15 to 20 are on display here, and an annual Spring Air Show features some of them in flight every March. There are also fascinating aviation exhibits, including aircraft from World Wars I and II and the Korean and Vietnam Wars. In addition, the museum is a working facility where vintage military aircraft are restored. The spruced-up classic planes appear in air shows and film and television productions. The gift shop here carries souvenirs and collectors' items. ♦ Admission. Daily. 6600 Tico Rd (south of Rte 405). 268.1941 &

66 Holiday Inn Kennedy Space Center $ The 118 rooms face either the pool or the Indian River, and all are furnished with two double beds. There's a restaurant and a laundry room, and fishing equipment is available for rent. ♦ 4951 S Washington Ave (between Riveredge Dr and Cheney Hwy). 269.2121, 800/465.4329; fax 267.4739; www.holiday-inn.com &

67 Best Western Space Shuttle Inn $ A good value, this motel has a restaurant, pool, sauna, and 126 rooms with king-size beds (there are even water beds for 1970s diehards). It offers easy access to I-95 near the **Kennedy Space Center.** ♦ 3455 Cheney Hwy (between Rte 405 and I-95). 269.9100, 800/523.7654; fax 383.4674; www.spaceshuttleinn.com &

Adventures in Outer Space

24 July 1950 The first missile launched from **Cape Canaveral** is a modified German V-2.

31 January 1958 *Explorer 1,* the first US satellite, discovers the Van Allen Radiation Belt.

17 March 1958 *Vanguard 1,* the second US satellite, determines that the Earth is slightly pear-shaped.

7 August 1959 *Explorer 6* sends back a crude image, the first photo of Earth taken in space.

1961 NASA begins acquiring land next to the **Cape Canaveral Air Force Station** on **Merritt Island** for its primary launch facility.

5 May 1961 Alan Shepard's suborbital flight aboard *Freedom 7,* the first Mercury flight in the US with a person on board, lasts 15 minutes.

20 February 1962 John Glenn becomes the first US astronaut to orbit the Earth, making three complete revolutions aboard *Friendship 7.*

23 March 1965 Virgil Grissom and John Young are the first to change orbital altitude. They are aboard the premier launch of the Gemini program.

3 June 1965 Edward White becomes the first American astronaut to walk in space, spending 21 minutes outside a *Gemini 4* capsule.

30 May 1966 *Surveyor 1* makes the first soft lunar landing in the Ocean of Storms and sends back 11,237 pictures.

27 January 1967 *Apollo 1* is gutted by a flash fire during launch-pad testing, killing astronauts Grissom, White, and Roger Chaffee.

11 October 1968 The first successful Apollo spaceship flight with people on board is launched; the astronauts on *Apollo 7* are Walter Schirra, Donn Eisele, and Walter Cunningham.

21 December 1968 *Apollo 8* goes to the moon, marking the first time humans leave the gravity of the Earth for another planetary body.

16 July 1969 *Apollo 11* is launched; its mission is to land men on the moon and return them safely to Earth—a national goal set in 1961 by President John F. Kennedy. The lunar landing occurs on 20 July. Neil Armstrong takes the first step on the moon at 10:56PM EDT on the same day.

11 April 1970 *Apollo 13* is launched to land on the moon but its mission is aborted because of an in-flight explosion. The astronauts return safely to Earth.

30 November 1971 *Mariner 9* is launched into orbit around Mars, sending back 6,876 pictures of the planet's surface.

3 March 1972 *Pioneer 10,* the first Jupiter probe, is launched and sends back close-up pictures of a Jovian moon.

14 May 1973 The *Skylab* space station is launched into orbit aboard a two-stage Saturn V rocket.

25 May 1973 The first of three astronaut teams that will use *Skylab* as a home and workshop is launched. Crew members are Pete Conrad Jr., Dr. Joseph Kerwin, and Paul Weitz.

3 November 1973 *Mariner 10* is launched and sends back the first TV pictures of Mercury.

17 July 1975 The *Apollo Saturn 210,* an American spacecraft, and the *Soyuz 19,* a Soviet spacecraft, launched 6,500 miles and seven-and-a-half hours apart, dock with each other 140 miles above Europe. Aboard *Apollo Saturn 210* are Donald Slayton, Thomas Stafford, and Vance Brand. Aboard *Soyuz 19* are Alexei Leonov, who was the first person to walk in space (on 18 March 1965), and Valeriy Kubasov.

20 August and 9 September 1975 *Viking 1* and *Viking 2* are sent to Mars in search of microscopic life in the planet's soil. Research finds no positive indications of life.

12 April 1981 *Columbia,* the first space shuttle, is launched.

4 April 1983 The *Challenger* is used for the first time in the sixth space-shuttle mission.

18 June 1983 Sally Ride becomes the first American woman in space.

30 August 1983 Guion Bluford becomes the first African-American in space.

7 February 1984 The first untethered space walk is accomplished by Bruce McCandless. Two hours later Robert Stewart does the same.

11 February 1984 The *Challenger* lands on Runway 15, the first end-of-mission landing at **Kennedy Space Center.**

6 April 1984 The *Solar Maximum Mission (SMM)* satellite, launched 14 February 1980 to study the sun, is the first satellite to be retrieved and repaired in space by a shuttle crew.

11 October 1984 Kathryn Sullivan becomes the first woman to walk in space.

28 January 1986 An explosion 73 seconds after liftoff kills the crew of *Challenger 10,* including Christa McAuliffe, a member of the "Teacher in Space" program.

24 April 1990 *Discovery 10* is launched to deploy the Hubble Space Telescope.

7 April 1991 The Gamma Ray Observatory is deployed from the *Atlantis* space shuttle. Also, astronauts perform space walks to test maneuverability of equipment while maintaining the proposed Space Station Freedom.

7 May 1992 *Endeavour,* the fourth and newest orbiter in the space-shuttle fleet, lifts off. May 16 marks the first time a drag chute is used on an orbiter during landing.

12 September 1992 *Endeavour's* second flight, the 50th shuttle mission, is the first to launch on time since the 23rd shuttle mission during November 1985. The first African-American woman to fly in space and the first married couple to participate in the same mission are among the seven-member crew.

5 May 1993 *Columbia,* NASA's oldest shuttle, reaches a milestone by accumulating one year's worth of time in space; the agency began using shuttle orbiters in 1981.

3 February 1994 *Discovery* flies the first Russian cosmonaut in the shuttle.

29 June 1995 *Atlantis* docks with the Russian space station *Mir.*

26 September 1996 Astronaut Shannon Lucid returns to Earth following her record-breaking 188 days in space.

7 December 1996 Space shuttle *Columbia* lands at Kennedy Space Center, after having completed the longest shuttle flight (17 days, 15 hours, 53 minutes, 18 seconds) to date. Astronaut Story Musgrave also sets the record for most shuttle flights (six).

12 January 1997 During the first space shuttle flight of 1997, *Atlantis* docks with *Mir,* and returns carrying the first plants to complete a life cycle in space—a crop of wheat grown from seed to seed.

4 June 1998 US space shuttle *Discovery* docks with *Mir* for the last time.

29 October 1998 Ohio senator John Glenn made history in 1962 as the first American to orbit the earth, completing three orbits aboard *Friendship 7;* he returns to space aboard space shuttle *Discovery* as a payload specialist and, at age 77, as the oldest person ever to travel in space.

KEELY EDWARDS

68 Ramada Inn and Suites Kennedy Space Center $ A hit with fans of shuttle launches and landings, the 124-room hotel has an exercise room, gameroom, sauna, and **Denny's** restaurant. ♦ 3500 Cheney Hwy (between Rte 405 and I-95). 269.5510, 800/228.3838; fax 269.3796; www.ramadaksc.com &

69 Luck's Way Inn $ This 114-room inn offers convenient access to I-95 and Cheney Highway and a good location for shuttle watching (you can see the launch from your room). Amenities include a pool, a restaurant, and a lounge. ♦ 3655 Cheney Hwy (just west of I-95). 269.7110; fax 268.6972

69 Days Inn Kennedy Space Center $ With a convenient location off the interstate, this 148-room motel has a large pool, one suite, a restaurant, and a lounge. ♦ 3755 Cheney Hwy (west of I-95). 269.4480; fax 383.0646 &

70 Miracle City Mall **Belk Lindsey** and **JCPenney** department stores anchor this 46-store mall. ♦ Daily. 2500 S Washington Ave (between Harrison and Jackson Sts). 269.7521

71 Titusville Playhouse An amateur community theater group presents two musicals and four dramas a year in this restored 1920s movie theater in downtown Titusville. ♦ 301 Julia St (at S Hopkins Ave). Box office 268.1125

72 North Brevard Historical Museum A surprisingly large number of articles detailing what life was like in the Titusville area at the turn of the century are on view at this storefront museum. Displays include farming equipment, pictures, and furniture. ♦ Free. Tu, Th, Sa 10AM-2PM. 301 S Washington Ave (at Main St). 269.3658

73 Dixie Crossroads ★$$ This eatery is much larger inside than it appears from the outside, and it's always crowded with locals. The menu features fresh seafood. Customers keep coming back for the all-you-can-eat rock shrimp (small, hard-shelled shrimp that taste a lot like lobster); the broiled or fried calico scallops with corn fritters is another favorite dish. ♦ Seafood ♦ Daily lunch and dinner. 1475 Garden St (between S Park and S Dixie Aves). 268.5000

74 Merritt Island National Wildlife Refuge/Canaveral National Seashore The national seashore and wildlife refuge are within easy reach of Orlando and the **Kennedy Space Center Visitor Complex.** The unspoiled beaches and the wildlife refuge—home to 310 species of birds, 25 species of mammals, 117 species of fish, and 23 species of migratory waterfowl—are a natural alternative to the expensive, manufactured attractions of the Orlando area. For backcountry hiking permits and details on the trails and beaches, stop by the **Visitors' Center.** ♦ Free. Daily. Route 402 (east of Washington Ave). 267.1110

At the Canaveral National Seashore:

Beaches Central Florida's hedonistic (there is nude bathing in certain areas), unsullied paradise, Playalinda Beach (Spanish for "pretty beach," but it's given the anglicized pronunciation "*play*-a-linda" by locals) offers plenty of sand, sun, and sea. Note: Playalinda is closed at times because of launches from **Cape Canaveral,** so call before you visit (867.2805, 267.1110). Lesser-known and less accessible than Playalinda, Apollo Beach is at the north end of **Canaveral National Seashore** in neighboring Volusia County. Take Interstate 95 or Highway 1 north to the city of New Smyrna Beach and head south on Route A1A to the beach. Both Apollo and Playalinda Beaches have parking areas and portable toilets; take water and food, since there's no snack bar. You can hike north from Playalinda Beach or south from Apollo Beach to the less populated Klondike Beach, which is accessible only by foot. Consult tide charts before setting out, however, since there may be little beach to walk on at high tide.

Drives The national seashore has two self-guided drives that offer good views of area wildlife. Both are near Titusville. The 30- to 45-minute Black Point Wildlife Drive meanders through pine woods and marshes and offers great opportunities for spotting waterfowl and wading birds, especially in the winter. The 20-minute Max Hoeck Creek Wildlife Drive (closed occasionally because of **Kennedy Space Center** operations) follows a railroad bed through a marsh and uplands just west of Playalinda Beach. If you're lucky, you'll get a glimpse of alligators and waterfowl, as well as some marsh and wading birds.

Hiking Trails The clearly marked paths afford rewarding glimpses of flora and fauna; distances are short enough even for small children. **Oak Hammock Trail** is a 30-minute loop that wanders through a hardwood hammock—a dense coastal forest. It lies off Route 402 about halfway between Titusville and Playalinda Beach. There's also a 15-minute hike at **Turtle Mound**, north of Apollo Beach, a two-acre heap of oyster shells piled up by ancient Indians..

Ranger Walks A great way to introduce yourself or your kids to Florida's wildlife is to participate in one of the ranger-sponsored hikes at **Canaveral National Seashore.** Rangers give one- to two-hour guided tours of hammocks and lead nature walks along the beach, dispensing interesting information about seashells, marine life, sand dunes, and beach vegetation. Instruction on fishing in the surf, including tips on proper equipment, bait, and how to cast your line, is also offered. Fishing equipment is provided for practice, or you can bring your own gear.

Camping If you want to rough it, the **Canaveral National Seashore** has a number of backcountry camping sites among the many islands in the northern part of Mosquito Lagoon. They can be reached only by boat or canoe, and those near Klondike Beach are closed from 15 May to 30 September to protect the sea turtle during its nesting period (see "Blinded by the Light" below). A backcountry hiking permit is required to stay overnight at campsites, but it is free. For permit information call 267.1110.

Blinded by the Light

"Save the baby loggerheads!" has become a rallying cry for nature lovers in **Brevard** and **Volusia Counties,** where thousands of endangered and threatened sea turtles nest from May through September. After baby sea turtles hatch in their beachside nests, they are instinctively drawn to the **Atlantic Ocean** by the moonlight shimmering off the water. Artificial lights, however, can confuse and disorient the hatchlings. Some head toward lights shining from condos, beachfront restaurants, or along the street, becoming easy prey for birds—if they aren't first squashed by cars in parking lots or on the street. Even if the little lost turtles survive their first night outside the ocean, they usually die from the intense heat of the sun the next day.

Both Volusia and Brevard Counties have enacted ordinances aimed at cracking down on lights that endanger the sea turtles. During the nesting season, residents and businesses in Brevard County coastal areas must turn off or shade bright oceanfront lights.

The female turtles that nest in Brevard County's sandy beaches are mostly loggerheads. Although the local loggerhead population fluctuates, it has been increasing in the last decade, an encouraging sign for the threatened species. Smaller green turtles and the occasional leatherback also nest in the area.

Typically, hatchlings incubate from 45 to 60 days and crawl out in the evening when the sand is damp and cool. Only about half of the hatchlings make it to the water; biologists are uncertain how many actually survive. You can watch the nesting turtles (some weighing as much as 350 pounds), but don't get too close to the female until she actually starts laying eggs. Nesting turtles are easily frightened, but once the female digs her nest and the process of egg-laying begins, spectators can approach without disturbing her. The turtle will lay as many as 120

eggs about the size of Ping-Pong balls. A female loggerhead may dig five nests in one season.

For more information about turtle-watching protocol, take a guided walk, usually scheduled from 9PM to midnight. Reservations are mandatory, and it's best to make them at least two weeks in advance. The following groups offer guided tours:

Brevard Turtle Preservation Society 676.1701
Canaveral National Seashore 267.1110
Merritt Island National Wildlife Refuge ..861.0667

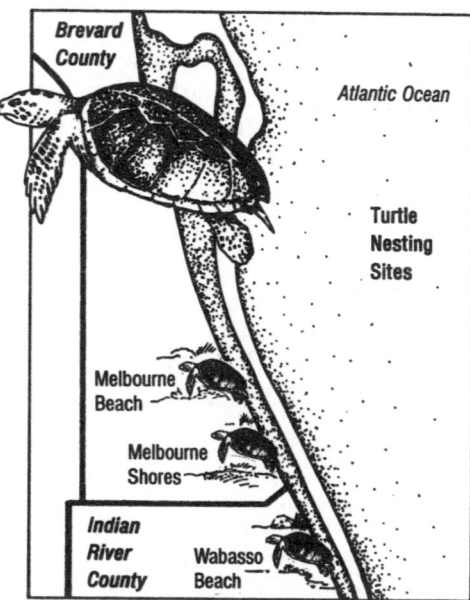

Daytona Beach Resort Area

Sand, sun, and speed are the main attractions in and around Daytona Beach, the largest city in Florida's **Volusia County.** The beaches here are among Central Florida's most dramatic, broad, and sweeping—in fact, they are so wide and have such hard-packed sand that some sections are open to auto traffic. Billed in these parts as "The World's Most Famous Beach," Daytona Beach is great for strolling any time of the day or night, and you can drive on it beginning an hour before sunrise and ending an hour after sundown. Park your car on the sand if you want—it's a tradition.

Every spring, successive waves of people flock to Daytona Beach. First come the auto-racing fans, who jam-pack **Daytona International Speedway** for Speed Weeks—three consecutive weekends of auto racing that climax in mid-February with the Daytona 500, the world's biggest and most lucrative stock-car race.

No sooner do the auto diehards leave than thousands of leather-clad motorcyclists roar into town from all over the country for Bike Week—seven days of motorcycle races in March, also held at the **Daytona International Speedway.** Most of the bikers—who represent a full spectrum of occupations and lifestyles—come to socialize at their unofficial headquarters: world-famous **Main Street,** Daytona Beach.

Before the bikers leave, the third wave of visitors has already arrived: college students on Spring Break, kicking back from the hectic pace of college life and ready to hit the beach. During a three-week period in March, thousands of students come to relax, meet new friends, party, and enjoy a wide variety of corporate-sponsored activities, including three-on-three basketball, beach volleyball, and seaside concerts. The bikers return in October for Biketoberfest, the newest of the area's motorcycle events. Highlights include racing, a Main Street rally, a motorcycle exposition, concerts, and swap meets.

Families or visitors who come merely to relax during any of these onslaughts can find quiet lodgings in the area's northern and southern stretches, especially **Ormond Beach** and **Daytona Beach Shores.** Still farther south, at the end of **Route A1A,** is **Ponce Inlet,** home of the area's best seafood restaurants. Also a bit removed from the action is the mainland part of Daytona Beach, across the **Halifax River** from the actual beach. Of particular note in mainland Daytona Beach is **Beach Street,** a strip of architecturally interesting buildings from the 1920s and 1930s. A more bucolic setting is found year-round in **West Volusia County,** site of two beautiful recreation areas. Don't miss **Blue Spring State Park** (two miles west of **Orange City**), where the endangered manatee can be seen from December through March.

Area code 904 unless otherwise noted.

West Volusia County

Sparsely populated except for the small towns that dot its western borders, this part of Volusia County is famous for its crystalline springs and swamp oaks dripping with moss.

1 Blue Spring State Park Once a riverboat stop on the St. Johns River, this 518-acre state park is now most notable as a manatee refuge. In fact, it's one of the best places in the world to see these rare aquatic mammals, whose closest living relative is the elephant. The manatees, which are about 12 feet long and weigh more than a ton, are drawn to the spring from November through March because of the constant 72-degree water temperature. The sea cows (as they're also called) are an endangered species, and rangers are on hand to make sure they are not harassed. Also of interest at the park is the **Thursby House.** Built on a mound of shells in 1872, it provides a look at life in the romantic steamboat days of the St. Johns River. The park offers camping, canoeing, fishing, nature trails, picnicking, rest rooms, a refreshment stand, and a public boat ramp outside of the park. When the manatees come to visit, no fishing or boating is allowed in Blue Spring, and swimming is permitted only

On the map:

Barberville (40)

(17)

(11)

to St. Augustine and Jacksonville

(1)

(95)

■ Tomoka State Park

Ormond Beach

For nos. 4-58, see pg. 145

Lake Woodruff

De Leon Springs State Recreation Area **3**

De Leon Springs

2

Holly Hill

Tomoka Wildlife Management Area

Daytona Beach

Glenwood ●

(40A)

(15A)

Delano Municipal Airport ✈

(92)

Daytona Beach Regional Airport ✈

(44)

De Land ●

(403A)

(4)

South Daytona

● **Port Orange**

(A1A)

Atlantic Ocean

(92)

Blue Spring State Park **1**

(17)

● Lake Helen

(44)

Spruce Creek Airport ✈

(415)

Halifax River

● **Orange City**

● Cassadaga

Samsula ●

(40A)

Ponce Inlet

DeBary ●

(4)

to Orlando ←

● Deltona

Enterprise

(44)

(415)

Farmton Wildlife Management Area

● **New Smyrna Beach**

Lake Monroe

Osteen

(415)

Edgewater

(442)

Indian River Lagoon

(46)

Midway ●

St. Johns River

Kalamazoo ●

(95)

(1)

to Titusville ↓ Oak Hill ●

Apollo ■ Beach

km/mi | 10 | 20
5 | 10

N

St. Johns River

---

in a designated area. A wheelchair accessible trail follows Blue Spring Run from the St. Johns River to the spring. ◆ Nominal fee. Daily. 2100 W French Ave (west of N Sparkman Ave). 775.3663

2 Karlings Inn ★★$$ A relaxing ride away from the hubbub of the beach and city, this restaurant, set in an old house, is definitely worth a detour. The dining room is reminiscent of a cozy German inn, wood paneled and decorated with the owner's collection of Hummel figurines and paintings of European landscapes. Traditional dishes from France, Spain, and other parts of Europe are featured. Everyone raves about the lobster fricassee with a cream, cayenne pepper, and scotch sauce. For an appetizer, try the escargots baked in garlic butter. The crème brûlée is a must for dessert. ◆ Continental ◆ Tu-Sa dinner. 4640 Hwy 17 N (between Fairport Rd and Dundee Ave), De Leon Springs. 985.5535 &

3 De Leon Springs State Recreation Area
The heart of this state park is a beautiful, 72-degree spring-fed pool that's good for swimming or snorkeling (scuba tanks aren't allowed, though). Canoes and kayaks can be rented for trips down the spring-fed run, and there's also a nature trail. ◆ Fee. Daily. 601 Ponce de Leon Blvd (at Burts Park Rd). 985.4212

Within the De Leon Springs State Recreation Area:

Old Spanish Sugar Mill & Griddle House ★★$ If you're in Central Florida for **Walt Disney World** but want a change of pace, put this at the top of your list. Once an old stone waterwheel house, this homey restaurant has specially built tables with big griddles in the middle. Guests order pitchers of marvelous pancake batter (don't miss the whole-wheat mix) and little bowls of mix-ins—such as blueberries, bananas, or peanut butter—and fry their own flapjacks. Even folks who've

143

forgotten how a kitchen works love it. Lines can be long if you arrive at midday. ♦ American ♦ Daily breakfast and lunch; last seating at 4PM. Reservations required for parties of 10 or more. 985.5644

Ponce Inlet

Located at the southern end of **Route A1A,** Ponce Inlet is one of the major charter fishing areas on Florida's east coast. Almost two dozen vessels, many private charter boats, are docked here. Sailfish, king mackerel, tuna, grouper, and red snapper can all be caught offshore. Not surprisingly, the seafood restaurants here serve nothing but the freshest the ocean has to offer.

4 Lighthouse Park Locals come here to get away from the crowded beaches. There's a playground, a picnic area, a nature trail, rest rooms, a marina, and a beach. ♦ Admission. Daily. 4931 S Peninsula Dr (at Lighthouse Dr). 756.7488

Within Lighthouse Park:

Ponce Inlet Lighthouse Mosquito Lights, built in 1834, was the first lighthouse in these parts, but it never opened. First, Indians vandalized it, then a storm swept it away. A more solid brick lighthouse, built north of the old structure across Ponce Inlet, first flashed its beacon in 1888. After years of using oil, the lighthouse was converted to electricity in the 1920s, when a revolving lens made in Paris in 1867 was installed. It flashed six times every 26 seconds and could be seen from as far away as 20 miles at sea. In 1970 the government decided the lighthouse was too costly to maintain and closed it down, but the city of Ponce Inlet was deeded the structure and has since fixed it up, along with the cottages on the grounds. The Coast Guard relit the lighthouse in 1982, and it is once again in use. The light can be seen from 16 miles at sea. Visitors willing to climb 203 steps to the top of the 175-foot lighthouse are rewarded with a sweeping view of the area. Pass through a white picket fence to the gift shop to start your tour. ♦ One admission fee covers the lighthouse and the three keepers' houses (see below). Daily. 761.1821 ɫ

On the Ponce Inlet Lighthouse grounds:

Head Lighthouse Keeper's House The building is now a sea museum, with displays on navigation, oceanography, marine biology, and fishing.

First Assistant Keeper's Cottage After restoration and refurnishing, this cottage looks as it did at the turn of the century.

Second Assistant Keeper's Cottage The original Ponce Inlet Lighthouse lens is housed here, along with other lighthouse artifacts. There are also exhibits on the history of Ponce Inlet.

5 Lighthouse Landing ★$$ At this charmingly rustic spot full of nautical memorabilia—a Spanish cannon, a pirate flag, sharks' jawbones—visitors can dine indoors on fresh mahimahi or farm-raised catfish, or eat shucked oysters outside under a spreading water oak (although the fare is not outstanding). Inside or out, you'll enjoy a sweeping view of the Halifax River and maybe see fisherfolk casting their nets at the water's edge. The bar is constructed from an old 35-foot boat, and another boat on the deck contains seating for diners. ♦ Seafood ♦ Daily lunch and dinner; closed January. 4940 S Peninsula Dr (at Sailfish Ave). 761.9271

6 Down the Hatch ★★$$ On a tree-shaded residential street at the end of the peninsula sits this rustic fishing-camp getaway. The chowder is terrific; follow it with fresh seafood or a steak and a cold drink while you take in the river view. If it's a scorching day, you can dine at big wooden tables indoors (where it's air-conditioned). But the ideal way to enjoy this scenic outpost is outside at a ceramic-tiled table, chasing raw oysters with a cold brew. ♦ Seafood ♦ Daily lunch and dinner. 4894 Front St (just north of Beach St). 761.4831

7 Oceandocks ★$$ Formerly **Brewster's,** this joint marks the spot where race-car drivers made a big turn in the days when all car racing took place on the beach. The big deck, part of which is enclosed with sliding glass doors, draws a lively, casual crowd. Live popular music jazzes things up on weekends, and the kitchen puts out good seafood and sandwiches. The view alone is worth a visit. ♦ Seafood ♦ M, W-Su lunch and dinner. 4511 S Atlantic Ave (between Cindy La and Seahaven Dr). 322.3258

Nearly 40,000 Native Americans live on reservations in Florida.

The St. Johns River in northeast Florida is the largest river in the state. It is one of the few rivers in the world that flows north.

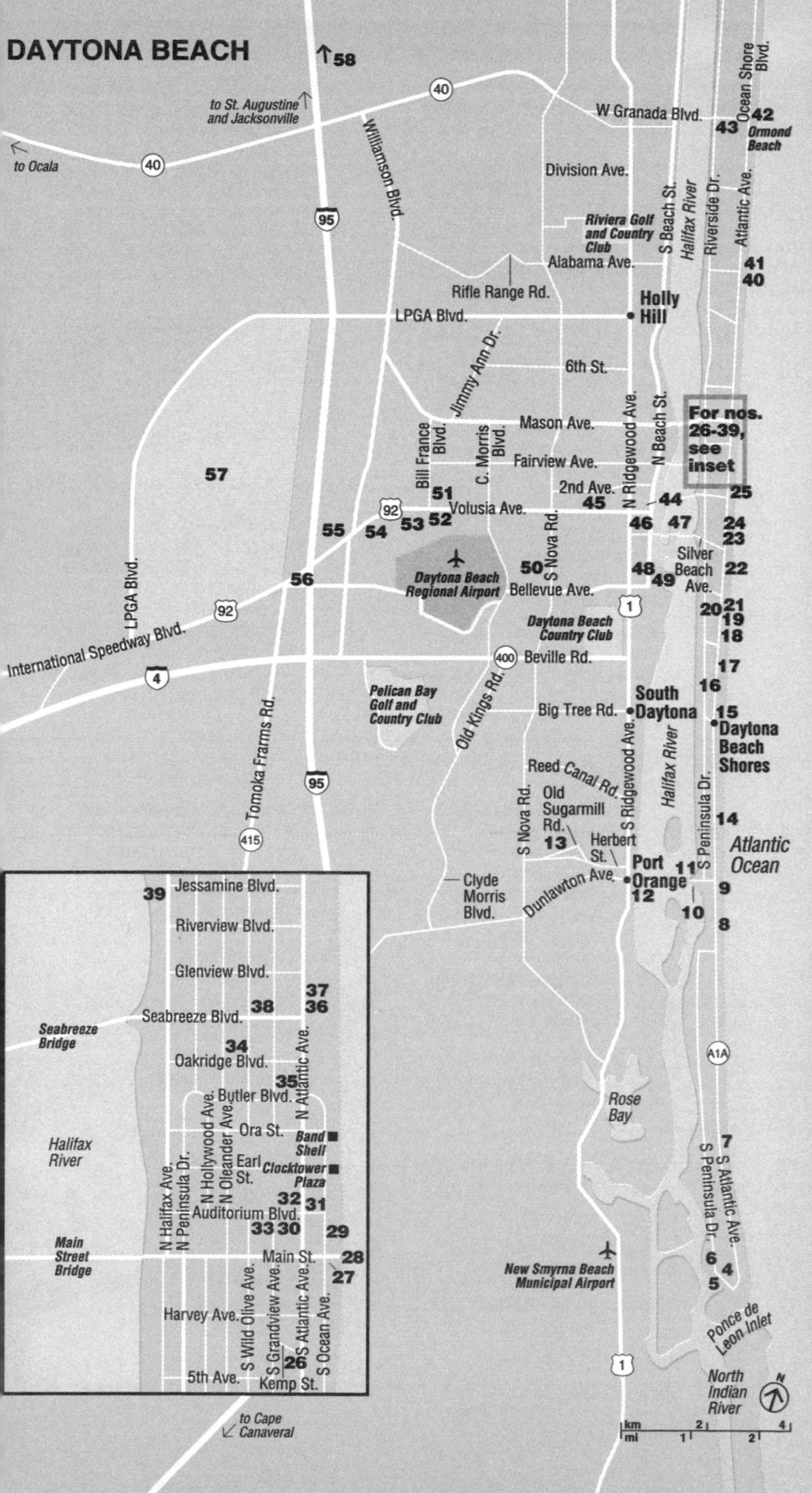

Daytona Beach Shores and Port Orange

Daytona Beach Shores officially begins near **Silver Beach Avenue** and extends south of **Dunlawton Boulevard**, but in reality the transition from **Daytona Beach** to Daytona Beach Shores is imperceptible. This section of the barrier island includes many waterfront condo developments and a beautiful stretch of sand that tends to be far less crowded than its neighbors to the north.

Across from Daytona Beach Shores on the mainland is the community of Port Orange. **Dunlawton Bridge** crosses the **Halifax River** and links the two towns; in these parts, "down under" refers to restaurants and other structures literally under this bridge.

8 **Royal Holiday Beach Motel** $ It's a basic 30-room motel, but it offers just about everything you need: efficiency units, suites, air-conditioning, color TV, wall-to-wall carpet, and a pool with an ocean view. The only thing missing is a restaurant. ♦ 3717 S Atlantic Ave (between Emilia and Phyllis Aves), Daytona Beach Shores. 761.5984

8 **Beach Quarters Resort** $$$ This five-story, 26-suite inn comes complete with a yellow clapboard exterior, white bedspreads, and oak furniture. Each suite has a living room with a queen-size sofa bed, a bedroom with two double beds or one queen-size bed, and a full kitchen with dishwasher and coffeemaker. Wicker rocking chairs beckon from the private balconies. **The Galley**, the inn's coffee shop, serves fresh baked goods and overlooks the heated swimming pool and the beach beyond. ♦ 3711 S Atlantic Ave (between Emilia and Phyllis Aves), Daytona Beach Shores. 767.3119, 800/332.3119; fax 767.0883

9 **Howard Johnson Pirate's Cove Hotel** $$ This beachfront hotel offers 121 rooms and efficiencies, each with a private balcony. Its heated pool, by the ocean, is ringed by a pleasant deck. The **Ocean Terrace Restaurant** serves breakfast, lunch, and dinner, while **Rum Runner's** offers drinks and live entertainment. ♦ 3501 S Atlantic Ave (at Dunlawton Blvd), Daytona Beach Shores. 767.8740, 800/233.2683 in Canada, 800/272.2683; fax 788.8609

Child's Play

Though Florida is known as the Sunshine State, it gets a considerable amount of rain—especially in June, July, and August, when afternoon showers occur almost daily. The rain is good for the lush, green vegetation, but it can be a drag when you've planned an outdoor adventure with the kids. In many cases, the precipitation lasts only a short time, so most of Central Florida's theme parks just carry on as usual. But on days when the weather's too wet for outdoor fun, here are a few suggestions that will keep children from getting restless.

Buckle yourself in a motion simulator and ride a roller coaster of your own design at **DisneyQuest**, a five-story entertainment center at **Downtown Disney West Side**.

Blow bubbles big enough to step in at the interactive **WonderWorks** attraction at **Pointe★Orlando** on **International Drive**.

Hop aboard a **St. Augustine Sightseeing Trains** trolley for a narrated trip around the city.

Use a computer to design and then test your own stock car at the interactive **Daytona USA** at the **Daytona International Speedway**.

Watch a movie about space exploration on one of the huge IMAX screens at the **Kennedy Space Center Visitor Complex**.

Step into the winds of a 74-mph hurricane in **Tampa's Museum of Science and Industry**, the largest science center in the Southeast.

Check out the latest blockbuster exhibition at the **Florida International Museum** in Tampa.

Get a dazzling view of the ocean 60 feet under at the Florida Coral Reefs exhibit at the **Florida Aquarium** in Tampa.

Board a full-scale space shuttle orbiter and take an interactive trip at the **US Astronaut Hall of Fame** near the **Kennedy Space Center**.

Observe moons, planets, and other astronomical events at evening sky watches at the **Orlando Science Center**.

10 Sinbad's Restaurant & Lounge ★$$
Beneath the bridge to Port Orange, right on the Halifax River, sits this "down under" restaurant. The specialty is seafood (don't pass up the deep-fried shrimp), but steak and prime rib also are served. When the weather is nice, dine on the deck that wraps around the restaurant and overlooks the water. The interior, which (not surprisingly) has a nautical decor, affords a beautiful view of the waterway too, and there's a large bar/lounge opening onto the deck with additional seating. Repeat visitors come to catch a glimpse of the dolphins that cavort nearby; occasionally a manatee is sighted. ♦ American ♦ Daily breakfast, lunch, and dinner. 78 Dunlawton Blvd (west of S Peninsula Dr), Port Orange. 756.2921

11 JC's Oyster Deck ★$$ Another "down under" restaurant, this modest spot is well known among locals as a great place to stop after a day at the beach. Raw or steamed oysters, clams, shrimp, and crab legs are available by the pound or by the bucket. Beer, burgers, and seafood sandwiches are served up, too. ♦ Seafood ♦ Daily lunch and dinner. 79 Dunlawton Blvd (west of S Peninsula Dr), Port Orange. 767.1881

12 Aunt Catfish's ★★$$ This blue and gray wood-frame riverside eatery is rambling and rustic, and the cooking is down-home and hearty, with catfish prepared just about every way you can imagine. Try the Florida Cracker Sampler, a platter with a crab cake, a whole catfish, fried shrimp, and a roasted chicken quarter. The flounder is also excellent. Sunday brunch is the talk of the town; flapjacks stuffed with blueberries, strawberries, and more come flying hot off an iron stove. Meals are served on the open-air deck and in the air-conditioned, glass-enclosed dining room. Arrive early to avoid lines. ♦ Seafood ♦ M-Sa lunch and dinner, Su brunch and dinner. Halifax Dr and Dunlawton Ave, Port Orange. 767.4768

Sugar Mill
BOTANICAL GARDENS

13 Sugar Mill Gardens Said to be the best-preserved sugar mill in the country, it sits in a 12-acre Volusia County park surrounded by oak, holly, and magnolia trees and, oddly enough, statues of dinosaurs. Back in 1946, when recent dinosaur discoveries had made the prehistoric beasts something of a national craze, two local businessmen decided to open a theme park here featuring life-size (and remarkably lifelike) dinosaur statues. The park—called "Bongoland" for its other star attraction, a talented trained baboon named Bongo—was a financial disaster, and the owners eventually turned it over to the county. The people from the **Botanical Gardens of Volusia,** who now care for the gardens, never removed the dinosaurs, so look for them as you walk down the shady paths. (One, a giant ground sloth, was added only a few years ago, presumably to represent at least one prehistoric animal that was actually known to have inhabited this area.)

Besides the flora and fauna, visitors can see the sugar mill building, vats, and machinery. The first sugar mill here was established by Patrick Dean, who was granted 995 acres by the Spanish government in 1804. (Florida didn't become part of the US until 1820.) The plantation changed hands twice beforeit was burned down in 1836 during the Second Seminole War. It was rebuilt in 1846 by John Marshall, who converted the refining process to steam. During the Civil War the Confederates used the big vats on the grounds to make salt from seawater. The gardens are open daily, but there aren't always people here to explain what you're seeing. A brochure helps, but it's a good idea to call beforehand if you want a guide. ♦ Donation. Daily. 950 Old Sugar Mill Rd (between Herbert St and Bird Dr), Port Orange. 767.1735

14 Landmark Hotel by the Sea $$ Each of the 115 rooms in this L-shaped, eight-floor motel has a balcony. A large sundeck surrounds a pool with stairs leading down to the beach, and there's a restaurant, lounge, gameroom, and gift shop. ♦ 3135 S Atlantic Ave (between Atares and Van Aves), Daytona Beach Shores. 767.8533, 800/822.7707; fax 788.1609

New Smyrna Beach, south of Daytona Beach, occupies a notable place in history as the site of the largest single attempt at colonial settlement in what is now the United States. Dr. Andrew Turnbull, a Scottish physician and entrepreneur, obtained a grant of land from the British Crown in 1768 and established a colony of 1,255 immigrants on a coastal plantation, where he began commercial production of corn, indigo, rice, hemp, and cotton. The colonial experiment lasted until 1777, when the colonists, plagued by disease and dissension, fled to St. Augustine.

15 Daytona Beach Hilton Oceanfront $$
This 214-room hotel still gets the nod as the best on the beach and it's even better after a $2 million renovation. The lobby now boasts a living room ambience and historical Florida cottage decor, with terra-cotta tile floors, whitewashed wood paneling, wicker chairs, gingerbread-style wooden trim, and bright colors everywhere. The **Blue Water Grille** also has an early Florida cottage theme, with more wicker and terra-cotta, French doors that open to reveal a view of the ocean, and a large outdoor eating area. The hotel boasts room service, refrigerators in each room, a beachside pool, an exercise room, nonsmoking rooms, and suites. ◆ 2637 S Atlantic Ave (between Richards La and Florida Shores Blvd), Daytona Beach Shores. 767.7350, 800/525.7350; fax 760.3651; www.hilton.com

16 Big Kahuna One of many surf shops that dot Atlantic Avenue, this two-story bright aqua and yellow store has a tropical grotto inside. It sells everything necessary for a day at the beach—from bikinis to baggy surfer shorts. ◆ Daily. 2540 S Atlantic Ave (at Sea Spray St), Daytona Beach Shores. 322.1143. Also at: 2739 N Atlantic Ave (north of Plaza Blvd), Daytona Beach. 677.6388; fax 677.8027

17 Sun Viking Lodge $$ Modest rates and a location on the beach are the biggest attractions at this 91-room lodging place, although an indoor heated pool keeps water enthusiasts happy even when it's raining outside. There's also an outdoor pool with a twisting, 60-foot water slide, plus basketball, shuffleboard, and volleyball courts. Room amenities include remote-controlled TV and kitchens with microwave ovens. The **Viking Kafe** is on-site. ◆ 2411 S Atlantic Ave (between Cheshire and Minerva Rds), Daytona Beach Shores. 252.6252, 800/874.4469; fax 252.5463; www.sunviking.com &

18 Best Western Aku Tiki Inn $$ Each of the 132 rooms and efficiency units has an ocean view and a private patio or balcony. There's also a large pool that overlooks the ocean, as well as a lounge and pool bar. **Trader's Restaurant** is open for breakfast, lunch, and dinner. ◆ 2225 S Atlantic Ave (between Minerva Rd and Browning Ave), Daytona Beach Shores. 252.9631, 800/258.8454; fax 252.1198; www.bestwestern.com

Florida: The Nation's Lightning Rod

Thanks to the regular pattern of thunderstorm activity, Florida is one of the lightning capitals of the world. Each year, an average of 10 people are killed and another 3 dozen are injured. Most fatalities occur at beaches or on golf courses. A towering thunderhead is a giveaway that a storm is in the vicinity.

(Remember that the storm needn't be right over you for lightning to be a threat; you should take precautions if you even suspect that a storm is in the area.)

The Hiker's Guide to Florida (Falcon Press; 1993) suggests taking the following steps in the event of a thunderstorm:

• Stay away from the beach or any type of water.

• Avoid tall trees in open fields, trees at the water's edge, or trees whose roots are in damp soil.

• Don't use oaks and pines for shelter; these trees are among the best natural lightning conductors because of their high starch content.

• Stay away from wire fences or any pieces of metal that could conduct lightning to you.

• A tingling sensation in your scalp is a warning that a bolt may be about to strike; quickly fall to the ground.

• July and August tend to be the peak lightning months, but lots of thunderstorms occur in June and September, too.

• If someone has been hit by lightning and is not breathing, administer cardiopulmonary resuscitation (CPR). However, leave the victim alone if he or she is still breathing. Note that being struck by lightning may cause a temporary loss of sight or hearing.

18 Perry's Ocean Edge $$ This is one of the few hotels in Central Florida that has an "indoor solarium"—a pool and spa topped with a retractable glass roof. In addition, there are two outdoor pools, as well as a putting green and a shuffleboard court. All of the 204 rooms face the ocean. Mornings begin with complimentary doughnuts and coffee, and the **Smokehouse** restaurant serves breakfast and lunch daily. ♦ 2209 S Atlantic Ave (between Minerva Rd and Browning Ave), Daytona Beach Shores. 255.0581, 800/342.0102 in FL, 800/447.0002; fax 258.7315; www.perrysoceanedge.com ♿

19 El Caribe Resort and Conference Center $$ The older rooms here continue to draw guests who return year after year, while the newer tower offers huge suites suitable for family groups. Many of the suites are loaded with amenities, including Jacuzzis, wraparound balconies, and full kitchens; some standard rooms also are equipped with kitchens. If you're in a romantic mood, ask for suite **1710** on the tower's top floor, which features a view of the ocean and the river, and a Jacuzzi beneath a skylight in the bathroom. There are two pools, plus a children's pool, but no restaurant or lounge. You can't miss this 154-room motel from the highway—look for the neon balloons on the exterior. ♦ 2125 S Atlantic Ave (between Minerva Rd and Browning Ave), Daytona Beach Shores. 252.1558, 800/445.9889; fax 254.1940; www.elcaribe.com

Within El Caribe Resort and Conference Center:

Third World Gift Shop Clothing, jewelry, and handicrafts from artisans of 30 nations can be found in this shop. ♦ Daily. 252.1558

20 Atlantic Red Snapper Restaurant and Lounge ★★$$ This traditional seafood restaurant has been around for 40 years, and it's the kind of place you go for fresh seafood, not for the ambience. The locals head here for the friendly service and the pan-fried red snapper, just one of the specialties. There are also New England clams, shrimp, scallops, Maine lobster, and steaks for landlubbers. Early birds save a couple of dollars on their entrées and get a free dessert between 4 and 6PM. ♦ Seafood ♦ Daily dinner. 2058 S Atlantic Ave (between Browning Ave and Sunrise Blvd), Daytona Beach Shores. 254.3130

21 Treasure Island Inn $$ This high-rise 236-room beachfront hotel offers plenty of goodies: ocean views from every room, in-

room refrigerators, two pools plus a children's pool, two whirlpools, a restaurant, a lounge, and a poolside bar. The lounge, **Hook's Landing,** features live entertainment. ♦ 2025 S Atlantic Ave (between Sunrise Blvd and Botefuhr Ave), Daytona Beach Shores. 255.8371, 800/874.7420, 800/543.5070; fax 255.4984; www.daytonahotels.com ♿

21 Bahama House $$ Among the newest hostelries on the beach, this property has 85 units done up island-style, with white rattan and bamboo furniture, tropical-print fabrics, and deep green carpeting. Each unit has a fully equipped kitchen (with a microwave oven, coffeemaker, and other full-size appliances), a Jacuzzi bathtub, and ceiling fans. A pool and whirlpool overlook the ocean. There's no restaurant, but continental breakfast and evening cocktails are included in the rate. There's also underground parking. ♦ 2001 S Atlantic Ave (at Botefuhr Ave), Daytona Beach Shores. 248.2001, 800/874.7420; fax 248.0991; www.daytonahotels.com ♿

Daytona Beach

The beach part of the city of Daytona Beach is a section of barrier island separated from the mainland by the **Halifax River.** However, the mainland part of town, directly across the river from the beach, is also called Daytona Beach—unlike Miami and Miami Beach, no distinction is made between the mainland and shore here. Locals have simplified (confused?) the situation further by calling the whole area—both mainland and beach—just plain Daytona. Whatever you call it, the sandy section of the city is where the action is.

22 Nautilus Inn $$$ Each of the large, pastel rooms in this 10-story building has a private balcony, a view of the ocean, a refrigerator, and a microwave oven. The upper floors offer terrific panoramas through floor-to-ceiling windows, and some of the units have kitchenettes. A complimentary continental breakfast buffet and evening cocktails are served in a spacious room overlooking the beach. Between the beach and the hotel are a pool and whirlpool; there are also shuffleboard courts. ♦ 1515 S Atlantic Ave (south of Silver Beach Ave). 254.8600, 800/245.2560

Restaurants/Clubs: Red	**Hotels:** Blue
Shops/ Outdoors: Green	**Sights/Culture:** Black

23 The Ocean Jewels Club $$ A little over a mile south of the Boardwalk, this condominium and hotel has 104 rooms for rent, most with private balconies. Efficiencies are also available. There's a huge pool deck with a bar, casual deli, and lounge. ♦ 935 S Atlantic Ave (between Silver Beach and Lenox Aves). 252.2581, 800/874.0136; www.oceanjewelsresort.com

24 Howard Johnson Plaza–Harbour Beach Resort $$ Formerly the **South Beach Resort,** this eight-story property has been completely revamped and is now one of the area's plusher beachfront lodging places. There are 115 studio efficiencies and suites, all with kitchens (some have microwaves instead of conventional ovens). There's an Olympic-size pool surrounded by a deck with a bar and lush tropical landscaping, as well as a restaurant, a Jacuzzi, a fitness center, and—for those who can't seem to get away from it all—a business center complete with computers and fax machines. The **Club Floor** offers added amenities such as complimentary continental breakfast. Children under 12 occupying the same room as their parents stay free. ♦ 701 S Atlantic Ave (at Revilo Blvd). 258.8522, 800/633.7010; fax 257.9122; www.hojo.com

25 Checkers Cafe & Club ★$ This casual nightclub and restaurant with a circular bar features a lively karaoke scene every night. Patrons take to the dance floor while a DJ spins oldies from a booth built into an actual 1959 Edsel. The menu offers standard favorites like barbecued ribs, fried chicken, steaks, and sandwiches. ♦ American ♦ Daily breakfast, lunch, and dinner; drinks and a bar menu available until 3AM. 219 S Atlantic Ave (between Broadway and S Ocean Ave). 239.0010

26 Streamline Hotel $ You can't miss this bright pink building, which resembles a ship. Amenities are few in the hotel's 49 rooms, but it's just a few blocks from the **Boardwalk.** ♦ 140 S Atlantic Ave (at Kemp St). 258.6937

27 Pit Stop $ This two-story wooden bar and restaurant opens onto the beach. There are a handful of tables where patrons can order standard fare like hamburgers and chicken wings. Entertainment is provided by the six pool tables and several TV sets that usually air highlights from memorable auto races. On weekend nights, there's live music, most often rock 'n' roll. ♦ American ♦ Daily lunch and dinner. 1114 Main St (east of S Ocean Ave). 258.8737

The Indians in the Caribbean used to call Florida "Bimini."

28 Main Street Pier Stretching a thousand feet out into the Atlantic from the end of Main Street, the pier is a good place to fish (although you do need a little luck).

On Main Street Pier:

Main Street Pier and Restaurant ★$ This blue-and-white frame structure at the end of the pier serves a varied menu—seafood platters, steaks, and sandwiches—in a casual atmosphere. You can eat inside or at one of the picnic tables outside. The bar looks out over the pier, and when the windows are open, it's cooled by ocean breezes. Occasionally there's live music on weekends. And as more of the Daytona Beach shoreline becomes restricted to on-beach driving, the popularity of this pedestrian area continues to grow. ♦ Seafood/Steaks ♦ Daily lunch and dinner. 238.1212

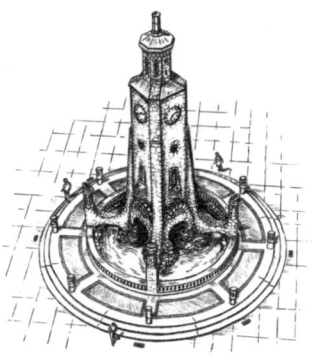

29 Boardwalk Stretching from Main Street to Ora Street, the Boardwalk was a project begun in 1936 by WPA workers and completed in 1938. Originally named the "Broadwalk," it came to be called the Boardwalk, like the popular seaside walkway in Atlantic City, even though there are no boards involved—it's a solid concrete slab. For a time more than a little seedy, the Daytona Beach Boardwalk has cleaned up its act, especially at the northern end. Though the south end retains some of its original flavor, with bars and amusement park rides, the "uptown" section near the **Adam's Mark Daytona Beach Resort** (formerly the **Marriott**) boasts the more upscale **Clocktower Plaza,** with several shops and restaurants. Just past the hotel, at the end of the Boardwalk, sits the 4,500-seat, open-air **Band Shell** (a local landmark since 1937), where free summer concerts are held. Basketball courts are at the rear. Another landmark, the **Clock Tower** (illustrated above), spells out "Daytona Beach" where the numbers should be. Between the coquina-rock **Band Shell** and the hotel is a public bathhouse, where you can change clothes if you want to take a dip. Most everything here opens late in the morning and closes about midnight. ♦ N Ocean Ave (between Main and Ora Sts) ♿

On the Boardwalk:

Space Needle A revolving ride to the top of the needle gives passengers a panoramic view of Daytona Beach. ♦ Admission. Daily

Gondola Though a far cry from the gondolas that ply the Grand Canal in Venice, this ride takes passengers out over the ocean waves and back again. ♦ Admission. Daily

Capt. Darrell's Oyster Bar $ Kids and the young at heart will love this place, where you can take a spin in a go-kart around a track on the roof. The menu offers all manner of steamed and fried seafood and raw oysters and clams. There are also such staples as hamburgers and Buffalo chicken wings. ♦ Seafood ♦ Daily lunch and dinner Feb-Aug; closed Tuesdays Sept-Jan. 255.5822

Bernkastel Festhaus Bavarian Pub ★ $$ The best of the **Clocktower Plaza** restaurants, it serves snacks, salads, and sandwiches, along with imported beer and wine. Try the Danish Delight, a turkey-and-cheese sandwich served warm on a croissant with havarti cheese. ♦ German ♦ Daily lunch and dinner. 255.8300

30 **Hog Heaven** $$ A great location—across the street from the **Ocean Center** and the Boardwalk, and three blocks from the **Peabody Auditorium**—but this casual eatery falls short of its claim of having the "World's Best Barbecue." Nevertheless, the barbecue sandwiches make a tasty lunch, and the ribs draw a dinner crowd. A standard breakfast is served during the high season. ♦ American ♦ Daily breakfast, lunch, and dinner. 37 N Atlantic Ave (at Auditorium Blvd). 257.1212

adam's mark®
daytona beach resort

31 **Adam's Mark Daytona Beach Resort** $$$ Right on the beach across from the **Ocean Center,** this sleek, 17-story pink hotel (formerly the **Marriott Daytona Beach**) boasts 402 rooms with ocean views. The split-level decks are great for soaking up sun, eating grilled sandwiches at the **Splash Bar and Grill,** or watching people parade down the beach. You can swim from the indoor part of the heated pool—which begins in a rock grotto—into the sunlight outdoors. The **Clocktower Restaurant** specializes in fresh fish served baked, poached, grilled, broiled, or Cajun-style; or grab a quick bite at the **Seaside Pavilion,** a cafeteria-style restaurant. After dark, guests can linger over drinks at the **Clocktower Lounge,** a piano bar that

overlooks the beach. The hotel has a concierge level and 25 suites. ♦ 100 N Atlantic Ave (at Auditorium Blvd). 254.8200, 800/872.9269; fax 253.8841; www.adamsmark.com

32 **Ocean Center** Conventions, sporting events, trade shows, and performances of all kinds take place in this busy center. It accommodates 9,500 for concerts and 8,400 for sporting events. ♦ 101 N Atlantic Ave (at Auditorium Blvd). Schedules and tickets 254.4545, convention information 254.4500, 800/858.6444

33 **Peabody Auditorium** Many people would rather attend a concert here than at the larger **Ocean Center.** The 2,560-seat auditorium plays host to the **Daytona Beach Symphony,** the civic ballet, and Concert Showcase, a series of concerts and Broadway performances. The **London Symphony Orchestra** returns every other year, a longtime tradition. ♦ Box office M-F. 600 Auditorium Blvd (at N Wild Olive Ave). 255.1314

34 **Seabreeze United Church** One of the most beautiful buildings in the area (pictured above), this church was known as the **Tourist Church** for years. It was designed by **Harry M. Griffin** in California Mission style in 1930, and although the rock it is built out of is sometimes passed off as coquina, it is actually bog rock that was mined near an area where prehistoric fossils have been discovered. Real coquina is made of limestone, usually mixed with shells and coral; bog rock—also called bog lime—is a soft grayish or whitish calcium carbonate taken from the bottom of freshwater lakes or ponds. It hardens as it dries and is often used as a cover for dirt roads because it won't wash away. The church changes color as the sun plays off the rock at different times of the day. ♦ 501 N Wild Olive Ave (at Oakridge Blvd). 252.6314

35 **Starlite Diner** $ This old-fashioned diner offers hamburgers and sandwiches, as well as a giant grilled-fish sandwich and good chili. You can't miss this one from the road—it has a sleek silver exterior and flashing neon lights. ♦ American ♦ Daily breakfast, lunch, and dinner. 401 N Atlantic Ave (at Butler Blvd). 255.9555

151

36 The Plaza Resort & Spa $$ Located on the beach, this salmon- and teal-colored high-rise offers guests relaxing surroundings featuring lush landscaping amid soothing tropical colors. There are 323 rooms, a full-service restaurant, three lounges, a full-service spa, a heated pool, and one of the largest pool decks along the strip. A gameroom, basketball court, shuffleboard court, and beach volleyball court provide more opportunities for fun and games. The two nightclubs, the **Oceanview Lounge** beach club and the progressive **600 North,** really rock during Spring Break. ♦ 600 N Atlantic Ave (at Seabreeze Blvd). 255.4471, 800/767.4471; fax 253.7543; www.daytonahotels.com &

37 Radisson Resort Daytona Beach $$ Each of the 206 rooms here has a private balcony and an ocean view. The hotel features one of the area's largest pool decks, as well as a restaurant, lounge, and coin-operated laundry. ♦ 640 N Atlantic Ave (between Seabreeze and Glenview Blvds). 258.5435, 800/874.7016; fax 253.0735; www.radisson.com

38 Oyster Pub $ Fans flock here to watch sports on big-screen TVs from little tables around a large horseshoe bar. The raw seafood bar and steak dishes are both popular. ♦ American ♦ Daily lunch and dinner. 555 Seabreeze Blvd (at N Grandview Ave). 255.6348

38 St. Regis Restaurant ★★$$$ Once a private residence—and some say it was a bawdy house—the former **St. Regis Hotel** no longer takes in overnight guests, but it's still an elegant dining spot with a quaint, intimate atmosphere. Simple preparation is the rule here; the favorite dish is the catch of the day. Steak lovers should try the filet mignon au poivre, served with a rich green-peppercorn sauce. ♦ American ♦ Tu-Sa dinner. Reservations recommended. 509 Seabreeze Blvd (between N Grandview and N Wild Olive Aves). 252.8743

THE DAYTONA PLAYHOUSE

39 Daytona Playhouse This 264-seat local theater, set right by the river, stages six shows per season (September through June). The offerings are usually familiar favorites— musicals, comedies, and dramas such as *Oklahoma, Fiddler on the Roof,* and *Arsenic and Old Lace.* ♦ Box office M-F 1-5PM during the season. 100 Jessamine Blvd (just west of N Halifax Ave). 255.2431

40 Best Western La Playa Resort $$ The rooftop lounge here has live entertainment nightly; it's a pleasant place to spend the evening after a day on the beach. The 239-room motel, directly on the beach, has outdoor and indoor pools, a Jacuzzi, an exercise room, and the **Verandah Restaurant,** with a relaxing, gardenlike setting. The motel is located across the street from the **Belair Plaza** shopping center. ♦ 2500 N Atlantic Ave (north of Williams Ave). 672.0990, 800/874.6996; fax 677.0982; www.bestwestern.com &

40 Howard Johnson Oceanfront $$ This sprawling hotel has 143 basic rooms with private balconies facing the ocean, and a pool. There's a member of the **Shoney's** restaurant chain on the premises. ♦ 2560 N Atlantic Ave (north of Williams Ave). 672.1440, 800/792.7309; fax 677.8811; www.daytonahowardjohnson.com &

41 Daytona Beach Resort and Conference Center $$ Two swimming pools overlook the beach at this establishment, which also offers a restaurant, lounge, and gameroom. Each of the 383 balconied rooms has an ocean view—some better than others— as well as the usual amenities, such as cable TV with HBO. Some efficiency units are available. Wednesday through Sunday the hotel offers a Hawaiian luau on the beach. ♦ 2700 N Atlantic Ave (north of Williams Ave). 672.3770, 800/272.6232; fax 673.7262; www.radisson.com

Ormond Beach

Less hectic and gaudy than **Daytona Beach,** Ormond Beach attracts visitors looking for a more subdued place to enjoy the sand and surf. This area traditionally has been a winter getaway for some of the nation's wealthiest vacationers. John D. Rockefeller built a house here, which is now a museum and cultural center.

42 T.G.I. Friday's $ This national chain offers an array of sandwiches and hearty meals in a festive environment. Sitting by a window, you might catch a glimpse of the surf. ♦ American ♦ Daily lunch and dinner. 255 E Granada Blvd (just east of Ocean Shore Blvd). 672.4121

43 The Casements Now a civic and cultural center, the white shingled 1912 mansion (pictured above) was the winter home of John

Rockefeller from 1918 until he died in 1937. Its name is derived from the rows of hinged casement windows that open outward. The first floor is often the site of concerts, art exhibits, and other special events. Upstairs is a Boy Scouts historical exhibit; a display of Hungarian arts, crafts, and historic artifacts; and a room set up the way it was when Rockefeller lived in the house. Across Riverside Drive, sloping toward the Halifax River, are two acres of formal gardens that have been restored to their original design. The building is listed on the National Register of Historic Places. ♦ Donation. M-Th 9AM-9PM; Fri 9AM-5PM; Sa 10AM-noon. Tours M-Th 10AM-2:30PM and by prior arrangement. 25 Riverside Dr (between Willis Dr and E Granada Blvd). 676.3216 ♿

Mainland Daytona Beach

This is the quieter section of the city, but it's not without its attractions. **Beach Street,** with its interesting early–20th-century architecture, is located here, as are several museums and historical homes. This is also the site of the **Daytona International Speedway,** home of the Daytona 500.

44 Downtown Post Office Take a few minutes to drive down Beach Street and marvel at the old buildings. The **Post Office** is particularly impressive—especially if you're a gargoyle fan. This Spanish Renaissance–style WPA project, designed by **Harry M. Griffin** in 1932, has seven gargoyles near its red terra-cotta roof. Step inside to see marble floors and wrought-iron grillwork. ♦ 220 N Beach St (between Bay St and Third Ave)

45 Mary McLeod Bethune Home Located on the **Bethune-Cookman College** campus, this two-story white frame house is where noted American educator Mary McLeod Bethune, daughter of a freed slave, lived for about 50 years until she died in 1955. She is buried next to the house. A strong proponent of education for African-American women and girls, Bethune founded **Daytona Normal and Industrial School for Girls** in 1904. The school merged with Jacksonville's **Cookman Institute for Boys** in 1924. Bethune's home, a National Historic Landmark, was the first Florida historical site commemorating an African-American citizen. The 1914 building is owned by the Mary McLeod Bethune Foundation and is open to visitors. In the front parlor is a display case filled with mementos: medals, an invitation sent by President Harry S. Truman, and a letter from Eleanor Roosevelt, a frequent guest. Bethune's bedroom upstairs is just as it was when she lived there, with her hat and gloves on a small table. The guest room is where Eleanor Roosevelt used to stay. ♦ Admission. M-F 10AM-noon and 1-4PM Jan-May, Sept-Dec; M-F 9-10AM and 1-5PM Jun-Aug. Bethune-

Cookman College, 640 Dr. Mary McLeod Bethune Blvd (between N Martin Luther King Jr. Blvd and N Lincoln St). 255.1401 ext 372

46 Halifax Historical Society and Museum Should you choose to spend a day in town rather than at the beach, be sure to visit this museum, if only to see the interesting architecture and the wood-carved miniature of the **Boardwalk** circa 1938. The building, embellished with an Ionic-pillared entrance, was designed by **W.B. Talley** in 1910 and first served as a **Merchants Bank.** The bank failed in 1929, and after a number of owners, the Halifax Historical Society purchased it in 1984. The two-story structure is built of gray sandstone and smooth cement stucco. There are two stained-glass skylights in the ceiling of the main room, as well as stained-glass windows on the south wall. On the north wall are six large murals depicting local scenes by Florida artist Don J. Emery and his son, Don W. Emery. The museum's exhibits range from 16th-century Spanish artifacts to World War II memorabilia. Several displays cover aspects of Daytona Beach history, including the life and work of Mary McLeod Bethune and the early days of auto racing. There's also a half-hour film presentation on the history of Daytona Beach. ♦ Admission. Tu-Sa 10AM-4PM. 252 S Beach St (between Orange and Magnolia Aves). 255.6976

47 Jackie Robinson Stadium A bronze statue of the first black major league baseball player was erected at the main entrance to this 4,200-capacity baseball stadium, formerly known as **City Island Park.** Robinson, as a member of the **Montreal Royals** (a **Brooklyn Dodgers** minor league team), played in Daytona Beach during a spring training game in 1946. The **Daytona Cubs** still play a regular season here from April through early September, making this the oldest minor-league stadium that's in use. There are no extant records pinpointing just when the stadium was built, but **Negro League** legend Buck O'Neal has said he remembers playing here in the 1930s. ♦ Box office M-F. 105 E Orange Ave (at City Island Pkwy). 257.3172

48 Coquina Inn $ This comfortable bed-and-breakfast inn is in a house designed by **S.H. Grove** in 1912. Each room is furnished with antiques and has a private bath. ♦ 544 S Palmetto Ave (at Cedar St). 254.4969

49 Chart House ★★$$$ A wood-trimmed skylit dining room overlooks the Halifax River. You can't go wrong with one of the tender steaks or the creatively prepared fresh fish. Watch the sunset from the outdoor deck, or top off the evening with an after-dinner drink in the convivial sunken lounge. ♦ American ♦ Daily dinner. 645 S Beach St (between Bellevue Ave and Marina Point Dr). 255.9022

50 Museum of Arts and Sciences Located on the grounds of the **Tuscawilla Nature Preserve,** this interesting juxtaposition of art and science features a planetarium and five galleries with collections ranging from outstanding examples of Cuban folk art to the skeleton of a 130,000-year-old giant ground sloth found only two miles from the museum. The **Cuban Art Gallery** displays works from the museum's permanent Cuban collection, which was brought to Florida by General Fulgencio Batista, the dictator who was overthrown by Fidel Castro. The collection isn't all-encompassing, but it contains some stunning pottery and beautifully detailed mid–19th-century lithographs that chronicle life on Cuba's great sugarcane plantations. Another room houses the museum's **American Art** collection. Notable here is a Duncan Phyfe silver serving set and Chippendale furniture once owned by George Washington. The museum's original wing houses the **Main Gallery** and a **Science Gallery;** exhibits here change every four to eight weeks. In the **Prehistory of Florida Gallery,** visitors can watch a short film about the giant ground sloth before walking through the gallery to see the skeleton of this Pleistocene-era vegetarian, which stood 13 feet tall and weighed more than three tons. Drawers in the gallery contain fossils and Indian artifacts, some for viewing and others for handling—for example, you can try to assemble the bones of a sloth's foot. The 260-seat planetarium offers regularly scheduled programs, including musical laser light shows. In front of the museum lies the **Frischer Public Sculpture Garden,** and in the back is the **Tuscawilla Nature Preserve,** a 60-acre coastal hammock with nature trails designed for short walks. A visit to this museum is more than just a rainy-day diversion—children and adults will be intrigued even on days when the sun is shining. It's a little tricky to find, though, so you may want to call ahead for detailed directions. ♦ Admission. Tu-F 9AM-4PM; Sa-Su noon-5PM; planetarium shows Tu-F 2PM; Sa-Su 1PM and 3PM. 1040 Museum Blvd (at S Seneca Blvd). 255.0285 &

51 Volusia Mall The largest mall in Volusia County is conveniently located near the intersection of two interstates on the main drag into town and across the street from **Daytona Beach Regional Airport.** There are more than 110 stores, including **Structure, Barnie's Coffee & Tea Co., The Disney Store, The Gap, Everything But Water** (great bathing suits), **The Limited, Belk Lindsey, Burdines,**

Dillard's, JCPenney, Gayfer's, and Sears. ♦ Daily. 1700 Volusia Ave (between Clyde Morris and Bill France Blvds). 253.6783

52 Olive Garden ★$$ Part of the national chain of casual Italian eateries, it offers standard Italian fare and especially good salad and breadsticks. If you like the one near your home, you will feel very comfortable here. ♦ Italian ♦ Daily lunch and dinner. 1725 Volusia Ave (at Midway Ave). 252.0621

53 Daytona International Speedway In 1959, car racing moved off the beaches and into this high-banked race track. Fans jam the stands—and the area's streets, beaches, and motels—during Speed Weeks in February, Camel Motorcycle Week in March, and for the Pepsi 400 in July. Speed Weeks begins with the Rolex 24 at Daytona, a 24-hour endurance race on the track's 3.56-mile road course, and concludes two weeks later with the Daytona 500, the country's biggest stock-car racing event (with the largest cash prize). The highlight of Cycle Week is the Daytona 200, which is the final event. The Pepsi 400 marks the halfway point of the **NASCAR** Winston Cup Series and is always held on the first Saturday of July. In addition to these big events, the speedway plays host to a number of other races, including the **World Karting Association's** Enduro World Championships. Tours are offered daily every half hour from 9:30AM to 4PM (weather permitting) except on racing days. The 30-minute narrated tour in a minibus takes you down the stretch, on the apron of a banked curve, and through the pits. A **Visitors' Center** with information on attractions, lodging, and events is on-site. **Daytona USA** is an $18-million interactive museum that offers a vivid presentation of the history of **NASCAR** stock racing, as well as road-, motorcycle-, and go-kart racing. Visitors can watch high-tech film presentations in three theaters, check out state-of-the-art displays, and participate in interactive exhibits (such as one that lets you experience what it's like to be in a pit crew). ♦ Fee for the speedway tour and museum; Visitors' Center free. Speedway daily (except when the track is in use); Visitors' Center daily; museum daily 9AM-7PM, with extended hours during holidays and events. 1801 Volusia Ave (between Midway Ave and Williamson Blvd). 254.2700 Ticket information 253.RACE (253.7223), 800/854.1234; Daytona USA 947.6800 &

54 Daytona Beach Greyhound Racing In the shadow of the **Daytona International Speedway,** this track hosts greyhound dog racing year-round. Buy a program as you enter; it explains the different wagers and list the racing record of each dog. **The Pavilion** restaurant allows visitors to watch and bet on the races while dining; chicken, shrimp, and steak dishes are served (children under six are not allowed in the restaurant). ♦ Nominal admission. Race times M, W, Sa 1PM, 7:45PM; Tu, Th-F 7:45PM. 2201 Volusia Ave (between Midway Ave and Williamson Blvd). 252.6484

55 Holiday Inn Indigo Lakes $$$ Set by a forest and lake off I-95, this resort, formerly the **Indigo Lakes Country Club,** has been downsized and is now a **Holiday Inn** property with opportunities for bicycling, tennis, swimming, and volleyball; there's also a golf course nearby (see below). The 151 rooms are large, and each has a balcony or patio. There is no restaurant on the premises, but four are within walking distance. ♦ 2620 International Speedway Blvd (between I-95 and Williamson Blvd). 258.6333; www.holiday-inn.com ♿

MARK MARTIN'S KLASSIX AUTO ATTRACTION

56 Mark Martin's Klassix Auto Museum A large collection of Corvettes is housed in this museum, which also features more than 40 vintage motorcycles from the early 1900s to the Harley years and beyond. Racing history is covered from the early years of steam and gas, through stock-car beach racing, to today's super-speedway races. There's a gift shop and an ice-cream parlor. ♦ Nominal admission. Daily. 2909 International Speedway Blvd (between Tomoka Farms Rd and I-95). 252.3800

57 LPGA International The centerpiece of this sprawling development, the national headquarters of the **Ladies Professional Golf Association,** is an 18-hole tournament-caliber golf course designed by Rees Jones

specifically for women's championship golf. Jones designed the course from the middle tees, adding the back tees later; the variety of tees allows play from 5,131 yards to 7,080 yards. The practice facilities are superb, with tees at both ends of the driving range, a large practice bunker, and a huge putting green; there's also a three-hole practice course. The annual $1.2-million Sprint Championship, one of the five major events on the **LPGA** tour, was played here for the first time in April of 1995. A second 18-hole golf course, designed by Arthur Hills, opened in the fall of 1998, and at press time a beautiful clubhouse was being built. Also included in future plans are a 985-room Radisson-owned golf resort and an **LPGA Golf Academy and Teaching Complex.** When the new residential and commercial areas around the complex are taken into account, the price tag for the entire development is expected to total a whopping $2 billion. ♦ Expensive greens fees. Open daily year-round. 300 Champions Dr (off LPGA Blvd). 274.6200; fax 257.9866

Palm Coast

Located just off **I-95** almost midway between **Daytona Beach** and St. Augustine, the 42,000-acre Palm Coast resort and residential community is known for its excellent golf courses.

58 Harbor Side Inn Palm Coast Resort $$ Guests here are kept busy with 18 tennis courts (clay, hard, and grass), four distinctly different championship 18-hole golf courses, a private beach club, a fitness center, an 80-slip marina, four swimming pools and two whirlpool spas, and racquetball courts. The four guest lodges have a total of 154 rooms and two-bedroom suites. There are also two restaurants on the premises. ♦ 300 Clubhouse Dr (north of Palm Coast Pkwy). 445.3000, 800/654.6538, 800/325.3535; www.palmcoastresort.com ♿

Daytona International Speedway

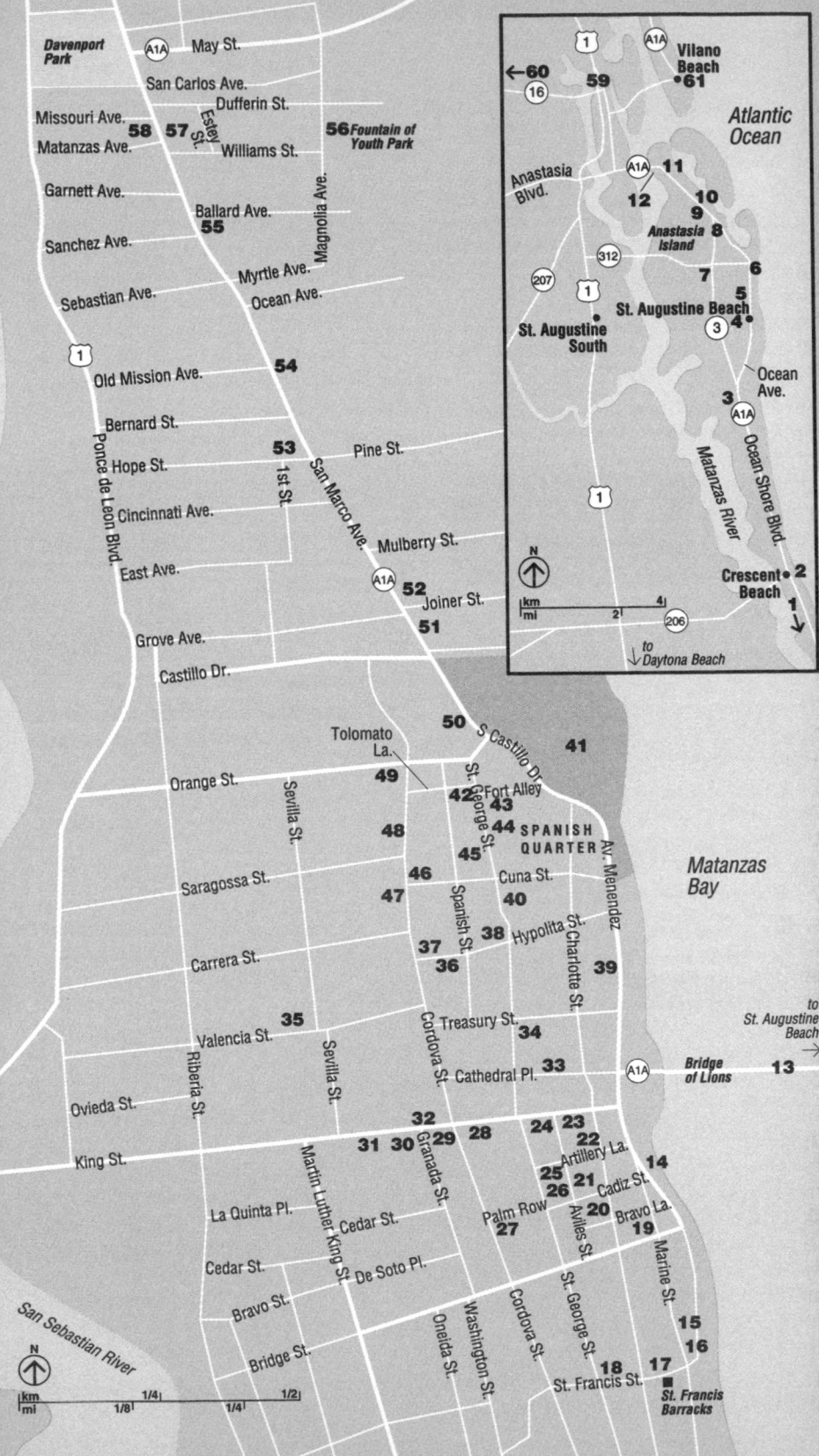

St. Augustine

St. Augustine is Florida's Williamsburg, just as authentic and reaching back even farther in history, to 1565. It's the oldest permanent settlement in what is now the continental United States, founded 42 years before the English colonized Jamestown and 55 years before the pilgrims landed at Plymouth Rock. Like any popular tourist destination, St. Augustine has more than its share of tourist kitsch; a plus here is that it's offset by interesting and varied architecture and enthralling history.

Juan Ponce de León was the first European to discover Florida and St. Augustine. Some historians say he was seeking gold or land he could claim for Spain when he anchored here in 1513. Others insist he was in search of the Fountain of Youth, which medieval legend placed in the Garden of Eden—then thought to be somewhere far to the east of Europe. Whatever his motive, Ponce de León came ashore between St. Augustine and the St. Johns River around Easter and named the new land La Florida, in honor of *Pascua Florida,* Spain's Eastertime Feast of Flowers. He then sailed down the coast.

Several Spaniards explored Florida in the ensuing years. In 1562 King Philip II of Spain decided to abandon the region, but he quickly changed his mind with the arrival of 150 Huguenots led by a French admiral, whose very presence in Florida challenged Spain's New World claims. In 1565, Philip II dispatched Pedro Menéndez and the largest armada of ships and colonists ever sent to Florida to drive the French out. On 4 September, after all the Spanish colonists were ashore, Mass was said and **San Augustin** (St. Augustine) was born.

The king's enforcers then set about attacking the French. In the course of two raids, they executed all captured soldiers who were not Catholic, took over the French Fort Caroline, and expelled the remaining Frenchmen.

Twenty-one years later, in 1586, Sir Francis Drake visited the then thriving Spanish settlement. The Englishman had sailed to the New World to capture Havana, but illness on board forced him to abandon that plan. Instead, his 23 warships and 2,000 men sailed up the coast of Florida and attacked St. Augustine. Drake and his crew eventually withdrew, but not before burning the city to the ground.

The next century didn't get any easier for the beleaguered inhabitants of St. Augustine. Between 1613 and 1617 the plague killed thousands of settlers as well as Native Americans, nearly wiping out the town; in 1640 famine ravaged what was left of the area's population. Ever fearful of attacks by the English and pirates, the Spanish began mining coquina (or shellstone) from a quarry on **Anastasia Island** to build **Castillo de San Marcos**, a fort designed to defend the city. The massive structure still dominates the northern entrance to the harbor from its vantage point on the west bank of the **Matanzas River,** opposite the north end of Anastasia Island.

Centuries later, railroad tycoon Henry Flagler ushered in the modern era and drastically changed St. Augustine's appearance when he brought the railroad to town. After visiting the city in 1883, Flagler was convinced he could transform it into an "American Riviera." By the end of that decade, the city's skyline had been dramatically altered by massive hotels and churches built in the Spanish Renaissance Revival style. **Hotel Alcazar**, now the **Lightner Museum**, is perhaps the most impressive example of the extravagant architectural style. For a time, St. Augustine was one of the favored winter resorts of the rich and famous. But as Flagler extended the railroad south, he transformed other Florida communities, and they soon stole the spotlight.

Today St. Augustine (pop. 105,000) is evolving into an art community, with about 20 galleries representing some 200 local artists. Although there are many quaint bed-and-breakfast inns in the southern end of the city, most hotels are concentrated around the downtown historic district, known as **Old St. Augustine,** and on nearby **St. Augustine Beach.** The historic district is one of the few remaining places in the US—along with New Orleans's French Quarter and, of course, Williamsburg—where visitors can get a true sense of what colonial life was like just by strolling around. The narrow, cobblestone streets are lined with well-preserved buildings from the Spanish era, many of which are now quaint shops and restaurants. There are also several historic monuments to visit, and aficionados of Spanish-style architecture—both the real thing and from the Revival period—will be in seventh heaven. A drive across the **Bridge of Lions** to St. Augustine Beach—the familiar beach resorts, miniature golf courses, and shopping malls—catapults visitors back into the modern world. Also of interest to visitors is the town of **Marineland,** located south of St. Augustine Beach. Its claim to fame was the country's first oceanarium, which opened in 1938 and closed in 1998.

Located just off **Interstate 95** south of Jacksonville, St. Augustine is the perfect antidote to the mechanical thrills of **Walt Disney World** and Florida's other amusement parks, though its historic district does have one thing in common with them: It requires lots of walking. Almost every street beckons, and the best way to navigate them is by foot or bicycle. Or take one of the trams or horse-drawn carriages that depart from in front of the **Castillo de San Marcos.** The point is to explore in a leisurely manner. Avoid driving in town; you'll just end up in a nerve-racking traffic jam.

For more information about St. Augustine and its environs, contact the **St. Augustine Chamber of Commerce** (653.2489, 800/OLD.CITY).

Area code 904 unless otherwise noted.

NATIONAL PARK SERVICE

1 Fort Matanzas The Spanish built this fort between 1740 and 1742 to protect St. Augustine from attack; it's now part of a 298-acre park. The Intracoastal Waterway is called the Matanzas River here because of a bloody incident that took place in 1565 near this spot (*matanza* is Spanish for "slaughter"). Having captured 276 French soldiers, Menéndez de Avilés executed all who were not Catholics—245 in total. A free ferry shuttles visitors out to the fort on Rattlesnake Island in the Matanzas River, and a ranger recounts its history. At the fort, visitors can explore the gun deck, enlisted men's quarters, officers' quarters, and an observation deck. Although it was never conquered, the fort wasn't used

after 1821; a little more than a century later it became a national monument. The park, about 15 miles south of St. Augustine, has rest rooms, hiking trails, and a beach. ◆ Free. Daily. 8635 A1A S (south of Rte 206). 471.0116

2 Beacher's Lodge $ All 132 rooms at this hostelry have a view of the ocean and come equipped with a kitchenette. Other amenities include an oceanfront pool, a private beach, and laundry facilities. ◆ 6970 A1A S, Crescent Beach. 471.8849; 800/527.8849; www.yp.bellsouth.com/beacherslodge

3 Salt Water Cowboys ★★$$ Built out over a saltwater marsh and complete with a wooden deck, tin roof, exposed beams, and planked floors, this rustic restaurant (pictured above) makes you feel as if you've stepped into a fishing camp. Best known for its soft-shell crabs, the place also serves a tasty redfish chowder. But while appetizers such as the Florida Cracker combo sound tempting, the frogs' legs, gator, and turtle are buried beneath too much breading. Enjoy a drink on the deck and watch the birds, fish, and turtles beyond the railing. The restaurant doesn't take reservations, and parking is limited, but the scenery and much of the food are great. At night, outside lights illuminate the nearby marsh. ♦ Seafood ♦ Daily dinner. 299 Dondanville Rd (west of Rte A1A), St. Augustine Beach. 471.2332

4 Comfort Inn $$ Although they answer the phone "Comfort Inn on the Beach," this is not beachfront property. It is, however, clean and comfortable, with 25-inch TVs in every room and a Jacuzzi and a pool on-site. You have to cross busy Route A1A and walk a bit to reach the sandy shore. There's no restaurant on the premises. ♦ 901 A1A (between A and 11th Sts), St. Augustine Beach. 471.1474, 800/221.2222; fax 461.9659; www.hotelchoice.com

4 Days Inn St. Augustine Beach $ This 50-room, Spanish-style motel, with its tropical pink walls and cool green doors and railings, stands out on this strip. If you don't want to cross Ocean Avenue to the beach, you can enjoy the pool and spa. There's no restaurant. ♦ 541 Ocean Ave (at Ninth St), St. Augustine Beach. 461.9990, 800/325.2525; fax 471.4774; www.daysinn.com

5 Sunset Grille ★★$ This popular hangout across the street from the ocean serves steaks, oysters, seafood, omelettes, and French toast rolled in Rice Krispies. Order from the walk-up window and eat at a picnic table or sit in the open-air lounge. There's also an air-conditioned dining room, a big-screen TV, and live entertainment on occasion. Early-bird specials are available. ♦ American ♦ Daily breakfast, lunch, and dinner. 421 Ocean Ave (between 14th and 15th Sts), St. Augustine Beach. 471.5555

6 Howard Johnson Resort Hotel $ The poolside rooms have views of the ocean (only a hundred yards away), and each of the 144 rooms has two double beds. There are also some efficiency units with kitchenettes. A dining room and lounge are on-site as well. ♦ 300 Beach Blvd (at Pope Rd), St. Augustine Beach. 471.2575, 800/752.4037 in FL; fax 471.1247; www.hojo.com ⟁

7 Antonio's Italian Restaurant ★$$ The cheese ravioli and the fettuccine Alfredo are both good at this low-key family place. You might want to finish your meal with a drink on the open porch. ♦ Italian ♦ Daily lunch and dinner. 1915 Rte 3 (at Rte 312), St. Augustine Beach. 471.3835

8 Cross and Sword An outdoor drama about the founding of St. Augustine in 1565, the play has been running since 1965. Written by Pulitzer Prize–winning playwright Paul

Green, it was designated Florida's Official State Play by the state legislature in 1973. It's performed from late July through August each year at the **St. Augustine Amphitheatre.** ♦ Admission. Tu-Su 8:30PM. Rte A1A (between Rte 312 and Anastasia Blvd), St. Augustine. 471.1965 ⟁

9 St. Augustine Alligator Farm In 1893, a pen of alligators was the main attraction at the **Museum of Marine Curiosities,** about a mile south of the St. Augustine lighthouse. The pen became an alligator farm, and as the area deteriorated, the farm was moved to its present location, whose entrance is a whitewashed, Mediterranean-style building with a red-tile roof. The hourly Florida Wildlife Show is entertaining, and visitors are allowed to feed and pet a number of the residents— goats, deer, and farm animals (not the alligators, though). **Land of Crocodiles** is said to be the world's only complete collection of all 22 living species of crocodile, each in its own habitat. The farm claims that Gomek, a giant 17.5-foot saltwater crocodile from New Guinea, is the largest in the Western Hemisphere. There's also a bird rookery, where you might see the endangered wood stork, as well as heron, ibis, and egret. A recently added attraction is the **Emu Exhibit,** housing the large flightless birds from Australia. Visitors also can walk through most of the lushly landscaped park on elevated wooden bridges. A snack bar and gift shop are on the premises. ♦ Admission. Daily. 999 Anastasia Blvd (between Old Quarry Rd and W Carver St), St. Augustine. 824.3337 ⟁

10 Lighthouse Park Restaurant $ Drive under large oak trees to the gray wooden building by the boat ramp. Inside you can sit in the air-conditioned, wood-paneled diner and order something off the grill—swordfish or blackened tuna, for example. Minorcan clam chowder is a specialty. If you're heading out for a day of fishing, bait and tackle are also available. ♦ American ♦ Daily breakfast, lunch, and dinner. 442 Ocean Vista Ave (at Lew Blvd), St. Augustine. 829.8172

The oldest library in Florida is the St. Augustine Free Public Library, opened in 1874.

Florida has favored the Democratic party for most of its history.

Restaurants/Clubs: Red   **Hotels:** Blue

Shops/♈ Outdoors: Green   **Sights/Culture:** Black

10 Lighthouse Museum of St. Augustine The inlet here is so treacherous that its shifting sands were called "crazy banks" by generations of sailors. Most of the time, visitors can pay for the privilege of climbing to the top of this lighthouse, but it's a lot more relaxing to walk through the **Keeper's House,** which is now a museum. The then–lighthouse keeper, his assistant, and their families resided in the two-story coquina-and-brick house from 1875 to 1955. A curving staircase leads down to its basement, where nautical artifacts, including beacons that once shone from the lighthouse, are on display. ♦ Admission for the lighthouse; Keeper's House free. Daily. 81 Lighthouse Ave (between E Carver and White Sts), St. Augustine. 829.0745

11 Gypsy Cab Company ★★★$$ This is the trendiest place in town—on weekends people wait in a line extending out to the street. The Art Deco facade is painted in cheerful tones of lavender, salmon, and turquoise and accented with neon and glass

bricks. The decor of the bustling dining room carries over the theme, with lots of original local art on the walls, black-and-white tile floors in one room, and a mural of taxicabs along one wall. The menu changes daily and draws from such diverse culinary styles as Cajun, French, Greek, and Italian. Perennial favorites include Angus New York strip steak with brandy peppercorn sauce, and Gypsy chicken (chicken breast stuffed with Swiss cheese and herb butter, breaded, baked, and topped with a mushroom sherry sauce). Regulars are known to request personal favorites—if the staff has the ingredients, they'll be happy to whip something up. ♦ Continental ♦ M, W-Sa lunch and dinner; Tu dinner; Su brunch and dinner. 828 Anastasia Blvd (between White St and Comares Ave), St. Augustine. 824.8244

11 Conch House Marina Resort $ Within walking distance of historic Old St. Augustine, this hostelry has been recently renovated and offers cozy rooms, studios, efficiencies, and suites, all decorated with driftwood and shell crafts. There's a pool and a 96-slip marina where guests can charter fishing or pleasure cruises. But the main attractions here are the hotel's restaurants and bars, fun places with good food. Dine indoors on fresh seafood, steaks, or pasta in the **Captain's Room,** with its romantic, secluded tables overlooking Salt Run. Or opt for one of the unique, private "pods," outdoor thatch gazebos set on pilings high above the water and connected by walkways to the main deck of the restaurant. The **Conch House Lounge,** an octagonal, cypress shanty on pilings at the end of the pier, has brass doors that are said to be from the **Hotel Alcazar,** now the **Lightner Museum.** The view from the **Crow's Nest,** up a spiral staircase, is great. A party barge tethered to the pier below serves grilled food and hosts a reggae band every Sunday afternoon and evening; there's a separate sports bar just across the deck from the lounge. ♦ 57 Comares Ave (between Anastasia Blvd and Inlet Dr), St. Augustine. 829.8646, 800/940.6256; fax 829.5414; www.conch-house.com ら

12 Anchorage Motor Inn $ Many visitors prefer to stay in a bed-and-breakfast inn or on the beach, but this blue-and-white motel is a good bet. It's at the east end of the Bridge of Lions, right on the Matanzas River. There are 38 rooms; ground-floor units have patios, and upstairs rooms have balconies with an outstanding view. A fishing pier and a pool are on the property. Although there's no restaurant on-site, there are plenty of good choices nearby. ♦ 1 Dolphin Dr (at Anastasia Blvd), St. Augustine. 829.9041

13 Bridge of Lions Designed and built in 1926 by Baltimore contractor **J.E. Greiner,** this drawbridge complements the Spanish Renaissance Revival architecture in Old St. Augustine. Four towers with tile roofs flank the span. The two marble lions on the city side of the bridge were gifts from Dr. Andrew Anderson, a local physician. The current bridge replaced a wooden structure that connected St. Augustine with Anastasia Island from 1895 to 1925.

14 Scenic Cruise Members of the Usina family have been taking tourists for historical cruises

on Matanzas Bay since the early 1900s. *Victory II,* a double-decker paddlewheel boat built in 1917 that was once a passenger ferry, is now strictly for sightseeing; both its decks are covered. *Victory III,* purchased a few years ago, has an open upper deck and an enclosed lower deck. Tours take about an hour and 15 minutes. Both vessels have refreshment stands and rest rooms aboard. ♦ Fee. Daily; call for departure times. City Yacht Pier, Av Menendez (south of King St), Old St. Augustine. 824.1806

15 Villas de Marin $ You get more than just a room here. All 16 units have sitting areas and kitchenettes (some large enough to eat in). All of the villas in this two-story, wooden-frame building have views of the Matanzas River, and some retain original features, including coquina walls, window seats, high ceilings, and porches. There's no restaurant, but the management offers discount vouchers good for breakfast at a nearby cafe. ♦ 142 Av Menendez (between St. Francis and Bridge Sts), Old St. Augustine. 829.1725

16 Westcott House $$ Because it offers some of the nicest rooms in St. Augustine, along with a great location for exploring the city, this bed-and-breakfast (pictured above) must be booked far in advance for weekend and holiday stays. Its nine rooms are warm and welcoming, with high-quality linens and beautiful furniture. All have private baths, and some have working fireplaces. Numbers **204** and **205** have a private stairway entrance. The charming attic room has a king-size bed and a full bath, but it's a steep climb. A continental breakfast is served in your room, on a side porch, or in a courtyard. Matanzas Bay is visible from the front and side porches. ♦ 146 Av Menendez (between St. Francis and Bridge Sts), Old St. Augustine. 824.4301, 800/513-9814; www.westcotthouse.com

17 Oldest House Take the time for a tour of this house, considered by many to be the oldest structure built by settlers in the New World. The house illustrates much of the city's history, showing both Spanish and British influences. The first structure on the site, a thatch-roofed wooden cottage built circa 1650, was replaced by the present

coquina stone building soon after the English burned St. Augustine to the ground in 1702. Tomas Gonzales y Hernandez, an artilleryman at **Castillo de San Marcos** (the fort), first lived here with his family. After Gonzales left, a British major named Peavetz and his wife purchased the house and added a second floor, turning the ground floor into a tavern, a shrewd move since there was (and still is) a barracks across the street. Maria Peavetz was widowed, then remarried, and lost the house when her young Irish husband was imprisoned in 1790 for gambling debts. The grounds are beautiful for picnicking. ♦ Admission. Daily. 14 St. Francis St (between Marine and Charlotte Sts). 824.2872 &

St. Francis Inn

18 St. Francis Inn $ A homey (but not luxurious) atmosphere is the hallmark of this 200-year-old, 14-room bed-and-breakfast establishment. Some rooms have kitchenettes, others have fireplaces, and there's a separate cottage that can accommodate up to two couples. The two-bedroom suite has a double-size bed for adults and twin-size beds for kids. All rooms have private baths, though the baths for the two lower-priced rooms (albeit private) are down the hall. The small parlor is complete with a piano. Breakfast includes fresh fruits, bagels, and a variety of pastries; the inn has a pool and provides bicycles for the use of guests. ♦ 279 St. George St (at St. Francis St), Old St. Augustine. 824.6068, 800/824.6062; www.stfrancisinn.com

19 Kenwood Inn $ Guests know they have made a wise choice when they step into the spacious and immaculately kept common rooms of this inn (pictured above). The guest quarters are also large and comfortable; the **Old English Room** has a king-size bed and a working fireplace, and all rooms have private baths. There are 14 units in total, including two suites—one with a view of the water. Period furnishings are found throughout without seeming cutesy or overdone. The pool is set in the walled-in courtyard, a nice place to relax with a good book. Innkeepers Mark, Kerianne, and Caitlin Constant serve a continental breakfast that includes homemade breads and cakes. ♦ 38 Marine St (between Bridge St and Bravo La), Old St. Augustine. 824.2116; fax 824.1689; www.oldcity.com/kenwood

20 Victorian House $ This charming bed-and-breakfast has four rooms in a two-story, yellow-frame house dating from 1890. There are also four suites in an adjoining building. The room most in demand has a queen-size canopy bed with carved posts, but all rooms are decorated in country Victorian style, with such welcome touches as handmade quilts and antique furniture. Continental breakfast is included in the rate and served daily in a main dining room; occasionally the inn offers a full breakfast on Sunday. ♦ 11 Cadiz St (between Charlotte and Aviles Sts), Old St. Augustine. 824.5214

21 Casa de Solana $$ One of the oldest houses in Florida, the **Don Manuel Solana House** was constructed in 1763. Each of its four rooms is actually a suite. Some boast fireplaces and others have balconies overlooking a lush garden; all have private baths with tub and shower. Innkeeper Faye McMurry serves a full breakfast and the inn is within walking distance of Old St. Augustine. ♦ 21 Aviles St (at Cadiz St), Old St. Augustine. 824.3555; www.oldcity.com/solana

22 Denoël French Pastry ★★★$ A real find, this eatery, in a historical house with European decor, serves light and wonderful lunch items from late morning to early evening. Order the juicy shrimp salad on a buttery croissant. The desserts, especially the dense cheesecake and the flaky chocolate éclairs, attract crowds, and the blueberry tortes are the best in town. It's a rare customer who leaves without a box of goodies to take along. ♦ French ♦ M, W-Su lunch (10AM-5PM). 212 Charlotte St (between Artillery La and King St), Old St. Augustine. 829.3974

COURTESY OF
HISTORIC ST. AUGUSTINE PRESERVATION BOARD

23 Spanish Military Hospital Enter through the side door, where a plaque explains that the hospital (pictured above) was originally a stable. When the English took over, William Watson converted the stables into a

residence, and when the Spanish returned in 1784, they turned the building into a hospital and pharmacy. Visitors can tour the apothecary to look at old instruments, the administrative office to see how the records were kept, and the herbarium to learn about the local plants used for medicinal purposes. Before leaving, stop at the five-bed ward (complete with a flowered chamber pot) that looks as it did more than 200 years ago, when this was the **Hospital of Our Lady of Guadalupe**. ♦ Nominal charge; free with a receipt from the Spanish Quarter Village. Daily. 3 Aviles St (between Artillery La and King St), Old St. Augustine. 825.6808

24 Potter's Wax Museum Opened in 1949 by George L. Packer, this establishment claims to be the oldest wax museum in the country. Whether that's true or not—and despite the fact that it has very little to do with St. Augustine—it's still fun to duck into this air-conditioned museum and, without peeking at the names, see if you can recognize the figures as you make your way through. Among the more than 170 renderings are: King Henry VIII with all six of his wives; Ulysses S. Grant, regal in uniform; Thomas Jefferson, seated behind a desk presumably writing the Declaration of Independence; writers Henry Wadsworth Longfellow and Alfred, Lord Tennyson; botanist George Washington Carver; Louis Pasteur, behind a desk and wearing a lab coat; and Leonardo da Vinci, with his long beard and flowing robe. The costumes are spectacular. A short theater presentation is shown occasionally throughout the day. The newest attraction, **Wax Works**, features a craftsperson designing wax figures. ♦ Admission. ♦ Daily, Sa-Su until 8PM. 17 King St (at Aviles St), Old St. Augustine. 829.9056 ♿

25 Oldest Store Museum You'll know this place by the cigar-store Indian out front. While a player piano tinkles turn-of-the-century hits such as "Peg o' My Heart," visitors can look at some of the store's original stock, including century-old buttonhook shoes and 1890s-era bathing suits. Another curious item is "The Bonebreaker," a massive 1850 bicycle with a heavy steel frame and large wooden-spoke wheels. ♦ Admission. Daily. 4 Artillery La (at St. George St), Old St. Augustine. 829.9729

26 Ximenez-Fatio House Built in 1798 by Andreas Ximenez, a Spanish merchant, this house originally contained a general store and tavern on the first floor and living quarters above. In 1830 Margaret Cook enlarged the building and turned it into a boardinghouse. Louise Fatio, who acquired the house in 1855, rented rooms to rich Northerners visiting for the winter, and its reputation as a fine hostelry soon grew. Now run by the Florida Chapter of the National Society of the Colonial Dames of America, the three-story, coquina-and-wood structure, with gabled roof and wooden balcony, is a boardinghouse museum, set up to look just as it did in the mid-1800s. ♦ Free. M, Th-Sa 11AM-4PM; Su 1-4PM; closed September. 20 Aviles St (at Cadiz St), Old St. Augustine. 829.3575

27 Old City House Inn $ Built in 1873 as a stable, the two-story brick, stucco, and wood building was converted to a guesthouse at the turn of the century. The rooms subsequently served as shops and offices until an inn was again established here in 1991. Each of the seven rooms is decorated differently and equipped with a TV, a modern bathroom, and a queen-size brass bed. Breakfast is served downstairs in the restaurant, and there's complimentary cheese and wine in the afternoon. There's a two-night minimum stay on weekends. ♦ 115 Cordova St (at Palm Row), Old St. Augustine. 826.0113; www.oldcityhouse.com

Within the Old City House Inn:

Old City House Restaurant ★★$$$
This casually elegant little restaurant serves a rack of New Zealand lamb that's always a big hit. The place has the feel of a New England country inn (the owners are from Connecticut), with a cozy gas fireplace surrounded by a couch and chairs, candlelit tables partially made of wood from the original 1873 structure, and lots of pleasant greenery. ♦ American ♦ Daily dinner. Reservations recommended. 826.0781

28 County Courthouse Originally the **Casa Monica Hotel,** this county building was designed and built in 1888 by millionaire Franklin Smith, who had already built the outrageous **Zorayda Castle** nearby (see below) as a winter home. Smith's medieval, Spanish-style hotel was a fine match for Henry Flagler's magnificent **Hotel Ponce de León** across the street. But Smith found himself overextended and sold his property to Flagler, who changed its name to the **Cordova Hotel.** Flagler then annexed the building to his **Hotel Alcazar** across Cordova Street. The hotel closed in 1932, and the Florida East Coast Hotel Company sold this structure to the St. Johns County Commission in 1961. ♦ M-F. King St (between St. George and Cordova Sts), Old St. Augustine

There are more than 2,000 restaurants in Central Florida.

29 Lightner Museum Plan on spending a long time here: This museum is simply irresistible. Built in 1888 by Henry Flagler as a winter retreat for Northerners and christened the **Hotel Alcazar,** the building was converted into a museum in 1948 by Otto C. Lightner, editor of *Hobbies* magazine. Like many smaller museums in Florida, the collection is an entertaining hodgepodge: Grand furniture sits near the entrance, including a mahogany-and-satinwood bureau built in the 1860s; nearby are musical instruments (including a player piano capable of mimicking an entire orchestra), which are demonstrated daily at 11AM and 2PM. For those interested in the exotic, shrunken heads are displayed on the second floor. An intact but nonfunctional turn-of-the-century steam room harkens back to the days when the building was a bustling hotel with a casino, a large indoor swimming pool, a dance floor, a gym, and a bowling alley. The casino and swimming pool area is now the **Lightner Antique Mall,** where antique furnishings, glassware, china, coins, and books are sold. The **Cafe Alcazar** specializes in soups, salads, sandwiches, and shrimp scampi. **City Hall** offices also are housed in the building. ♦ Admission. Daily. 75 King St (between Cordova and Granada Sts), Old St. Augustine. 824.2874 &

30 Museum of Weapons and Early American History Gun lovers and Civil War buffs will be interested in this museum. It's essentially one big room with antique rifles hung on the walls and small firearms, antique coins, newspapers, and Civil War memorabilia enclosed in display cases. Even non-enthusiasts appreciate the beautiful flintlock pistols dating back to 1770, and there are several touching letters home from Civil War soldiers. One anomaly in the collection: President John Tyler's piano, circa 1830. ♦ Admission. Daily. 81-C King St (between Granada and Martin Luther King Sts), Old St. Augustine. 829.3727

31 Zorayda Castle Much of Henry Flagler's inspiration for transforming St. Augustine into the "American Riviera" came from Boston millionaire Franklin W. Smith, famed for his interest in exotic architecture. In 1883, after a trip to Spain, Smith created this "castle" as a winter home, basing the design on a wing of the Alhambra in Granada. He named the castle after a daughter of King Mohammed el Hazare, one of the Moorish rulers who had occupied the Alhambra. One of the first all-concrete buildings in the country, the structure was purchased by Abraham S. Mussallem, an Egyptian consul, in 1913. Mussallem opened it as a gambling casino in 1923, then in 1936 turned it into a museum displaying the rare artifacts he had collected from around the world. Mussallem's sons own the castle to this day. Highlights downstairs include the **Harem's Prayer Room,** with a Chinese teakwood fountain; a damascene brass lamp in the **Second Prayer Room;** and, in the **Hall of Justice,** a game table made of sandalwood, satinwood, rosewood, mother of pearl, and ivory. The gift shop is off the **Hall of Justice.** ♦ Admission. Daily. 83 King St (between Granada and Martin Luther King Sts), Old St. Augustine. 824.3097

32 Flagler College Henry Flagler chose architects **Thomas Hastings,** the 25-year-old son of an old business acquaintance, and **John M. Carrère** to design the **Ponce de León Hotel** in 1888. The structure, in a style the young architects dubbed "Spanish Renaissance Revival," was the first major building in the country to be constructed of poured concrete—a mix of cement, native coquina, and sand. The project established the reputations of **Hastings** and **Carrère,** who went on to become among the top architects of the early 1900s. The soaring spires of the hotel—which in 1968 became **Flagler College,** an independent, coeducational liberal arts school—were matched by the elegance within. Murals by George W. Maynard decorate the rotunda, formerly the hotel's lobby, while the grand parlor, now called the **Flagler Room,** boasts illusionist canvases painted in France by Virgilio Tojetti;

take a close look at these intriguing paintings, which contain birds that seem to fly toward you and a girl holding a rabbit whose eyes seem to follow you as you circle the room. The **Flagler Room** also contains memorabilia from the building's heyday as a hotel. The 150-foot oval dining room is spectacular, with floor-to-ceiling stained-glass windows by Louis Tiffany; in fact, the college has the largest collection of Tiffany glass anywhere in the country. A statue of Flagler marks the entrance. ♦ Free. Courtyard and rotunda open daily year-round. Free guided tours through the restored areas (the rotunda, Flagler Room, and dining room) on the hour from 10AM to 4PM, May-Aug; tours at other times of the year are available by prior arrangement. 74 King St (between Cordova and Sevilla Sts), Old St. Augustine. 829.6481

33 Basilica Cathedral of St. Augustine The building dates from 1791, but parish registers go back to 1594 and are said to be the oldest written records in the United States. After a fire in 1887, a bell tower and transept were added. ♦ Daily. Guided tours are offered in the afternoon. 40 Cathedral Pl (between Charlotte and St. George Sts), Old St. Augustine. 829.0620

34 Dr. Peck House The first floor of this structure, also known as the **Peña-Peck House,** was built in 1746 in the typical Spanish colonial style for the Royal Treasurer of Spain, Estevan de Peña. During the British period, the house served as the residence of Governor John Moultrie. In 1837, Dr. Seth Peck bought it and added a second story in the Cape Cod style (Peck was a native New Englander). The house remained in the Peck family for nearly a century, until Dr. Peck's granddaughter, Anna Burt, left the house to the city in 1931. The Women's Exchange conducts tours of the house, which is filled with antique furnishings. ♦ Donation. Daily. 143 St. George St (at Treasury St), Old St. Augustine. 829.5064

Flagler College

St. George Street Shopping

ORANGE STREET

ST. GEORGE STREET

Candle Creations
George's Treasures
Gatekeeper Souvenirs

TOLOMATO LANE

Grist Mill Gifts

museum **Oldest Wooden Schoolhouse**

FORT ALLEY

Casa de Martin Martinez Gallegos
part of Spanish Quarter Village
Casa de Lorenzo Gómez
part of Spanish Quarter Village
Casa de Maria Triay
entrance to Spanish Quarter Village
Spanish Quarters Cafe

Casa de Geronimo de Hita y Salazar
part of Spanish Quarter Village

Venetian glass necklaces **Casa Rodriguez**

Casa Avaro *St. Photios Chapel*
Casa de Antonio de Mesa
part of Spanish Quarter Village

St. Augustine Art Glass and Craft Gallery

Spanish Quarter Village Store
Peso de Burgo-Pellicer
part of Spanish Quarter Village

American restaurant **The Monk's Vineyard**

European arts and crafts **Spanish Dutch Convoy**

CUNA STREET

gifts **J.R. Benet**

handmade rugs **Dreamweavers**

Florida Cracker Cafe *American restaurant*

exotic earrings **The Pirate and His Lady**

Sea Gems of St. Augustine *shells/coral/jewelry*

metal sculpture **The Secret Cove**

The Columbia Gift Shop

The Pink Petunia *handcrafts*

Spanish **Columbia Restaurant**

HYPOLITA STREET

shops **St. George's Row**
earrings **Unique by Edith**
purses **The Bag Lady**
sportswear **Bay Bags**

Sunburst Crystal
The Ancient Mariner *nautical gifts*

St. George Souvenir Shop

Maronel's Shoes
The Bunnery

teddy bears/collectibles **The Bear Connection**
Cuzzins Sandwich Shop
Moeller's Jewelers
Sonico Tourist Shopping Spot
World of Flags
sportswear **East Coast–West Coast**

The Fringe *clothing*
Donna's *womenswear*

PK's Cafe & Coffee House
The House of Ireland

TREASURY STREET

Kilwin's Fudge and Chocolate

ST. GEORGE STREET

Dr. Peck House

Churchyard

shops/food court **Heritage Walk**

CATHEDRAL PLACE

Memorial Presbyterian
Church

35 Memorial Presbyterian Church Built
in 1889, this house of worship is another
fine example of Henry Flagler's preferred
architectural style: Spanish Renaissance
Revival. St. Mark's Basilica in Venice, with
its dome, elaborate ornamentation, rounded
arches, and towers, was the inspiration for
its design. ♦ Tours available M-Sa; Su noon–
4:30PM. 36 Sevilla St (at Valencia St), Old St.
Augustine. 829.6451

36 Schmagel's Bagels ★★$ There's no
better way to start your morning than by
munching on an authentic New York–style
bagel while enjoying the view of historic
St. Augustine from this eatery sited right
in its center. In fact, your hardest decision
of the day just might be deciding which
of the 10 bagel varieties to select. Lunch
is just as delicious, featuring homemade
soups and bagel sandwiches. ♦ American
♦ Daily breakfast and lunch. 69 Hypolita St
(at Spanish St), Old St. Augustine. 824.4444

37 Scarlett O'Hara's ★$ This old house,
reportedly constructed in the late 1700s, is
now a popular pub. Folks come for the drinks,
live entertainment, outdoor deck with rocking
chairs, and rustic interior. The old house next
door has been linked to the main building,
providing more room for dining. The menu
offers several seafood dishes; the fresh fish
of the day, served with red beans and rice and

garlic bread, is a good value. Then there are
the usual pub staples, such as chicken wings,
nachos, and hamburgers with all the fixins.
♦ American ♦ Daily lunch and dinner. 70
Hypolita St (at Cordova St), Old St. Augustine.
824.6535

38 Columbia Restaurant ★★$$ Diners
surrounded by stone fountains, hand-painted
ceramic tiles, and handcrafted furnishings feast
on black bean soup, *arroz con pollo* (yellow
rice and chicken), and *paella à la Valenciana*.
Huge crowds line up for the fiesta brunch on
Sundays. ♦ Spanish ♦ M-Sa lunch and dinner,
Su brunch and dinner. 98 St. George St (at
Hypolita St), Old St. Augustine. 824.3341

39 Casa de la Paz $ A fine example of
Spanish Renaissance Revival architecture,
this bed-and-breakfast inn offers three rooms
with sweeping views of the Matanzas Bay
and three rooms with a private veranda.
The rooms are extremely well outfitted, with
high-quality linens, antiques, and private
baths. A complete, hot breakfast buffet is
included in the rate, but there's no restaurant.
♦ 22 Av Menendez (between Treasury and
Hypolita Sts), Old St. Augustine. 829.2915;
www.casadelapaz.com

39 Casa Blanca $$ An elegant bed-and-
breakfast, this 81-year-old house has a guest
parlor, a breakfast room, a front porch with

rocking chairs overlooking the bay, and 12 rooms (including two suites) furnished with antiques; each room has its own deck or balcony (some with bay views) and a private entrance. One of the suites has a double Jacuzzi and a decorative fireplace; the other has a covered deck facing the bay with a double hammock, in addition to a private sunbathing deck to the rear of the house. ♦ 24 Av Menendez (between Treasury and Hypolita Sts), Old St. Augustine. 829.0928; fax 826.1892; www.casablancainn.com

40 Florida Cracker Cafe ★$ Enjoy juicy burgers, garden salads, conch fritters, sandwiches, and other light fare, accompanied by freshly made lemonade in the summertime or a Jamaican Red Stripe beer, at this small, casual cafe. An eight-table outdoor patio right off St. George Street has a lemonade stand that caters to passing pedestrians. Inside the dining room, which is decorated with works by local artists, there are 12 more tables and a bar. ♦ American ♦ M-Th lunch; F-Su lunch and dinner. 81 St. George St (between Hypolita and Cuna Sts), Old St. Augustine. 829.0397

41 Castillo de San Marcos National Monument The chance to walk around this imposing gray-walled fort is reason enough to visit St. Augustine. Built by the Spanish between 1672 and 1695, the **Castillo** was originally intended to be a way station in North Florida for treasure-filled Spanish ships bound home from the Caribbean (St. Augustine had one of the few operating harbors along the southern Atlantic Coast). At the time Spanish forts were usually made of wood, but after pirates sacked St. Augustine in 1668, Spanish engineers constructed the sturdy **Castillo** out of coquina. Wars between Spain and England led to two serious sieges in 1702 and 1740, but the fort was never captured. In 1924 the **Castillo** was declared a national monument. After crossing a bridge and entering the fort, visitors can study displays that explain its history. The exhibits also chronicle some less-than-illustrious incidents in the fort's past: During the 1835 Seminole Wars, the US Army kept more than 300 Indians imprisoned here; and Great Plains Indians were incarcerated here after the Civil War. From the promenade, volunteers clad in Spanish colonial uniforms fire cannons on select weekends (call ahead). Carriages offering tours of St. Augustine gather on the street outside the fort entrance. Red carriages are for sightseeing, green for historical tours. ♦ Nominal fee; free for children under 16 and seniors over 61. Daily. 1 S Castillo Dr (between Av Menendez and San Marco Ave), Old St. Augustine. 829.6506 &

Castillo de San Marcos National Monument

42 Oldest Wooden Schoolhouse Built more than 225 years ago of cypress and red cedar joined by wooden pegs, this schoolhouse stands on its original site despite the wars, fires, and hurricanes that St. Augustine has endured. It was only in recent years that a heavy chain was placed around the top of the building, anchoring it to the ground to protect it from being blown away. Before entering the schoolhouse, walk into the garden in the back to see the outhouse. Also behind the school is the kitchen, situated away from the main building to prevent accidental fire and excess heat in the summer. The trees and plants are all identified, and there is an old school bell visitors can ring. During the 1834-41 Seminole Wars, the school was turned into a guardhouse and shelter for the sentries at the City Gate; 15 years later it was converted back into a school. Inside, the floors are the original tabby (concrete made of crushed oyster shells and mortar). When you push a button, life-size mannequins dressed in original costumes describe what school was like back in the old days. For insurance reasons, visitors are no longer allowed in the schoolmaster's residence upstairs, but a mirror placed at the top of a steep flight of stairs provides a substantial view. As you leave through the gift shop, pick up a complimentary diploma. ♦ Nominal fee. Daily. 14 St. George St (at Tolomato La), Old St. Augustine. 824.0192 &

Spanish Quarter.

43 Spanish Quarter Village Based on archaeological and historical research, this museum, managed by the City of St. Augustine, re-creates life as it was here in the mid-1700s, successfully mixing education and entertainment without being hokey. Visitors see how ordinary citizens and soldiers lived; there are also demonstrations by weavers, blacksmiths, and woodworkers dressed in period costumes. Enter the museum next to the **Casa de Maria Triay.**
♦ Admission. Daily. St. George St (between Cuna St and Fort Alley), Old St. Augustine. 825.6830 &

Within the Spanish Quarter Village:

Casa de Maria Triay This reconstructed two-room Spanish colonial home is typical of those owned by families from the island of Minorca in the late 1700s. It is not open to the public.

Casa de Lorenzo Gómez A foot soldier lived here in 1740. One corner of the small house served as a store to help the family supplement its income.

Casa de Martin Martinez Gallegos Next door to the **Gómez House,** this is the reconstructed home of Artillery Sergeant Martin Martinez Gallegos.

Blacksmith Shop At this site, notice how close you are to the fort that protected the inhabitants. The blacksmith who works here produces whatever metal objects are needed for the Spanish Quarter (hinges, hooks, fireplace pokers, and such); his techniques are those used in the 18th century. Some replicas are sold at the **Spanish Quarter Village Store.**

Taberna This one-room building has been furnished to replicate a typical 18th-century tavern.

Casa de Antonio de Mesa Originally a two-room house owned by Antonio de Mesa in the mid-1700s, this home was given a second story during the second Spanish Period (1783-1821), when it was owned by Juan Sanchez. It's now furnished as it was in the early 1800s, illustrating how a middle- or upper-middle-class American family lived in St. Augustine at that time. ♦ Guided tours offered daily; schedule varies according to season

Peso de Burgo/Pellicer House On one side of this duplex designed in the late 1700s lived Jose Peso de Burgo, a Corsican merchant and shopkeeper, and on the other, Francisco Pellicer, a Minorcan carpenter. Today the building houses an exhibit that chronicles Minorcan immigration to St. Augustine.

Casa de Geronimo de Hita y Salazar Another typical soldier's home of the mid–18th century, this one was a bit larger, probably to accommodate a big family. Here you can watch a woodworker demonstrate his craft. After leaving the house, pass through the gate to return to St. George Street. The next building on your left is **St. Photios Chapel** (see below).

44 St. Photios Chapel This chapel is part of the **St. Photios National Greek Orthodox Shrine** housed in the 1749 **Casa Avaro**. The first Greeks arrived in St. Augustine in 1768, and later most of them moved 65 miles down the coast to New Smyrna. But after several difficult years of hurricanes and other disasters, the survivors returned to St. Augustine and used the **Casa Avaro** for worship. The house was bought in 1965 by the Greek Orthodox Archdiocese of North and South America partially because of its significance to St. Augustine's Greek community. Construction of the chapel began in 1979 and was completed in 1982. While the outside is of Spanish design, the interior is filled with Byzantine-style frescoes, which are highlighted with gold and depict scenes from the life of Christ. There's also a museum with an audiovisual presentation and exhibits illustrating the struggle of Greek immigrants in the United States. ♦ Donation. Daily. 41 St. George St (between Cuna St and Fort Alley), Old St. Augustine. 829.8205

45 The Monk's Vineyard ★★$ One of the most inviting places to eat along touristy St. George Street, this restaurant serves a substantial bean chowder, hearty salads (the usually ubiquitous iceberg lettuce is absent here), and big burgers. Sit in the air-conditioned dining room or at one of the little wooden tables outside on a veranda facing the street. The helpful servers are dressed as monks, and the whimsical decor evokes the atmosphere of an abbey grape arbor, with light fixtures in the shape of grape clusters, latticework and grapevines overhead, stained glass, and plenty of "monkabilia" adorning the walls. Upstairs, there's a wine store that specializes in the finest wines from small West Coast vineyards; you also can purchase monk paraphernalia and the restaurant's house wine, Blushing Monk. ♦ American ♦ M-Tu, Th-Su

lunch. 56 St. George St (between Cuna St and Tolomato La), Old St. Augustine. 824.5888

Bed & Breakfast

46 Carriage Way Bed & Breakfast $ Brass and four-poster canopied beds add to the Victorian ambience of this nine-room inn. All rooms have private baths (two lower-priced ones have baths down the hall). A full breakfast is included, and bicycles are available for exploring the district. There's a two-night minimum stay on weekends. ♦ 70 Cuna St (at Cordova St), Old St. Augustine. 829.2467; fax 826.1461; www.carriageway.com

47 Old Powder House Inn $ Set in the shade of towering pecan trees, this fancy bed-and-breakfast offers big breakfasts, afternoon sweets, and complimentary wine and hors d'oeuvres. Each of the eight rooms (including two suites) is decorated with antiques and has its own theme: The upstairs **Grandma's Attic** is done up in pastels, with a king-size bed, old photos, and vintage hats and other clothing hanging from wall pegs. **Queen Anne's Lace** has a four-poster queen-size pedestal bed with a tester canopy and is decorated in lace and shades of pink. One room has a kitchenette, and some have private entrances off the inn's veranda. All rooms have private baths, most with a tub and shower, some with a shower only. Other extras include cable TV, a Jacuzzi, and bicycles (including a bicycle for two) for exploring. ♦ 38 Cordova St (between Carrera and Saragossa Sts), Old St. Augustine. 824.4149, 800/447.4149; www.oldpowderhouse.com

48 Southern Wind Bed & Breakfast $$ Owners Bob and Alana Indelicato make visitors feel right at home in their Victorian bed-and-breakfast inn. The 10 rooms are furnished with antiques, cable TV, and queen-size beds; all have private baths. The inn furnishes bicycles for touring the historic district. ♦ 18 Cordova St (between Saragossa and Orange Sts), Old St. Augustine. 825.3623; www.southernwindinn.com

48 Cordova House $$ The three rooms at this bed-and-breakfast are filled with antiques, and the place has a luxury most of the competition doesn't: a swimming pool. The rooms have private baths (one is across the hall from the room). Innkeepers Carole and Hal Schroeder serve a full breakfast, complimentary wine, and iced tea. The sprawling verandas are a great place to unwind. There's a two-night minimum stay on weekends. ♦ 16 Cordova St (between Saragossa and Orange Sts), Old St. Augustine. 825.0770; www.innformation.com/fl/cordova

49 Authentic Old Drugstore A don't-miss tourist spot, this drugstore museum displays some of its original stock, including a concoction that was guaranteed to cure "loose operation" (diarrhea). People over the age of 50 usually chuckle at the bottles of Hadacol, recalling how it was hawked by a Louisiana entrepreneur. It didn't really cure anything, but the 12-percent–alcohol solution helped patients forget their aches and pains. The drugstore began as a trading post but grew into a general store and by 1872 had become a pharmacy. Now, the only things for sale here are the usual souvenirs from the museum's gift shop. ♦ Free. Daily. 31 Orange St (at Cordova St), Old St. Augustine. 824.2269

50 Visitor Information Center Stop in to pick up some brochures and watch the 15-minute orientation film. It's also worth the time (and the nominal fee) to see the 52-minute film *Dream of Empire,* which explains why the Spanish settled in this area and relates the true story of a family that lived here in the late 16th century. Next door is a half-acre burial ground, established for Protestants who died in 1821 from a yellow-fever epidemic. Try to arrive early, when there is plenty of parking. There's a smaller **Visitor Information Center** downtown in the **Government House** (St. George St and Cathedral Pl, 825.5079). ♦ Daily. 10 S Castillo Dr (between Orange St and Castillo Dr), Old St. Augustine. 825.1000.

51 Ripley's Believe It or Not! Museum Videos briefly extol Ripley's curiosities; less interesting are the matchstick London Tower Bridge and the toothpick model of the Eiffel Tower. The museum ends with a nifty trick involving a nude woman and mirrors (see it for yourself) and a walk through a revolving tunnel—guaranteed to give you vertigo. Built as a private residence by a business associate of Henry Flagler, the house was known for years as **Warden Castle.** Later it became a hotel owned by novelist Marjorie Kinnan Rawlings, author of *The Yearling.* ♦ Admission. Daily. 19 San Marco Ave (between Shenandoah and Joiner Sts), Old St. Augustine. 824.1606 ♿

52 Le Pavilion ★★$$ This large yet intimate upscale eatery serves a number of tasty dishes, including chicken curry Bombay (served with rice pilaf and sprinkled with bananas, chutney, coconut, and raisins), chicken pavilion (sautéed and topped with a fresh mushroom sauce), and bouillabaisse with fresh fish, crabmeat, mussels, shrimp, and vegetables. The onion soup also hits the spot, and the crepes are delicate and flavorful.

The ambience is European, with seven dining rooms graced with crisp white tablecloths, candles, and flowers on the tables. ♦ Continental ♦ Daily lunch and dinner. Reservations recommended. 45 San Marco Ave (between Joiner and Mulberry Sts). 824.6202

53 Raintree ★★★$$$ When the MacDonald family immigrated from England in 1980, they opened a restaurant in this stately Victorian house. Since then, the place has become one of St. Augustine's most successful dining spots. Many selections on the menu change each month, but the catch of the day is always good, especially when served à la Raintree—in white wine, mushrooms, and cream. Another favorite is the flaky Florida grouper, whose delicacy isn't overwhelmed by the rich crawfish cream sauce. The main dining room has Victorian furniture and an attractive blue and burgundy color scheme. A second dining room has dark green, mauve, and gold decor, with lustrous wood paneling and a decorative fireplace. There's also a lovely, glass-enclosed atrium and a banquet room upstairs. The restaurant is named for the tree-shaped fountain out front. ♦ American ♦ Daily dinner. Reservations recommended. 102 San Marco Ave (between Hope and Bernard Sts), Old St. Augustine. 824.7211

54 Mission Nombre de Dios Founded in 1565 by Spanish explorer Pedro Menéndez de Avilés, who landed nearby with a group of settlers and priests, this pretty little mission church is set on tranquil grounds. Early missions built on the site were destroyed by pirates, hurricanes, and English gunfire; the present structure, built in 1915, is a reconstruction of the original. Inside the mission chapel is a statue of the Virgin Mary, brought from Spain in the 17th century. Nearby is a 208-foot-high stainless-steel cross that was erected in 1965 to celebrate the city's 400th birthday. ♦ Donation. Daily. San Marco Ave (between Pine St and Ocean Ave), Old St. Augustine. 824.2809

55 Howard Johnson Express Inn $ This 80-room hotel is noted for the lovely 500-year-old oak tree, called "Old Senator," that sits in the center of the grounds. The inn is a typical no-frills motel, but the location can't be beat: It's within walking distance of the **Fountain of Youth Park** and other local attractions. All rooms have coffeemakers and two have kitchenettes. There's no restaurant, but a free continental breakfast is offered each morning in the lobby. The **St. Augustine Sightseeing Trains** pick up passengers at the front entrance. ♦ 137 San Marco Ave (between Myrtle and Ballard Aves), Old St. Augustine. 824.6181, 800/446.4656; fax 825.2774

56 Fountain of Youth Park Legend has it that in 1513 Juan Ponce de León came ashore here in search of the Fountain of Youth. This park has a path to the site where the explorer is thought to have landed and a spring that's said to be the one Ponce de León believed was the Fountain of Youth (visitors are welcome to take a drink). There's also a diorama of the Spaniard's landing, and several Fountain of Youth–related items, such as old cartoons and letters, are displayed behind glass. Near the spring are 27 rocks laid out in the shape of a cross—15 down and 13 across—supposedly placed by Ponce de León to mark the fountain and the year it was discovered. A ranger explains the history of the area in a brief lecture, and *Discovery Globe,* a movie about the first hundred years of European exploration in America, is screened in a small auditorium. In addition, the presentation at the **Navigator's Planetarium** explains astronomical sailing techniques used by the early explorers. Long before Ponce de León made his appearance, the Timucuan Indians had a settlement here called Seloy. In 1976 archaeologists discovered hut foundations that suggest that the Timucuan were here a thousand years before the Spaniard's arrival. Artifacts such as Indian dugout canoes and Spanish anchors are labeled and placed around the grounds of the park. ♦ Admission. Daily. 11 Magnolia Ave (between Ballard Ave and Dufferin St), Old St. Augustine. 829.3168 ᕹ

57 Old Jail The **St. Johns County Jail** was built in 1890 on land purchased by Henry Flagler because the previous jail was too close to his fancy **Ponce de León Hotel.** In use until 1953, this jail is now a museum. Big yellow footprints painted in the prison yard lead visitors on a self-guided tour that includes the imposing Queen Anne–style house that served as living quarters for the jailer and his family, as well as the jailhouse itself. The building is creepy enough, but the cells are downright eerie. Weapons used in murders and other crimes are displayed at the jailhouse entrance. ♦ Admission. Daily. 167 San Marco Ave (between Williams and Dufferin Sts), Old St. Augustine. 829.3800

58 St. Augustine Sightseeing Trains Although it's just as easy to devise your own

walking tour of St. Augustine's historic area, these open-air trolley tours are worth considering for a narrative history of the district. There are eight tours to choose from, ranging from one to six hours and at various prices. Trains leave from sites all over town, but the stop across the street from the **Old Jail** is handy because there's plenty of parking there. Tickets include stop-off privileges at major attractions. ♦ Fee. Daily. 170 San Marco Ave (at Missouri Ave), Old St. Augustine. 829.6545 ᕹ

59 Days Inn Historic $ Only minutes away from the action, this 124-room inn is a quiet oasis after a hectic day of sightseeing. There's a large pool, a playground, and a flower garden (all shaded by large oak trees), as well as a restaurant on the premises. Sightseeing trams leave right from the hotel. ♦ 2800 Ponce de Leon Blvd (between Rte 16 and San Marco Ave), St Augustine. 829.6581, 800/325.2525; fax 824.0135; www.daysinn.com ᕹ

60 St. Augustine Outlet Center Shop in almost a hundred outlet stores, conveniently located right off the interstate. Anchoring the mall is a **West Point Pepperell Mill Store,** a linen outlet featuring such name brands as **Lady Pepperell, Martex, Stevens,** and **Utica.** Also find **Sunglass Hut, Bon Worth, Brooks Brothers, Coach, Reebok, Corning/Revere, J.Crew, DKNY, Calvin Klein, Nautica, London Fog, Mikasa, Nine West, The Gap, Samsonite, Laura Ashley, Toy Liquidators,** and **Van Heusen,** along with other housewares shops, clothing and shoe stores, and bookstores. A tourist information booth is located in the small food court, along with rest rooms and telephones. ♦ Daily. 2700 Rte 16 (just west of I-95), St Augustine. 825.1555

61 Fiddler's Green ★★$$$ Large windows offer a fabulous view of the Atlantic Ocean, and a cozy stone fireplace sets the mood at this eatery. Delicate snails baked in butter and herbs or succulent oysters Rockefeller are perfect appetizers for a meal of crabs fried in a light tempura batter. The menu also offers chicken and pasta dishes and steaks. ♦ Seafood/American ♦ Daily dinner. Reservations recommended. 50 Anahma Dr (east of Rte A1A), Vilano Beach. 824.8897

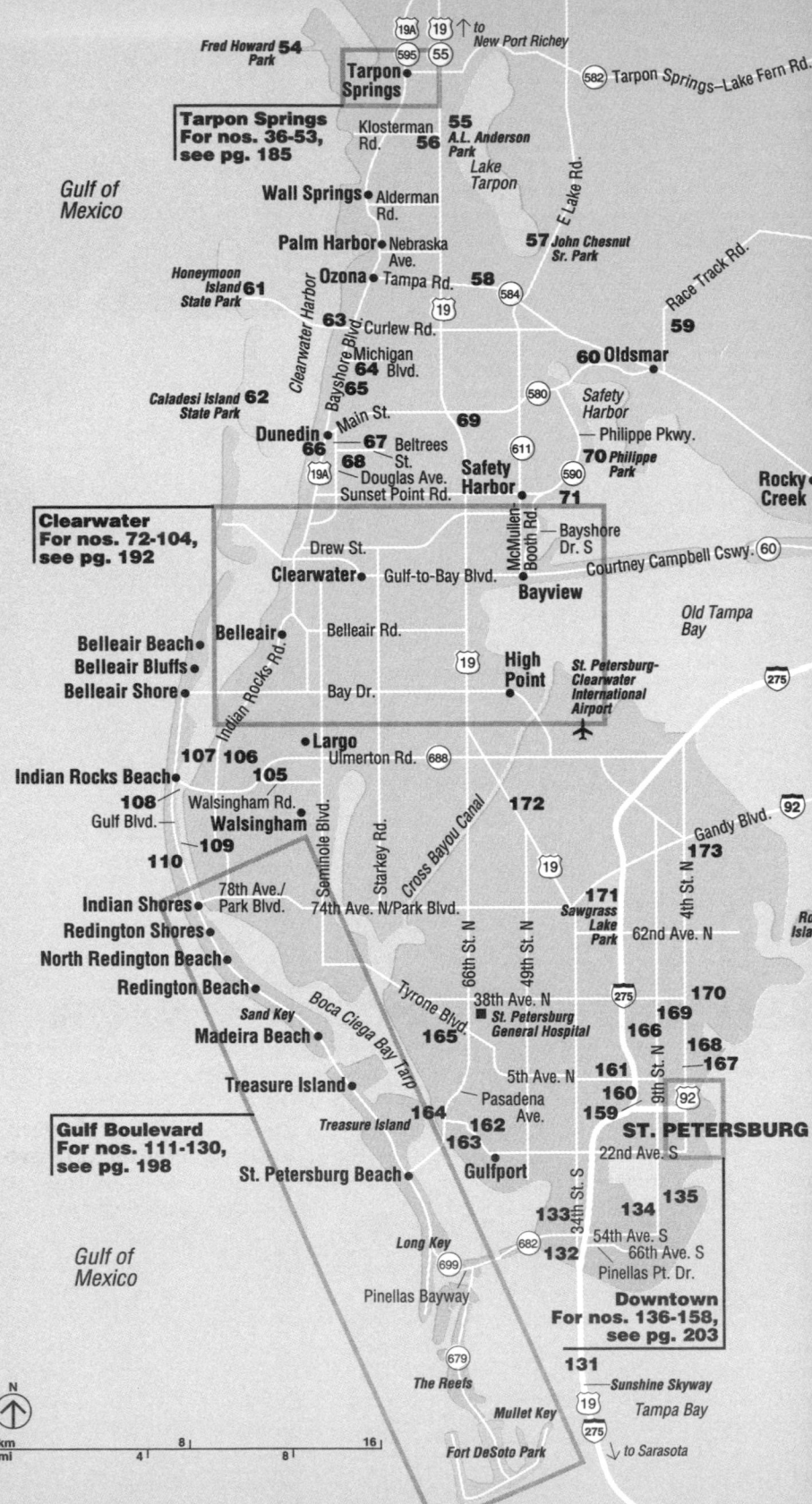

Fred Howard **54**
Park

19A 19 ↑ to New Port Richey

595 55

582 Tarpon Springs–Lake Fern Rd.

**Tarpon
Springs**

**Tarpon Springs
For nos. 36-53,
see pg. 185**

Klosterman
Rd. **56**

55
A.L. Anderson
Park

Lake
Tarpon

*Gulf of
Mexico*

Wall Springs
Alderman
Rd.

E Lake Rd.

Palm Harbor
Nebraska
Ave.

57 John Chesnut
Sr. Park

Race Track Rd.

Ozona
Tampa Rd.

58
584

59

*Honeymoon
Island* **61**
State Park

63
Curlew Rd.

Bayshore Blvd.

Clearwater Harbor

Michigan
Blvd. **64**

60 **Oldsmar**

Caladesi Island **62**
State Park

65
Main St.

580

69

*Safety
Harbor*

Philippe Pkwy.

Dunedin
66

67 Beltrees
St.

611

70 *Philippe
Park*

**Rocky
Creek**

19A

68
Douglas Ave.
Sunset Point Rd.

590

**Safety
Harbor**

71

**Clearwater
For nos. 72-104,
see pg. 192**

Drew St.

McMullen-Booth Rd.

Bayshore
Dr. S

Courtney Campbell Cswy.
60

*Old Tampa
Bay*

Clearwater
Gulf-to-Bay Blvd.

Bayview

Belleair Beach
Belleair Bluffs
Belleair Shore

Belleair

Belleair Rd.

19

**High
Point**

St. Petersburg-
Clearwater
International
Airport

275

Bay Dr.

Largo
Ulmerton Rd.
688

Indian Rocks Rd.

107 106
Indian Rocks Beach
105

172

Gandy Blvd.
92

108
Gulf Blvd.
Walsingham Rd.

173

4th St. N

Walsingham

109

Seminole Blvd.

Starkey Rd.

Cross Bayou Canal

19

171
*Sawgrass
Lake
Park*

62nd Ave. N

*Ros
Islan*

110

78th Ave./
Park Blvd.

74th Ave. N/Park Blvd.

169
170

Indian Shores
Redington Shores
North Redington Beach
Redington Beach

Tyrone Blvd.

38th Ave. N
St. Petersburg
General Hospital

275

166

168
167

Sand Key

Madeira Beach

Boca Ciega Bay Tarp

165

66th St. N
49th St. N

161

160
159

9th St. N

92

Treasure Island

164

162
163

5th Ave. N
Pasadena
Ave.

ST. PETERSBURG

**Gulf Boulevard
For nos. 111-130,
see pg. 198**

Treasure Island

St. Petersburg Beach

Gulfport

22nd Ave. S

133

132

682

134 **135**

54th Ave. S
66th Ave. S
Pinellas Pt. Dr.

*Gulf of
Mexico*

Long Key
699

34th St. S

**Downtown
For nos. 136-158,
see pg. 203**

Pinellas Bayway

679

131

N

The Reefs

Sunshine Skyway

19

Tampa Bay

km
mi
4   8   8   16

Mullet Key

275

↓ to Sarasota

Fort DeSoto Park

Tampa/St. Petersburg Area

Known as the "Suncoast" for its year-round excellent weather and as a mecca for baseball players in spring training, the Tampa/St. Petersburg area is that and much more. It probably has as many distinct nationalities per square mile as Miami—from the Greek communities in **Tarpon Springs** to Scots near **Clearwater** to the Cuban enclave of **Ybor City.** And although the region's two main cities—Tampa and St. Petersburg—are often spoken as one word, they are separate urban districts offering a variety of cultural activities. Beautiful beaches, parks, and other attractions abound in the surrounding areas.

Located on the **Gulf of Mexico** coast in the center of the state, the area has enjoyed one of the fastest-growing economies in the US during the past decade. Although tourism is largely accountable for this upswing—**Busch Gardens** in Tampa is the biggest tourist attraction on Florida's west coast—other industries are also important. Tampa is one of the largest and busiest ports in the country and boasts Florida's largest shrimp fleet. Cigar making, phosphorus mining, brewing, and the headquarters of the US Operations Command at **MacDill Air Force Base** are other major sources of economic activity.

Long before tourists began flocking here and before Cuban immigrants arrived to set up the world's largest cigar factory, Spanish explorers scouted an area Native Americans called "Tanpa," which translated variously as "sticks of fire" and "land by the water." Finding neither gold nor other mineral wealth, the Spanish had little to conquer and no reason to settle the area. Its prime attraction, even then, was the soothing quality of the weather and the water. In the first half of the 15th century Hernan de Soto, discovering mineral springs near what is now **Safety Harbor**, named **Tampa Bay** "La Bahía del Espíritu Santo" (Bay of the Holy Spirit), believing, as the local Indians did, that the waters held special healing powers. For the next 200 years or so, these springs were enjoyed exclusively by the pirates and rumrunners who were the only Europeans to visit the region. In 1773, the area became British when the Spanish traded Havana for Florida, and the river, bay, and county on the east side of Tampa Bay were named after Lord Hillsborough, a British diplomat.

When Florida became a US territory in the 1820s, the west coast functioned primarily as a military area. **Fort Brooks** was built on the site of what is today downtown Tampa. A community sprang up around the fort, and one of the settlers—Dr. Odet Philippe—imported grapefruit from the Bahamas and planted Florida's first citrus groves. By the time Florida became a state in 1845, the settlement around **Fort Brooks** had grown into the thriving town of Tampa.

The area was destroyed during the Civil War but rebuilt soon after. A tremendous wave of Cuban immigration followed; among the new arrivals was Vincente Martínez Ybor, who built a cigar factory that made Tampa the "cigar capital of the world." In 1875, General John Williams followed his doctor's orders and headed from Detroit to Florida in search of milder weather as a cure for his asthma. With Tampa already bustling, Williams bought land west of the city and set out to build a new community—today's St. Petersburg.

Railroad tycoon Henry B. Plant brought the **Southern Florida Railroad** to Tampa in 1884, and transformed western Florida. The railroad not only made Tampa accessible from the north, it also hastened the development of Tampa's deep water port by linking it directly to the rest of the country. That same year, a prominent physician presented a well-publicized paper to the American Medical Society calling the Tampa Bay area the "healthiest place on earth." With this kind of endorsement, and a new railroad, the only thing lacking was suitable accommodations. Plant stepped in to build something suitable—for a king. In 1891, Plant, who was known for his ambition but not his modesty, opened the castlelike **Tampa Bay Hotel.** With 511 rooms filled with art, antiques, and the rich and famous, the hotel put Tampa on the tourist map. Today, the building and its minarets, now a museum and administrative office of the **University of Tampa**, still dominate the downtown skyline.

Meanwhile, west of Tampa, General Williams was building up his new community. The arrival of the **Orange Belt Railroad** from eastern Florida in 1888 opened a direct link to his settlement in west Tampa Bay. Legend has it that Williams and Peter Demens, a Russian immigrant who was a partner in the railroad company, drew lots to determine who would name the new community. Demens won and christened the settlement after his hometown in Russia. Plant, who was in the midst of a building frenzy, put up the **Belleview Hotel** (which later became the **Belleview Biltmore**), just north of the newly dubbed St. Petersburg.

The Spanish-American War brought 30,000 troops to the Tampa Bay area, including Teddy Roosevelt, who commandeered the **Tampa Bay Hotel** for his headquarters. Many of the soldiers stayed on, contributing to a construction and population boom that lasted until the 1930s. After World War II, peace, prosperity, and the automobile ushered in a second golden age of construction and a soaring population. As overseas travel grew increasingly more accessible in the 1960s and 1970s, Tampa and St. Petersburg experienced a lull, becoming less attractive to young vacationers and more renowned as a retirement spot. But an impressive revival that began in the 1980s has shown no signs of slowing. The sleek lines of new buildings and exciting museums in the two metropolitan areas complement the carefully restored Spanish colonial architecture. The **Tampa Performing Arts Center, Florida Aquarium, Bayfront Center, Dalí Museum, Florida International Museum, The Pier,** and **Tropicana Field** are only some of the attractions that have helped redefine Tampa/St. Petersburg. The two cities and their outlying areas offer a bit of everything, from major league baseball to major league beaches, museums, and restaurants. And as Hernan de Soto discovered, the weather is perfect.

Tampa

The economic center of western Florida, Tampa sits on the **Hillsborough River** and **Hillsborough** and **Tampa Bays.** It offers spectacular waterfront views, charming ethnic neighborhoods, sleek new architecture, and a rich cultural life.

With a population of about 280,000, Tampa is one of the nation's fastest growing cities—in the midst of an economic and cultural revival. At the center of it all is the neatly laid-out **Downtown** area—the city's business and financial center—dominated by the silhouette of the old **Tampa Bay Hotel** (now part of the **University of Tampa** campus). East of downtown is **Ybor City,** Tampa's once-again vibrant Latin Quarter. Home to a large Cuban community, many Spanish and Latin American restaurants, clubs, and a burgeoning art scene, Ybor City is also where cigar factories dominated Tampa from the 1880s to the 1930s. West of downtown is **Tampa International Airport** (which added a new terminal as part of a $110-million expansion). North of downtown is **Busch Gardens,** Florida's second-largest theme park and the area's largest single tourist attraction. Another worthwhile place for the whole family to visit is the **Museum of Science and Industry (MOSI),** a fascinating science center that has tripled in size after a $35-million expansion.

Area code 813 unless otherwise noted.

1 Saddlebrook $$ Just a half-hour from **Tampa International Airport** is this inland 480-acre golf and tennis resort. Golfers can choose between two 18-hole golf courses designed by Arnold Palmer, and tennis buffs can participate in the Harry Hopman/Saddlebrook International Tennis clinics and play on 45 courts. The sprawling resort features 165 one- and 247 two-bedroom villas with a living room and fully equipped kitchen, and 131 hotel rooms, all decorated in pastels and many with a patio or balcony. Other sports facilities include a 500,000-gallon pool, fitness center, and bicycle rentals. The four restaurants serve a variety of fare—from seafood buffet to Italian to mixed grill; there are also two lounges. ♦ 5700 Saddlebrook Way (at Rte 54), Wesley Chapel. 973.1111, 800/729.8383; fax 973.4504; www.saddlebrookresort.com &

2 Skipper's Smokehouse Restaurant ★★$ Alligator, catfish, Jamaican chicken, and seafood are served on a wooden deck under spreading oaks at this popular eatery. Regulars also rave about the oyster bar and Key lime pie. Big-name musicians play reggae on Wednesday, Friday, and Saturday, and blues on Sunday. ♦ Seafood ♦ Cover for shows. Tu-Su lunch and dinner. 910 Skipper Rd (at Nebraska Ave). 971.0666

3 Museum of Science and Industry (MOSI) The museum and planetarium offer more than 30 hands-on displays combining education and entertainment, including *WaterCycles*—an exhibit that focuses on water conservation and resources—and a simulation of a space shuttle. A $35-million expansion has tripled the space, adding several additional attractions: a 350-seat **IMAX-Dome Theater** that projects movies with a 180° fish-eye lens on an 85-foot-high domed screen; two high-tech, multipurpose theaters; the

Back Woods, featuring exhibits on Florida and its environment; the Butterfly Encounter, with a greenhouse on 47 acres of outdoor exhibit space; a science store; and a public library. ◆ Admission. Daily. 4801 Fowler Ave (between N 50th and N 46th Sts). 987.6100, 800/995.6674 &

4 Lucy Ho's Bamboo Garden ★$
An eclectic blend of Mandarin, Cantonese, and Szechuan specialties—General Tso's chicken, chicken with cashews, beef with orange flavor—are served at this restaurant. Mongolian beef is also on the menu. ◆ Chinese ◆ Daily lunch and dinner. 2740 Fowler Ave (between Bruce B. Downs Blvd and 17th St). 977.2783

5 DoubleTree Guest Suites Hotel Tampa/Busch Gardens $$ Conveniently located near **Busch Gardens,** this hotel has 129 one-bedroom suites, each with a queen-size bed in the bedroom, sofa bed in the living room, mini-bar, refrigerator, and microwave. There's also a heated pool and Jacuzzi. Breakfast and a shuttle to **Busch Gardens** are complimentary. It's a perfect setup for families. Be sure to ask about lower rates on weekends. ◆ 11310 Bruce B. Downs Blvd (at E 113th Ave). 971.7690, 800/362.2779; fax 971.7690; www.doubletree.com &

6 Best Western Resort & Conference Center $ This 255-room hotel loaded with amenities is popular with families headed to **Busch Gardens.** The guest rooms wrap around an atrium that's filled with cafes, fountains, and bars. Facilities include a lounge, restaurant, indoor and outdoor heated pools, two Jacuzzis, four lighted tennis courts, sauna, exercise room, gameroom, and laundry room. There's a free shuttle to **Busch Gardens.** ◆ 820 E Busch Blvd (between Ninth St and Nebraska Ave). 933.4011, 800/777.1700; fax 932.1784; www.bestwesterntampa.com &

7 Busch Gardens One of the top five theme parks in Florida, this place combines a naturalistic zoo and thrill rides on its 300 acres 15 minutes north of downtown Tampa. The first of the Anheuser-Busch theme parks, its nine areas aim to capture the spirit of turn-of-the-century Africa, as well as provide entertainment for children. As an accredited member of the American Association of Zoological Parks and one of the nation's top zoos, it does a splendid job of displaying animals—more than 2,700—and sometimes has special guest appearances by animals on loan, such as the guest pandas from China. Plan on spending five to six hours in the park. It's best to arrive early and go straight to **Egypt,** featuring the 60-mile-an-hour **Montu,** the world's longest and tallest inverted roller coaster; the cars are attached to ride below the track instead of riding on it. Next, hop on the monorail around **Serengeti Plain** to view the roaming animals (the animals from Africa are more active in the morning). A highlight in the **Serengeti** is the new $20-million **Edge of Africa,** where visitors stroll through a village seemingly taken over by wild animals—lions, hyenas, meerkats, and more. Then head to the **Nairobi Train Station** and climb aboard the **Trans-Veldt Railroad** train, which circles part of the park. Get off at the **Congo Train Station** and walk back to the front, passing through **Congo, Timbuktu,** and **Nairobi.** Go next to the **Land of the Dragons,** where a huge tree house dominates a fairy-tale land, complete with dragons. Follow with a brewery tour, which includes two free glasses of beer next door in the **Hospitality House.** Don't forget to see the koalas (this is one of the few places in the country where they can be found), which live in the **Bird Gardens** area; pet the snake charmer's python in **Morocco;** admire the 2,000-pound Clydesdales at **Clydesdale Hamlet;** and stand in awe before two white tigers in **Congo.** At the park you may purchase a **FlexTicket** (see "International Drive"), which admits you to **Busch Gardens, Universal Studios Escape, SeaWorld,** and **Wet 'n Wild.** ◆ Admission. Parking fee. Daily; extended hours in summer. 3000 E Busch Blvd (at Bruce B. Downs Blvd). 987.5000, recorded information 987.5082 &

Museum of Science and Industry

BUSCH GARDENS

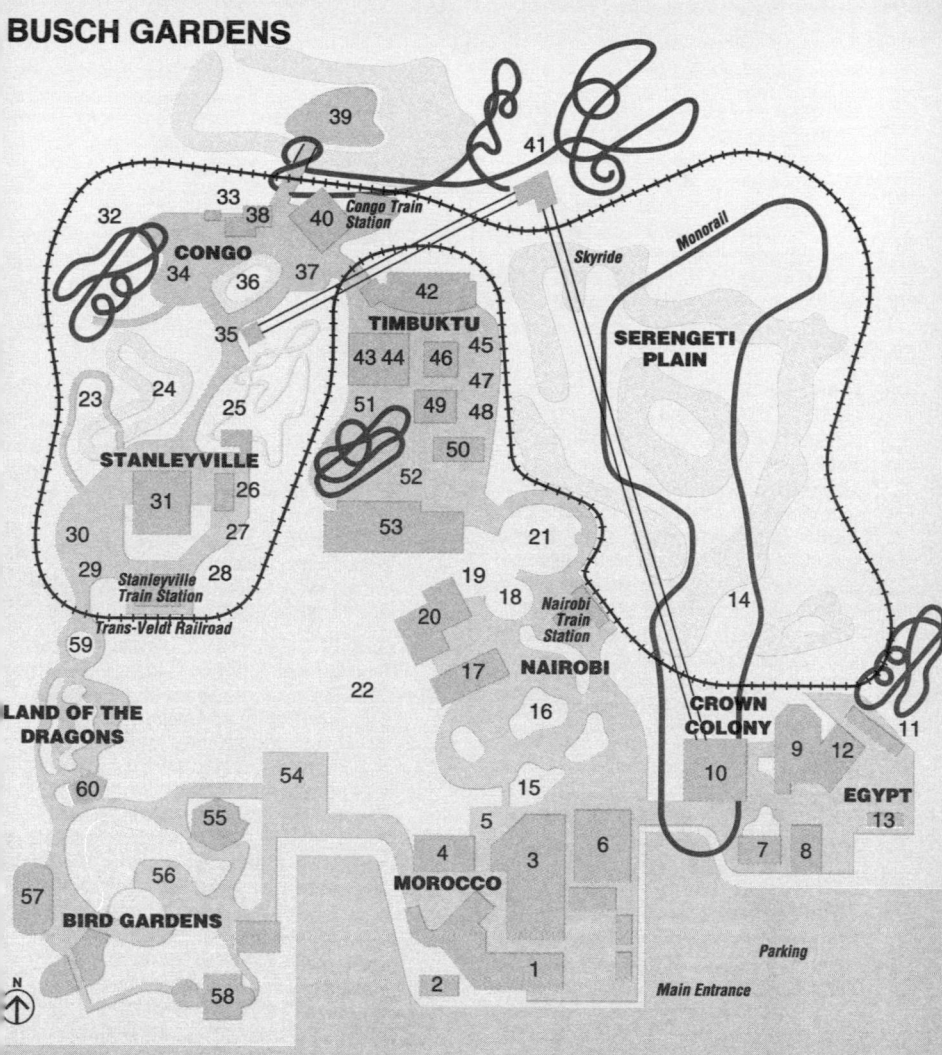

MOROCCO
1 Guest Services
2 Marrakesh Theater
3 Boujad Bakery
4 Zagora Cafe
5 Sultan's Tent
6 Moroccan Palace Theater

CROWN COLONY
7 Clydesdale Hamlet
8 Akbar's Adventure Tour
9 Crown Colony House
10 Skyride & Monorail Station

EGYPT
11 Montu
12 Tut's Tomb
13 Sand Dig

SERENGETI PLAIN
14 Edge of Africa

NAIROBI
15 Myombe Reserve
16 Curiosity Caverns
17 Animal Nursery

18 Tortoise Habitat
19 Petting Zoo
20 Show Jumping Hall of Fame/
   Reptiles
21 Elephant Habitat
22 Gwazi

STANLEYVILLE
23 Orchid Canyon
24 TanganyikaTidal Wave
25 Stanley Falls Log Flume
26 Bazaar Cafe
27 Stanleyville Smokehouse
28 Warthog Habitat
29 Orangutans
30 Zambezi Pavilion
31 Stanleyville Theate

CONGO
32 Python
33 Congo Bongo Fun Center
34 Python Ice Cream
35 Skyride
36 Claw Island
37 Kiddie Rides
38 Vivi Restaurant
39 Congo River Rapids

40 Ubanga-Banga Bumper Cars
41 Kumba

TIMBUKTU
42 Dolphin Theater
43 Games Area
44 Oasis Juice Bar
45 Crazy Camel
46 Carousel Caravan
47 Phoenix
48 Kiddie Rides
49 Electronic Arcade
50 Gift Shop
51 Scorpion
52 Sandstorm
53 Festhaus

BIRD GARDENS
54 Eagle Canyon
55 Hospitality House
56 Bird Show Theater
57 Aviary
58 Koala Habitat
59 Lory Landing

LAND OF THE DRAGONS
60 Dragon's Tale Theater

Within Busch Gardens:

Morocco At the main entrance to the park are Moroccan craft demonstrations and snake charmers. The very popular Mystic Sheiks of Morocco Marching Band performs here daily and the area has three theaters with impressive live shows. Lockers, a bank machine, guest relations, rest rooms, and the lost and found are also located here. For snacks, choose from the **Boujad Bakery,** the open-air **Zagora Cafe,** and an ice-cream parlor.

Crown Colony Overlooking the **Serengeti Plain,** this section of the park features a hospitality center and the **Crown Colony House**—the park's only table-service restaurant. Stop in at **Clydesdale Hamlet** for a close-up look at the massive draft horses. Nearby, **Akbar's Adventure Tour,** a computer-controlled flight simulator, takes you on a hilarious trek to—and through—some of Egypt's most recognizable landmarks. The wacky show stars the actor and comedian Martin Short. Children love the ride—and, although it lasts only six minutes, it's wild enough to please thrill-seeking teens and jaded adults, too.

Egypt The newest themed land features a record-breaking ride. Traveling at speeds in excess of 60 mph, **Montu** is the world's longest and tallest inverted roller coaster. In **Tut's Tomb,** guests walk through a replica of the famous excavation site as it appeared to archaeologists in the 1920s. The **Sand Dig** gives children the opportunity to unearth Egyptian "antiquities."

Serengeti Plain Nearly 800 African animals, including hippos, giraffes, antelopes, dromedary camels, Nile crocodiles, flamingos, and ostriches, are found in this 80-acre veldtlike plain. It's also a breeding ground for several endangered species, including the black rhino. If the heat bothers you, see this area from the air-conditioned monorail, steam locomotive, sky ride, or promenade. The new 15-acre **Edge of Africa** puts you close to the animals. On a self-guided tour, you'll see hippos, giraffes, lions, baboons, meerkats, crocodiles, hyenas, and other species. Throughout the journey, roaming guides offer educational facts about the animals and Africa.

Nairobi A great place to take children, the **Nairobi Animal Nursery** is home to baby birds and other infant animals. It looks like a Dr. Livingstone–era African hospital, but inside, modern equipment provides care to diapered baby chimpanzees, young gazelles, cape buffaloes, and other animals. At the **Nairobi Train Station** is a petting zoo with reptile displays. An unusual and fascinating feature is **Curiosity Caverns,** where creatures of the night are exhibited inside a cavelike environment. Here reside bush babies, sloths, fruit bats, hedgehogs, and an assortment of poisonous American snakes as well as pythons and boa constrictors. Near the entrance is **Tortoise Habitat,** featuring the last survivors of their species. The huge creatures can weigh up to 300 pounds and live more than a hundred years. The **Myombe Reserve** is a three-acre habitat where six lowland

Busch Gardens

gorillas and eight common chimpanzees, both endangered species, roam freely in a tropical forest. New to this area is **Gwazi,** a huge double wooden roller coaster. Up to 22 Asian elephants share the **Elephant Habitat** in Nairobi's northernmost sector. Elephant washes are scheduled several times daily; zoo education aides are available to answer questions.

Stanleyville Skip the shopping bazaar here and head for the two water rides, **Tanganyika Tidal Wave** and **Stanley Falls Log Flume.** The former, a boat ride, concludes with a 55-foot plunge into a splash pool, while the latter is an outstanding water-flume ride. Snack stops include **Stanleyville Smokehouse** and **Bazaar Cafe,** where you can grab a barbecued-beef sandwich or succulent ribs.

Congo Billed as the largest and fastest steel roller coaster in the southeastern US, the **Kumba** takes riders upside down seven times and reputedly features the world's largest loop. Also located here is the **Congo River Rapids,** a white-water boat ride, and the **Python,** a roller coaster with a 360° double spiral. **Claw Island** displays rare white Bengal tigers in a natural setting; if you're lucky, the tigers will be in a playful mood, cooling off in the waterfall. Strawberry waffle-cone sundaes are the specialty at **Python Ice Cream.**

Timbuktu Don't miss the wild **Phoenix** boat ride here—a thrill for the hardiest—as well as the **Scorpion,** another 360° loop roller coaster. A shopping bazaar features African artisans at work. Corned-beef sandwiches, German sausages, and cold beer are served at the 1,200-seat **Festhaus** German beer hall.

Bird Gardens At this popular attraction nearly 2,000 exotic birds are on display; some perform in the park's *World of Birds* show, and others can be seen in **Eagle Canyon,** a natural habitat display that is home to American bald eagles. The free-flight aviary is full of exotic birds and greenery. Also in this section is an exhibit featuring Australian wallabies and koalas. The new **Lory Landing** allows bird lovers to feed nectar to colorful lorikeets, a type of parakeet, and you can see the production of the TV show "Jack Hanna's Animal Adventures." Stop in the **Anheuser-Busch Hospitality House** for pizza, sandwiches, and complimentary Anheuser-Busch products.

Land of the Dragons This fantasyland features Dumphrey, a charming and frolicsome dragon, who roves an enchanted forest looking for children (and adults) to play with. The main focus of Dumphrey's domain is a three-story-tall tree house filled with adventurous activities, including a babbling brook with stepping stones, an echo chamber, and brilliant crystals that give off music

when trod upon. Outside the abode are rides, including a Ferris wheel, a dragon carousel, slides, and a rope climb, among others. In addition, there's a children's theater where the allegorical world of dragons is presented.

8 Adventure Island For the best aquatic thrill rides on Florida's west coast, visit this 25-acre water park with 17 attractions run by **Busch Gardens.** Start with **Aruba Tuba,** an inner tube adventure that carries riders over, under, and around other existing slides in the park. **Calypso Coaster** is a twisting flume from a 45-foot tower that ends in a splash pool. Other favorites are the **Caribbean Corkscrew,** a four-story ride through a 240-foot translucent tube that crisscrosses another tube, and the **Everglides,** a 35-foot drop on a surf toboggan that zips you down a 72-foot slide and then skims across a hundred feet of water. There is also a championship volleyball complex, snack bars, picnic areas, surf shop, video games, and locker rooms. ♦ Admission. Daily mid-Mar–early Sept; Sa-Su mid-Sept–late Oct; closed November through mid-March. 10001 Malcolm McKinley Dr (at E Linebaugh Ave). 987.5660

9 Rumpelmayer's German Restaurant ★ **$$** This 110-seat Old World restaurant offers Wiener schnitzel, sauerbraten, and various sausages, as well as Polish stuffed cabbage, *schweinebraten* (pork tenderloin roast with a sweet stuffing), chicken schnitzel, and smoked mackerel. ♦ Bavarian ♦ Daily lunch and dinner. Reservations recommended. 4812 E Busch Blvd (between Ashlee La and Connechusett Rd). 989.9563

10 Days Inn Busch Gardens Maingate $ A half-mile west of **Busch Gardens,** this motel has 174 standard rooms surrounding a pool, and laundry service. In addition to a **Denny's,** there's an adjacent 24-hour coffee shop. ♦ 2901 E Busch Blvd (between N 30th and N 27th Sts). 933.6471, 800/325.2525; fax 932.0261; www.daysinn.com

11 Lowry Park Zoo With more than 1,500 animals of 375 different species in an open-air, natural habitat, this park ranks among the top three zoos of its size (24 acres) in North America. Its most popular attraction is the **Manatee and Aquatic Center,** where two large viewing tanks afford close-up looks at the five resident manatees. The **Asian Domain** boasts such animals as Sumatran tigers, Indian rhinos, and Persian leopards. More than a dozen different species, including chimpanzees, orangutans, and baboons, are found in the **Primate World.** Not only native Florida animals are found in the **Florida Wildlife Center,** but also species from elsewhere in North America that adapt well to Florida's climate—river otters, black bears, and so forth. There's also an aviary with 65 species of subtropical birds, and a petting zoo. ◆ Admission. Daily. 7530 North Blvd (between W Sligh Ave and W Patterson St). 932.0245

12 Tampa Airport Hilton at MetroCenter
$$ This 12-story, 238-room hotel is situated in a commercial area halfway between the airport and downtown. The contemporary rooms have a separate vanity area in the bathrooms, and a section of the hotel is reserved for nonsmokers. Other facilities include a restaurant, lobby bar, heated pool, hot tub, and tennis court. There's free parking and a courtesy airport shuttle. ◆ 2225 N Lois Ave (at International Dr). 877.6688, 800/445.8667; fax 879.3264; www.hilton.com &

13 Hyatt Regency Westshore $$ Most of the 445 rooms here overlook Tampa Bay and offer stunning views of the evening sunset. Other highlights include three restaurants, three lounges, two heated pools, two lighted tennis courts, a sauna, whirlpool, health club, and jogging trails. There's also a 35-acre nature preserve. Ask for a cost-saving weekend rate or package. A courtesy airport shuttle is provided. ◆ 6200 Courtney Campbell Cswy (between Eisenhower Blvd and Rocky Point Dr). 874.1234, 800/233.1234; fax 281.9618; www.hyatt.com &

Within the Hyatt Regency Westshore:

Armani's ★★★$$$ Residents flock to this elegant dining spot atop the hotel for both the lovely view of Old Tampa Bay and the gourmet creations, including housemade fresh pasta. The cuisine ranges from filet mignon with gorgonzola to veal with wild mushrooms and creamy black-truffle sauce. There's an ample wine list and antipasto bar. ◆ Northern Italian ◆ M-Sa dinner. Reservations recommended. 281.9165

As a young English journalist, Winston Churchill was sent to Tampa to report on developments on the Cuban front of the Spanish-American War.

Oystercatchers ★★$$$ Set in a Key West–style building in the nature preserve and connected to the hotel by a boardwalk, this restaurant sports a casual ambience. Enjoy the catch of the day mesquite-grilled, poached, sautéed, or blackened, either inside or outdoors. Nonaquatic offerings include steak, lamb, and duck. ◆ Seafood ◆ M-Sa lunch and dinner; Su brunch. Reservations recommended. 281.9116

14 Embassy Suites Tampa Airport Westshore $$ Located in the Westshore business district, this 16-story, 221-unit hotel is about two miles from the airport but convenient to downtown. The exterior is white stucco and glass; inside, there are archways and Florida artwork. Each suite has a separate bedroom and living room with kitchen. Other facilities include a cafe, lounge, heated pool, sundeck, saunas, whirlpool, exercise room, and library. A cooked-to-order breakfast and evening cocktails are included in the rates. Courtesy airport shuttle service is provided. ◆ 555 N Westshore Blvd (at I-275). 875.1555, 800/EMBASSY; fax 287.3664; www.embassysuites.com &

15 WestShore Plaza The closest shopping venue to downtown Tampa, this center has more than a hundred specialty and department stores, as well as an international food court and self-service post office. ◆ Daily. N Westshore and W JFK Blvds. 286.0790

16 Donatello ★★★$$$ The plain white stucco building doesn't give a hint of the elegance inside this restaurant. A red rose on each table enhances the sophisticated main dining room, where diners enjoy a range of food, from Northern Italian dishes to veal, rack of lamb, and chicken, all served by tuxedo-clad waiters. If you have room for dessert, spend your calories on the Amaretto ice cream. For a final touch, each woman is presented with a long-stemmed red rose as she leaves. ◆ Italian ◆ Daily lunch and dinner. Reservations recommended. 232 N Dale Mabry Hwy (at B St). 875.6660

Ybor City

Don Vicente Martínez Ybor, a Spanish-born cigar maker from Key West, via Cuba, created Ybor City (pronounced Ee-bor) in 1886. He developed a planned industrial community based on cigar manufacturing, and employed nonunionized Cuban immigrants in order to keep his costs low. From then until the city's decline in the 1930s, one-fifth of Ybor City's 20,000 residents worked at the cigar factory. But the Depression, the rising popularity of cigarettes, and the invention of cigar-rolling machines hit Ybor City hard. Today, you can experience the legacy of Ybor City, a National Landmark Historic District (and still buy a hand-rolled cigar), with free walking tours that are offered every Thursday and Saturday morning (248.3712). During the day, tourists and locals alike shop and dine on **Seventh Avenue,** Ybor City's main street, or in **Ybor Square,** the upscale shopping area in the old cigar factory. After dark, Ybor City has a variety of clubs that cater to all tastes. Seventh Avenue is closed to vehicular traffic on Friday and Saturday nights. The **Columbia Restaurant,** one of Ybor City's architectural splendors, also offers flamenco dancing on most nights.

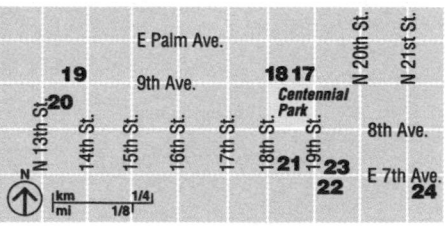

17 Ybor City State Museum The first stop in Ybor City should be the state museum, which is housed in the **Ferlita Bakery** building. Displayed here are historic pictures of the founding of Ybor City and the rise and fall of the cigar industry. A small formal garden connects the museum with the **Cigar Worker's Cottage.** ◆ Nominal admission. Tu-Sa. 1818 Ninth Ave (between 19th and 18th Sts). 247.6323

18 Cigar Worker's Cottage Three cottages built on Fifth Avenue around 1895 were moved here to re-create a turn-of-the-century streetscape. This narrow home has a shingle roof and has been restored to its original appearance. Enter through the picket gate. The front room extends the width of the abode, and the hallway leads back to the kitchen, passing two bedrooms on the right. Water now comes from a pump, but when the houses were originally built there was no electricity, heat, or water. Window shutters were closed to keep the house as cool as possible, and cheesecloth served as screens. ◆ Nominal admission. Tu-Sa. 1804 Ninth Ave (between 19th and 18th Sts). 247.1434

19 Cafe Creole ★★$$ Gumbo, Louisiana oysters, and crawfish are served at this casual restaurant. There's a courtyard for alfresco dining, and live jazz is an attraction Wednesday through Saturday evenings. ◆ Cajun/Creole ◆ M-Sa lunch and dinner. 1330 Ninth Ave (between 14th and N 13th Sts). 247.6283

20 Ybor Square Restaurants and shops are squeezed into Don Vicente Martínez Ybor's original cigar factory, which still consists of three buildings—**The Stemmery, The Factory,** and **The Warehouse.** Be sure to note the five-globe light posts here that are prevalent in Ybor City. ◆ M-Sa; Su noon-5:30PM. N 13th St (between Eighth and Ninth Aves). 247.4497 ✦

Within Ybor Square:

The Stemmery It was in this three-story redbrick building that the stems were removed from the tobacco leaves, most of which were imported from Cuba. It now houses shops and restaurants.

Within The Stemmery:

Chevere Clothes by Christine St. Rick of California, unique colorful and comfortable designer clothes from Guatemala, and Indonesian as well as Maya folk art are sold here. ◆ Daily. First floor. 247.1339

Tampa Rico Cigar Co. The sign inside says it all: "Thanks for smoking." Notice the cigar-store Indian on the right as you walk in; on the left a cigar maker rolls cigars behind a counter Tuesday through Friday until 3PM. ◆ Tu-Su. Second floor. 248.0218

The Warehouse Formerly the storage facility of the cigar factory, it now boasts a restaurant on the first floor, and offices on the second.

Within The Warehouse:

Spaghetti Warehouse Restaurant ★$ Part of an international chain, this large restaurant draws a casual, young crowd. The menu features more than a dozen pasta dishes, as well as chicken parmigiana and Italian sausage. ◆ Italian ◆ Daily lunch and dinner. 1911 N 13th St. 248.1720

The Factory As the name implies, this is where the cigars were made. Today it houses offices on the second floor, and a variety of shops, eateries, and a jazz club on the first level.

21 La Tropicana Cafe ★★$ This informal restaurant has been a hotbed of political activism ever since the Spanish-American War, and it is still the place to be seen and make deals if you're a local politician. In a back corner is a table set apart from the others with a nameplate on it that reads: "Reserved for Roland Manteiga." Manteiga is the editor of *La Gaceta,* an Ybor City weekly printed in Spanish and English that includes a page of news in Italian. (A painting of him in his trademark white-linen suit hangs on the restaurant wall.) The paper was begun by his father as a Spanish-language daily in 1922. It would be worth it to poke your head in just for the atmosphere, but the cafe also serves great Cuban sandwiches, spicy crab cakes, and stuffed potatoes. ◆ Cuban ◆ M-Sa breakfast and lunch. 1822 E Seventh Ave (between 19th and 18th Sts). 247.4040

22 Ovo Cafe ★★$ Eclectic and whimsical, this 150-seat restaurant is divided into three separate dining rooms, each decorated with antique kitchen utensils that the owner collects. Food is "clean American cuisine"— no microwaving or frying here. They make pizza from scratch and offer five kinds of pierogis (pasta pockets stuffed with mashed potatoes and other ingredients, like spinach or ham). Salads are a hit, especially the California chopped salad and the sweet-and-sour Chinese chicken salad. "Wafffles with a Splash," flavored with a splash of liquor, are a specialty, and they offer 40 varieties of martini and 32 kinds of wine by the bottle or glass. ◆ American ◆ Daily lunch and dinner. 1907 E Seventh Ave (between N 20th and 19th Sts). 248.6979

23 Blues Ship Live blues and jazz are presented here in the heart of Tampa's Latin Quarter. Pub grub is also served, but most come for the music. ◆ Cover. Tu-Su 3PM-3AM. 1910 E Seventh Ave (between N 20th and 19th Sts). 248.6097

At least 51 million tons of cargo are carried through Tampa Bay each year.

Baseball spring training started in 1888, when the precursors of the Minnesota Twins tried to get a jump on the competition by practicing in Jacksonville, Florida, during the spring. Now, between 20 and 26 major league baseball teams hold spring training in Florida.

Restaurants/Clubs: Red   **Hotels:** Blue

Shops/♟ Outdoors: Green   **Sights/Culture:** Black

24 Columbia Restaurant ★★$$$ Billed as "America's Oldest Spanish Restaurant," this place dates back to 1905 and is a favorite, especially with tourists. It was so successful that the original spot has burgeoned into a Florida chain. The eatery grew from **The Corner Cafe** to a restaurant that now occupies a whole city block and has 11 serving rooms, seating a total of 1,660 people. Ornate chandeliers hang from the ceiling, and the walls are covered with brightly colored Spanish tiles. The waiters wear dinner jackets even at lunch. In the evening there is live entertainment, including a flamenco show Monday through Thursday at 8:30PM and at various times Friday and Saturday. Cuban black-bean soup and Spanish bean soup are recommended, as is the 1905 salad, paella, red snapper fillet *alicante* (baked in a garlic, onion, and wine sauce, and covered with roasted almonds), and flan. ◆ Spanish ◆ Daily lunch and dinner. 2117 E Seventh Ave (between N 22nd and N 21st Sts). 248.4961. Also at: The Pier, 800 Second Ave NE (east of Bayshore Dr), St. Petersburg. 822.8000

Downtown

Commerce, finance, art, and culture are housed side by side in temples of steel, granite, and glass in the heart of Tampa. With the opening of the **Garrison Seaport Center,** a new 30-acre complex featuring cruise-ship terminals, the **Florida Aquarium,** the **Ice Palace,** and restaurants, more and more people are flocking downtown not only for business, but for entertainment as well.

Although most of the buildings are new, the structure that dominates the skyline is the former **Tampa Bay Hotel,** a 13-minaret castle built by railroad tycoon Henry B. Plant over a hundred years ago. The hotel closed in 1930 and was taken over and converted into a museum by the **University of Tampa.**

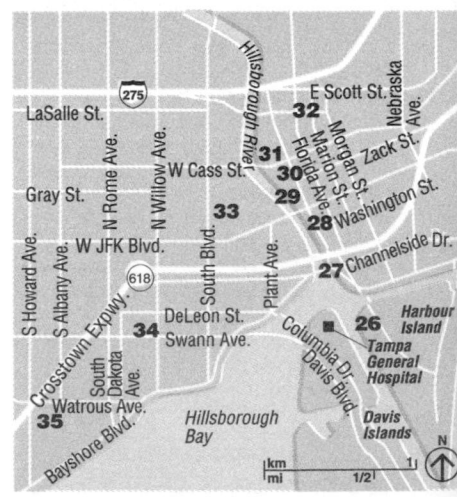

It's a Bet: Parimutuel Wagering

KEELY EDWARDS

Although Florida voters once again rejected casino gambling in a 1994 referendum, three sports involving parimutuel betting have long ›en associated with the Sunshine State: jai alai, ›eyhound racing, and thoroughbred horse racing.

i alai, promoted as the world's fastest sport, is known for its many players from Spain, South America, and Mexico, who display a particular interest in and aptitude for the game. Originally a 17th-century Basque sport, the game involves throwing a hard ball (called a pelota) against a wall and catching it before it bounces using a wicker basket called a *casta* that's strapped to the player's hand. Two teams compete against one another, with individual members playing either singles or doubles matches (similar to Davis Cup tennis). Spectators bet on the teams involved. A good player can propel a ball as fast as 150 mph. The game is played year-round at the **Orlando Jai**

Alai and Racebook (6405 S Hwy 17, at Semoran Blvd, 407/339.6221) in **Fern Park.**

Greyhound racing is similar to horse racing: The first one around the track and across the finish line wins. A fast-moving mechanical rabbit is used to motivate the dogs to run at their top speed from the moment they break out of the gate. Races are held at several locations throughout Central Florida. The **Sanford-Orlando Kennel Club** (301 Dog Track Rd, between Hwy 17 and County Rd 427, 407/831.1600), in **Longwood,** holds races November through April. From May through November, the dogs run at the **Super Seminole Greyhound Park** (2000 Seminole Blvd, east of Lake Dr, 407/699.4510), in adjoining **Casselberry.** In **St. Petersburg** at **Derby Lane** (10490 Gandy Blvd, between San Martin Blvd and Fourth St N, 813/576.1361), the greyhounds race from January through June; the **Tampa Greyhound Track** (8300 Nebraska Ave, between E Bird St and E Waters Ave, 813/932.4313) holds races Monday through Saturday July through December; and the dogs run from November through April at the **Melbourne Greyhound Park** (1100 N Wickham Rd, between Sarno Rd and Eau Gallie Blvd, 407/259.9800).

For aficionados of thoroughbred horse racing, the only track in the area is **Tampa Bay Downs** (11225 Race Track Rd, north of W Hillsborough Ave, 813/855.4401), which holds meets daily from December through early May.

25 Tampa/Ybor Trolley Six 30-seat, rubber-tire trolleys connect Ybor City with downtown, and the port area to the **Tampa Convention Center** (S Franklin and E Platt Sts). ♦ 254.4278

25 Garrison Seaport Center Work continues on this $300-million waterfront and entertainment complex that covers 30 acres in downtown Tampa. The center includes three state-of-the-art cruise ship terminals, one the home of **Carnival Cruise Lines;** the **Florida Aquarium;** a waterfront amphitheater with 5,000 seats; and restaurants. ♦ Channelside Dr (south of Adamo Dr). 272.0555

Within Garrison Seaport Center:

Florida Aquarium One of the largest (4.3 acres), most modern aquariums in the nation, this $84-million, three-story attraction was designed by **Hellmuth, Obata & Kassabaum (HOK)** and **Esherick, Homsey, Dodge & Davis (EHD&D).** The 80-foot-high glass roof is shaped like a seashell and contains the **Wetlands Gallery,** one of four galleries housing more than 4,300 plants and animals native to Florida. The focus is on Florida's waterways and follows a drop of water from freshwater springs through wetlands and finally to the ocean. Each gallery concentrates

on a different habitat: **Florida Wetlands, Florida Bays and Beaches, Florida Coral Reefs,** and **Florida Offshore.** There is also an interpretive theater, book and gift shop, and waterfront restaurant. ♦ Admission. Daily. 701 Channelside Dr. 273.4000; fax 224.9583

Ice Palace This new sports arena is the venue for the **Tampa Bay Lightning National Hockey League** franchise, as well as for concerts and meetings. ♦ 401 Channelside Dr. 223.6100

26 Wyndham Harbour Island Hotel $$ Most of the 300 rooms and suites at this property have a waterfront view. Amenities include a restaurant, several eateries, tennis, racquetball, squash, an outdoor pool, exercise room, five-mile jogging trail along Bayshore Boulevard, marina, and spas. ♦ 725 S Harbour Island Blvd (south of S Franklin St). 229.5000, 800/631.4200, 800/822.4200 in Canada; fax 229.5322; www.wyndham.com ♿

27 Tampa Bay History Center Exhibits of five centuries of Florida history are displayed in the center's new and permanent home on Franklin Street. Featured are the Timucuan Indians, Spanish exploration, the Spanish-American War, and World War II. There's also a display on Henry B. Plant that includes his

183

role in starting the **Tampa Bay Hotel,** and the Tampa railroad is shown in photographs and railcar models. ♦ Free. Daily. 225 S Franklin St (at E Platt St). 228.0097

28 Hyatt Regency Tampa $$$ This hotel is Tampa's largest, with 518 rooms. The striking atrium lobby boasts a graceful waterfall and many plants. Facilities include a pool, health club, in-room movies, two restaurants, and two lounges. There's also a complimentary airport shuttle. ♦ 211 N Tampa St (between Washington and Jackson Sts). 225.1234; 800/233.1234; fax 273.0234; www.hyatt.com &

29 Tampa Museum of Art A 5,000-square-foot appendix to this museum—the **Florida Gallery**—showcases Florida's recognized and emerging artists. A library-resource center has also been added, and the museum store has been enlarged. Also, a special-events courtyard and sculpture garden with a reflecting pool recently opened, together with the seven-acre **Curtis Hixon Park** and a river walk along the Hillsborough River connecting the park to the museum. Future plans include extending the riverwalk to the **Tampa Convention Center.** The changing exhibits range from classical antiquities to contemporary art. ♦ Free. Donations accepted. Tu-Sa 10AM-5PM; Su 1-5PM. 600 N Ashley Dr (between W JFK Blvd and Gasparilla Plaza). 274.8130 &

SINCE 1926

30 Tampa Theatre A restored 1926 movie palace listed in the National Register of Historic Places, this theater has perennially twinkling stars on the ceiling and is dotted with Greek and Roman sculpture representations and ornate colonnades. This is *the* place in the Tampa Bay area to see foreign, alternative, and classic films in style. Concerts and shows are often held here as well. ♦ 711 N Franklin St (between Zack and Polk Sts). Box office 274.8286, recorded information 274.8981

31 Tampa Bay Performing Arts Center This $57-million complex on the banks of the Hillsborough River is considered the best of the three area performance halls—the acoustics are nearly perfect. The 3,000-square-foot, 100-seat **Off-Center Theater** has been added to the center. It hosts shows by local theater groups, musicians, poets, dancers, and others. Other performance arenas include the 2,400-seat **Festival Hall,** a 900-seat playhouse, and a 300-seat theater featuring Broadway shows, concerts, and ballets. ♦ 1010 W.C. MacInnes Pl (between W Tyler and W Fortune Sts). 222.1000, 800/955.1045

32 Museum of African-American Art The first of its kind in Florida, this museum boasts more than 80 artists represented in 140 works of sculpture, watercolors, and paintings. The **Barnett-Aden Collection,** valued at $7.5 million, is regarded as the country's foremost African-American collection. ♦ Donation. Tu-Sa; Su 1-4:30PM. 1308 Marion St (between E Laurel and E Scott Sts). 272.2466 &

Tampa Bay Performing Arts Center

Henry B. Plant Museum

33 Henry B. Plant Museum The onion-shaped minarets on this structure have been a Tampa landmark since railroad tycoon Henry Plant opened it as the **Tampa Bay Hotel** in 1891. Inspired by the Alhambra Palace in Spain, the hotel awed guests and locals with its exotic design, and the then mind-boggling price tag of $2 million. It was filled with priceless art and furnishings from Asia, and visited by socialites from the US and Europe. Today the hotel has a museum in the south wing with cabinets once owned by Queen Isabella of Spain, chairs that belonged to Marie Antoinette, and antiques and furnishings from the hotel. The other end of the building is the site of the main administrative offices of the **University of Tampa**. ◆ Museum: Admission. Tu-Su. University of Tampa, 401 W JFK Blvd (at University Dr). 254.1891 &

34 Old Hyde Park Village Tampa's upscale mall has about 60 stores, restaurants, and theaters on one level. Shops include **Jacobson's, Ann Taylor, Brooks Brothers, Banana Republic, Polo Ralph Lauren, Structure, Laura Ashley, Talbots, The Sharper Image, Williams-Sonoma,** and **Godiva Chocolatier.** ◆ M-W, Sa; Th-F 10AM-9PM; Su noon-5PM. 1509 Swann Ave (between S Oregon and South Dakota Aves). 251.3500

Within Old Hyde Park Village:

Cactus Club ★$$ Try the unusual thin-crust Texas pizza at this eatery. One variety comes with fresh tomatoes and basil; another with red and green peppers, spicy chorizo, and monterey jack cheese. Burgers and Mexican platters are favorites, as are the *chiles rellenos* (Anaheim peppers stuffed with cheese, covered with a light batter, and fried). ◆ Tex-Mex ◆ Daily lunch and dinner. 251.4089

Selena's ★★$$$ This pretty restaurant serves zesty Creole and hearty Italian fare in several antiques-filled dining rooms. Spicy red beans and rice with sausage won't leave you hungry. For a lighter meal, try the catch of the day prepared Creole-style and laced with plenty of garlic and lemon butter. You can't go wrong with any of the delicate pasta dishes. Live music Monday through Saturday nights adds to the ambience. ◆ Creole/Italian ◆ Daily lunch and dinner. 251.2116

Joffrey's Coffee & Tea ★★$ Spend an hour with a novel in this famous gourmet coffeehouse, where wonderful desserts and confections are offered. ◆ Coffeehouse ◆ M-W 8AM-11PM; Th-Sa 8AM-midnight; Su 9AM-11PM. 251.3315

35 Bern's Steak House ★★★$$$$ Tampa's famous steak haven also has a phone-book–size wine list with more than 6,800 selections, and vegetables grown on owner Bern Laxer's organic farm. Order your beef from a chart according to cut, thickness, and weight. Don't let the garishness of red velvet, antiques, and assorted statuary put you off—this restaurant's worth at least one visit, and more if you're a steak purist. Seafood from live tanks is also on the menu. There are private booths upstairs for dessert only. ◆ American ◆ Daily dinner. Reservations recommended. 1208 S Howard Ave (between Marjory and Watrous Aves). 251.2421, 800/282.1547 in FL

Tarpon Springs

The town of Tarpon Springs was founded in 1876, but it wasn't until 1905 that John Cocoris brought Greek sponge divers from Key West to settle the area. Today the natural sponge industry is still thriving and Tarpon Springs remains a Greek enclave. To learn more about this business, walk along **Dodecanese Boulevard** among the heaps of newly harvested sponges drying on the docks. Buy the soft, natural sponges in every imaginable size in nearby shops. Leave time to enjoy a Greek meal (don't forget to try the delicious desserts) in one of the cafes, tearooms, or restaurants here, and to pay a visit to the Byzantine **St. Nicholas Greek Orthodox Cathedral.**

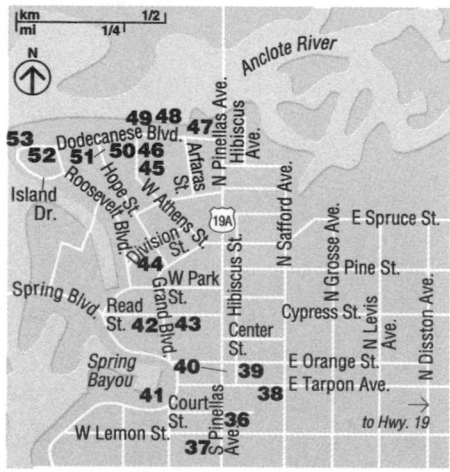

With more than 50 miles of waterfront, Tarpon Springs is sometimes called the "Venice of the South." Don't miss the historic waterfront mansions in the **Spring Bayou** (also known as "Golden Crescent") area to get a flavor of how the wealthy lived in their summer retreats during the 19th century.

Area code 727 unless otherwise noted.

36 Tarpon Springs Cultural Center Built in 1914 to serve as city hall, today this 84-seat theater features films, music performances, dance troupes, and children's operettas. There are also gallery exhibits pertaining to the town's culture and history. ♦ Tu-Sa. 101 S Pinellas Ave (at E Court St). 942.5605

37 The Frog Prince—Puppetry Arts Center & Theatre Frog Prince Frederick, Chester the Jester, Whoo-ty Owl, Randy Russell Raccoon, and Harry the Hare entertain at this theater-cum–enchanted forest. All shows are performed by professional puppeteers. The gift shop sells volunteer-made puppets, coloring books, tapes, and supplies for making puppets. ♦ Nominal fee. Call for show times. The Arcade, 210 S Pinellas Ave (between W Boyer and W Lemon Sts), Suite 158. 942.2222

38 Tarpon Springs Historical Society Museum A renovated railroad station displays historic photos and memorabilia of the area. ♦ Free. Tu, Th 2-4PM; Sa 11AM-3PM. 168 E Tarpon Ave (at S Safford Ave). 938.3711

39 Oxford House ★$ This English tearoom doubles as a gift shop with homemade accessories and crafts. Sandwiches, salads, muffins, and scones are served in the best British tradition. It's a good place to stop after touring **St. Nicholas Greek Orthodox Cathedral.** ♦ Tearoom ♦ M-Sa lunch and tea. 118 E Orange St (between N Safford Ave and Hibiscus St). 937.0133

40 St. Nicholas Greek Orthodox Cathedral A scaled-down reproduction of the famed St. Sophia's in Istanbul, this structure is an outstanding example of Byzantine architecture. The present cathedral was built by **P. Pipinos** in 1943 after the original wooden structure (constructed in 1907) had burned to the ground in the late 1930s. The interior contains stained glass and elaborate icons placed within sculptured Grecian marble fronting the altar. The marble came from the Greek exhibit at the 1939 New York World's Fair. Although all the images have religious significance, the weeping icon of St. Nicholas is the most famous: On 5 December 1970 (the day before the name day of St. Nicholas), drops of moisture were noticed around the halo and on the eyes and cheeks. ♦ 36 N Pinellas Ave (between E Tarpon Ave and E Orange St). 937.3540 ♿

Weathering a Hurricane

Orlando has never suffered from a truly devastating hurricane, but the fearsome storms have swept up out of the **Gulf of Mexico,** the Caribbean, and the Atlantic to batter cities on both Florida coasts. **Tampa** and Miami residents may whip out the hurricane tracking maps the minute they hear about a storm, but Central Floridians living inland tend to shrug their shoulders. They're fond of telling newcomers that hurricanes aren't so bad and that you can outrun them a lot easier than you can a tornado. But don't you be quite so blasé about it. On the remote chance that one is headed your way, here are a few precautions you can take: If you're staying in a beachside hotel or condo, you'll want to head inland. If you expect to have to evacuate, make sure your car has a full tank of gas, refill important prescriptions, and get some cash (automatic teller machines may not work if the power goes out). Florida has well-planned evacuation routes, which you can learn about from the local news media. The hurricane season lasts from June to November, with September historically being the month with the most tropical-cyclone activity.

41 Spring Bayou/Golden Crescent During the late 1800s, Tarpon Springs flourished as an exclusive retreat for the wealthy, who came to escape the harsh climate of the North. Spring Boulevard forms a horseshoe, or crescent, around the lavish mansions along the water's edge, which date from 1885 to 1905 and may be viewed from the outside. A booklet detailing a walking tour of the area known as Spring Bayou (or "Golden Crescent") is available from the **Tarpon Springs Cultural Center** (see page 186).The bayou itself is an ocean inlet with some freshwater springs; manatees make their home here during the winter. The neighborhood comes into its own on Epiphany, celebrated annually on 6 January. The Orthodox version of the holiday commemorates the baptism of Christ in the River Jordan, when the Holy Spirit descended upon him in the form of a dove. A morning service at the **St. Nicholas Greek Orthodox Cathedral** (see page 186) is followed by a procession to the sponge docks at the bayou, where a white dove is released and the archbishop casts a lead-weighted white wooden crucifix into the water. Greek youths dive to retrieve it, and the one who finds it receives the church's blessing for the next year. The afternoon is given over to a *glendi* (party) with traditional Greek dancing, food, and music. ♦ Spring Blvd (between W Lemon St and Riverside Dr)

42 Safford House Anson Safford was an early developer of Tarpon Springs. His home began as a simple frame cottage when it was constructed in 1883. In 1887 it was expanded to two stories, and by 1890 several elaborate Victorian touches had been added. The house was moved from the original site on North Spring Boulevard to its present location 13 years later. Originally called **The Miramar,** the building is a prime example of wood-frame vernacular domestic architecture in Central Florida. The rectangular house consists of a balloon structure and a pier-type foundation. Hip-roofed porches with post supports and balustrades are attached to the southern, eastern, and western sides of the house. The gabled main roof is part shingle and part tin. The structure is the only private residence in Tarpon Springs listed on the National Register of Historic Places. ♦ Parkin Ct and Grand Blvd

43 Inness Paintings The largest collection of works—11 in all—by American landscape artist George Inness Jr. is on display in the **Universalist Church.** Inness had a home nearby and painted numerous scenes of Tarpon Springs between the 1890s and 1920s. Themes of spirituality and love of nature predominate. ♦ Donation. Tu-Su 2-5PM; closed June through September. 57 Read St (at Grand Blvd). 937.4682

44 Shrine of St. Michael An 11-year-old boy, Steve Tsalichis, became ill with a high fever in 1939. Efforts by 15 physicians to diagnose the child's condition failed, and his health worsened. Hospitalized, in a coma, with virtually no hope of recovery, Steve suddenly awoke one day and told his mother that a vision had appeared to him through one of the family's icons. The vision told the boy that he would be completely healed if his mother constructed a shrine to St. Michael. The promise was kept and young Steve recovered. Today, people of all faiths visit the shrine, which was built next to the family's home, and many have claimed miraculous healings. ♦ 113 Hope St (between Grand Blvd and Division St)

45 Paul's Shrimp House ★★$ Some of the best shrimp in the area is offered here—seasoned with lemon juice, olive oil, and Greek spices—as well as a tasty shrimp burger. Other specialties include conch salad, Greek salad, broiled octopus, and fried squid. Everything on the small menu is very good. ♦ Seafood ♦ Daily lunch and dinner. 530 W Athens St (between Acacia St and Dodecanese Blvd). 938.5093

46 St. Nicholas Boat Line Take a 30-minute ride down the Anclote River for a simulation of sponge harvesting, complete with a diver in an old-time orange suit. ♦ Daily. 693 Dodecanese Blvd (at W Athens St). 942.6425

47 Louis Pappas' Riverside Restaurant ★ $$ Long a tradition here, this 40,000-square-foot restaurant spawned from a roadside cafe in the 1920s. Specialties include leg of lamb, prime rib, Greek kabobs, and moussaka. The unusual Greek salad with chunks of potato is a meal in itself. All the wines are authentic. ♦ Greek ♦ Daily lunch and dinner. Reservations recommended. 10 Dodecanese Blvd (at Hwy 19A). 937.5101

Thelma "Butterfly" McQueen, best known for her role as Prissy in *Gone With the Wind*, was born in 1911 in Tampa.

After its factories in Key West burned to the ground in 1886, the cigar industry relocated the bulk of its manufacturing activity to Tampa.

Restaurants/Clubs: Red   **Hotels:** Blue
Shops/♀ Outdoors: Green   **Sights/Culture:** Black

48 Spongeorama This complex houses a museum and gift shop in an old sponge factory on the main tourist strip of Dodecanese Boulevard. Although the display is nothing fancy, the tour of the factory is the best way to understand the Greek community's roots and learn about sponge diving. A film on the sponge industry is shown in an adjacent building. ♦ Free. Daily. 510 Dodecanese Blvd (between Arfaras and W Athens Sts). 943.9509 &

Behind Spongeorama:

Island Wind Tours No reservations are required for this hour-long excursion on a 60-foot catamaran along the Anclote River and the Gulf of Mexico. You might spot dolphins, manatees, and several species of birds, including eagles, along the way. The boat also travels past Anclote Key, which has a scenic lighthouse. ♦ Schedule varies according to season. 600 Dodecanese Blvd. 934.0606

49 Golden Docks ★★$ Good food is offered in this casual, upbeat wharfside taverna adjacent to the **Sponge Docks**. For a sampling of Aegean dishes, try the combination platter—moussaka, gyro, and spinach pie. Other dishes include souvlaki and grilled seafood (scallops, squid, etc.) dishes. ♦ Greek ♦ Daily breakfast, lunch, and dinner. 698 Dodecanese Blvd (at W Athens St). 938.5155

50 Sponge Exchange Originally a trading post for sponges, this place has been restructured into a stylish open-air shopping center with touristy shops and restaurants. The merchandise sold is mostly women's clothing, souvenirs, and gifts. At the front is a walk-in exhibit on sponge auctions. ♦ 735 Dodecanese Blvd (between W Athens and Hope Sts). 934.9262

51 Hellas Bakery ★★★$ The *St. Petersburg Times*'s "Talk of the Town" column rates this bustling dining spot with indoor and outside seating ". . . one of the very best restaurants in the Tampa area." Try a house specialty, such as fresh grouper, red snapper, or lamb chops prepared the way the Greeks do—marinated in a tangy sauce and broiled. The pies, baklava, and apple turnovers are delicious. There's also a children's menu and a wine list with Greek and California offerings. ♦ Greek ♦ Daily lunch and dinner. 785 Dodecanese Blvd (at Hope St). 934.8400

52 Bill's Lighthouse ★★$$ Specialties at this casual and relaxed place are dolmas (stuffed grape leaves), flaming shish kebab, souvlaki, a good selection of fresh seafood, and such wonderful Greek pastries as baklava. ♦ Greek/American ♦ Daily lunch and dinner. 813 Dodecanese Blvd (between Roosevelt Blvd and Island Dr). 938.4895

53 Konger Coral Sea Aquarium This aquarium features a 120,000-gallon tank filled with fish found in the waters off Florida, including nurse shark, lemon shark, spiny lobster, and grouper. The four daily feedings are a major attraction, and there are petting tanks for small stingrays and sharks. Three smaller tanks showcase other marine life, including lionfish, eels, and sea anemones. ♦ Admission. Daily. 852 Dodecanese Blvd (between Roosevelt Blvd and Island Dr). 938.5378

54 Fred Howard Park Tarpon Springs's best beach can be reached by a milelong causeway. There are facilities for picnics, barbecues, fishing, and boating, as well as a children's playground. ♦ Howard Park Cswy (northwest of Sunset Dr). 937.4938

55 A.L. Anderson Park A 128-acre park on Salmon Bay and the shores of Lake Tarpon, this spot has a boat ramp, children's playground, barbecue grills, and covered picnic tables. ♦ Hwy 19 (between Tooke Rd and E Oakwood St)

Safety Harbor to Clearwater Harbor

Stretching from the shores of Safety Harbor to the waters of Clearwater Harbor, this area is certain to satisfy travelers with a hankering for sports activities, shopping, and dining. Whether your taste is for world-class horse racing (check out **Tampa Bay Downs**), championship-caliber golf (don't miss the **Westin Innisbrook Hilton Resort**), taking the waters (visit **Safety Harbor Resort & Spa**), beautiful nature preserves (**Caladesi Island** is one of the few remaining undisturbed barrier islands in Florida), or great shopping or eating (the award-winning **Bon Appétit** facing Clearwater Harbor is a must), you'll find it here.

Area code 727 unless otherwise noted.

56 Westin Innisbrook Hilton Resort $$$ Even if golf (the three courses here consistently rank high on national sports lists) and tennis aren't your games, this heavily wooded 1,200-acre property is one of Florida's best inland resorts. The $100-million, 1,200-condo complex also provides three excellent restaurants, six heated swimming pools, 15 tennis courts, racquetball courts, a fitness center, fishing, cycling, a regular beach shuttle, children's programs, and jogging trails. Money-saving packages are available; rates are lowest in summer. ◆ 36750 Hwy 19N (at Klosterman Rd), Palm Harbor. 942.2000, 800/456.2000; fax 942.5577; www.westin-innisbrook.com &

57 John Chesnut Sr. Park With 400 feet of sand on Lake Tarpon, this is the only freshwater beach in Pinellas County. There's also a bathhouse, 30-foot-high lookout tower, boat dock, canoe trails, and more than a mile of boardwalks. Nature trails wind through the park. ◆ Daily 7AM to sunset. 2200 E Lake Rd (between Rte 584 and Sandy Point Rd). 784.4686

58 Shoppes at Cloverplace Somewhat upscale stores and two notable restaurants are found in this strip mall. ◆ Tampa Rd (between Lake St. George Dr and W Lake Rd), Palm Harbor. No phone

Within the Shoppes at Cloverplace:

Sea Grill ★★$$ You won't go wrong if you choose calamari, grouper, or the catch of the day at this informal dining spot. Have your choice prepared charcoal grilled, sautéed, or baked. Steaks and lamb tenderloin are also on the menu. There's a fine wine list, too. ◆ Seafood ◆ Daily dinner. 787.6129

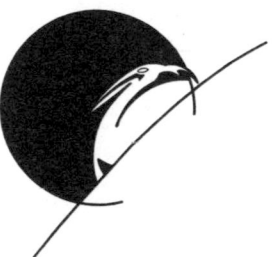

Blue Heron ★★★$$ Thai, Latin, and Jamaican spices are blended to near perfection at this casual spot for fine dining. The spices show up in such unusual dishes as Chinatown steak (marinated in mustard and soy sauce), grouper fillet *cardinale* (stuffed with lobster, shrimp, scallops, and served with lobster sauce and goat cheese), and Pacific Coast salmon over angel hair with fresh parmesan cheese. The roast chicken and the pork chops are good for less adventurous diners. ◆ American ◆ Tu-Su dinner. Reservations recommended. 789.5176

59 Tampa Bay Downs The only horse-racing course on Florida's west coast, this is where the Tampa Bay Derby, a preparation race for the Triple Crown, is held in March. There are as many as 10 races daily during the regular racing season, which normally runs from December to early May. Facilities include a restaurant, lounge, and gallery with big screens for replays. ◆ Nominal admission;

women and seniors free one day a week (call for the day). M, Th-Su. 11225 Race Track Rd (north of W Hillsborough Ave). 813/855.4401

60 Boston Cooker ★★★$$ This casual and relaxed place is a true find, where seafood specials are served with a big helping of Southern hospitality. Such New England dishes as fresh scrod au gratin and big-belly Ipswich clams (rare in Florida), along with fried scallops, mussels, and steamers, highlight the menu, as does lobster. There are unlimited refills of salad and hot rolls at dinnertime. ◆ Seafood ◆ M-Sa lunch and dinner. Reservations recommended. 3682 Tampa Rd (between Forest Lakes Blvd and Curlew Rd), Oldsmar. 855.2311

61 Honeymoon Island State Park This recreation area is suited for swimming, shelling, fishing, picnicking, or nature study. ◆ Nominal admission. Daily. 1 Causeway Blvd (west of Bayshore Blvd), Dunedin. 469.5942

62 Caladesi Island State Park One of the few remaining undisturbed barrier islands in Florida, this park lies off the coast of Dunedin in the Gulf of Mexico and can be reached only by boat. It's an ideal setting for shelling, fishing, picnicking, or beachcombing, with its three miles of undeveloped beaches. A self-guided nature trail winds through the interior. A ferry travels between the ranger station and **Honeymoon Island State Park.** Call 734.1501 for times and other locations. ◆ Admission. Daily until sunset. 469.5918

63 Classic Boutique Gallery An authorized dealer for such collectors' clubs as Hummel and Lladro, this shop features an extensive assortment of plates, figurines, crystal, Armani, Dept 56, Swarovski, and other collectibles. ◆ Daily Oct-May; M-Sa June-Sept. Causeway Plaza, 2632 Bayshore Blvd (at Causeway Blvd), Dunedin. 736.1444

64 Dunedin Fine Arts Center This bright, open center showcases exhibits of proven and emerging artists in two galleries. ◆ M-F, Su. 1143 Michigan Blvd (at Pinehurst Rd), Dunedin. 738.1892

Clara Barton established hospital headquarters in Tampa to aid the military during the Spanish-American War.

Florida's oldest restaurant is the Columbia in Ybor City, serving Spanish delicacies in ornately tiled, Old World surroundings.

Jazz musician David Sanborn, who as a child battled polio and as an adult played with such stars as Stevie Wonder, Paul Simon, and David Bowie, was born in Tampa.

From Comedy to Culture: The Ringling Museum of Art

Just 53 miles south of Tampa in **Sarasota** is Florida's official state art museum—the **John and Mable Ringling Museum of Art** (5401 Bayshore Rd, at Ringling Pl, 941/359.5700). A true delight for art and circus lovers alike, the museum features the couple's winter home, art and circus galleries, and a theater. John Ringling left the estate, including the various buildings and art collections, to the state of Florida after his death in 1936.

John and Mable Ringling were so in love with anything Venetian (Mable Ringling even had a gondola docked at the foot of marble steps leading to a pier on **Sarasota Bay**) that their mansion, the **Ca' d'Zan** ("House of John" in Venetian dialect), is based on the Doges' Palace in Venice. Built by **Dwight James Baum** in 1926, the residence contains many graceful embellishments and furnishings ranging from Venetian Gothic to Italian and French Renaissance to Baroque. The main decorative element used was terra-cotta, because it was felt that the glaze on the tiles could best weather the bright Florida sun. All the windows are handmade tinted Venetian glass.

After making a substantial fortune on real estate, railroads, and the still world-famous circus he shared with his brothers, Ringling spent five years in Europe amassing works for his 22-room **Art Galleries,** and spent an estimated $3 million for 500 pieces of art. Housed in a pink, Italian Renaisssance-style villa built by **John H. Phillips,** the collection boasts works by El Greco and Rembrandt, pieces from the late Middle Ages and the Renaissance, as well as the finest assortment of Rubens and 17th-century Baroque art in the United States. There are also antiquities from Cyprus, European and American prints, photographs, sculpture, jewelry, and some contemporary objects.

The **Circus Museum** houses 18th-century prints and colored drawings of circuses, spangled costumes, painted carved wagons, a scale model of the **Ringling Brothers Barnum and Bailey Circus** from the 1930s, posters, photographs, and memorabilia of the bygone days of circus life. None of these pieces had been in the Ringlings' personal collection, but the museum acquired the works and placed them here as a tribute to the man who brought the **Ringling Brothers Barnum and Bailey Circus** to Sarasota in the winter.

Purchased by the museum in 1950, the 18th-century **Asolo Theater** was moved, piece by piece, from just outside Venice to the Ringling estate and reassembled. The theater had been taken down in 1930 after renowned actors and actresses had performed on its stage for more than a century. A Venetian antiques dealer bought the theater and kept it in storage until the museum acquired the contents. Seating only 300, the hall is Rococo in style and boasts gold ornaments and a frieze of famous Italians.

The museum is open daily; there is an admission charge, except for children 12 years old and younger.

65 Andrews Memorial Chapel Built in 1888 at a site several miles south of its present locale, this chapel has undergone two relocations in its history. In 1926 it was first moved to a different spot on the same lot to make room for the **First Presbyterian Church.** The chapel was later saved from demolition by the local historical society in 1970 and underwent a difficult transfer to **Hammock Park,** where it was subsequently restored. It remains a fine example of Florida Gothic architecture, most evident in the tall, pointed windows and wood framing. The chapel is listed on the National Register of Historic Places. ♦ Su 2-4PM Jan-May, Oct-Dec. 1899 San Mateo Dr (between Mira Vista and Buena Vista Drs), Dunedin

66 Bon Appétit ★★★$$$ This award-winning waterfront restaurant facing St. Joseph's Sound presents French classics—rack of lamb, veal, and Dover sole—as well as Wiener schnitzel. The cuisine and service never fail to please, and there is an extensive wine list. Dine outside in the casual cafe or indoors at the more formal dining room. ♦ French/German ♦ Daily lunch and dinner. Reservations recommended; jackets recommended inside. 148 Marina Plaza (just west of Edgewater Dr), Dunedin. 733.2151

67 J.O. Douglas House One of the few remaining original homesteads along Edgewater Drive and Dunedin's oldest house (1878), this structure remains remarkably unaltered considering its age. It was the first house in Dunedin constructed of milled lumber rather than logs, and is a fine example of a typical late–19th-century dwelling in Central Florida. Douglas, along with other men of Scottish ancestry, petitioned the government for a post office to be named Dunedin, which is Gaelic for Edinburgh, Scotland's capital. This privately owned house is listed on the National Register of Historic Places. ♦ 209 Scotland St (between Broadway Way and Edgewater Dr), Dunedin

68 Grant Field The spring training site for the **Toronto Blue Jays** from mid-February to April becomes home to the **Dunedin Blue Jays,** a member of the Class A **Florida State League,** the rest of the year. The ballpark seats 6,200 people. ♦ 373 Douglas Ave (at Beltrees St), Dunedin. 733.0429

69 Countryside Mall This 155-store mall is one of the area's largest, with an eye toward the middle-income and affluent shopper. Such shops as **Structure, Victoria's Secret, Dillard's,** and **Burdine's** are represented, as well as gourmet-food outlets, including **Schnickel Fritz,** which sells 180 kinds of cheese and 60 types of smoked meats and sausages. There's also a **McDonald's** for a quick, inexpensive bite. An ice-skating rink in the middle of the mall offers a fun diversion. ♦ Daily. Hwy 19 and Main St, Clearwater. 796.1079

70 Philippe Park Overlooking Old Tampa Bay, this park is named for Count Odet Philippe, a Frenchman who was the first white settler on the Pinellas Peninsula ("pinellas" comes from the Spanish *punta pinal*—point of pines). Count Philippe is credited with introducing the first grapefruit trees to the New World. Before he settled here in the 1830s, the site was occupied by Indians, and a sizable ceremonial mound from those first inhabitants can be seen today. Facilities include picnic shelters, picnic tables, and a children's playground. The archaeological site is listed on the National Register of Historic Places. ♦ Daily 7AM-sunset. Philippe Pkwy (at N Bayshore Dr), Safety Harbor. 726.2700

SAFETY HARBOR

71 Safety Harbor Resort and Spa $$$ Said to have been discovered by Hernando de Soto in 1539, the four mineral springs called **Espíritu Santo Springs** (Springs of the Holy Spirit) provide the setting for this full-scale, 22-acre spa. The spa has been in existence since 1926 and offers 35 fitness classes for spa guests, including exercises designed for the professional boxers who occasionally train here. Facilities include heated indoor and outdoor pools, nine tennis courts, a driving range, **Clarins Institut de Beauté,** saunas, steam baths, and a full range of health and beauty treatments. Three nutritional meals a day are generally included (except the corporate rate). Prices are steepest in the winter. ♦ 105 Bayshore Dr N (at Philippe Pkwy), Safety Harbor. 726.1161, 800/237.0155; www.safetyharborspa.com 占

Florida offers 70 public hunting lands, the largest system in the US. Popular prey include deer, turkey, and wild hogs.

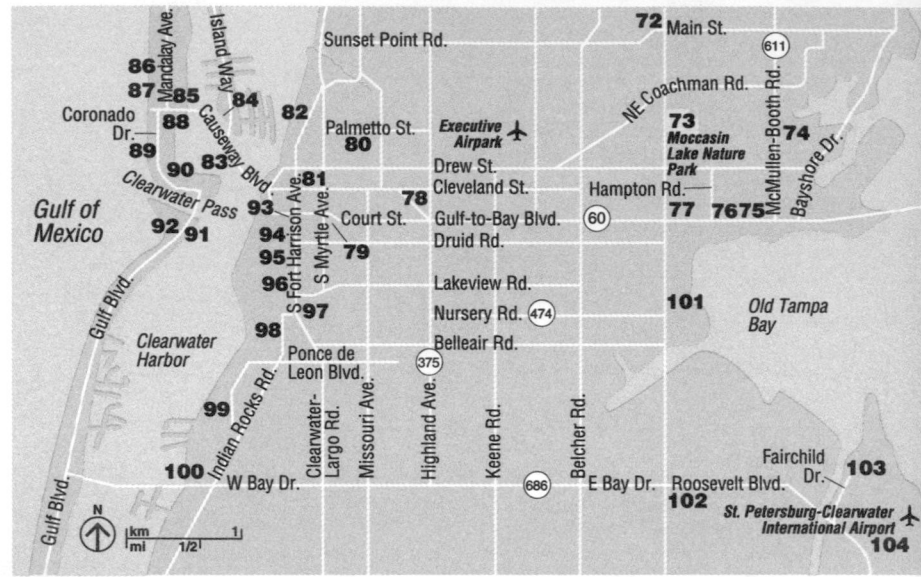

Clearwater/ Clearwater Beach Area

The largest beaches in the Tampa/St. Petersburg area are located about 22 miles from, and halfway between, the two cities. Clearwater's sandy beaches are wide, long (nearly four miles), and warmed by the calm waters of the **Gulf of Mexico.** Although the beaches are popular and can get pretty crowded, ample parking is available off **Gulfview Boulevard,** and on the street from **15th** to **27th Avenues** and on **First** and **Eighth Avenues.** In addition to the area's fine beaches, a wide variety of reasonably priced hotels and ethnically diverse restaurants is another draw.

Area code 727 unless otherwise noted.

72 Forbidden City ★$$ For those restricting their caloric intake, chicken with broccoli and Mandarin-style fish are real treats at this Chinese dining spot. However, "Seven Stars around the Moon," an entrée that includes jumbo shrimp dipped in batter, wrapped in bacon, and fried with sautéed Chinese vegetables, lobster, chicken, and scallops, is for eaters unconcerned with fat. Another good choice is Kung-Fu Twins au poivre—pepper steak with a Chinese twist. ♦ Chinese ♦ Daily lunch and dinner. 25778 Hwy 19N (at Main St), Clearwater. 797.8989

73 Moccasin Lake Nature Park: An Environmental and Energy Education Center A milelong nature trail winds through this 50-acre park filled with wax myrtle, laurel oaks, water oaks, live oaks, cypresses, slash pines, and wildflowers. Animals include alligators, bald eagles, barn owls, screech owls, burrowing owls, flying squirrels, possums, snapping turtles, and armadillos. ♦ Admission. Tu-Su. 2750 Park Trail La (just west of Beachwood Ave), Clearwater. 462.6024

74 Ruth Eckerd Hall Concerts, ballets, Broadway shows, and other events are staged year-round at this modern performing arts center seating 2,000 people. There's one design inconvenience—no center aisle. ♦ 1111 McMullen-Booth Rd (between San Bernardino St and 10th St S), Clearwater. 791.7400

75 Tio Pepe's ★★★$$ This lovely hacienda, filled with antiques, fine art, and Victorian furniture, is always jammed with customers indulging in the excellent Spanish cuisine. Try the black-bean soup and a spectacular 22-ounce pork chop, both of which go well with rich black bread and a salad mixed at your table. There is a good choice of wines, including red and white sangria. The bakery in the foyer makes bread and apple tarts. Ask to be seated in the front room away from the crowds and noise. ♦ Spanish ♦ Tu-Su lunch and dinner. 2930 Gulf-to-Bay Blvd (between Bayview Ave and Hampton Rd), Clearwater. 799.3082

76 Hooters ★$ This is the original of the finger-food chain where the female servers are clothed in brief, tight T-shirts and shorts. The menu consists mostly of chicken wings, steamed shrimp, and sandwiches. It's quick and inexpensive. ♦ American ♦ Daily lunch and dinner. 2800 Gulf-to-Bay Blvd (at Hampton Rd), Clearwater. 797.4008. Also at: Numerous locations throughout the area

Florida has more golf courses than any other state in the US—more than 1,100 and counting.

77 Key West Grill ★$$ The fish of the day is grilled or blackened in this casual eatery. Servings are generous, and the muffins are fresh. Start with one of the soups and tiny homemade rolls with strawberry butter. The conch fritters are flavorful but can be tough. ◆ Seafood ◆ Daily lunch and dinner. 2660 Gulf-to-Bay Blvd (between Hampton Rd and Hwy 19), Clearwater. 797.1988

78 A Blue Moon Rare and old books, decorative maps, prints, records, and posters are for sale here. Appraisals are also available. ◆ M-Sa. 1415 Cleveland St (between S San Remo and S Hillcrest Aves), Clearwater. 443.7444

79 Bilgore Groves A fine selection of fruit, especially citrus, is offered here for shipment only from the company's groves in Indian River County on the Atlantic coast. ◆ M-Sa. 807A Court St (between S Prospect and S Myrtle Aves), Clearwater. 442.2171

80 Jack Russell Stadium The **Philadelphia Phillies** hold their spring training here from mid-February through April. Then the 7,000-seat stadium becomes home to the **Clearwater Phillies,** a Class A **Florida State League** team. ◆ 800 Phillies Dr (at Seminole St), Clearwater. 441.8638

81 Cleveland Street Post Office This Mediterranean Revival building is representative of the 1929-39 federal public works program that commissioned local professionals and industries. Still in use, it is listed on the National Register of Historic Places. ◆ 650 Cleveland St (at N East Ave), Clearwater

81 Ottavio's Place ★★$$$ Fireplaces, bookshelves, and wine bottles decorate this intimate trattoria in downtown Clearwater. Start with fettuccine with smoked salmon and then move on to any of the veal dishes—veal is a specialty here—or try the shrimp marinara. Pasta, desserts, and bread are homemade. ◆ Italian ◆ Daily lunch and dinner. 45 N Fort Harrison Ave (at Hendricks St), Clearwater. 442.6659

82 Bill Irle's ★★$$ A native German touch is evident in the dishes served at this casual, family-style restaurant. Try the sauerbraten, Wiener schnitzel, potato pancakes, and Black Forest cake. The salads are fresh and desserts homemade. ◆ German ◆ Daily lunch and dinner. 1310 N Fort Harrison Ave (at Engman St), Clearwater. 446.5683

83 Jesse's Seafood House ★★★$$ This crowded fish house boasts a young, family-oriented clientele in a somewhat noisy setting. As for the food, you can't beat it—salmon, crab, mahimahi, grouper, and snapper are among the choice picks. Dishes may be cooked to order—fried, broiled, charbroiled, or blackened. ◆ Seafood ◆ Daily lunch and dinner. Reservations recommended. 345 Causeway Blvd (southeast of Island Way), Clearwater Beach. 736.2611

84 Clearwater Marine Aquarium Live and model displays of area marine life are on exhibit at this nonprofit research and rehabilitation center. One of the more popular tanks holds baby sea turtles. There are also stingrays, small sharks, and dolphins. Children will like the "touching tank" with hermit crabs and other creatures. ◆ Admission. Daily. 249 Windward Passage (at Island Way), Clearwater Beach. 447.0980, 441.1790 ⑤

85 Swim & Play An extensive selection of beach clothes and resortwear for women, including hard-to-find sizes, are offered at this shop. ◆ Daily. 407 Mandalay Ave (between Marianne and Papaya Sts), Clearwater Beach. 461.4499

85 Bob Heilman's Beachcomber ★★$$$ An area mainstay for 50 years, this restaurant has a resort elegance that encourages diners to dress up a bit for dinner—no beachwear here. The kitchen offers a wide array of fresh seafood, including panfried rainbow trout, broiled salmon with béarnaise sauce, and grouper baked in parchment. Steaks and prime ribs are also tops. The fried chicken (an old family recipe) is one of the most popular menu items; it's served with mashed potatoes and muffins. The only drawback here is that there's no view of the water; a plus is a separate dining room for nonsmokers. ◆ American ◆ M-Sa lunch and dinner. 447 Mandalay Ave (between Papaya and Baymont Sts), Clearwater Beach. 442.4144

86 Palm Pavilion $ This renovated 1940s, 29-unit hotel with a pool still retains its pink-and-blue Art Deco exterior. All the accommodations, including two efficiencies, feature custom-built furniture. Adjacent to the property is the **Palm Pavilion,** a classic beach pavilion (not to be confused with the hotel) that opened in 1926 and has a gift shop and snack bar that serves beer and wine. ◆ 18 Bay Esplanade (just west of Mandalay Ave), Clearwater Beach. 446.6777, 800/433.PALM; fax 446.4255; www.palmpavilioninn.com

87 Clearwater Beach Hotel $$ Some of the 160 rooms in the oldest hotel on Clearwater Beach have small kitchens. Part of the building dates from the turn of the century, though the property was redone in 1988. Other features include a heated pool, library, and sundeck. ◆ 500 Mandalay Ave (at Baymont St), Clearwater Beach. 441.2425, 800/292.2295; fax 449.2083 ♿

Within the Clearwater Beach Hotel:

Clearwater Beach Hotel Dining Room ★★★$$$ You'll enjoy grand dining in a turn-of-the-century beach setting at this casual restaurant, with its oversize wicker chairs, Victorian accents, and beautiful view of the gulf. Contemporary and nouvelle cuisine recipes elevate such old favorites as filet mignon, veal Marsala, broiled swordfish, and Gulf shrimp scampi to new heights. A full wine list complements the menu. ◆ American ◆ Daily breakfast, lunch, and dinner. 443.2180

87 Hilton Clearwater Beach Resort $$ Hardly your standard roadside hostelry, this 427-room hotel (formerly the **DoubleTree Inn Clearwater Beach Surfside**) is a good value. It sits right on 10 acres of prime beachfront with ample water-sports rentals, volleyball, a swimming pool, sundeck, and restaurant. The property is within walking distance of the many restaurants and shops at the beach's north end. ◆ 400 Mandalay Ave (between Marianne and Papaya Sts), Clearwater Beach. 461.3222, 800/465.4329; fax 461.0610 ♿

88 Starlite Majesty Very enjoyable sight-seeing luncheon and dinner-dance cruises are offered on this 300-passenger, triple-deck vessel that cruises the Intracoastal Waterway along Clearwater Beach, turns around in the Gulf of Mexico, and returns to dock at the **Clearwater Beach Marina.** A narrative history of the area accompanies the afternoon cruise. Schedules vary according to season. ◆ Admission. Causeway Blvd and Coronado Dr, Clearwater Beach. 462.2628, 800/444.4814

The Florida aquifer, a vast underground river, creates the most extensive system of underwater caves and tunnels in the entire US.

89 Seafood & Sunsets at Julie's ★$$ Beach dress is the order of the day at this relaxed Key West–style place. Fish-and-chips, clam strips, grouper sandwiches, burgers, conch fritters, and a wide range of other kinds of seafood are served. Come here to watch the beach activities or catch the sunset. ◆ Seafood ◆ Daily lunch and dinner. 351 S Gulfview Blvd (between Fifth and Third Sts), Clearwater Beach. 441.2548

90 Best Western Sea Stone Suites Resort $$ There are 43 one-bedroom suites with kitchens in this six-story, waterfront hotel on the bay side of the island, as well as 65 rooms located in the older **Gulfview** structure. Other features include a pool, private dock, sundeck, small marina, restaurant, whirlpool, and guest laundry service. Supervised children's programs are available June through August. ◆ 445 Hamden Dr (between S Gulfview Blvd and Bayside Dr), Clearwater Beach. 441.1722, 800/444.1919; fax 461.1680; www.bestwestern.com ♿

90 Best Western Sea Wake Inn $$ This 110-room hotel has a heated pool, restaurant, children's playground, supervised children's program June through August, and cabana rentals. Meals can be enjoyed on the tree-draped patio that overlooks the beach— a nice break if it's hot out. ◆ 691 S Gulfview Blvd (at Parkway Dr), Clearwater Beach. 443.7652, 800/444.1919; fax 461.2836; www.bestwestern.com ♿

91 Shops at Sand Key Fine restaurants and several specialty shops can be found in this Clearwater Harbor mall. ◆ M-Sa 9AM-9PM; Su noon-5PM. 1241 Gulf Blvd (south of S Gulfview Blvd), Clearwater Beach. No phone

91 Radisson Suite Resort $ Set on 7.5 acres, this $40-million hotel offers 220 one-bedroom suites, each with two televisions, a wet bar, coffeemaker, microwave, and private balcony. Resort facilities include a free-form swimming pool with a waterfall and daytime grill, sundeck, child-care center, fitness center, and continental dining room. ◆ 1201 Gulf Blvd (south of S Gulfview Blvd), Clearwater Beach. 596.1100, 800/333.3333; fax 595.4292; www.radisson.com ♿

92 Sheraton Sand Key Beach Resort $$ A beautiful, clean, and secluded beach is the drawing card to this 390-room resort that has long been a favorite among international visitors. There's also a heated swimming pool children's pool, Jacuzzi, volleyball court, and a wide selection of water sports. Young people (including kids) particularly like this place—they can take part in supervised fun activities all the day. There's also a coffee shop, restaurant, snack bar, gameroom, bar, and entertainment lounge. ♦ 1160 Gulf Blvd (south of S Gulfview Blvd), Clearwater Beach. 595.1611, 800/325.3535, 800/456.SAND; fax 596.8488; www.beachsand.com ♿

93 Pinellas County Courthouse This courthouse, built in 1917 and representing Neo-Classical Revival style, served the county's needs exclusively until 1960, when a second structure was erected to share the caseload. The original building was recently redone as judges' chambers. ♦ 324 S Fort Harrison Ave (at Court St), Clearwater

94 South Ward School Built in 1906, this elementary school is Florida's oldest county school continuously operating in the same building. It is listed on the National Register of Historic Places. ♦ 610 S Fort Harrison Ave (between Hamilton Crescent and Turner St), Clearwater

95 Clearwater Harbor Oaks Historical District Many fine old homes of various architectural styles are still standing in this three-block stretch of Fort Harrison Avenue that was developed in the 1920s. It's a pleasant detour on the way to the beaches. ♦ S Fort Harrison Ave (between Lotus Path and Druid Rd), Clearwater

96 Louis Ducros House Railroad tycoon Henry B. Plant had a number of cottages constructed along a railroad spur for men working on his nearby grand **Belleview Biltmore** hotel (see below). Louis Ducros was Plant's official photographer and possibly the first resident of Clearwater. Built in the 1890s, this structure is a rare example of Carpenter Gothic architecture, with its gable roof, bay windows, and veranda stretching across the front of the house. Listed on the National Register of Historic Places, the house is not open to the public. ♦ 1324 S Fort Harrison Ave (at B St), Clearwater

97 A Place for Cooks An exhaustive collection of bakeware, gadgets, and unusual specialty foods is available here. ♦ M-Sa. 1447 S Fort Harrison Ave (at Belleview Blvd), Clearwater. 446.5506

98 Belleview Biltmore $$ Perched on a mainland bluff overlooking Clearwater Harbor, this 292-room resort first opened in 1897 as a grand seasonal hotel built by railroad tycoon Henry Plant. Legend has it that this is the world's largest continuously occupied wooden structure. (Truth is, the wooden shutters have been converted to aluminum siding to reduce costs and maintenance.) Renovations by former and current owners have achieved a much-needed modernization, but a good deal of the spirit of other eras was lost in the process. Still, guests will find themselves in a relaxing environment surrounded by Tiffany glass, chandeliers, gables, and peaked roofs. The **Terrace Cafe** serves breakfast, lunch, and dinner. Facilities include an 18-hole golf course, croquet, four tennis courts, a swimming pool, and health spa. ♦ 25 Belleview Blvd (west of Indian Rocks Rd), Clearwater. 442.6171, 800/237.8947; fax 441.4173; www.belleviewbiltmore.com

Pinellas County Courthouse

99 Florida Gulf Coast Arts Center This regional arts center on 12 wooded acres shows contemporary works by nationally recognized artists. Visitors can wander through the studios and watch potters, sculptors, and painters at work. ♦ Tu-Sa; Su noon-4PM; closed August. 222 Ponce de Leon Blvd (between Magnolia and Manatee Rds), Belleair. 584.8634

100 E&E's Steakout Grill ★$$ At this Southwestern-style steak house, formerly **Eugen's,** you'll find good steak, but the fresh seafood is popular too. Try the Black-and-Blue sirloin appetizer (seared sirloin on wasabi sauce). For dessert, the Million-Dollar Cake is a must. ♦ American ♦ Daily lunch and dinner. Plaza Shopping Center, 100 N Indian Rocks Rd (between W Bay Dr and Sunset Blvd), Belleair Bluffs. 585.6399

101 Hops Grill & Bar ★★$$ Of the four beers brewed here, the British-style pale ale is a standout. And for those interested in home brewing, a miniature brewery is on display. The pasta, soup, and steaks are excellent. ♦ American ♦ Daily lunch and dinner. 1451 Hwy 19 S (between Nursery Rd and Harn Blvd), Clearwater. 531.5300

102 Bay Area Outlet Mall Everything from paper goods to books to clothes is available at bargain prices in this 70-store emporium. ♦ M-Sa; Su most stores. 15579 Hwy 19 N (at Roosevelt Blvd). 535.2337

103 Boatyard Village A favorite tourist destination, this re-created 1890s fishing village nestled in a cove on Tampa Bay has restaurants, boutiques, and galleries with tin roofs and weathered wood exteriors. The **Boatyard Stage,** a 176-seat theater, holds performances year-round. ♦ Daily. 16100 Fairchild Dr (northeast of 49th St N). 535.4678 ♿

flightshops

104 Flightshops Aviation books and charts may be purchased at this store near the **St. Petersburg–Clearwater International Airport.** ♦ Daily. Roosevelt Blvd and Terminal Pkwy. 530.1415

105 Heritage Park & Museum A schoolhouse, train depot, and houses ranging from a log cabin to a Victorian mansion have been restored and collected on 21 wooded acres at this site. About 20 structures have been moved from other parts of the county, including a turn-of-the-century bandstand. The historical museum depicts the county's pioneer lifestyle, and tours are led by guides in period dress. Spinning, weaving, and other crafts exhibits are held regularly. The garden for the visually impaired, where fragrant plants surround a gazebo, is an unusual feature. The annual Country Jubilee is held on the fourth Saturday in October. ♦ Donation. Tu-Sa; Su 1-4PM. 11909 125th St (between Walsingham Rd and 121st Ave), Largo. 582.2123

Heritage Park & Museum

Gulf Boulevard Beach Communities

A 15-mile ribbon of beach communities on barrier islands fronting the **Gulf of Mexico** runs along **Gulf Boulevard** in southern **Pinellas County.** Constant sunshine, clean white sand, and warm shallow waters make this area popular with families who vacation at the small, independent hotels and motels along the beach. For nourishment, fresh and simple is the theme around here, often right off the boat. Public access and metered parking is available from **141st** to **148th Avenues** for **Madeira Beach County Park;** at **John's Pass Village & Boardwalk;** and from **77th** to **127th Avenues.**

Area code 727 unless otherwise noted.

109 Hungry Fisherman ★★$$ Sporting a weathered wood facade, this restaurant isn't fancy, but it offers more than 40 seafood varieties at low prices. Selections include Danish lobster tails, Alaskan salmon, scallops, and snapper. ◆ Seafood ◆ Daily lunch and dinner. No credit cards accepted. 19915 Gulf Blvd (north of 197th Ave E), Indian Shores. 595.4218

109 Scandia ★★$$ Paned windows, timbered walls, and Scandinavian items dress up this small chalet that doubles as a gift shop and restaurant. The Norwegian smoked salmon, Swedish marinated herring, and Danish roast pork loin are hard to beat. The owner offers a cook's tour of his native Denmark and other Scandinavian countries for travelers interested in those lands' cuisines. ◆ Scandinavian ◆ Tu-Su lunch and dinner. Reservations recommended. 19829 Gulf Blvd (north of 197th Ave E), Indian Shores. 595.5525

110 Holiday Villas II $$ These 72 fully furnished condos with kitchens are right on the beach. There's a four-night minimum rental and no restaurant, but maid service, a laundry, and pool are provided. ◆ 19610 Gulf Blvd (south of 197th Ave W), Indian Shores. 596.4852, 800/428.4852

111 Holiday Villas III $$ A three-night minimum is required at this beachside complex with 75 condos and seven efficiencies. There's a pool, gameroom, laundry, and private dock, but no restaurant. ◆ 18610 Gulf Blvd (between 183rd Terr and Park Blvd), Indian Shores. 595.0770; fax 595.1932

112 Suncoast Seabird Sanctuary  This refuge for sick and injured birds is known worldwide for its preservation and rehabilitation of wild and endangered species. The goal is to rehabilitate these birds so they can be released. Visitors can observe brown pelicans, cormorants, white herons, birds of prey, songbirds, and other species. ◆ Free. Daily dawn to dusk. 18328 Gulf Blvd (at 183rd Terr), Indian Shores. 391.6211 ♿

106 Sturgeon Memorial Rose Garden In 1985 this park was approved by All-America Rose Selections as a public display garden, one of less than a hundred in the country. The only other accredited rose gardens in Florida are at **Walt Disney World, Cypress Gardens,** and Orlando's **Harry P. Leu Gardens.** There are approximately 850 bushes representing more than a hundred varieties. Don't be put off: The garden is inside **Serenity Gardens Memorial Park,** a cemetery. The best months to visit are October and November. ◆ Daily sunrise to sunset. 13401 Indian Rocks Rd (between Wilcox Rd and Harbor Heights Dr), Largo. 595.2914

107 Keegan's Seafood Grille ★$ This modest restaurant with decent prices presents seafood ranging from seviche to grilled fish. (Note: The portions can be modest, too.) ◆ Seafood ◆ Daily lunch and dinner. 1519 Gulf Blvd (between 15th and 16th Aves), Indian Rocks Beach. 596.2477

108 Crabby Bill's ★★★$$ While the atmosphere may be bare bones, there's nothing lacking in the seafood dishes at this dining spot, which are available at rock-bottom prices. Favorites are steamed shrimp, crab cakes, oysters, clams on the half shell, oyster stew, and catfish. Matt Loder says his family decided to name the restaurant after his father, Bill, because he's "crabby all the time," and, of course, because they serve crab. This is part of an eight-building complex that also includes other eateries, retail food shops, a gift shop, and warehouse. There are no reservations, so be prepared to wait. ◆ Seafood ◆ Daily lunch and dinner. 401 Gulf Blvd (between Fourth and Fifth Aves), Indian Rocks Beach. 595.4825

The geographic center of Florida lies 12 miles northwest of Brooksville, in Hernando County.

113 Lobster Pot ★★★$$$ As you can imagine, lobster, prepared any number of ways, is the house specialty. Standouts include lobster bisque and lobster stuffed with shrimp and scallops. Fish chowder, escargots, red snapper, and grouper are also excellent. Come for the food, not the ambience—the place is small and noisy. ♦ Seafood ♦ Daily dinner. Reservations recommended. 17814 Gulf Blvd (at Atoll Ave), Redington Shores. 391.8592

114 Redington Long Pier Both those who like to cast a fishing line and sightseers enjoy this pier, which stretches more than a thousand feet into the Gulf of Mexico. Equipment rental, a snack bar, and rest rooms are available. It's also the best place to park for the Redington beaches. ♦ Admission. Daily 24 hours. 17490 Gulf Blvd (between 173rd Ave and 176th Ave W), Redington Shores. 391.9398

114 Wine Cellar Restaurant ★★★$$$ A casual beach atmosphere accompanies serious food and quality wines at this dining spot. Start with avocado and crab bisque, Hungarian goulash, or soused shrimp in the rough (soaked in olive oil, garlic, and dry Vermouth, with the tail portion left on). Entrées include Wiener schnitzel, beef Wellington, and Idaho rainbow trout. As you would expect, there's an extensive wine list, including labels from California, Australia, France, and Italy. ♦ Continental ♦ Tu-Su dinner. Reservations recommended. 17307 Gulf Blvd (at 173rd Ave), Redington Shores. 393.3491

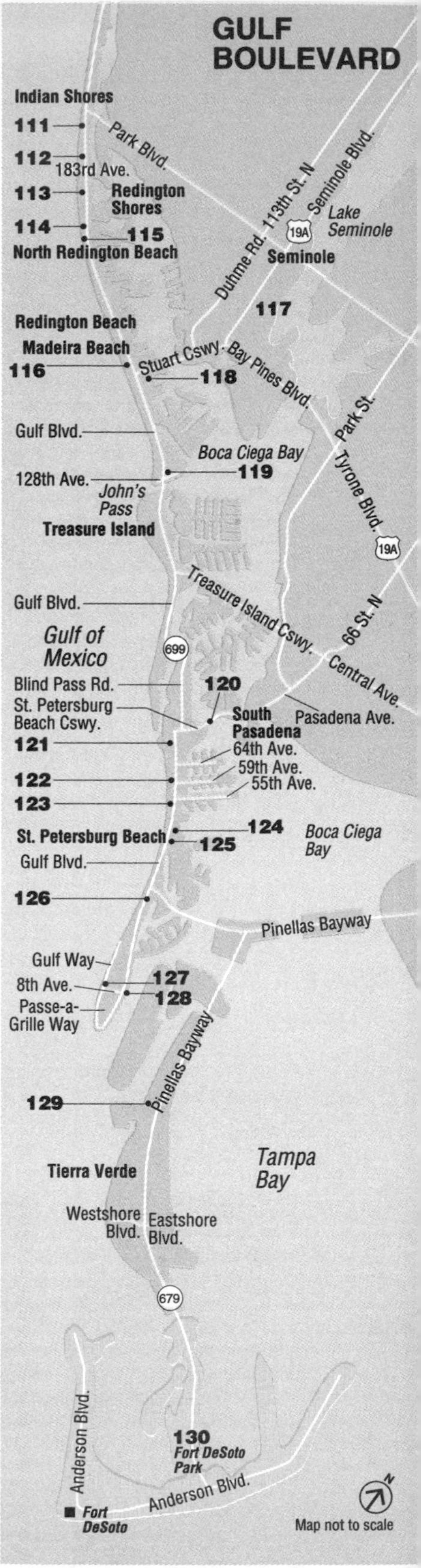

Restaurants/Clubs: Red   **Hotels:** Blue
Shops/♥ Outdoors: Green   **Sights/Culture:** Black

GULF BOULEVARD

Indian Shores
111 — Park Blvd.
112 — 183rd Ave.
113 — Redington Shores
114 — 115
North Redington Beach
Seminole Blvd.
113th St. N
Duhme Rd.
19A Lake Seminole
Seminole
117

Redington Beach
Madeira Beach
116 — Stuart Cswy · Bay Pines Blvd.
118
Park St.
Gulf Blvd. —
Boca Ciega Bay
119
Tyrone Blvd.
128th Ave. — John's Pass
Treasure Island
19A

Gulf Blvd. —
Treasure Island Cswy.
66 St. N
Gulf of Mexico 699
Central Ave.
Blind Pass Rd. — 120
St. Petersburg Beach Cswy.
121
South Pasadena Ave.
Pasadena
64th Ave.
122
59th Ave.
123
55th Ave.
124
St. Petersburg Beach · 125
Boca Ciega Bay
Gulf Blvd. —
126 —

Gulf Way —
8th Ave. — 127
Passe-a-Grille Way 128
Pinellas Bayway

129 —
Pinellas Bayway
Tampa Bay
Tierra Verde
Westshore Blvd. Eastshore Blvd.
679

Anderson Blvd.
130
Fort DeSoto Park
■ Fort DeSoto
Anderson Blvd.
N
Map not to scale

115 North Redington Beach Hilton $$ Each of the 125 slickly decorated rooms at this hotel has a balcony with a view of either the Gulf of Mexico or Boca Ciega Bay, as well as a service bar, large bathroom, and separate dressing room. Located on its own 125 feet of beach, the hotel also boasts a pool and deck, and **Gulf Front Steakhouse**. Parking is free. ◆ 17120 Gulf Blvd (between 171st and 173rd Aves), North Redington Beach. 391.4000, 800/445.8667, 800/447.7263; fax 397.0699; www.hilton.com &

116 Holiday Inn Madeira Beach $ All 149 rooms have a balcony or patio with a full or partial view of the hotel's 600 feet of beach. A restaurant and lounge overlook the Gulf of Mexico. Other features include a heated pool, lighted tennis court, and such beachside rentals as cabanas and water-sports equipment. ◆ 15208 Gulf Blvd (between Madeira Way and 153rd Ave), Madeira Beach. 392.2275, 800/465.4329; www.holiday-inn.com

117 London Bus Pub ★$ This British tavern is just like an English pub—complete with darts and a selection of British beers and cider. The menu is filled with authentic dishes, including pasties, steak-and-kidney pie, shepherd's pie, and bangers (sausages). ◆ British ◆ M-Sa lunch and dinner; Su dinner. 5667 Seminole Blvd (between Pineapple Rd and Orange Blossom La), Seminole. 399.1122

118 Leverock's on the Bay ★★$$ Good, fresh seafood is served at affordable prices in this simple restaurant. For a real taste delight, try scrod Jason (broiled in a wine sauce with cheese, garlic butter, and bread crumbs). The waterfront view and good service also make dining here a delightful experience. ◆ Seafood ◆ Daily lunch and dinner. 565 150th Ave (northeast of Gulf Blvd), Madeira Beach. 393.0459

119 John's Pass Village & Boardwalk More than 60 shops and several outstanding seafood restaurants can be found in this converted fishing village of tin-roof buildings. It overlooks "fish famous" **John's Pass**, a natural strait connecting the Gulf of Mexico and the Intracoastal Waterway, and home to a large commercial and charter fishing fleet. The 1,000-foot boardwalk provides a scenic view of the pass. Some shops carry the predictable tourist merchandise, but the majority are antiques, arts and crafts, and handicraft shops selling woodwork, glassware, and jewelry. **The Bronze Lady**, a longtime art gallery here, is said to be the world's largest single dealer of works by comedian and artist Red Skelton. ◆ Daily. 12901 Gulf Blvd (at 129th Ave), Madeira Beach &

At John's Pass Village & Boardwalk:

 Captain Hubbard's Marina Try your hand at fishing—from the docks, catwalks, or a party boat. Fishing sage Captain Wilson Hubbard claims that on 9 days out of 10, more fish are landed on boats here than on any other vessels along the Florida coast. It's a good idea to reserve in advance for half-day, full-day, or overnight trips. ◆ Schedules vary. 393.1947

At Captain Hubbard's Marina:

Friendly Fisherman ★$$ Amberjack, mullet, stone crabs, and other seafood have been brought in daily by the fleet of Captain Hubbard, the "friendly fisherman," for more than 50 years. Dine indoors or out on the boardwalk. ◆ Seafood ◆ Daily breakfast, lunch, and dinner. 391.6025

119 Sea Cruz Five- or six-hour lunch or dinner cruises into the Gulf of Mexico are offered on this 440-passenger luxury ship. Casino gambling is allowed once the ship passes the state territorial limit, 9.1 miles offshore in the Gulf of Mexico. ◆ Schedules vary. 129th Ave and Gulf Blvd, Madeira Beach. 800/688.7529

St. Petersburg Beach Area

Take your pick of activities here: Ride a gondola at the **TradeWinds Resort**, stroll through the turn-of-the-century resort village of **Passe-a-Grille**, or wander around 900 acres of pristine parkland and three miles of beaches in **Fort DeSoto Park**. When you're in the mood to hit the sand, get out quarters for the meters and head for the three-milelong St. Petersburg Beach, just off **Gulf Boulevard**. Among your best beach bets are: **Bella Vista Beach**, with access at **46th Avenue; Upham Beach**, with parking at **68th Avenue;** and Passe-a-Grille, where you can park on **Eighth Avenue.**

Area code 727 unless otherwise noted.

120 Starlite Princess A nice way to visit the area: This three-deck, 106-foot, Victorian-style paddle wheeler built in 1986 offers a variety of cruises for sight-seeing, dancing, lunch, or dinner. The ship leaves once a week for a six-hour trip to **The Pier** in St. Pete. Breakfast and a sit-down lunch are included. The boat is also available for charter. ◆ Schedule varies. Reservations required. 3400 Pasadena Ave S (at Sailboat Key Blvd), South Pasadena. 462.2628, 800/444.4814

121 Woody's Waterfront ★$ Burgers, fried shellfish, and grouper are the favorites at this popular beach bar. ♦ American ♦ Daily lunch and dinner. 7308 Sunset Way (between 73rd and Corey Aves), St. Petersburg Beach. 360.9165

TradeWinds

122 TradeWinds Sandpiper Beach Resort $$ Toasters, coffeemakers, small refrigerators, and wet bars come with many of the 159 accommodations at this modern beachfront hotel. Suites have a separate living room and full kitchen. Other facilities on the well-kept grounds include two restaurants, a beachfront pool, enclosed heated pool, air-conditioned racquet-sport courts, supervised children's activities, water-sports rentals, a gameroom, and exercise room. ♦ 6000 Gulf Blvd (between 59th Ave and Gulfwinds Dr), St. Petersburg Beach. 360.5551, 800/237.0707, 800/333.3333; fax 367.4567; www.tradewindsresort.com ✦

123 TradeWinds Resort $$$ Guests can ride motorized gondolas to their rooms on the meandering waterways that cut through the 18 acres of beach property at this resort hotel. All 577 guest rooms are outfitted with coffeemakers, toasters, and wet bars; each suite has a separate living room and fully equipped kitchen. Recreational facilities include five pools, Jacuzzis, a sauna, fitness center, racquet sports, water-sports rentals, and supervised activities for children. There are two restaurants and two lounges in addition to the **Palm Court**. ♦ 5500 Gulf Blvd (at 55th Ave), St. Petersburg Beach. 367.6461, 800/237.0707; fax 367.4567; www.tradewindsresort.com ✦

Within TradeWinds Resort:

Palm Court ★★$$$ Grouper, salmon, lamb, and roast duckling prevail on the dinner menu of this informal dining room. French overtones blend well with fresh Florida ingredients. Lunch choices are lighter—pasta salad, and a chicken and brie sandwich. ♦ American ♦ Daily breakfast, lunch, and dinner. Reservations required. 367.6461

123 Best Western Sirata Beach Resort $ This 155-room hotel was built on the site of the old **El Sirata Hotel,** constructed in the 1930s. The hotel's original Art Deco theme was beautifully revived in peach and turquoise hues. Most of the guest rooms have a beach view. Sports facilities include parasails, wave runners, and an exercise room. ♦ 5390 Gulf Blvd (between 52nd and 55th Aves), St. Petersburg Beach. 367.2771, 344.5999; fax 360.6799; www.siratabeachresort.com ✦

Within the Best Western Sirata Beach Resort:

Bill Nagy's on the Beach ★★$$ Bill Nagy creates tasty culinary concoctions at this seaside restaurant. Try the spinach salad, roasted duck with currant sauce, or any of the fresh seafood creations. ♦ Continental ♦ Daily dinner. 367.2771

124 Swim & Play This store has a huge inventory of beachwear, including swimsuits from such brands as Roxanne and Gottex, as well as hard-to-find sizes. ♦ Daily. 4785 Gulf Blvd (between 46th and 50th Aves), St. Petersburg Beach. 367.1713

125 Kinjo ★★$$$ Great sushi, plus an extensive menu of tempura, shrimp, and chicken prepared at a *teppanyaki* grill, are the culinary highlights at this tranquil dining spot. ♦ Japanese ♦ Daily dinner. 4615 Gulf Blvd (between 46th and 50th Aves), St. Petersburg Beach. 866.6515

126 Don CeSar Beach Resort & Spa $$$ With its striking pink-stucco structure with towers and high-arched windows, this beachfront grande dame is a real traffic stopper. The attractive and imposing "Don," as it's called locally, was opened in 1928 as a seasonal winter hotel by Irishman **Thomas J. Rowe,** one of the great figures in the 1925 land boom in St. Petersburg. **Rowe** built it in gratitude for the money he made in the city and named it after his favorite opera character. Closed down in 1941 and used as an army hospital in 1942, the hotel was slated for the wrecker's ball in 1969 and again in 1975, but preservationists intervened and several renovations followed, among them a $14-million overhaul that replaced the old Spanish-style interior with luxurious and aristocratic English carpet, Italian crystal chandeliers, French furniture, and French and Italian marble. After the fix-up, some claimed to have seen **Rowe**'s ghost at the hotel. The most recent renovation included refurbishment of the guest rooms, and the addition of a wellness center, spa, second swimming pool, shopping arcade, and two restaurants—the **Maritana Grille** and the **Sea Porch Cafe.** The 275 rooms, including two grandiose penthouses, have marble baths and ocean views, and the other swimming pool and tennis courts are right on the beach. There are also various water-sports rentals on the beach here, and a children's program. The hotel is listed on the National Register of Historic Places. The most recent addition to the resort is the beachfront **Don CeSar Beach House,** an all-suite, 70-room luxury hotel just a short stroll away. Formerly condominium rentals, the **Beach House** has been refurbished and painted the legendary pink of the original **Don CeSar.** Bright and airy, the suites are furnished in florals, and each

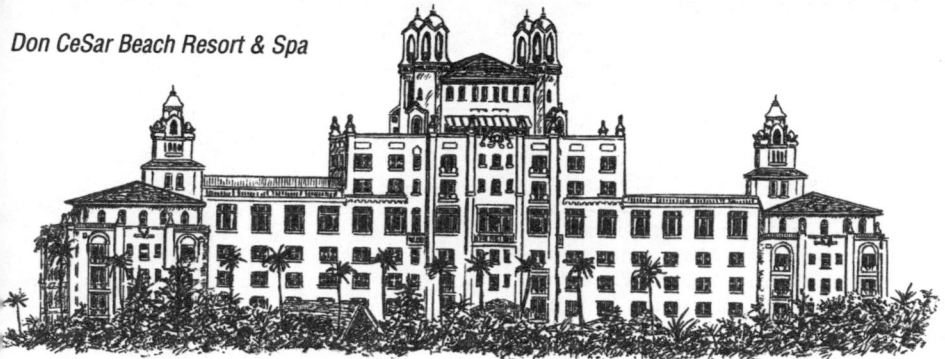

Don CeSar Beach Resort & Spa

includes a fully equipped kitchen. Guests of the **Beach House** share privileges with those staying at the original building, including the **Beach Club & Spa,** swimming pools, shopping arcade, and restaurants. ◆ 3400 Gulf Blvd (at 34th Ave), St. Petersburg Beach. 360.1881, 800/282.1116; fax 367.7597; www.doncesar.com &

127 Passe-a-Grille Started around the turn of the century, this tiny beach community at the southern tip of Long Key was the area's first resort. Made up of old-fashioned, single-family homes, it's little more than a block wide from bay to beach. To get there, take the series of bridges spanning the mouth of Boca Ciega Bay. Day-trippers can park on Eighth Avenue, where there's access to the public beach. ◆ St. Petersburg Beach

127 Hurricane Seafood Restaurant ★★★ $$$ Without a doubt, the area's best and freshest grouper sandwiches are served at this informal gulfside cafe with an upstairs deck. Equally excellent are the grouper amandine, crab cakes, steamed crab claws, and various pasta dishes. ◆ Seafood ◆ Daily breakfast, lunch, and dinner. 807 Gulf Way (between Eighth and Ninth Aves), St. Petersburg Beach. 360.9558

127 Keystone Motel & Apartments $ The 36 units in this complex right across from the beach in the heart of Passe-a-Grille include eight apartments and four efficiencies. Guests have use of a pool and laundry. ◆ 801 Gulf Way (at Eighth Ave), St. Petersburg Beach. 360.1313

127 Evander Preston Contemporary Jewelry Celebrities Carl Reiner, Peter Max, and Jimmy Buffett have found their way to this oasis outside Passe-a-Grille for creative one-of-a-kind jewelry. Visitors are treated to a glass of white sangria as they peruse the chic inventory—prices range from $100 to $25,000. ◆ Daily. 106 Eighth Ave (between Passe-a-Grille and Gulf Ways), St. Petersburg Beach. 367.7894

128 Shell Key Shuttle Shuttle service on a 32-passenger vessel is offered to Shell Key, an unspoiled, half-milelong island just south of Passe-a-Grille that provides excellent shelling. Schedules vary daily; a sunset cruise is sometimes included. ◆ Admission. 801 Passe-a-Grille Way (at Eighth Ave), St. Petersburg Beach. 360.1348

129 Good Times Continental Restaurant ★★★$$ Tucked away near **Fort DeSoto Park,** this eatery—owned by Czechs—is frequented by a loyal local clientele, but word of the fine dining here continues to travel. In addition to pork, roast duckling, bratwurst, and homemade desserts, the restaurant offers nearly 30 soups. ◆ Continental ◆ Tu-Sa dinner. No credit cards accepted. 1130 Pinellas Bayway (at 12th St W). 867.0774

130 Fort DeSoto Park This park consists of 900 unspoiled acres on five islands. There are three miles of beach and two fishing piers, as well as picnic and 200-plus camping areas, a concession stand, and rest rooms. Although there are no boat rentals, there is a boat ramp and seawall tie-up areas for those who bring boats. The fort itself was built during the Spanish-American War and offers panoramic views. It is listed on the National Register of Historic Places. ◆ Free. Daily sunrise to sunset. Pinellas Bayway and Anderson Blvd. 582.2267

St. Petersburg

Also called "St. Pete," St. Petersburg was named for the home town of Piott A. Dementieff, a Russian immigrant. In 1887, Dementieff—who changed his name to Peter Demens—was instrumental in building the **Orange Belt Railroad** down the **Pinellas Peninsula** to its tip. He also constructed a rail pier that connected docking ships with the main railroad artery—the tracks ran atop the pier itself. The area became a focal point of St. Petersburg life, with other piers being turned over to shops and restaurants. The most prominent was **Million Dollar Pier,** built in 1926. It was so named because of the district's popularity among the rich of St. Petersburg, who discovered the area during the 1920s. In 1989, when a new building for shops, restaurants, and an aquarium was added at the end of the half-mile promenade, it was named **The Pier**, and this inverted pyramid remains one of St. Pete's top attractions.

Today a city of about a quarter-million residents, St. Pete hops in the spring with the Festival of States, a three-week party coinciding with major league baseball's spring training. The gala includes such events as a competition among high school bands from around the country, parades, various free concerts, a fishing tournament, and a regatta. Call 898.3654 for more information.

But what St. Pete was really waiting to celebrate all these years was the acquisition of a major league baseball team. Finally, in 1995, the city was awarded the **Tampa Bay Devil Rays,** who play at the elaborate **Tropicana Field** stadium. The arena is also host to other sports events, rock concerts, and shows.

St. Petersburg also has a number of fine museums, some located downtown within easy walking distance of each other. The latest addition to this group is the **Florida International Museum.** Opened in 1995, the museum features excellent temporary art exhibits from the world over.

Finally, St. Pete is a place of quiet leisure. Walk around and visit the area's parks and gracious old houses, many listed on the National Register of Historic Places.

Area code 727 unless otherwise noted.

131 Sunshine Skyway Modeled after the Bretonne Bridge over the Seine River in France, Florida's first suspension bridge connects Pinellas County with Manatee County to the south. An older bridge alongside it has been converted into the state's longest fishing pier—more than four miles long and lined with 83 artificial fishing reefs that were created from old cars, boats, chunks of concrete, and steel girders. The middle of the old bridge's southbound span was knocked out by a freighter one foggy night in 1980, and 35 people lost their lives. The state subsequently built this $244-million, 4.1-mile replacement bridge in 1987; its yellow cables, resembling inverted fans, are illuminated at night.

132 Skyway Jack's Restaurant ★★$ Situated in a small marina, this likable place is the top choice in town for breakfast. It's best known for SOS—gravy and biscuits served with potatoes. Everything is prepared to order, so expect to wait during tourist season. ♦ American ♦ Daily breakfast and lunch. 6701 34th St S (south of Pinellas Point Dr). 866.3217

133 Leverock's Maximo Moorings ★$$ The service is friendly and the portions ample at this waterside restaurant, which is cozily surrounded by private fishing docks. Try the salmon Wellington (salmon coated with light bread crumbs mixed with butter and garlic), Alaska crab legs, shrimp, or crab cakes. ♦ Seafood ♦ Daily lunch and dinner. 4801 37th St S (between Fuller Cir and 46th Ave). 864.3883

134 Boyd Hill Nature Park Six trails meander through 216 acres of various Florida ecosystems in this park: oak hammock, red maple swamp, cattail/willow marsh, pine flatwood, scrub, and lake. Wildlife abounds here—nesting bald eagles, gopher tortoises, flying and gray squirrels, possums, raccoons, snakes, frogs, and alligators—and photo opportunities pop up on every trail. Other facilities include a playground, picnic area, four aquariums, and an observation beehive at the nature center building. ♦ Admission. Daily. 1101 Country Club Way S (west of Ninth St). 893.7326

135 Munch's ★★$ This community restaurant offers home-style cooking—burgers, grouper salad, and creamy milk shakes. Local memorabilia dominate the otherwise nondescript decor. You can still order a 99-cent breakfast special on Monday, Wednesday, and Friday. ♦ American ♦ Daily breakfast and lunch. 3920 Sixth St S (between 40th and 39th Aves). 896.5972

The Chattaway

136 The Chattaway ★★$ This funky outdoor burger stand with a sense of humor is a tradition among locals. The sign outside says, "It only looks expensive." Choose from burgers or Southern cooking; a British breakfast is served on weekends. Onion rings are juicy but not greasy. There's a small sit-down area inside; picnic tables and a bar are outside. ♦ American ♦ M-Sa lunch and dinner Sa-Su breakfast, lunch, and dinner. 358 22nd Ave S (at Fourth St). 823.1594

137 Bayboro House Bed and Breakfast $ Located on the bay in a quiet residential nook south of Bayboro Harbor, this many-gabled house was built at the turn of the century and has three rooms and a suite with a sitting area and kitchen. Each guest room is furnished in a different decor with antiques, linens, and lace, and has a private bath and television. A complimentary continental breakfast is served in the dining room or on the wraparound porch. The *Miami Herald* has rated it one of the top ten bed-and-breakfasts in Florida. ♦ 1719 Beach Dr SE (between 18th and 17th Aves). 823.4955; www.bbdirectory.com

Florida has more golf courses than any other state in the US—more than 1,100 and counting.

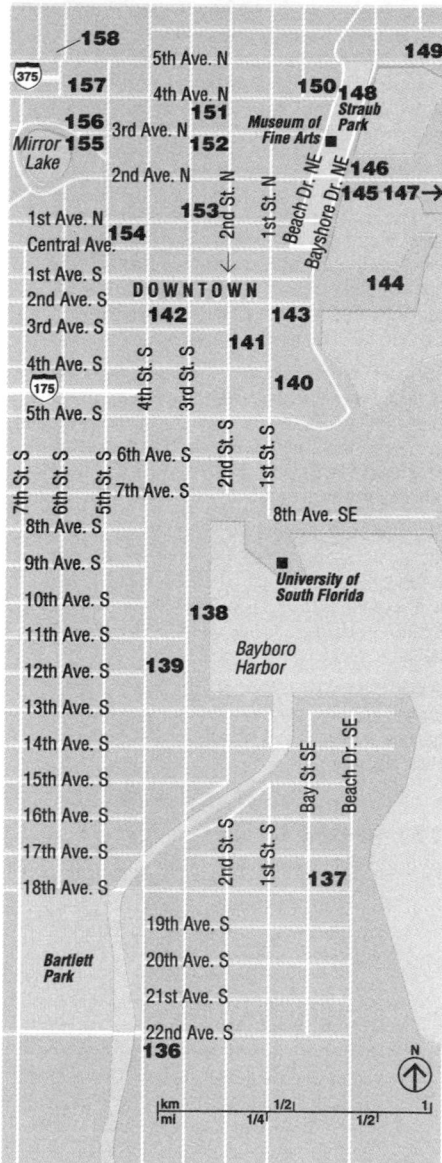

138 Salvador Dalí Museum The bold, sometimes controversial work of Salvador Dalí (1904-89), the world-famous Spanish surrealist artist, may seem slightly out of sync in sedate St. Pete but it's a real treat to view his masterpieces here. This is the world's largest collection of his work—it encompasses 94 oils, more than 100 watercolors and drawings, and 1,300 other pieces ranging from graphics and sculptures to objets d'art—and is valued at more than $125 million. When you enter the gallery, proceed clockwise around the museum to appreciate Dalí's work chronologically. Start with his early pieces (1914), move through his transitional period, and end up with his masterful surrealistic works. Among his most interesting is *The Three Ages*. Look carefully for the faces of Infancy, Adolescence, and Old Age, which Dalí painted using double images. Against the back wall are his floor-to-ceiling masterworks, painted between 1948 and 1970, including *The Discovery of America by Christopher Columbus* (1958), *Nature Morte Vivante* (1956), *Ecumenical Council* (1960), *Velázquez Painting the Infanta Margarita with the Lights and Shadows of His Own Glory* (1958), and *Hallucinogenic Toreador* (1970). Try to take the docent tour, which can be highly entertaining. Reproductions of the artist's work, posters, T-shirts, and books are sold in the museum store. ♦ Admission. M-Sa; Su noon-5:30PM. 1000 Third St S (between 13th and 7th Aves). 823.3767 &

139 Great Explorations, The Hands-On Museum More for children than for adults, perhaps, this hands-on museum is educational and entertaining for both. Exhibits include a long, dark touch tunnel and laser pinball games, as well as sensory experiences and challenging puzzles. There's also a deli and gift shop. ♦ Admission. Daily. 1120 Fourth St S (between 13th and 11th Aves). 821.8885 &

140 Bayfront Center Celebrity entertainment, special exhibits, ice shows, and plays are staged in this facility on the downtown waterfront. The **Bayfront Center Arena** seats 8,400 and the **Mahaffey Theater** 2,000 people. ♦ 400 First St S (between Fifth and Second Aves SE). 825.3333

141 St. Petersburg Bayfront Hilton $$ This 15-story hotel overlooking Tampa Bay is decorated in marble, crystal, and tile and is within walking distance of bayfront attractions, museums, and entertainment facilities. The 333 rooms have views of the bay or city. Guests staying on the concierge level enjoy extras—bathrobes, shoe-shine machines, and a miniature TV/radio in each bathroom. There's also a restaurant, deli, lobby bar, fitness center, outdoor heated pool, patio deck, Jacuzzi, and sauna. ♦ 333 First St S (between Fourth and Second Aves). 894.5000, 888/843.6929 in FL, 800/445.8667; fax 894.7655; www.hilton.com &

142 American Stage Co. St. Petersburg's resident professional theater presents drama, comedy, and experimental plays in a former tobacco factory. A *Shakespeare in the Park* series takes place in **Straub Park** in the spring. It's considered the best local production company on the Pinellas side of the bay. ♦ 211 Third St S (between Third and Second Aves). 823.1600

143 Al Lang Stadium The **St. Louis Cardinals** use this as their spring training ground from mid-February through April. ♦ 230 First St S (between Fifth and Second Aves). 893.7490

144 Demens Landing This 611-slip municipal marina provides permanent slips, along with an additional transit dock facility that can be rented. Boat supplies, fuel, and rental power boats and sailboats are some of the other amenities. There's also a nine-acre waterfront park with picnic facilities and a children's playground. ♦ First Ave SE and Bayshore Dr

145 Apropos Bistro & Bar ★$$ This Art Deco–style restaurant with great views of the waterfront sits right on the approach to **The Pier.** Plenty of fresh herbs flavor the cuisine, which ranges from lamb chops and herbed chicken breast to fresh seafood, salads, and sandwiches. ♦ American ♦ Tu-Sa breakfast, lunch, and dinner; Su brunch. 300 Second Ave NE (at Bayshore Dr). 823.8934

146 St. Petersburg Historical Museum The history of commercial aviation is presented here in hands-on and walk-in exhibits. In addition to a permanent exhibition area chronicling the area's history, an intimate gallery houses rotating displays that reflect such topics as early architecture in St. Petersburg. The focal point, however, is the **Benoist Pavilion,** which contains a full-size replica of the historic aircraft *Benoist Airboat,* suspended from a 38-foot ceiling. The original, which flew from St. Petersburg to Tampa in 1914, was the world's first regularly scheduled passenger flight. ♦ Admission. Daily. 335 Second Ave NE (just east of Bayshore Dr). 894.1052 ও

147 The Pier A city landmark, this five-level inverted pyramid overlooks Tampa Bay and provides sweeping views of the water and the city skyline. A free trolley runs between the entrance and nearby parking lots. The merchandise in the complex's shops ranges from art and jewelry to souvenirs and crafts. Other features include restaurants, a food court, an observation deck, boat and water-sports rentals, public boat docks, and two catwalks for fishing. On the second-level aquarium, giant tubes bubble with native and tropical fish, sharks, and invertebrates. ♦ Donation for the aquarium. Daily. 800 Second Ave NE (east of Bayshore Dr). 821.6164 ও

At The Pier:

Columbia Restaurant ★$$$ Specialties at this casual branch of Tampa's famous Spanish dining spot include salmon Adele (fillet cooked in tomato sauce and topped with melted cheese), and beef stuffed with sausage and topped with brown gravy. ♦ Spanish ♦ Daily lunch and dinner. 822.8000. Also at: 2117 E Seventh Ave (between N 22nd and N 21st Sts), Tampa. 248.4961

148 Straub Park This 36-acre park on the bay was named in honor of William Straub, the local newspaper editor who led the campaign for public ownership of the city's waterfront in the early 1900s. Concerts are held here occasionally, and *Shakespeare in the Park* performances take place in the spring. ♦ Bounded by Bayshore and Beach Drs NE, and First and Fifth Aves

The Pier

Hello, Dalí

You might say it was the power of the press that helped bring the **Salvador Dalí Museum** to **St. Petersburg.** When the *Wall Street Journal* reported that Cleveland industrialists A. Reynolds and Eleanor Morse were searching for a permanent home for their collection of Salvador Dalí works, the paper's headline read: "US Art World Dillydallies Over Dalís."

The article caught the attention of St. Petersburg attorney James W. Martin, who spearheaded a group that mobilized city and state support to bring the collection to St. Petersburg. An old waterfront warehouse was renovated in 1982, and now the two-story building houses a museum, community room for workshops, hurricane-proof vault, library, conference room, and office space (see **Salvador Dalí Museum** on page 202).

The real story behind the **Salvador Dalí Museum** began in 1941, however, when A. Reynolds Morse and his fiancée Eleanor Reese first viewed a traveling exhibit of Dalí's early work in Cleveland. Excited about what they saw, the couple arranged a meeting with the painter in New York in 1942. That rendezvous was the start of a lifelong friendship between the Morses and Salvador and Gala Dalí.

The Morses purchased their first Dalí oil painting, titled *Daddy Longlegs of the Evening . . . Hope!,* on the occasion of their wedding anniversary in 1943. So began a lifetime of collecting that resulted in the world's largest private collection of Dalí's art.

Within Straub Park:

Museum of Fine Arts It's worth a visit to this Greco-Roman–style museum just to see the collection of French Impressionist paintings, which include Renoirs and Cézannes. There is also an important collection of American photographers, featuring Ansel Adams, Margaret Bourke-White, and Philippe Halsman; and a gallery of Steuben glass and period rooms with antiques and historical furnishings. ◆ Donation. Tu-Su. 255 Beach Dr NE. 896.2667 ♿

49 Renaissance Vinoy Resort $$$ Aymer Vinoy Laughner, a Pennsylvania oilman, developed this Mediterranean Revival–style building as a luxury resort in 1925. His bayfront property hosted the likes of F. Scott Fitzgerald, Babe Ruth, and Calvin Coolidge. The 360-room pink hotel features 65 mythological creatures on the moldings, two heated pools, a fitness center, 16 tennis courts, an 18-hole Ron Garl–designed golf course, 74-slip marina, two croquet courts, and several restaurants. It's headquarters of the **Women's Tennis Association** and is listed on the National Register of Historic Places. ◆ 501 Fifth Ave NE (between Bayshore and Beach Drs). 894.1000, 800/HOTELS1; fax 822.2785; www.renaissancehotels.com ♿

50 The Glass Canvas In this modern gallery, the favored medium is glass sculpture, while the theme leans toward the sea, including fish and shells. Paintings and craft items are also featured. ◆ Daily. 233 Fourth Ave NE (at Beach Dr). 821.6767

151 Veillard House This rusticated block structure was commissioned in 1901 by Ralph Veillard, a local merchant and political activist who ingeniously combined Bungalow and Queen Anne styles. It is one of the earliest surviving Bungalow-style structures in St. Petersburg and is listed on the National Register of Historic Places. ◆ 262 Fourth Ave N (between Second and Third Sts)

152 Heritage Holiday Inn $$ Known as the **Martha Washington Hotel** when it was built in the 1920s, this elegant restored inn is now allied with Holiday Inn. Located in a quiet tree-shaded residential area within a few blocks of the heart of downtown, it has 71 guest rooms and suites that still retain pieces of the original furniture. A wide veranda with a series of etched-glass French doors leads to the lobby. Other facilities include a small heated pool, Jacuzzi, and lobby bar. Guests can dine at the hotel's restaurant, **Heritage Grille** (see below). A continental breakfast served in the foyer is included in the weekend rate. ◆ 234 Third Ave N (between Second and Third Sts). 822.4814, 800/283.7829

152 Heritage Grille ★★$$ American cuisine is given new life in this old home with an updated, snazzy decor. Favorites include sautéed artichoke hearts filled with blue-crab meat, and seafood and andouille sausage fettuccine. Soups are made fresh daily. ◆ American ◆ M-F lunch and dinner; Sa dinner. 256 Second St N (between Second and Third Aves). 823.6382

153 Florida International Museum *Treasures of the Czars,* billed as the most significant collection of royal treasures ever to leave the Kremlin Museums in Moscow, was the opening exhibition when this $4-million museum debuted in 1995. Housed in the former **Maas Brothers** department store, the museum does not have a permanent collection but hosts exhibits from around the world. There's also a 200-seat theater, a restaurant, and an outdoor cafe. ♦ Admission. Daily. Reservations recommended. 100 Second St N (at First Ave). 821.1448, 800/777.9882

154 Snell Arcade This Mediterranean Revival–style shopping arcade and office building was built in 1926 by land developer Perry Snell. The interior arcade serves as a passage to the post office and was restored in 1982. It is listed on the National Register of Historic Places. ♦ 405 Central Ave (between Fourth and Fifth Sts N)

154 US Post Office Once notable as the country's only open-air post office (part of it is now enclosed), this structure was built in 1917 in the Mediterranean Revival style and designed locally by **George Stewart.** It is listed on the National Register of Historic Places. ♦ M-F. 76 Fourth St N (between Central and First Aves). 823.7558

155 Mirror Lake Library The city's first library building was built with a Carnegie Foundation grant in 1915. The Beaux Arts–style old section was designed by **Henry Whitfield** of New York and is listed on the National Register of Historic Places. ♦ M-Sa. 300 Fifth St N (at Mirror Lake Dr). 893.7268

156 St. Petersburg Shuffleboard Club This shuffleboard club, the world's largest, dates from 1924 and houses the **National Shuffleboard Hall of Fame.** The sport was invented in Florida around 1912, and the courts are open to the public. It's located in the **Mirror Lake Park** club building. ♦ Nominal admission. M-F 9AM-noon. 559 Mirror Lake Dr (between Fifth and Seventh Sts). 822.2083

157 Coliseum Ballroom This Mediterranean Revival–style building houses one of the country's oldest continuously operating big band–era dance halls. Since it was built in 1924, many thousands have danced on the 13,000-square-foot maple ballroom floor, one of the country's largest. This downtown landmark was featured in the break-dancing sequence of the movie *Cocoon*. Antiques shows and exhibits are also held here. ♦ Admission. Schedule varies. 535 Fourth Ave N (between Fifth and Sixth Sts). 892.5202

158 Boone House Built in 1910 in the Classical Revival style by pioneer land developer Benjamin Boone, this restored structure houses private offices. It is listed on the National Register of Historic Places. There are no tours. ♦ 601 Fifth Ave N (at Sixth St)

159 Gas Plant Antique Arcade More than 70 dealers are housed in this four-story complex, a former gas plant that is now one of the largest antiques malls on Florida's west coast. Everything from toys and dolls to art and furniture is sold here. Beware: The proprietor asks that handbags be checked into lockers at the front of the store, so if this strict policy seems bothersome, you may want to shop elsewhere. ♦ Daily. 1246 Central Ave (between 11th and 13th Sts N). 895.0368

159 Tropicana Field When St. Petersburg's newly acquired major league baseball team—the **Tampa Bay Devil Rays**—started playing here in 1998, this 45,000-seat stadium, formerly the **ThunderDome,** was ready to host them with a vengeance. The city waited a long time to have its own squad, and spent $138 million on this arena in preparation for the big day. A variety of events, including other sports events, are also held here. ♦ M-F hours vary according to events. First Ave S and 16th St. 825.3100

160 Haslam's Undoubtedly Florida's best general bookstore, this shop also claims to be the state's largest and specializes in finding out-of-print books. There are more than 300,000 volumes in this librarylike emporium—hardcover, paperback, new, and used. The store has been in operation since 1933. Spend an afternoon here browsing for bargains. ♦ M-Sa. 2025 Central Ave (between 20th and 21st Sts N). 822.8616

161 Central (St. Petersburg) High School Designed by **William B. Ittner** in the Mediterranean Revival style, this high school was built in 1925 during the Florida land boom at a cost of $1 million. It is listed on the National Register of Historic Places. ♦ 2501 Fifth Ave N (at 25th St)

162 Stetson University College of Law This Mediterranean Revival–style structure was built as the **Rolyat Hotel** ("Taylor" spelled backward) in 1925. It was the climactic achievement of I.M. "Handsome Jack" Taylor, one of the chief figures in the frenzied St. Petersburg real estate boom of 1925. **Paul Reed,** a young Miami architect, based his concept for the hotel on a walled medieval village. It opened in a blaze of glory; guests included golfer Walter Hagen, baseball's Babe Ruth, and prima donna Frieda Hempel. The building also served as a military academy before becoming a law school in 1954. ♦ 1401 61st St S (between 15th and 13th Aves), Gulfport. 345.1300

163 Ted Peters' Famous Smoked Fish ★★★$ Some say this landmark sidewalk cafe serves the best smoked fish in Florida. Try the mullet or Spanish mackerel, served with hot German potato salad, thick slices of onion and tomato, and whole-wheat bread. Diners enjoy it all at tables set up in open-air pavilions. ♦ Seafood ♦ M, W-Su lunch and dinner. 1350 Pasadena Ave S (between Shore Dr and Gulfport Blvd), South Pasadena. 381.7931

164 Horse & Jockey ★★$$ The Tampa Bay area's largest British pub offers fish-and-chips, meat pies, and other traditional pub fare. There are 11 British beers on tap. High tea is served on weekdays, and Sunday dinner usually includes roast beef and Yorkshire pudding. ♦ British ♦ Daily lunch and dinner. Reservations required a day ahead for high tea. 1155 Pasadena Ave S (at Sunset Dr), South Pasadena. 345.4995

165 Tyrone Square Mall More than 150 stores—including bookstores, jewelers, and boutiques—and such department stores as **Dillard's, Burdine's,** and **JCPenney,** make up this mall. ♦ Daily. 6901 22nd Ave N (between 66th and Anvil Sts). 347.3889

166 Wilson's Book Store New and rare comic collectibles are on sale here at one of the Southeast's largest dealers of paperback and comic selections for a quarter-century. ♦ M-Sa. 2394 Ninth St N (at 24th Ave). 896.3700

167 Fourth Street Shrimp Store ★★$ Oilcloth-covered tables and a down-home decor are the setting for copious quantities of shrimp, crab, and other seafood cooked to perfection. ♦ Seafood ♦ Daily lunch and dinner. 1006 Fourth St N (between 10th Ave and Joyce Terr). 822.0325

Sunken Gardens

168 Sunken Gardens Once a sinkhole, this seven-acre garden has been converted into a tourist attraction with 5,000 varieties of orchids, palms, and other exotica. There is also an aviary filled with spoonbills, macaws, and other rare birds. Alligators are displayed in tanks and natural habitats, including a gator pool. The only entrance forces you to trek through one of the largest and tackiest collections of souvenirs in Florida. ♦ Admission. Daily. Bird shows 11:15AM,

noon, 1:15PM, 2PM, 3:15PM, 4PM, and 5PM. 1825 Fourth St N (between 18th and 20th Aves). 896.3186 ⑆

169 El Cap ★★$ At this local hangout for residents and major league baseball teams during spring training, you'll find great grilled cheese sandwiches and chili, but it's definitely the place to have one of the area's best hamburgers—thick and juicy. Baseball memorabilia is displayed throughout. ♦ American ♦ M-Sa lunch and dinner. 3500 Fourth St N (at 35th Ave). 521.1314

Pepín

170 Pepín ★★★$$ This place, attractively decorated with Dalí and Picasso prints, is resounding proof that all the area's good Spanish restaurants are not located in Tampa. The chicken with yellow rice, *pompano à la sal* (baked in salt), and steak *milanesa* (breaded, sautéed, and served with a tomato sauce) are always good. The salads and hearty brown bread are also memorable. ♦ Spanish ♦ Daily lunch and dinner. 4125 Fourth St N (between 41st and 42nd Aves). 821.3773

171 Sawgrass Lake Park A mile of elevated boardwalk winds through a swamp filled with maple trees in this 400-acre park. An observation tower provides a panoramic view of Sawgrass Lake. Pick up a booklet for self-guided tours of nature trails at the park's office/classroom. ♦ Daily 7AM-sunset. 7400 25th St N (north of 68th Ave). 527.3814

172 Joyland For a toe-tapping good time, the area's only country-and-western ballroom features live bands, well-known performers, and free dance lessons nightly. ♦ Admission. Tu-Su 7PM-1AM. 11225 Hwy 19 S (between 110th and 115th Aves N). 573.1919

173 Derby Lane Founded in 1925, this greyhound-racing track claims to be the world's oldest in continual operation. There are 14 races run daily. Facilities include a lounge and restaurants. ♦ Nominal admission. M, W, Sa 11:30AM-11PM; Tu, Th-F 6-11PM; closed July-December. 10490 Gandy Blvd (between San Martin Blvd and Fourth St N). 576.1361

American wine making began in Florida in 1562, when some French Huguenot settlers started fermenting wild muscadine grapes near present-day Jacksonville.

Restaurants/Clubs: Red   Hotels: Blue
Shops/🌳 Outdoors: Green   **Sights/Culture:** Black

History

1497 European explorers see Florida for the first time.

1502 Florida appears as a peninsula on a Spanish map.

1513 In March, Ponce de León sees land, and in April, in the vicinity of present-day **St. Augustine,** he names the land **"Pascua Florida,"** meaning "during the time of the feast of Easter."

1565 In August, Pedro Menéndez de Avilés of Spain enters a harbor and calls it **San Augustin,** which becomes St. Augustine, the first continuously inhabited settlement in the New World.

1763 Florida is given to the British, as the Spanish swap it for Havana.

1783 Florida is given back to the Spanish.

1821 The Spanish turn Florida over to the United States—with General Andrew Jackson as governor—after the 1819 agreement reached by American Secretary of State John Quincy Adams and Spanish minister Luís de Onis has been ratified by both nations.

1845 On 3 March, Florida is granted statehood.

1886 Henry M. Flagler buys the first link in his chain of railroad and hotel properties, which will become a network of commerce down the east coast of the state. At about the same time, Henry Plant builds his railroad line from Jacksonville to **Tampa.**

1912 Flagler's railroad reaches Key West.

1914 On New Year's Day, the world's first scheduled airline service begins, with regular flights from **St. Petersburg** to Tampa.

1950s Thanks to the invention of the air conditioner, Florida's population grows an astounding 78 percent. By the decade's end it is the 10th most populous state.

1958 *Explorer I,* the first satellite to orbit Earth, is launched by the United States as the **National Aeronautics and Space Administration (NASA)** begins its operations at **Cape Canaveral.**

1959 Cubans fleeing Fidel Castro begin arriving in Miami. **Busch Gardens Tampa** opens.

1963 Cape Canaveral is renamed **Cape Kennedy** by President Lyndon Johnson and the **John F.**

Kennedy Space Center is installed in honor of the assassinated president. (Cape Kennedy later reverted to its former name.)

1971 **Walt Disney World** opens near **Orlando.**

1973 **Sea World** opens in Orlando.

1981 The first space shuttles carrying people are launched from **Kennedy Space Center.**

1982 **Epcot** opens at **Walt Disney World.**

1987 Orlando and Miami are awarded **National Basketball Association** franchises—the **Miami Heat** and the **Orlando Magic.**

1989 **Disney-MGM Studios** opens at **Walt Disney World.**

1990 **Universal Studios Florida,** a theme park and working film studio, opens.

1992 Hurricane Andrew hits South Florida, causing $1 billion in damage.

1995 Hurricane Opal hits the Florida Panhandle, causing extensive damage.

1998 **Disney's Animal Kingdom** opens at **Walt Disney World.** The workforce at **Walt Disney World** surpasses 50,000 employees, making it the largest employer in the state.

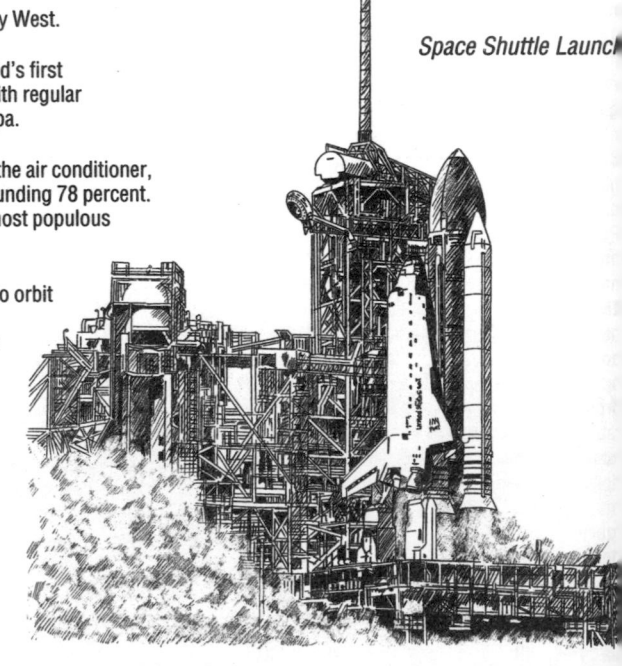

Space Shuttle Launch

Index

Index

Restaurants

Only restaurants with star ratings are listed below. All restaurants are listed alphabetically in the main (preceding) index. Always call in advance to ensure a restaurant has not closed, changed its hours, or booked its tables for a private party. The restaurant price ratings are based on the average cost of an entrée for one person, excluding tax and tip.

★★★★ An Extraordinary Experience
★★★ Excellent
★★ Very Good
★ Good

$$$$ Big Bucks ($25 and up)
$$$ Expensive ($15-$25)
$$ Reasonable ($10-$15)
$ The Price Is Right (less than $10)

Hotels

The hotels listed below are grouped according to their price ratings; they are also listed in the main index. The hotel price ratings reflect the base price of a standard room for two people for one night during the peak season.

Index